Understanding
Business Accounting

FOR
DUMMIES®
3RD EDITION

by John A Tracy and Colin Barrow

WILEY

Understanding Business Accounting For Dummies® 3rd Edition

Published by
John Wiley & Sons, Ltd
The Atrium
Southern Gate
Chichester
West Sussex
PO19 8SQ
England
www.wiley.com

For general information on our other products and services, please contact our Customer Care Department within the U.S. at 877-762-2974, outside the U.S. at 317-572-3993, or fax 317-572-4002.

For technical support, please visit www.wiley.com/techsupport.

Wiley publishes in a variety of print and electronic formats and by print-on-demand. Some material included with standard print versions of this book may not be included in e-books or in print-on-demand. If this book refers to media such as a CD or DVD that is not included in the version you purchased, you may download this material at http://booksupport.wiley.com. For more information about Wiley products, visit www.wiley.com.

British Library Cataloguing in Publication Data: A catalogue record for this book is available from the British Library

ISBN 978-1-119-95128-5 (pbk); ISBN 978-1-119-95384-5 (ebk); ISBN 978-1-119-95385-2 (ebk); ISBN 978-1-119-95386-9 (ebk)

Printed and bound in Great Britain by TJ International Ltd

10 9 8 7 6 5 4 3 2 1

About the Authors

John A Tracy is Professor of Accounting, Emeritus, in the College of Business and Administration at the University of Colorado in Boulder. Before his 35-year tenure at Boulder he was on the business faculty for four years at the University of California in Berkeley. He has served as staff accountant at Ernst & Young and is the author of several books on accounting, including The Fast Forward MBA in Finance and How To Read a Financial Report. Dr Tracy received his MBA and PhD degrees from the University of Wisconsin and is a CPA in Colorado.

Colin Barrow was until recently Head of the Enterprise Group at Cranfield School of Management, where he taught entrepreneurship on the MBA and other programmes and where he is still a visiting fellow. He is also a visiting professor at business schools in the US, Asia, France and Austria. His books on entrepreneurship and business have been translated into over twenty languages including Russian and Chinese. He worked with Microsoft to incorporate the business planning model used in his teaching programmes into the software program, Microsoft Business Planner, bundled with Office. He is a regular contributor to newspapers, periodicals and academic journals such as The Financial Times, The Guardian, Management Today and the International Small Business Journal.

Thousands of students have passed through Colin's start-up and business growth programmes, raising millions in new capital and going on to run successful and thriving enterprises. Some have made it to *The Sunday Times* Rich List. He has been a non-executive director of two venture capital funds, on the board of several small businesses, and serves on a number of Government Task Forces. Currently he is a non-executive director in several private firms and works with family businesses in the Middle East on succession planning.

Dedication

For all my grandchildren.

John A Tracy

Authors' Acknowledgments

From John: I'm deeply grateful to everyone at Wiley who helped produce this book. Their professionalism and their unfailing sense of humour and courtesy were much appreciated. I owe a debt of gratitude to a faculty colleague at Boulder, an accomplished author in his own right, Professor Ed Gac. He offered very sage advice. Ed was always ready with a word of encouragement when I needed one, and I'm very appreciative.

I often think about why I like to write books. I believe it goes back to an accounting class in my undergraduate days at Creighton University in Omaha. In a course taught by the Dean of the Business School, Dr Floyd Walsh, I turned in a term paper and he said that it was very well written. I have never forgotten that compliment. I think he would be proud of this book.

From Colin: I would like to thank everyone at Wiley for the opportunity to write this book, as well as their help, encouragement, feedback and tireless work to make this all happen.

Publisher's Acknowledgments

We're proud of this book; please send us your comments at http://dummies.custhelp.com. For other comments, please contact our Customer Care Department within the U.S. at 877-762-2974, outside the U.S. at 317-572-3993, or fax 317-572-4002.

Some of the people who helped bring this book to market include the following:

Acquisitions, Editorial, and Vertical Websites

Project Editor: Rachael Chilvers
    (Previous Edition: Steve Edwards)

Commissioning Editor: Claire Ruston

Assistant Editor: Ben Kemble

Proofreader: James Harrison

Production Manager: Daniel Mersey

Publisher: David Palmer

Cover Photos: iStock / Jonathan Maddock

Cartoons: Ed McLachlan

Composition Services

Project Coordinator: Kristie Rees

Layout and Graphics: Joyce Haughey,
    Lavonne Roberts

Proofreader: Lauren Mandelbaum

Indexer: Christine Karpeles

Publishing and Editorial for Consumer Dummies

    Kathleen Nebenhaus, Vice President and Executive Publisher

    Kristin Ferguson-Wagstaffe, Product Development Director

    Ensley Eikenburg, Associate Publisher, Travel

    Kelly Regan, Editorial Director, Travel

Publishing for Technology Dummies

    Andy Cummings, Vice President and Publisher

Composition Services

    Debbie Stailey, Director of Composition Services

Contents at a Glance

Table of Contents

Part II: Getting a Grip on Financial Statements *85*

Introduction

Welcome to *Understanding Business Accounting For Dummies*, 3rd Edition. We've written this book for people who need to understand accounting information and financial reports, quickly. Unsurprisingly the business climate at the end of the first decade of the 21st Century has made this a hot topic – not quite in the Stieg Larsson league but every bit as scary in its own way. While it's *not* for accountants and bookkeepers, they should find this book very interesting and a good refresher course. This book is for people who need to use and understand accounting information – business managers and entrepreneurs, for example, who need to raise money, make profit, turn profit into cash flow and control the assets and liabilities of their venture. If you're running a business or you're a business unit manager, we're probably preaching to the converted when we say that you need a basic familiarity with accounting and financial statements in order to make good business decisions.

Business investors, lawyers, business consultants – pretty much anyone who reads (or aspires to read) *The Financial Times* – can also benefit from a solid understanding of how to read financial reports and how accounting works.

About This Book

Understanding Business Accounting For Dummies, 3rd Edition lifts the veil of obscure terminology and lays bare the methods of accounting. This book takes you behind the scenes and explains the language and methods of accounting in a down-to-earth and light-hearted manner – and *in plain English*.

Each chapter in this book is designed to stand on its own. Each chapter is self-contained, and you can jump from chapter to chapter as you please (although we encourage you to take a quick tour through the chapters in the order that we present them). We bet you'll discover some points that you may not have expected to find in a book about accounting.

Conventions Used in Financial Reports

Much of this book focuses on profit and how a business makes profit. Because profit and other financial aspects of a business are reported in *financial statements*, understanding some basic notations and conventions used in these financial reports is important.

We use the following condensed profit and loss account to illustrate some conventions that you can expect to see when reading financial reports. (The actual format of a profit and loss account includes more information about expenses and profit.) These conventions are the common ways of showing figures in financial reports just as saying hello and shaking hands are common conventions that you can expect when you greet someone.

Abbreviated Profit and Loss Account		
Sales revenue		£25,000,000
Cost of goods sold expense	15,000,000	
Gross margin	£10,000,000	
Marketing expenses	£4,000,000	
Other expenses	2,000,000	6,000,000
Profit		£4,000,000

✔ You read a financial statement from the top down. In this sample profit and loss account, for example, sales revenue is listed first followed by cost of goods sold expense because this particular expense is the first expense deducted from sales revenue. The other two expenses are listed below the first profit line, which is called gross margin.

✔ The sample profit and loss account includes two columns of numbers. Note that the 6,000,000 total of the two expenses in the left column is entered in the right column. Some financial statements display all figures in a single column.

✔ An amount that is deducted from another amount – like cost of goods sold expense in this sample profit and loss account – may have parentheses around the amount to indicate that it is being subtracted from the amount just above it. Or, financial statements may make the assumption that you know that expenses are deducted from sales revenue – so no parentheses are put around the number. You see expenses presented both ways in financial reports. But you hardly ever see a minus or negative sign in front of expenses – it's just not done.

✔ Notice the use of pound signs in the sample profit and loss account. Not all numbers have a pound sign in front of the number. Financial reporting practices vary on this matter. We prefer to use pound signs only for the first number in a column and for a calculated number. In some financial reports, pound signs are put in front of all numbers, but usually they aren't.

✔ To indicate that a calculation is being done, a single underline is drawn under the bottom number, as you see below the 15,000,000 cost of goods sold expense number in the sample profit and loss account.

✔ The final number in a column is usually double underlined, as you can see for the £4,000,000 profit number in the sample profit and loss account. This is about as carried away as accountants get in their work – a double underline. Again, actual financial reporting practices are not completely uniform on this point – instead of a double underline on a bottom-line number, the number may appear in **bold.**

✔ Sometimes statements note that the amounts shown are in thousands (this prevents clogging up neat little columns with loads of noughts). So if a statement noting 'amounts in thousands' shows £300, it actually means £300,000. And that can make quite a difference!

When we present an accounting formula that shows how financial numbers are computed, we show the formula indented, like this:

Assets = Liabilities + Owners' Equity

Terminology in financial reporting is reasonably uniform, thank goodness, although you may see a fair amount of jargon. When we introduce a new term in this book, we show the term in *italics* and flag it with an icon (see the section 'Icons Used in This Book' later in this Introduction). You can also turn to Appendix A to look up a term that you're unfamiliar with.

Foolish Assumptions

While this book is designed for all of you who have that nagging feeling that you really should know more about accounting, we have made a few assumptions about you.

You don't want to be an accountant, nor do you have any aspirations of ever sitting for the FCA (Fellow of the Institute of Chartered Accountants) exam. But you worry that ignorance of accounting may hamper your decision-making, and you know deep down that learning more about accounting would help.

We assume that you have a basic familiarity with the business world, but we take nothing for granted in this book regarding how much accounting you know. Even if you have some experience with accounting and financial statements, we think you'll find this book useful – especially for improving your communication with accountants.

We assume that you need to *use* accounting information. Many different types of people (business managers, investors and solicitors, to name but three) need to understand accounting basics – not all the technical stuff, just the fundamentals.

We assume that you want to know something about accounting because it's an excellent gateway for understanding how business works, and it gives you an indispensable vocabulary for moving up in the business and investment worlds. Finding out more about accounting helps you understand earnings reports, mergers and takeovers, frauds and pyramid schemes, and business restructurings.

 Let us point out one other very practical assumption that we have regarding why you should know some accounting. We call it the *defensive* reason. A lot of people out there in the cold, cruel financial world may take advantage of you, not necessarily by illegal means, but by withholding key information and by diverting your attention away from unfavourable aspects of certain financial decisions. These unscrupulous characters treat you as a lamb waiting to be fleeced. The best defence against such tactics is to learn some accounting basics, which can help you ask the right questions and understand the financial points that tricksters don't want you to know.

How This Book Is Organised

This book is divided into parts, and each part is further divided into chapters. The following sections describe what you can find in each part.

Part 1: Accounting Basics

Part I of *Understanding Business Accounting For Dummies*, 3rd Edition introduces accounting to non-accountants and discusses the basic features of bookkeeping and accounting record-keeping systems. This part also talks about taxes of all kinds that are involved in running a business, as well as accounting in the everyday lives of individuals.

Part II: Getting a Grip on Financial Statements

Part II moves on to the end product of the business accounting process – *financial statements*. Three main financial statements are prepared every period – one for each financial imperative of business: making *profit*, keeping *financial condition* in good shape and controlling *cash flow*. The nature of profit and the financial effects of profit are explained in Chapter 5. The assets, liabilities and owners' capital invested in a business are reported in the *balance sheet*, which is discussed in Chapter 6. Cash flow from profit and the *cash flow statement* are explained carefully in Chapter 7. The last chapter in this part, Chapter 8, explains what managers have to do to get financial statements ready for the annual financial report of the business to its owners.

Part III: Accounting in Managing a Business

Business managers should know their financial statements like the backs of their hands. However, just understanding these reports is not the end of accounting for managers. Chapter 9 kicks off this part with an extraordinarily important topic – building a basic profit model – that clearly focuses on the key variables that drive profit. This model is absolutely critical for decision-making analysis.

Chapter 10 discusses accounting-based planning and control techniques, especially budgeting. Business managers and owners have to decide on the best business ownership structure, which we discuss in Chapter 11. Managers in manufacturing businesses should be wary of how product costs are determined – as Chapter 12 explains. This chapter also explains other economic and accounting costs that business managers use in making decisions. Chapter 13 identifies and explains the alternative accounting methods for expenses and how the choice of method has a major impact on profit for the period, and on the cost of stock and fixed assets reported in the balance sheet.

Part IV: Financial Reports in the Outside World

Part IV explains financial statement reporting for investors. Chapter 14 presents a speed-reading approach that concentrates on the key financial ratios to look for in a financial report. The scope of the annual audit and what to look for in the auditor's report are explained in Chapter 15, which also explains the role of auditors as enforcers of financial accounting and disclosure standards.

Part V: The Part of Tens

This part of the book presents four chapters. Chapter 16 presents some practical ideas for managers to help them put their accounting knowledge to use while Chapter 17 lists various sources of finance available to the business. Chapter 18 gives business investors some handy tips on things to look for in a financial report – tips that can make the difference between making a good investment and a not-so-good one. Chapter 19 provides our take on reading the stars. Sure, no one knows everything about the financial future, but here we outline some ways you can spot a cloud before it becomes a thunder storm.

Part VI: Appendixes

At the back of the book, you can find two helpful appendixes that can assist you on your accounting safari. Appendix A provides you with a handy, succinct glossary of accounting terms. Appendix B fills you in on the accounting software programs available for your business.

Icons Used in This Book

For Dummies books always include little icons in the margins to draw your attention to paragraphs of particular significance:

This icon calls your attention to particularly important points and offers useful advice on practical financial topics. This icon saves you the cost of buying a yellow highlighter pen.

This icon serves as a friendly reminder that the topic at hand is important enough for you to put a note about it in the front of your wallet. This icon marks material that your lecturer might put on the board before the class starts, noting the important points that you should remember at the end of the class.

Accounting is the language of business, and, like all languages, the vocabulary of accounting contains many specialised terms. This icon identifies key accounting terms and their definitions. You can also check the glossary (Appendix A) to find definitions of unfamiliar terms.

This icon is a caution sign that warns you about speed bumps and potholes on the accounting highway. Taking special note of this material can steer you around a financial road hazard and keep you from blowing a fiscal tyre. In short – watch out!

We use this icon sparingly; it refers to very specialised accounting stuff that is heavy going, which only an FCA could get really excited about. However, you may find these topics important enough to return to when you have the time. Feel free to skip over these points the first time through and stay with the main discussion.

This icon alerts you that we're using a practical example to illustrate and clarify an important accounting point. You can apply the example to your business or to a business in which you invest.

This icon points out especially important ideas and accounting concepts that are particularly deserving of your attention. The material marked by this icon describes concepts that are the building blocks of accounting – concepts that you should be very clear about, and that clarify your understanding of accounting principles in general.

Where to Go from Here

If you're new to the accounting game, by all means, start with Part I. However, if you already have a good background in business and know something about bookkeeping and financial statements, you may want to jump right into Part II of this book, starting with Chapter 5. Part III is on accounting tools and techniques for managers and assumes that you have a handle on the financial statements material in Part II. Part IV stands on its own; if your main interest in accounting is to make sense of and interpret financial statements, you can read through Part II on financial statements and then jump to Part IV on reading financial reports. If you have questions about specific accounting terms, you can go directly to the glossary in Appendix A.

We've had a lot of fun writing this book. We sincerely hope that it helps you become a better business manager and investor, and that it aids you in your personal financial affairs. We also hope that you enjoy the book. We've tried to make accounting as fun as possible, even though it's a fairly serious subject. Just remember that accountants never die; they just lose their balance. (Hey, accountants have a sense of humour, too.)

Part I
Accounting Basics

'So for all you eager investors, our latest financial report will be read to you by our new accountant, Mr Mesmero.'

In this part . . .

Accounting is important in all walks of life, and it's absolutely essential in the world of business, never more so than when the economy goes pear shaped. Accountants are the bookkeepers, scorekeepers, and occasionally the gatekeepers of business. Without accounting, a business couldn't function, wouldn't know whether it's making a profit or loss, wouldn't know its financial situation, or if it was in danger of running out of cash.

Bookkeeping – the record-keeping part of accounting – must be managed well to make sure that all the financial information needed to run the business is complete, accurate, and reliable, especially the numbers reported in financial statements and tax returns. Wrong numbers in financial reports and tax returns can cause all sorts of trouble.

Speaking of taxes, you can't take more than three or four steps before bumping into dreaded taxes. No one likes to pay taxes, but managers must collect and pay taxes as part of running a business. In addition to income taxes, accounting plays a bigger role in your personal financial affairs than you might realise. This part of the book explains all this and more.

Chapter 1

Introducing Accounting to Non-Accountants

*M*ost medium to large businesses employ one or more accountants. Even a very small business could find value in having at least a part-time accountant. Have you ever wondered why? Probably what you think of first is that accountants keep the books and the records of the financial activities of the business. This is true, of course. But accountants perform other very critical but less well-known functions in a business:

✔ Accountants carry out vital back-office operating functions that keep the business running smoothly and effectively including payroll, cash receipts and cash payments, purchases and stock, and property records.

✔ Accountants prepare tax returns, including VAT (value-added tax) returns for the business, as well as payroll and investment tax returns.

✔ Accountants determine how to measure and record the costs of products and how to allocate shared costs among different departments and other organisational units of the business.

✔ Accountants are the *professional profit scorekeepers* of the business world, meaning that they are the ones who determine exactly how much profit was earned, or just how much loss the business suffered, during the period. Accountants prepare reports for business managers, keeping them informed about costs and expenses, how sales are going, whether the cash balance is adequate and what the stock situation is. Most importantly, accountants help managers understand the reasons for changes in the bottom-line performance of a business.

✔ Accountants prepare *financial statements* that help the owners and shareholders of a business understand where the business stands financially. Shareholders wouldn't invest in a business without a clear understanding of the financial health of the business, which regular financial reports (sometimes just called *the financials*) provide.

In short, accountants are much more than bookkeepers – they provide the numbers that are so critical in helping business managers make the informed decisions that keep a business on course toward its financial objectives.

Business managers, investors and others who depend on financial statements should be willing to meet accountants halfway. People who use accounting information, like spectators at a football game, should know the basic rules of play and how the score is kept. The purpose of this book is to make you a knowledgeable spectator of the accounting game.

Accounting Everywhere You Look

Accounting extends into virtually every walk of life. You're doing accounting when you make entries in your cheque book and fill out your income tax return. When you sign a mortgage on your home you should understand the accounting method the lender uses to calculate the interest amount charged on your loan each period. Individual investors need to understand some accounting in order to figure the return on capital invested. And every organisation, profit-motivated or not, needs to know how it stands financially. Accounting supplies all that information.

Many different kinds of accounting are done by many different kinds of persons or entities for many different purposes:

✔ Accounting for organisations and accounting for individuals.

✔ Accounting for profit-motivated businesses and accounting for non-profit organisations (such as hospitals, housing associations, churches, schools and colleges).

✔ Income tax accounting while you're living and estate tax accounting after you die.

✔ Accounting for farmers who grow their products, accounting for miners who extract their products from the earth, accounting for producers who manufacture products and accounting for retailers who sell products that others make.

✔ Accounting for businesses and professional firms that sell services rather than products, such as the entertainment, transportation and health care industries.

✔ Past-historical-based accounting and future-forecast-oriented accounting (that is, budgeting and financial planning).

✔ Accounting where periodic financial statements are mandatory (businesses are the primary example) and accounting where such formal accounting reports are not required.

✔ Accounting that adheres to cost (most businesses) and accounting that records changes in market value (investment funds, for example).

✔ Accounting in the private sector of the economy and accounting in the public (government) sector.

✔ Accounting for going-concern businesses that will be around for some time and accounting for businesses in bankruptcy that may not be around tomorrow.

Accounting is necessary in any free-market, capitalist economic system. It's equally necessary in a centrally controlled, socialist economic system. All economic activity requires information. The more developed the economic system, the more the system depends on information. Much of the information comes from the accounting systems used by the businesses, individuals and other institutions in the economic system.

The Basic Elements of Accounting

Accounting involves bookkeeping, which refers to the painstaking and detailed recording of economic activity and business transactions. But *accounting* is a much broader term than *bookkeeping* because accounting refers to the design of the bookkeeping system. It addresses the many problems in measuring the financial effects of economic activity. Furthermore, accounting includes the *financial reporting* of these values and performance measures to non-accountants in a clear and concise manner. Business managers and investors, as well as many other people, depend on financial reports for vital information they need to make good economic decisions.

Accountants design the *internal controls* in an accounting system, which serve to minimise errors in recording the large number of activities that a business engages in over the period. The internal controls that accountants design can detect and deter theft, embezzlement, fraud and dishonest behaviour of all kinds. In accounting, internal controls are the gram of prevention that is worth a kilo of cure.

An accountant rarely prepares a complete listing of all the details of the activities that took place during a period. Instead, he or she prepares a *summary financial statement,* which shows totals, not a complete listing of all the individual activities making up the total. Managers may occasionally need to search through a detailed list of all the specific transactions that make up the total, but this is not common. Most managers just want summary financial statements for the period – if they want to drill down into the details making up a total amount for the period, they ask the accountant for this more detailed backup information. Also, outside investors usually only see summary-level financial statements. For example, they see the total amount of sales revenue for the period but not how much was sold to each and every customer.

Financial statements are prepared at the end of each accounting period. A period may be one month, one quarter (three calendar months), or one year. One basic type of accounting report prepared at the end of the period is a 'Where do we stand at the end of the period?' type of report. This is called the *balance sheet.* The date of preparation is given in the header, or title, above this financial statement. A balance sheet shows two aspects of the business.

One aspect is the *assets*, or economic resources, of the business. The other aspect of the balance sheet is a breakdown of where the assets came from, or the sources of the assets. The asset *values* reported in the balance sheet are the amounts recorded when the assets were originally acquired. For many assets these values are recent – only a few weeks or a few months old. For some assets, the values as reported in the balance sheet are the costs of the assets when they were acquired many years ago.

Assets are not like manna from heaven. They come from borrowing money in the form of loans that have to be paid back at a later date and from owners' investment of capital (usually money) in the business. Also, making profit increases the assets of the business; profit retained in the business is the third basic source of assets. If a business has, say, £2.5 million in total assets (without knowing which particular assets the business holds) you know that the total of its liabilities, plus the capital invested by its owners, plus its retained profit, adds up to £2.5 million.

In this particular example suppose that the total amount of the liabilities of the business is £1.0 million. This means that the total amount of *owners' equity* in the business is £1.5 million, which equals total assets less total liabilities. Without more information we don't know how much of total owners' equity is traceable to capital invested by the owners in the business and how much is the result of profit retained in the business. But we do know that the total of these two sources of owners' equity is £1.5 million.

The financial condition of the business in this example is summarised in the following *accounting equation* (in millions):

£2.5 Assets = £1.0 Liabilities + £1.5 Owners' Equity

Looking at the accounting equation you can see why the statement of financial condition is also called the balance sheet; the equal sign means the two sides have to balance.

Double-entry bookkeeping is based on this accounting equation – the total of assets on the one side is counter-balanced by the total of liabilities, invested capital and retained profit on the other side. Double-entry bookkeeping is discussed in Chapter 2.

Other financial statements are different from the balance sheet in one important respect: They summarise the significant *flows* of activities and operations over the period. Accountants prepare two types of summary flow reports for businesses:

- ✔ The **profit and loss account** summarises the inflows of assets from the sale of products and services during the period. The profit and loss account also summarises the outflow of assets for expenses during the period leading down to the well-known *bottom line* (the final profit or loss) for the period.

- ✔ The **cash flow statement** summarises the business's cash inflows and outflows during the period. The first part of this financial statement calculates the net increase or decrease in cash during the period from the profit-making activities reported in the profit and loss account.

The balance sheet, profit and loss account, and cash flow statement constitute the hard core of a financial report to those persons outside a business who need to stay informed about the business's financial affairs. These individuals have invested capital in the business, or the business owes them money and therefore they have a financial interest in how well the business is doing. These three key financial statements are also used by the managers of a business to keep themselves informed about what's going on and the financial position of the business. They are absolutely essential to helping managers control the performance of a business, identify problems as they come up, and plan the future course of a business. Managers also need other information that is not reported in the three basic financial statements. (Part III of this book explains these additional reports.)

The jargon jungle of accounting

Financial statements include many terms that are reasonably clear and straightforward, like *cash, debtors* and *creditors.* However, financial statements also use words like *retained earnings, accumulated depreciation, accelerated depreciation, accrued expenses, reserve, allowance, accrual basis* and *current assets.*

This type of jargon in accounting is perhaps too common: It's everywhere you look. If you have any doubt about a term as you go along in the book, please take a quick look in Appendix A, which defines many accounting terms in plain English.

Accounting and Financial Reporting Standards

Experience and common sense have taught business and financial professionals that uniform financial reporting standards and methods are critical in a free-enterprise, private, capital-based economic system. A common vocabulary, uniform accounting methods and full disclosure in financial reports are the goals. How well the accounting profession performs in achieving these goals is an open question, but few disagree that they are worthy goals to strive for.

The emergence of international financial reporting standards (IFRS)

The accounting professional bodies, with a little prodding from governments, are responsible for ensuring that accounting reports conform to what are known as Generally Accepted Accounting Practices (GAAP). A newish entrant, International Accounting Standards, is challenging that term itself as GAAP rules have been interpreted differently on different continents and indeed largely ignored on others. The whole subject of accounting standards is still being thrashed out. In October 2010 the Accounting Standards Board issued a Financial Reporting Exposure Draft (FRED) proposing a new financial reporting standard to replace current UK and Republic of Ireland financial reporting standards.

The rule book has to be adapted to accommodate changes in the way business is done. For example, international business across frontiers is now the norm, so rules on handling currency and reporting taxable profits in different countries have to be accommodated within a company's accounts in a consistent manner.

Although you aren't usually expected to know all the rules – unless you're the accountant responsible for preparing your organisation's figures, try to get up-to-date before any meetings where the subject is likely to come up. You can keep track of changes in company reporting rules on the Institute of Chartered Accountants website (`www.icaew.com/en/technical/financial-reporting`).

In the UK there's a large degree of conformity between domestic and international standards, and the Accounting Standards Board considers each new international standard carefully before deciding whether or not to include it in the domestic standard. Topics that have been the cause of disagreement in the recent past are the treatment of goodwill, deferred tax and pension costs.

The role of the Accounting Standards Board (ASB) is to issue accounting standards. It took over the task of setting accounting standards from the Accounting Standards Committee (ASC) in 1990. The ASB also collaborates with accounting standard-setters from other countries and the International Accounting Standards Board (IASB) both in order to influence the development of international standards and in order to ensure that its standards are developed with due regard to international developments. You can keep up with its work at `www.frc.org.uk/asb/`.

Why accounting rules are important

Business managers should know the basic features of the accounting rules applying in their area – though certainly not all the technical details – so that they understand how profit is measured. Managers get paid to make profit, and they should be very clear on how profit is measured and what profit consists of. The amount of profit a business makes depends on how *profit* is defined and measured.

For example, a business records the purchase of products at cost, which is the amount it paid for the products. *Stock* is the name given to products being held for sale to customers. Examples include clothes in a department store, fuel in the tanks in a petrol station, food on the shelves in a supermarket, books in a bookstore, and so on. The cost of products is put in the stock asset account and kept there until the products are sold to customers. When the products are eventually sold, the cost of the products is recorded as the cost of goods sold expense, at which time a decrease is recorded in the stock asset account. The cost of products sold is deducted from the sales revenue received from the customers, which gives a first-step measure of profit. (A business has many other expenses that need to be factored in, which you can read about in later chapters.)

Now, assume that before the business sells the products to its customers the replacement cost of many of the products being held in stock awaiting sale increases. The replacement cost value of the products is now higher than the original, actual purchase cost of the products. The company's stock is worth more, is it not? Perhaps the business could raise the sales prices that it charges its customers because of the cost increase, or perhaps not. In any case, should the increase in the replacement cost of the products be recorded as profit? The manager may think that this holding gain should be recorded as profit. But the accepted accounting standards say that no profit is earned until the products are sold to the customers.

What about the opposite movement in replacement costs of products – when replacement costs fall below the original purchase costs? Should this development be recorded as a loss, or should the business wait until the products are sold? As you'll see, the accounting rule that applies here is called *lower of cost or market*, and the loss is recorded. So the rule requires one method on the upside but another method on the downside. See why business managers and investors need to know something about the rules of the game? We should add that accounting rules are not all crystal-clear, which leaves a lot of wriggle room in the interpretation and application of these accounting standards. But first a quick word about accounting rules and income tax accounting.

Income tax and accounting rules

Generally speaking (and we're being very general when we say the following), HM Revenue & Customs' income tax accounting rules for determining the annual taxable income of a business are in agreement with the accounting rules applied in most other developed economies. In other words, the accounting methods used for figuring taxable income and for figuring business profit before income tax are in general agreement. Having said this, we should point out that several differences do exist. A business may use one accounting method for filing its annual income tax returns and a different method for measuring its profit, both for management reporting purposes and for preparing its external financial statements to outsiders.

Flexibility in accounting standards

An often-repeated accounting story concerns three accountants being interviewed for an important position. The accountants are asked one key question: 'What's 2 plus 2?' The first candidate answers, 'It's 4,' and is told, 'Don't call us, we'll call you.' The second candidate answers, 'Well, most of the time the answer is 4, but sometimes it's 3 and sometimes it's 5.' The third candidate answers: 'What do you want the answer to be?' Guess who got the job?

The point is that accounting rules are not entirely airtight or cut-and-dried, and are being updated. Many accounting standards leave a lot of room for interpretation. *Guidelines* would be a better word to describe some accounting rules. Deciding how to account for certain transactions and situations requires flexibility, seasoned judgement and careful interpretation of the rules. Furthermore, many estimates have to be made.

Sometimes, businesses use what's called *creative accounting* to make profit for the period look better. Like lawyers who know where to find legal loopholes, accountants sometimes come up with inventive solutions but still stay within the guidelines. We warn you about these creative accounting techniques – also called *massaging the numbers* – at various points in this book. Articles in financial newspapers and magazines regularly focus on such accounting abuses.

Enforcing Accounting Rules

As we mentioned in the preceding sections, when preparing financial statements a business must follow generally accepted accounting principles – the authoritative ground rules for measuring profit and for reporting values of assets and liabilities. Everyone reading a financial report is entitled to assume that the country's accepted accounting standards have been followed (unless the business clearly discloses that it is using another so-called comprehensive basis of accounting).

The basic idea behind sticking closely to the accepted accounting standards is to measure profit and to value assets and liabilities *consistently* from business to business – to establish broad-scale uniformity in accounting methods for all businesses. The idea is to make sure that all accountants are singing the same tune from the same hymnbook. The purpose is also to establish realistic and objective methods for measuring profit and putting values on assets and liabilities. The authoritative bodies write the tunes that accountants have to sing.

All systems of accounting standards include minimum requirements for *disclosure*, which refers to how information is classified and presented in financial statements and to the types of information that have to be added to the financial statements in the form of footnotes. Chapter 8 explains these disclosures that are required in addition to the three primary financial statements of a business (the profit and loss account, balance sheet and cash flow statement).

The Accounting Standards Board, the body responsible for setting accounting standards in the UK, is undertaking a programme of gradually ripping up UK GAAP and replacing it with international financial reporting standards. Today, companies with outside shareholders in the UK and across Europe have bitten the bullet and are adopting international accounting standards, known as International Financial Reporting Standards (IFRS). International standards sound like a great idea – especially with the introduction of a single European currency and the emergence of pan-European equity markets. In fact most financial directors of public companies want to be able to adopt IFRS ahead of time. The UK's Accounting Standards Board is pressing ahead with a programme to 'converge' UK accounting standards so that they match the international standards – almost. You can keep track of changes in company reporting rules on the Institute of Chartered Accountants' website at www.icaew.com/en/technical/financial-reporting. How do you know if a business has actually followed the rules faithfully? We think it boils down to two factors. First is the competency and ethics of the accountants who prepared the financial reports. No substitute exists for expertise and integrity. But accountants often come under intense pressure to massage the numbers from the higher-level executives that they work for.

Which leads to the second factor that allows you to know if a business has obeyed the dictates of accounting standards. Businesses have their financial statements audited by independent chartered or management accountants. In fact, limited companies are required by law to have annual audits and many private businesses hire accountants to do an annual audit, even if not legally required. The Companies Act 2006 has introduced some tough rules on how auditors, amongst others, should report on company accounts. Chapter 15 explains audits and why investors should carefully read the auditor's report on the financial statements.

Protecting investors: Sarbanes-Oxley and beyond

A series of high profile financial frauds in US-based businesses such as Enron and WorldCom in the mid to late 1990s badly shook people's confidence in US businesses. In response, the US government introduced the Sarbanes-Oxley Act, known less commonly but better understood as 'the Public Company Accounting Reforms and Investor Protection Act – 2002'.

The central tenet of the Sarbanes-Oxley Act is to ensure truthfulness in financial reporting – a quest the accounting profession has been pursuing since Pacioli set out the rules of double-entry bookkeeping five centuries ago. The act closes the loopholes that creative accountants opened up, which made it difficult (and sometimes impossible) for shareholders to see how a business was performing until after the baddies had made off with the loot. The act applies to any business with shares listed on an American stock market that does business in the US – not just to US companies.

The British version, 'the Companies (Audit, Investigations, and Community Enterprise) Act – 2004', is causing the accounting profession to clutch its collective head. This knock-on effect from Sarbanes-Oxley means that all companies selling shares to the public have to make changes to their accounts and accounting standards. You can read up on the UK rules at `www.legislation.gov.uk/ukpga/2004/27/contents`.

The Accounting Department: What Goes On in the Back Office

As we discussed earlier in this chapter, bookkeeping (also called *record-keeping*) and financial reporting to managers and investors are the core functions of accounting. In this section, we explain another basic function of a business's accounting department: the back-office functions that keep the business running smoothly.

Most people don't realise the importance of the accounting department. That's probably because accountants do many of the back-office, operating functions in a business – as opposed to sales, for example, which is front-line activity, out in the open, and in the line of fire.

Typically, the accounting department is responsible for:

- **Payroll:** The total wages and salaries earned by every employee every pay period, which are called *gross wages* or *gross earnings,* have to be determined. In short, payroll is a complex and critical function that the accounting department performs; the correct amounts of income tax, social security tax and other deductions from gross wages have to be calculated.

- **Cash inflows:** All cash received from sales and from all other sources has to be carefully identified and recorded, not only in the cash account but also in the appropriate account for the source of the cash received. In larger organisations, the *Chief Accountant* may be responsible for some of these cash flow and cash-handling functions.

- **Cash payments:** A business writes many cheques during the course of a year to pay for a wide variety of items including local business taxes, paying off loans and the distribution of some of its profit to the owners of the business. The accounting department prepares all these cheques for the signatures of the officers of the business who are authorised to sign cheques, and keeps the relevant supporting documents and files for the company's records.

- **Purchases and stock:** Accounting departments are usually responsible for keeping track of all purchase orders that have been placed for stock (products to be sold by the business) and all other assets and services that the business buys – from postage stamps to forklift trucks. The accounting department also keeps detailed records on all products held for sale by the business and, when the products are sold, records the cost of the goods sold.

- **Capital accounting:** A typical business holds many different assets called *capital* – including office furniture and equipment, retail display cabinets, computers, machinery and tools, vehicles, buildings and land. The accounting department keeps detailed records of these items.

The accounting department may be assigned other functions as well, but we think that this list gives you a pretty clear idea of the back-office functions that the accounting department performs. Quite literally, a business could not operate if the accounting department did not do these functions efficiently and on time.

Focusing on Business Transactions and Other Financial Events

Understanding that a great deal of accounting focuses on business transactions is very important. *Transactions* are economic exchanges between a business and the persons and other businesses with which the business deals. Transactions are the lifeblood of every business, the heartbeat of activity that keeps the business going. Understanding accounting, to a large extent, means understanding the basic accounting methods and practices used to record the financial effects of transactions.

A business carries on economic exchanges with six basic groups:

- Its **customers,** who buy the products and services that the business sells.

- Its **employees,** who provide services to the business and are paid wages and salaries and provided with a broad range of benefits such as a pension plan and paid holidays.

✔ Its **suppliers** and **vendors,** who sell a wide range of things to the business, such as legal advice, electricity and gas, telephone service, computers, vehicles, tools and equipment, furniture, and even audits.

✔ Its **debt sources of capital,** who loan money to the business, charge interest on the amount loaned, and have to be repaid at definite dates in the future.

✔ Its **equity sources of capital,** the individuals and financial institutions that invest money in the business and expect the business to earn profit on the capital they invest.

✔ The **government agencies** that collect income taxes, payroll taxes, value-added tax and excise duties from the business.

Figure 1-1 illustrates the interactions between the business and the other parties in the economic exchange.

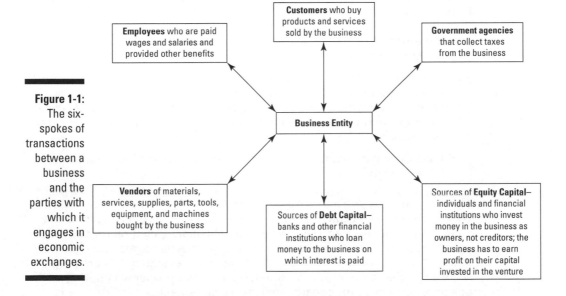

Figure 1-1: The six-spokes of transactions between a business and the parties with which it engages in economic exchanges.

Even a relatively small business generates a surprisingly large number of transactions, and all transactions have to be recorded. Certain other events that have a financial impact on the business have to be recorded as well. These are called *events* because they're not based on give-and-take bargaining – unlike the something-given-for-something-received nature of economic exchanges. Events such as the following have an economic impact on a business and have to be recorded:

✔ A business may lose a lawsuit and be ordered to pay damages. The liability to pay the damages should be recorded.

✔ A business may suffer a flood loss that is uninsured. The water-logged assets may have to be written off, meaning that the recorded values of the assets are reduced to nil if they no longer have any value to the business.

✔ A business may decide to abandon a major product line and downsize its workforce, requiring that severance be paid to laid-off employees.

Taking a Closer Look at Financial Statements

As we mention in the preceding sections, accountants prepare certain basic financial statements for a business. The three basic financial statements are the following:

✔ **Balance Sheet:** A summary of the financial position of the business at the end of the period.

✔ **Profit and loss account:** A summary of sales revenue and expenses that determines the profit (or loss) for the period just ended. This is also called the *income statement,* or simply abbreviated to the *P&L statement.* (Alternative titles also include the *operating statement* and the *earnings statement.*)

✔ **Cash flow statement:** A summary of cash inflows and cash outflows for the period just ended.

This section gives you a description of these statements that constitute a business's financial centre of gravity. We show you the general format and content of these three accounting reports. The managing director and chief executive officer of a business (plus other top-level managers and financial officers) are responsible for seeing that the financial statements are prepared according to financial reporting standards and that proper accounting methods have been used to prepare the financial statements.

If a business's financial statements are later discovered to be seriously in error or misleading, the business and its top executives can be sued for damages suffered by lenders and investors who relied on the financial statements. For this reason, business managers should understand their responsibility for the financial statements and the accounting methods used to prepare the statements. In a court of law, they can't plead ignorance.

We frequently meet managers who don't seem to have a clue about the three primary statements. This situation is a little scary; a manager who doesn't understand financial statements is like an aeroplane pilot who doesn't understand the instrument readouts in the cockpit. A manager *could* run the business and 'land the plane safely', but knowing how to read the vital signs along the way is much more prudent.

In short, business managers at all levels – from the board of directors down to the lower rungs on the management ladder, and especially managers of smaller businesses who have to be jacks-of-all-trades in running the business – need to understand financial statements and the accounting methods used to prepare the statements. Also, lenders to a business, investors in a business, business lawyers, government regulators of business, entrepreneurs, employees who depend on the continued financial success of the business for their jobs, anyone thinking of becoming an entrepreneur and starting a business, and, yes, even economists, should know the basics of financial statement accounting. We've noticed that even experienced business journalists, who ought to know better, sometimes refer to the balance sheet when they're talking about profit performance. The bottom line is found in the profit and loss account, not the balance sheet!

The balance sheet

The balance sheet is the essential financial statement that reports the main types of assets owned by a business. Assets are only half the picture, however. Almost all businesses borrow money. At the date of preparing the balance sheet, a business owes money to its lenders, who will be paid sometime in the future. Also, most businesses buy many things on credit and at the balance sheet date owe money to their suppliers, which will be paid in the future. Amounts owed to lenders and suppliers are called *liabilities*. A balance sheet reports the main types of liabilities of the business, and separates those due in the short term and those due in the longer term.

Could total liabilities be greater than a business's total assets? Well, not likely – unless the business has been losing money hand-over-fist. In the vast majority of cases a business has more total assets than total liabilities. Why? For two reasons: (1) its owners have invested money in the business, which is not a liability of the business; and (2) the business has earned profit over the years and some of the profit has been retained in the business. (Profit increases assets.) The sum of invested capital from owners and retained profit is called *owners' equity*. The excess of total assets over total liabilities is traceable to owners' equity. A balance sheet reports the make-up of the owners' equity of a business.

You generally see the balance sheet in the following layout:

Basic Format of the Balance Sheet

Assets, or the economic resources the business owns: examples are cash on deposit, prod ucts held for sale to customers, and buildings.	**Liabilities,** which arise from borrowing money and buying things on credit.
	Owners' Equity, which arises from two sources: money invested by the owners, and profit earned and retained by the business.

One reason the balance sheet is called by this name is that the two sides balance, or are equal in total amounts:

Total Recorded Amount of Assets = Total Recorded Amount of Liabilities + Total Recorded Amount of Owners' Equity

Owners' equity is sometimes referred to as *net worth*. You compute net worth as follows:

Assets – Liabilities = Net Worth

Net worth is not a particularly good term because it implies that the business is worth the amount recorded in its owners' equity accounts. Though the term may suggest that the business could be sold for this amount, nothing is further from the truth. (Chapter 6 presents more information about the recorded value of owners' equity reported in the balance sheet, and Chapter 14 discusses the market prices of shares, which are units of ownership in a business corporation.)

The profit and loss account

The profit and loss account is the all-important financial statement that summarises the profit-making activities (or operations) of a business over a time period. In very broad outline, the statement is reported like this:

Basic Format of the Profit and Loss Account

Sales Revenue (from the sales of products and services to customers)

Less Expenses (which include a wide variety of costs paid by the business, including the cost of products sold to customers, wages and benefits paid to employees, occupancy costs, administrative costs and income tax)

Equals Net Income (which is referred to as the *bottom line* and means final profit after all expenses are deducted from sales revenue)

The profit and loss account gets the most attention from business managers and investors – not that they ignore the other two financial statements. The very abbreviated versions of profit and loss accounts that you see in the financial press, such as in *The Financial Times,* report only the top line (sales revenue) and the bottom line (net profit). In actual practice, the profit and loss account is more involved than the basic format shown here. Refer to Chapter 5 for more information on profit and loss accounts.

The cash flow statement

The cash flow statement presents a summary of the sources and uses of cash in a business during a financial period. Smart business managers hardly get the word *profit* out of their mouths before mentioning *cash flow.* Successful business managers can tell you that they have to manage both profit *and* cash flow; you can't do one and ignore the other. Business is a two-headed dragon in this respect. Ignoring cash flow can pull the rug out from under a successful profit formula. Still, some managers become preoccupied with making profit and overlook cash flow.

For financial reporting, cash flows are divided into three basic categories:

Basic Format of the Cash Flow Statement

(1) **Cash flow** from the profit-making activities, or *operating activities,* for the period (***Note:*** *Operating* means the profit-making transactions of the business.)

(2) **Cash inflows and outflows** from *investing activities* for the period

(3) **Cash inflows and outflows** from the *financing activities* for the period

You determine the bottom-line net increase (or decrease) in cash during the period by adding the three types of cash flows shown in the preceding list.

Part 1 explains why net cash flow from sales revenue and expenses – the business's profit-making operating activities – is more or less than the amount of profit reported in the profit and loss account. The *actual* cash inflows from revenues and outflows for expenses run on a different timetable than the sales revenue and expenses, which are recorded for determining profit. It's like two different trains going to the same destination – the second train (the cash flow train) runs on a later schedule than the first train (the recording of sales revenue and expenses in the accounts of the business). Chapter 7 explains the cash flow analysis of profit as well as the other sources of cash and the uses of cash.

Part 2 of the cash flow statement sums up the major long-term investments made by the business during the year, such as constructing a new production plant or replacing machinery and equipment. If the business sold any of its long-term assets, it reports the cash inflows from these divestments in this section of the cash flow statement.

Part 3 sums up the financing activities of the business during the period – borrowing new money from lenders and raising new capital investment in the business from its owners. Cash outflows to pay off debt are reported in this section, as well as cash distributions from profit paid to the owners of the business.

The cash flow statement reports the net increase or net decrease in cash during the year (or other time period), caused by the three types of cash flows. This increase or decrease in cash during the year is never referred to as the *bottom line*. This important term is strictly limited to the last line of the profit and loss account, which reflects net income – the final profit after all expenses are deducted.

Imagine you have a highlighter pen in your hand, and the three basic financial statements of a business are in front of you. What are the most important numbers to mark? Financial statements do *not* have any numbers highlighted; they don't come with headlines like newspapers. You have to find your own headlines. *Bottom-line profit* in the profit and loss account is one number you would mark for sure. Another key number is *cash flow from operating activities* in the cash flow statement, or some variation of this number. Cash flow has become very important these days. Chapter 7 explains why this internal source of cash is so important and the various definitions of *cash flow* (did you think there was only one meaning of this term?).

Accounting as a Career

In our highly developed economy, many people make their living as accountants – and here we're using the term *accountant* in the broadest possible sense. Despite the introduction of new technology, the number of people employed in accountancy as a profession has shown extensive growth in the past three decades. Accountants work in many areas of business and the public sector in roles ranging from sole practitioner to chief executive of a multinational company. In public practice firms, from small high street to large international practices, accountants provide professional services to a wide range of fee-paying clients from the private individual to large commercial and public sector organisations. These services include audit/assurance, accountancy, tax, business advisory and other management services.

In commerce/industry and the public sector, chartered accountants work in a variety of financial management and financial reporting roles. It is possible for accountants to set up their own firm or become a partner in a private practice. This requires a Practising Certificate, which is awarded by one of the relevant qualifying bodies to accountants with at least two years' experience. There are also opportunities to work abroad.

Because accountants work with numbers and details, you hear references to accountants as bean counters, digit heads, number nerds and other names we don't care to mention here. Accountants take these snide references in their stride and with good humour. Actually, accountants come out among the most respected professionals in many surveys.

Chartered accountant (CA)

In the accounting profession, the mark of distinction is to be a *CA*, which stands for *chartered accountant*. The majority of chartered accountants train in public practice and the first three years are devoted to achieving the chartered qualification. The training involves completion of professional exams together with a period of structured work experience. The professional exam training is provided by the Institute of Chartered Accountants in England and Wales (ICAEW) (www.icaew.co.uk), which is the largest, the Institute of Chartered Accountants of Scotland (ICAS) (www.icas.org.uk), and the Chartered Accountants Ireland (ICAI) (www.icai.ie) – Dublin Office. The structure of the exams and methods of training delivery vary slightly between the institutes and full details can be found on their websites. However, the qualifications cover broadly similar syllabuses and are of equal status and recognition, all leading to the designation 'chartered accountant' (ACA or CA). The syllabuses cover subjects such as accounting, audit, business finance, taxation, law and business management, which are assessed primarily through formal exams. Chartered accountants must remain up-to-date on technical and business issues, so there is a strong emphasis on continuing professional development after qualification.

Other professional bodies that train accountants and are useful to know about include the Chartered Institute of Management Accountants (www.cimaglobal.com), who focus on accounting for and in business, the Chartered Institute of Public Finance and Accountancy (www.cipfa.org.uk), who specialise in the public sector, and the Association of Accounting Technicians (www.aat.org.uk), whose 36,000 members assist chartered accountants in their work, or can themselves join a chartered institute after further study.

The financial controller: The chief accountant in an organisation

After working for an accountancy firm in public practice for a few years, most CAs leave public accounting and go to work for a business or other organisation. Usually, they start at a mid-level accounting position with fairly heavy accounting responsibilities, but some step in as the top accountant in charge of all accounting matters of a business. The top-level accountant in a business organisation is usually called the *financial controller*, or *chief accountant*.

The financial controller designs the entire accounting system of the business and keeps it up-to-date with changes in the tax laws and changes in the accounting rules that govern reporting financial statements to outside lenders and owners. Controllers are responsible for hiring, training, evaluating, promoting and sometimes firing the persons who hold the various bookkeeping and accounting positions in an organisation – which range from payroll functions to the several different types of tax returns that have to be filed on time with different government agencies.

The controller is the lead person in the financial planning and budgeting process of the business organisation. Furthermore, the financial controller designs the accounting reports that all the various managers in the organisation receive – from the sales and marketing managers to the purchasing and procurement managers. These internal reports should be designed to fit the authority and responsibility of each manager; they should provide information for managers' decision-making analysis needs and the information they need to exercise effective control.

The controller also designs and monitors the accounting reports that go to the business's top-level executives, the chief executive officer of the business, and the board of directors. All tough accounting questions and problems get referred to the controller. The controller needs good people management skills, should know how to communicate with all the non-accounting managers in the organisation and at the same time should be an 'accountant's accountant' who has deep expertise in many areas of accounting.

Smaller businesses may have only one or two 'accountants'. The full-time bookkeeper or office manager may carry out many of the duties that would belong to the financial controller in a larger organisation. Smaller businesses often call in a chartered accountant in public practice to advise their accountants. The chartered accountant may function more or less as a part-time controller for a small business, preparing the annual income tax returns and helping to prepare the business's external financial reports.

Accounting branches: Treasury, tax and audit

Accounting from a career perspective can be broken down into three main branches, with some overlap between, particularly in smaller enterprises where, in effect, all three areas are the responsibility of a single person or department:

- ✔ **Financial accounting** is concerned with preparing financial statements summarising past events, usually in the form of profit and loss accounts and balance sheets. These historic statements are mainly of interest to outside parties such as investors, loan providers and suppliers.

- ✔ **Management accounting** involves assembling much more detailed information about current and future planned events to allow management to carry out their roles of planning, control and decision-making. Examples of management accounting information are product costs and cost data relevant to a particular decision, say, a choice between make or buy. Also included in management accounting are preparing and monitoring budgeted costs relating to a product, activity or service. Management accounting information is rarely disclosed to outside parties, though bankers and private equity providers often ask for monthly management accounts as a condition of funding.

- ✔ **Financial management** covers all matters concerning raising finance and ensuring it is used in the most efficient way. For example it would be financially inefficient to raise a long-term loan or sell shares just to finance a short-term increase in sales. It would be the role of financial management to select and use a more cost-effective funding source such as an overdraft. The cost of capital is influenced by both the capital structure adopted as well as the risk of the investments undertaken.

Within these three broad areas of accounting there may be further subsets of accounting relating either to one specific activity, or across the whole spectrum. For example:

- ✔ **Treasury** is a finance function usually only found in a very large company or group of companies. For example, the managing of bank balances to get the maximum interest on positive balances or to minimise the payment of interest on negative balances would be a typical treasury task. This might involve lending money overnight on the money markets. Treasury activity would also be concerned with the managing of exchange risk where financial transactions in foreign currencies are involved.

✔ **Taxation** in a small company is included in the duties of the financial accountant who may need to call on outside professional advice from time to time. Corporation tax on company profits isn't straightforward and the system of capital allowances can be complex for some large companies, groups of companies or multinational companies. The ramifications of value added tax (VAT), sales tax where it applies, employee tax and other related deductions such as National Health Insurance and director benefits in kind, often call for the services of a specialist accountant, or team of accountants. Large companies usually use the services of such firms to minimise the pain and maximise the gain from such taxes and allowances.

✔ **Audit** is another accounting function mainly found in larger organisations. Internal auditors monitor that accounting procedures, documents and computerised transactions are carried out correctly. This work is additional or complementary to that undertaken by external auditors who take a broader approach in providing an independent report to shareholders in the annual report. See Chapter 15 where we discuss this subject in greater depth.

Chapter 2

Bookkeeping 101: From Shoe Boxes to Computers

. . . .

In This Chapter

▶ Understanding the difference between bookkeeping and accounting

▶ Following the steps in the bookkeeping cycle

▶ Managing the bookkeeping and accounting system

▶ Getting down the basics of double-entry accounting

▶ Deterring and detecting errors, irregularities and outright fraud

. . . .

Most people are pretty terrible bookkeepers just because they really don't do much bookkeeping. Admit it. Maybe you balance your chequebook against your bank statement every month and somehow manage to pull together all the records you need for your annual income tax return. But you probably stuff your bills in a drawer and just drag them out once a month when you're ready to pay them. (Hey, that's what we do.) And you almost certainly don't prepare a detailed listing of all your assets and liabilities (even though a listing of assets is a good idea for insurance purposes). We don't prepare a summary statement of our earnings and income for the year or a breakdown of what we spent our money on and how much we saved. Why not? Because we don't need to! Individuals can get along quite well without much bookkeeping – but the exact opposite is true for a business.

One key difference between individuals and businesses is that a business must prepare periodic *financial statements*, the accuracy of which is critical to the business's survival. The business uses the accounts and records generated by its bookkeeping process to prepare these statements; if the accounting records are incomplete or inaccurate, the financial statements will be incomplete or inaccurate. And inaccuracy simply won't do.

Obviously, then, business managers have to be sure that the company's bookkeeping and accounting system is adequate and reliable. This chapter shows managers what bookkeepers and accountants do – mainly so that you can make sure that the information coming out of your accounting system is complete, timely and accurate.

Bookkeeping versus Accounting

Bookkeeping is essentially the process (some would say the drudgery) of recording all the information regarding the transactions and financial activities of a business – the record-keeping aspects of accounting. Bookkeeping is an indispensable subset of accounting. The term *accounting* goes much further, into the realm of designing the bookkeeping system in the first place, establishing controls to make sure that the system is working well, and analysing and verifying the recorded information. Bookkeepers follow orders; accountants give orders.

Accounting can be thought of as what goes on before and after bookkeeping. Accountants prepare reports based on the information accumulated by the bookkeeping process – financial statements, tax returns and various confidential reports to managers. Measuring profit is a very important task that accountants perform, a task that depends on the accuracy of the information recorded by the bookkeeper. The accountant decides how to measure sales revenue and expenses to determine the profit or loss for the period. The tough questions about profit – where it is and what it consists of – can't be answered through bookkeeping alone.

The rest of this book doesn't discuss bookkeeping in any detail – no talk of debits and credits and all that stuff. All you really need to know about bookkeeping, as a business manager, is contained in this chapter alone.

Pedalling through the Bookkeeping Cycle

Figure 2-1 presents an overview of the bookkeeping cycle side-by-side with elements of the accounting system. You can follow the basic bookkeeping steps down the left-hand side. The accounting elements are shown in the right-hand column. The basic steps in the bookkeeping sequence, explained briefly, are as follows. (See also 'Managing the Bookkeeping and Accounting System,' later in this chapter, for more details on some of these steps.)

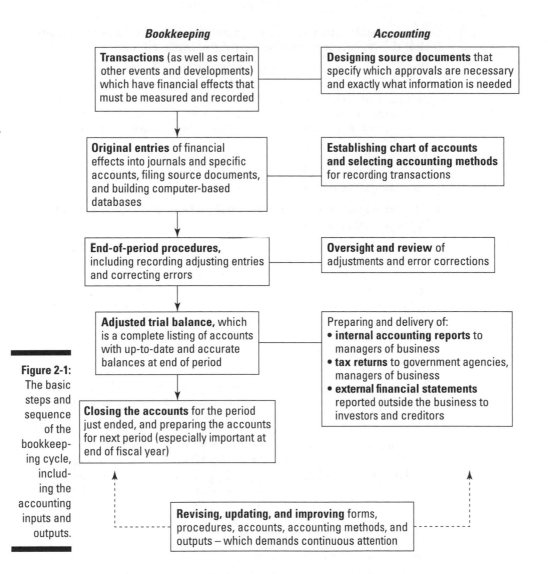

Figure 2-1: The basic steps and sequence of the bookkeeping cycle, including the accounting inputs and outputs.

1. **Record *transactions* – the economic exchanges between a business and the other people and businesses that it deals with.**

   Transactions have financial effects that must be recorded – the business is better off, worse off or at least 'different off' as the result of its transactions. Examples of typical business transactions include paying employees, making sales to customers, borrowing money from the bank and buying products that will be sold to customers. The bookkeeping process begins by identifying all transactions and capturing the relevant information about each transaction.

2. **Prepare and collect *source documents* – transaction documentation that the bookkeeper uses to record the transactions.**

   When buying products, a business gets a *purchase invoice* from the supplier. When borrowing money from the bank, a business signs for an *overdraft*, a copy of which the business keeps. When a customer uses a credit card to buy the business's product, the business gets the *credit card slip* as evidence of the transaction. When preparing payroll cheques, a business depends on *salary schedules* and *time cards.* All of these key business forms serve as sources of information into the bookkeeping system – in other words, information the bookkeeper uses in recording the financial effects of the transaction.

3. **Record original entries (the financial effects of the transactions) into journals and accounts.**

   Using the source document(s) for every transaction, the bookkeeper makes the first, or original, entry into a journal and then into the business's accounts. Only an official, established book of accounts should be used in recording transactions. A *journal* is a chronological record of transactions in the order in which they occur – like a very detailed personal diary. In contrast, an *account* is a separate record for each asset, each liability and so on. One transaction affects two or more accounts. The journal entry records the whole transaction in one place; then each piece is recorded in the two or more accounts changed by the transaction.

   Here's a simple example that illustrates recording of a transaction in a *journal* and then *posting* the changes caused by the transaction in the *accounts.* Expecting a big demand from its customers, a retail bookshop purchases, on credit, 50 copies of *Understanding Business Accounting For Dummies* from the publisher, John Wiley & Sons, Ltd. The books are received and placed on the shelves. (50 copies are a lot to put on the shelves, but our relatives promised to rush down and buy several copies each.) The bookshop now owns the books and also owes John Wiley £600.00, which is the cost of the 50 copies. You look only at recording the purchase of the books, not recording subsequent sales of the books and paying the bill to John Wiley.

   The bookshop has established a specific stock or account called 'Stock-Trade Paperbacks' for books like this. And the purchase liability to the publisher should be entered in the account 'Creditor-Publishers'. So the journal entry for this purchase is recorded as follows:

Stock-Trade Paperbacks	+ £600.00
Creditor-Publishers	+ £600.00

   This pair of changes is first recorded in one journal entry. Then, sometime later, each change is *posted,* or recorded, in the separate accounts – one an asset and the other a liability.

   Not so long ago, bookkeepers had to record these entries by hand, and even today there's nothing wrong with a good hand-entry (manual) bookkeeping system. But bookkeepers can now use computer programs that take over many of the tedious chores of bookkeeping. Computers have come to the rescue – of course, typing has replaced hand cramps with repetitive strain injury, but at least the work gets done more quickly and with fewer errors! (See Appendix B for more about popular accounting software packages for personal computers.)

We can't exaggerate the importance of entering transaction data correctly and in a timely manner. For example, an important reason that most retailers these days use cash registers that read bar-coded information on products is to more accurately capture the necessary information and to speed up the entry of this information.

4. **Perform end-of-period procedures – preliminary steps for preparing the accounting reports and financial statements at the end of every period.**

A *period* can be any stretch of time – from one day to one month to one quarter (three months) to one year and is determined by the needs of the business. A year is usually the longest period of time that a business would wait to prepare its financial statements. As a matter of fact, most businesses need accounting reports and financial statements at the end of each quarter, and many need monthly financial statements.

Before the accounting reports can be prepared at the end of the period (see Figure 2-1), the bookkeeper needs to bring the accounts of the business up-to-date and complete the bookkeeping process. One step, for example, is recording the *depreciation expense* for the period (see Chapter 6 for more on depreciation). Another step is getting an actual count of the business's stock so that the stock records can be adjusted to account for shoplifting, employee theft and so on.

The accountant needs to take the final step and check for errors in the business's accounts. Data entry clerks and bookkeepers may not fully understand the unusual nature of some business transactions and may have entered transactions incorrectly. One reason for establishing *internal controls* (discussed in 'Protect the family jewels: Internal controls', later in this chapter) is to keep errors to an absolute minimum. Ideally, accounts should contain very few errors at the end of the period, but the accountant can't make any assumptions and should make a final check for any errors that fell through the cracks.

5. **Prepare the adjusted trial balance for the accountants.**

After all the end-of-period procedures have been completed, the book-keeper prepares a complete listing of all accounts, which is called the *adjusted trial balance.* Modest-sized businesses maintain hundreds of accounts for their various assets, liabilities, owners' equity, revenue and expenses. Larger businesses keep thousands of accounts, and very large businesses may keep more than 10,000 accounts. In contrast, external financial statements, tax returns and internal accounting reports to managers contain a relatively small number of accounts. For example, a typical external balance sheet reports only 20 to 25 accounts, and a typical income tax return contains less than 100 accounts.

The accountant takes the adjusted trial balance and telescopes similar accounts into one summary amount that is reported in a financial report or tax return. For example, a business may keep hundreds of separate stock accounts, every one of which is listed in the adjusted trial balance. The accountant collapses all these accounts into one summary stock account that is presented in the external balance sheet of the business.

In short, the large number of specific accounts listed in the adjusted trial balance is condensed into a comparatively small number of accounts that are reported in financial statements and tax returns. In grouping the accounts, the accountant should comply with established financial reporting standards and income tax requirements.

6. *Close the books* – **bring the bookkeeping for the fiscal year just ended to a close and get things ready to begin the bookkeeping process for the coming fiscal year.**

   Books is the common term for *accounts*. A business's transactions are a constant stream of activities that don't end tidily on the last day of the year, which can make preparing financial statements and tax returns challenging. The business has to draw a clear line of demarcation between activities for the year (the 12-month accounting period) ended and the year yet to come by *closing the books* for one year and starting with fresh books for the next year.

The business may have an *accounting manual* that spells out in great detail the specific accounts and procedures for recording transactions. But all businesses change over time, and they occasionally need to review their accounting system and make revisions. Companies do not take this task lightly; discontinuities in the accounting system can be major shocks and have to be carefully thought out. Nevertheless, bookkeeping and accounting systems can't remain static for very long. If these systems were never changed, bookkeepers would still be sitting on high stools making entries with quill pens and ink in leather-bound ledgers.

Managing the Bookkeeping and Accounting System

In our experience, far too many business managers either ignore their bookkeeping and accounting systems or take them for granted – unless something obvious goes wrong. The managers assume that if the books are in balance, then everything is okay. The section 'Recording transactions using debits and credits', later in this chapter, covers just exactly what 'the books being in balance' means – it does *not* necessarily mean that everything is okay.

To determine whether your bookkeeping system is up to scratch, check out the following sections, which, taken as a whole, provide a checklist of the most important elements of a good system.

Categorise your financial information: The chart of accounts

Suppose that you're the accountant for a company and you're faced with the daunting task of preparing the annual income tax return for the business. This demands that you report the following kinds of expenses (and this list contains just the minimum!):

- Advertising
- Bad debts
- Charitable contributions
- Compensation of directors
- Cost of goods sold
- Depreciation
- Employee benefits
- Interest
- Pensions and profit-sharing plans
- Rents
- Repairs and maintenance
- Salaries and wages
- Taxes and licenses

You must provide additional information for some of these expenses. For example, the cost of goods sold expense is determined in a schedule that also requires stock cost at the beginning of the year, purchases during the year, cost of labour during the year (for manufacturers), other costs and stock cost at year-end.

Where do you start? Well, if it's March 1 and the tax return deadline is March 15, you start by panicking – unless you were smart enough to think ahead about the kinds of information your business would need to report. In fact, when your accountant first designs your business's accounting system, he or she should dissect every report to managers, the external financial statements and the tax returns, breaking down all the information into categories such as those we just listed.

For each category, you need an *account*, a record of the activities in that category. An account is basically a focused history of a particular dimension of a business. In bookkeeping this means a basic category of information in which the financial effects of transactions are recorded and which serves as the source of information for preparing financial statements, tax returns and reports to managers.

The term *general ledger* refers to the complete set of accounts established and maintained by a business. The *chart of accounts* is a term used to describe a formal index of these accounts – the complete listing and classification of the accounts used by the business to record its transactions. *General ledger* usually refers to the actual accounts and often to the balances in these accounts at some particular time.

The chart of accounts, even for a relatively small business, normally contains 100 or more accounts. Larger business organisations need thousands of accounts. The larger the number, the more likely that the accounts are given number codes according to some scheme – all assets may be in the 100–300 range, all liabilities in the 400–500 range and so on.

As a business manager, you should make sure that the person in charge of accounting (or perhaps an outside chartered accountant) reviews the chart of accounts periodically to determine whether the accounts are up-to-date and adequate for the business's needs. Over time, income tax rules change, the company may go into new lines of business, the company could decide to offer additional employee benefits and so on. Most businesses are in constant flux, and the chart of accounts has to keep up with these changes.

Standardise source document forms and procedures

Businesses move on paperwork. Whether placing an order to buy products, selling a product to a customer or determining the earnings of an employee for the month – virtually every business transaction needs paperwork, known as *source documents*. Source documents serve as evidence of the terms and conditions agreed upon by the business and the other person or organisation that it's dealing with. Both parties receive some kind of source document. For example, for a sale at a cash register, the customer gets a sales receipt, and the business keeps a running record of all transactions in the register.

Clearly, an accounting system needs to standardise the forms and procedures for processing and recording all normal, repetitive transactions and should control the generation and handling of these source documents.

From the bookkeeping point of view, these business forms and documents are very important because they provide the input information needed for recording transactions in the business's accounts. Sloppy paperwork leads to sloppy accounting records, and sloppy accounting records just won't do when the time comes to prepare tax returns and financial statements.

Check out a business office-supply store to see the kinds of forms that you can buy right off the shelf. You can find many – maybe all – of the basic forms and documents that you need for recording business transactions, although most firms have to design at least some of their own forms. Also, personal computer accounting software packages (see Appendix B for more detail) provide templates for common business forms.

Don't be penny-wise and pound-foolish: The need for competent, trained personnel

What good is meticulously collecting source documents if the information on those documents isn't entered into your system correctly? You shouldn't try to save a few pounds by hiring the lowest-paid people you can find. Bookkeepers and accountants, like all other employees in a business, should have the skills and knowledge needed to perform their functions. No-brainer, right? Well, determining what that level is *can* be difficult. Here are some guidelines for choosing the right people to enter and manipulate your business's data and for making sure that those people *remain* the right people:

- ✔ **University degree:** Many accountants in business organisations have a degree in accounting. However, as you move down the accounting department you find that more and more employees do not have a degree and perhaps even haven't taken any courses in accounting.

- ✔ **ACA, ACCA or CIMA:** The main professional accounting credentials are: ACA sponsored by the Institute of Chartered Accountants; ACCA sponsored by the Association of Chartered Certified Accountants; and CIMA sponsored by the Chartered Institute of Management Accountants. All of these qualifications are evidence that the person has passed tough exams and has a good understanding of business accounting and income tax. The Association of Chartered Certified Accountants (www.accaglobal.com, click on 'Public Interest' and then on 'Find an Accountant') and the Institute of Chartered Accountants (www.icaewfirms.co.uk) have online directories of qualified accountants. You can search these directories by name (useful if you have a personal recommendation from a colleague you respect), location (handy if you just want someone nearby), the business sector you're in (helpful for tapping into specialist skills) or any specific accountancy skills or knowledge you're looking for.

- ✔ **Accounting technicians:** These people assist chartered accountants in their work, or can join a chartered institute themselves after further study. The Association of Accounting Technicians' website (`www.aat.org.uk`, then click on 'Employers' and 'Recruitment') provides guidance on pay structures and tips on how to find an accountant.

- ✔ **Bookkeepers:** These are the lowest-cost players in this game. They perform the basic entry work covering anything from simply recording the transactions in your books through to producing accounts, preparing the VAT return or doing the Payroll. The International Association of Book-keepers (`www.iab.org.uk`) and the Institute of Certified Bookkeepers (`www.book-keepers.org`) offer free matching services to help small businesses find a bookkeeper to suit their particular needs.

- ✔ **Continuing education:** Many short-term courses, e-learning and home-study programmes are available at very reasonable costs for keeping up on the latest accounting developments. Accountancy bodies that give practising certificates, which allow accountants to work with businesses in public practice, will expect them to take continuing education in approved courses in order to keep their practising certificates.

- ✔ **Integrity:** What's possibly the most important quality to look for is also the hardest to judge. Bookkeepers and accountants need to be honest people because of the amount of control they have over your business's financial records.

Protect the family jewels: Internal controls

Every accounting system should establish and vigorously enforce *internal controls* – basically, additional forms and procedures over and above what's strictly needed to move operations along. These additional controls serve to deter and detect errors (honest mistakes) and all forms of dishonesty by employees, customers, suppliers and even managers themselves. Internal controls are like a public weighbridge that makes sure that a heavy goods vehicle's load doesn't exceed the limits and that the vehicle has a valid licence. You're just checking that your staff are playing by the rules.

For example, to prevent or minimise shoplifting, most retailers now have video surveillance, tags that set off the alarms if the customer leaves the store with the tag still on the product, and so on. Likewise, a business has to implement certain procedures and forms to prevent, as much as possible, any theft, embezzlement, scams and fraud (and simple mistakes) by its own employees and managers.

In our experience, smaller businesses tend to think that they're immune to embezzlement and fraud by their loyal and trusted employees. Yet a recent study found that small businesses are hit the hardest by fraud and usually can least afford the consequences. Your business, too, should put checks and balances into place to discourage dishonest practices and to uncover any fraud and theft as soon as possible. For example, virtually every retailer that deals with the general public installs protection against shoplifting. Likewise, every business should guard against 'internal shoplifting' or fraud by its employees and managers.

Keep the scales in balance with double-entry accounting

A business needs to be sure that *both* sides of the economic exchange are recorded for all its transactions. Economic exchanges involve a give and take, or something given for something received. Businesses (and other entities as well) use the *double-entry accounting method* to make sure that both sides of their transactions are recorded and to keep their books in balance. This method, which has been used for hundreds of years, involves recording certain changes as debits and the counterbalancing changes as credits. See 'Double-Entry Accounting for Non-Accountants,' later in this chapter, for more details.

Check your figures: End-of-period procedures checklist

Like a pilot before take-off, an accountant should have a clear checklist to follow at the end of each period and especially at the end of the accounting year. Two main things have to be done at the end of the period:

- ✔ **Normal, routine *adjusting entries* for certain expenses:** For example, depreciation isn't a transaction as such and therefore hasn't been recorded as an expense in the flow of transactions recorded in the day-to-day bookkeeping process. (Chapter 6 explains depreciation expense.) Similarly, certain other expenses and some revenues may not have been associated with a specific transaction and will not have been recorded. These kinds of adjustments are necessary for providing complete and accurate reports.

✔ ***Careful sweep of all matters* to check for other developments that may affect the accuracy of the accounts:** For example, the company may have discontinued a product line. The remaining stock of these products may have to be removed from the asset account, with a loss recorded in the period. Or the company may have settled a long-standing lawsuit, and the amount of damages needs to be recorded. Layoffs and severance packages are another example of what the chief accountant needs to look for before preparing reports.

Lest you still think of accounting as dry and dull, let us tell you that end-of-period accounting procedures can stir up controversy of the heated-debate variety. These procedures require that the accountant make decisions and judgments that upper management may not agree with. For example, the accountant may suggest recording major losses that would put a big dent in the profit for the year or cause the business to report a loss. The outside auditor (assuming that the business has an audit of its financial statements) often gets in the middle of the argument. These kinds of debates are precisely why you business managers need to know some accounting: to hold up your end of the argument and participate in the great sport of yelling and name-calling – strictly on a professional basis, of course.

Keep good records: Happy audit trails to you!

The happy trails that accountants like to walk are called *audit trails.* Good bookkeeping systems leave good audit trails. An audit trail is a clear-cut path of the sequence of events leading up to an entry in the accounts; an accountant starts with the source documents and follows through the bookkeeping steps in recording transactions to reconstruct this path. Even if a business doesn't have an outside accountant do an annual audit, the firm's management accountant has frequent occasion to go back to the source documents and either verify certain information in the accounts or reconstruct the information in a different manner. For example, suppose that a salesperson is claiming some suspicious-looking travel expenses; the accountant would probably want to go through all this person's travel and entertainment reimbursements for the past year.

If HM Revenue and Customs comes in for a field audit of your business, you'd better have good audit trails to substantiate all your expense deductions and sales revenue for the year. Rules exist about saving source documents for a reasonable period of time (usually at least five years) and having a well-defined process for making bookkeeping entries and keeping accounts. Think twice before throwing away source documents. Also, ask your accountant to demonstrate, and lay out for your inspection, the audit trails for key transactions – such as cash collections, sales, cash disbursements, stock purchases and so on. Even in computer-based accounting systems, the importance of audit trails is recognised. Well-designed computer programs provide the ability to backtrack through the sequence of steps in the recording of specific transactions. The HM Revenue and Customs website (go to `www.hmrc.gov.uk` and click on 'Businesses and corporations') gives you the lowdown on which books to keep and for how long. You can search for info about any unlisted topics by using the search panel at the top of the homepage.

Look out for unusual events and developments

Business managers should encourage their accountants to be alert to anything out of the ordinary that may require attention. Suppose that the debtor balance for a particular customer is rapidly increasing – that is, the customer is buying more and more from your company on credit but isn't paying for these purchases quickly. Maybe the customer has switched more of his or her company's purchases to your business and is buying more from you only because he or she is buying less from other businesses. But maybe the customer is planning to stuff your business and take off without paying his or her debts. Or maybe the customer is secretly planning to go into bankruptcy soon and is stockpiling products before the company's credit rating heads south. To some extent, accountants have to act as the eyes and ears of the business. Of course, that's one of your main functions as business manager, but your accounting staff can play an important role as well.

Design truly useful accounting reports for managers

We have to be careful in this section; we have strong opinions on this matter. We have seen too many hit-and-miss accounting reports to managers – difficult to decipher and not very useful or relevant to the manager's decision-making needs and control functions.

Part of the problem lies with the managers themselves. As a business manager, have you told your accounting staff what you need to know, when you need it, and how to present it in the most efficient manner? Probably not. When you stepped into your position you probably didn't hesitate to rearrange your office and maybe even insisted on hiring your own support staff. Yet you most likely lay down like a lapdog regarding your accounting reports.

Maybe you've assumed that the reports have to be done a certain way and that arguing for change is no use.

On the other hand, accountants bear a good share of the blame for the poor reports. Accountants should proactively study the manager's decision-making responsibilities and provide the information that is most useful, presented in the most easily digestible manner.

In designing the chart of accounts, the accountant should also keep in mind the type of information needed for management reports. To exercise control, managers need much more detail than what's reported on tax returns and external financial statements. And, as Chapter 9 explains, expenses should be regrouped into different categories for management decision-making analysis. A good chart of accounts looks to both the external and the internal (management) needs for information.

So what's the answer for a manager who receives poorly formatted reports? Demand a report format that suits your needs! See Chapter 9 for a useful profit analysis model (and make sure that your accountant reads that chapter as well).

Double-Entry Accounting for Non-Accountants

A business is a *two-sided* entity. It accumulates assets on one side – by borrowing money, persuading investors to put money in the business as owners, purchasing assets on credit and making profit. Profit (net income) is essentially an increase in assets, not from increasing liabilities and not from additional capital infusion from owners, but rather as the net result of sales revenue less expenses. Assets don't fall on a business like manna from heaven. Assets have *sources*, and these sources are *claims* of one sort or another on the assets of a business. A business needs to keep track of the sources of assets, according to the type of claim each source has against the assets. This is precisely the reason for and nature of *double-entry accounting*.

The two-sided nature of a business entity and its activities

In a nutshell, double-entry accounting means *two-sided* accounting. Both the assets of a business and the sources of and claims on its assets are accounted for. Suppose that a business reports £10 million in total assets.

That means the total sources of and claims on its assets are also reported at a total of £10 million. Each asset source has a different type of claim. Some liabilities charge interest and some don't; some have to be paid soon, and other loans to the business may not come due for five or ten years. Owners' equity may be mainly from capital invested by the owners and very little from retained earnings (profit not distributed to the owners). Or the mix of owners' equity sources may be just the reverse.

The sources of and claims on the assets of a business fall into two broad categories: *liabilities* and *owners' equity*. With a few technical exceptions that we won't go into, the amount of liabilities that the business reports are the amounts that will be paid to the creditors at the maturity dates of the liabilities. In other words, the amounts of liabilities are definite amounts to be paid at certain future dates.

In contrast, the amounts reported for owners' equity are *historical* amounts, based on how much capital the owners invested in the business in the past and how much profit the business has recorded. Owners' equity, unlike the liabilities of a business, has no maturity date at which time the money has to be returned to the owners. When looking at the amount of owners' equity reported in a balance sheet, don't think that this amount could be taken out of the business. Owners' equity is tied up in the business indefinitely.

So one reason for double-entry accounting is the two-sided nature of a business entity – assets are on one side and the sources of and claims on assets are on the other side. The second reason for double-entry accounting is the *economic exchange* nature of business activities, referring to the give-and-receive nature of the transactions that a business engages in to pursue its financial objectives. Consider a few typical transactions:

- A business borrows £10 million. It receives money, so the company's cash increases. In exchange, the business promises to return the £10 million to the lender at some future date so the company's debt increases. Interest on the loan is paid in exchange for the use of the money over time.

- The business buys products that it will later resell to its customers: It gives money for the products (the company's cash decreases) and receives the products (the company's stock increases).

- The business sells products: It receives cash or promises of cash to come later (the company's debtors increase), and it gives the products to the customer (the company's stock decreases). Of course, the business should sell the products for more than cost. The excess of the amount received over product cost is called *gross profit*, from which many other expenses have to be deducted. (Chapter 5 explains the profit-making transactions leading to bottom-line profit or loss.)

Recording transactions using debits and credits

Using *debits and credits* is a marvellous technique for making sure that both sides of exchanges are recorded and for keeping both sides of the accounting equation in balance. The recording of every transaction requires the same value for the debits on one side and the credits on the other side. Just think back to maths class in your schooldays: What you have on one side of the equal sign (in this case, in the accounting equation) must equal what you have on the other side of the equal sign.

See the table for how debits and credits work in the balance sheet accounts of a business. The rules of debits and credits:

Changes	In Assets	In Liabilities and Owners' Equities
Increases	Debit	Credit
Decreases	Credit	Debit

Note: Sales revenue and expense accounts, which aren't listed, also follow debit and credit rules. A revenue item increases owners' equity (thus is a credit), and an expense item decreases owners' equity (thus is a debit).

As a business manager, you don't need to know all the mechanics and technical aspects of using debits and credits. Here's what you do need to know:

✔ **The basic premise of the accounting equation:** Assets equal the sources of the assets and the claims on the assets. That is, the total of assets on the one side should equal the sum of total liabilities and total owners' equity on the other side.

✔ **The important difference between liabilities and owners' equity accounts:** Liabilities need to be paid off at definite due dates in the future. Owners' equity has no such claims for definite payments at definite dates. As such, these two accounts must be kept separate.

✔ **Balanced books don't necessarily mean correct balances:** If debits equal credits, the entry for the transaction is correct as far as recording equal amounts on both sides of the transaction. However, even if the debits equal the credits, other errors are possible. The bookkeeper may have recorded the debits and credits in a wrong account, or may have entered wrong amounts, or may have missed recording an entry altogether. Having balanced books simply means that the total of accounts with debit balances equals the total of accounts with credit balances. The important thing is whether the books (the accounts) have *correct* balances, which depends on whether all transactions and other developments have been recorded and accounted for correctly.

Making Sure the Books Don't Get Cooked

Cooked is a catch-all term; we're using the term in its broadest sense to include any type of dishonest, unethical, immoral or illegal practice. Our concern here is with the effects of distortion on a business's accounting records, not with the broader social and criminal aspects of fraudulent accounting – which are very serious, of course, but which are outside the scope of this book.

A business should capture and record faithfully all transactions in its accounting records. Having said this, we have to admit that some business activities are deliberately *not* accounted for or are accounted for in a way that disguises their true nature. For example, *money laundering* involves taking money from illegal sources (such as drug dealing) and passing it through a business to make it look legitimate – to give the money a false identity. This money can hardly be recorded as 'revenue from drug sales' in the accounts of the business.

Fraud occurs in large corporations and in one-owner/manager-controlled small businesses – and every size business in between. Some types of fraud are more common in small businesses, including *sales skimming* (not recording all sales revenue, to deflate the taxable income of the business and its owner) and the recording of personal expenses through the business (to make these expenses deductible for income tax). Some kinds of fraud are committed mainly by large businesses, including paying bribes to public officials and entering into illegal conspiracies to fix prices or divide the market. The purchasing managers in any size business can be tempted to accept kickbacks and under-the-table payoffs from vendors and suppliers.

We should mention another problem that puts accountants in the hot seat: In many situations, two or more businesses are controlled by the same person or the same group of investors. Revenue and expenses can be arbitrarily shifted among the different business entities under common control. For one person to have a controlling ownership interest in two or more businesses is perfectly legal, and such an arrangement often makes good business sense. For example, a retail business rents a building from a property business, and the same person is the majority owner of both businesses. The problem arises when that person arbitrarily sets the monthly rent to shift profit between the two businesses; a high rent generates more profit for the property business and lower profit for the retail business. This kind of manoeuvre may even be perfectly legal, but it raises a fundamental accounting issue.

Readers of financial statements are entitled to assume that all activities between the business and the other parties it deals with are based on what's called *arm's-length bargaining*, meaning that the business and the other parties have a purely business relationship. When that's not the case, the financial report should – but usually doesn't – use the term *related parties* to describe persons and organisations who are not at arm's length with the business.

According to financial reporting standards, your accountant should advise you, the business manager, to disclose any substantial related-party transactions in your external financial statements.

In short, fraud occurs in the business world. Most of these schemes require *cooking the books* – which means altering entries in the accounts to cover the fraud or simply not recording certain entries that should be recorded. If you saw an expense account called *bribes,* you would tend to be a little suspicious, but unethical bookkeepers and accountants are usually a tad cleverer than that. You can find several tips on uncovering and preventing fraud in 'Managing the Bookkeeping and Accounting System' earlier in this chapter.

When the books have been cooked, the financial statements prepared from the accounts are distorted, incorrect and probably misleading. Lenders, other creditors and the owners who have capital invested in the business rely on the company's financial statements. Also, a business's managers and board of directors (the group of people who oversee a business enterprise) may be misled – assuming that they're not a party to the fraud, of course – and may also have liability to third-party creditors and investors for their failure to catch the fraud. Creditors and investors who end up suffering losses have legal grounds to sue the managers and directors (and perhaps the auditors who did not catch the fraud) for damages suffered.

The Sarbanes-Oxley Act, a new set of rules and regulations designed to ensure truthful accounting in companies listed on the American stock market, came into force in 2002. Chapter 1 gives you information about Sarbanes-Oxley.

Chapter 3

Taxes, Taxes and More Taxes

· ·

In This Chapter

▶ Paying taxes as an employer and a property owner

▶ Putting on your tax collector hat and collecting Value Added Tax (VAT)

▶ Determining how much of business profit goes to the government

▶ Allowing company tax methods to override good accounting methods

▶ Looking at the different ways company tax works for different business structures

· ·

As an employer, a business pays taxes. As a property owner or occupier, a business pays taxes. As a seller of goods and services, a business collects Value Added Tax paid by customers and remits the amounts to the government's Customs and Excise Department. And, of course, a business, or its owners, must pay corporate income tax. Yikes! Is there no escaping the tax millstone?

Nope, afraid not (short of resorting to illegal activity or a sly move to another country – you'll have to find another book to tell you about those options). But you can take advantage of the many options in tax laws that can minimise how much you pay and delay your payment (a perfectly legal strategy known as *tax avoidance*). This chapter starts you on your way by explaining the various types of taxation that a business faces.

We say that this chapter '*starts* you on your way' because we can't possibly provide you with exhaustive detail in one chapter. And besides, no one can give you good tax advice without first looking at your specific situation – consult a professional tax expert for that.

Taxing Wages and Property

Even if you don't earn a profit in your business, you still have to pay certain taxes. Unlike corporation tax, which is a *contingent* or *conditional* tax that depends on whether a business earns taxable income for the year, the two major types of non-income taxes – *employer payroll taxes* and *business rates* – always have to be paid. (See 'Taxing Your Bottom Line: Company Taxes,' later in this chapter, for more about income tax.)

Putting the government on the payroll: Employer taxes

In addition to deducting income tax from employees' wages and remitting those amounts to the proper government agencies, businesses need to pay National Insurance for all employees, yourself included. (Actually, National Insurance isn't really a tax, but we won't get technical.)

National Insurance

Most people don't realise that they usually pay less than half of their National Insurance bill – the employer picks up the rest of the tab. The idea is that the burden should be shared almost evenly, but with the employer generally picking up a little more of the tab.

We don't want to get into a debate about the National Insurance system and the financial problems it's facing; we'll just say that the amount you'll pay in National Insurance almost certainly won't diminish in the future. Here's an idea of what a business pays in National Insurance: In 20011/12, the first £5,315 of annual wages were exempt from any National Insurance charges. Then, up to a ceiling of £42,475, the employer pays 13.8 per cent.

Employment tax

Employing people requires you to manage a PAYE (Pay As You Earn) system. If your business is a limited company, the owner (you) is also liable for PAYE. You will also have to deduct National Insurance. Both these tasks will involve some additional record keeping, as, once again, owner-managers are being asked to act as unpaid tax collectors. There are serious penalties for getting it wrong.

PAYE

Income tax is collected from employees through the PAYE system, or Pay As You Earn. The employee's liability to income tax is collected as it is earned instead of by tax assessment at some later date. If the business is run as a limited company, then the directors of the company are employees. PAYE must be operated on all salaries and bonuses paid to them, yourself included.

The way to an employee's heart is through the payroll department

Remember the first time you received a real pay cheque? Your jaw dropped when you compared the *gross wages* (the amount before deductions) and the *net,* or *take-home pay* (the amount you actually received), right? A business's accountants need to track how much of the following, by law, to deduct from employees' pay cheques:

✔ National Insurance.

✔ Pay As You Earn (PAYE) taxes on income, which go to the Government.

✔ Other, non-tax-related withholdings that the employee agrees to (such as union dues,

pension plan contributions, and health insurance costs paid by the employee).

✔ Other non-tax-related withholdings required by a court order (for example, a business may be ordered to withhold part or all of an employee's wages and remit the amount to a legal agency or a creditor to which the employee owes money).

For all these deductions, a business serves as a collection agent and remits the appropriate amount of wages to the appropriate party. As you can imagine, this task requires lots of additional accounting and record-keeping.

HM Revenue and Customs now issues booklets in reasonably plain English explaining how PAYE works. The main documents you need to operate PAYE are:

✔ **Form P11,** a deduction working sheet for each employee.

✔ **The PAYE Tables.** There are two books of tax tables in general use, which are updated in line with the prevailing tax rates.

   • Pay Adjustment Tables show the amount that an employee can earn in any particular week or month before the payment of tax.

   • Taxable Pay Tables show the tax due on an employee's taxable pay.

✔ **Form P45,** which is given to an employee when transferring from one employment to another.

✔ **Form P46,** which is used when a new employee does not have a P45 from a previous employment (for example, a school-leaver starting work for the first time).

✔ **Form P60,** which is used so that the employer can certify an employee's pay at the end of the income tax year in April.

✔ **Form P35,** the year-end declaration and certificate. This is used to summarise all the tax and National Insurance deductions from employees for the tax year.

✔ **Form P6,** the tax codes advice notice issued by the Inspector of Taxes telling you which tax code number to use for each employee.

You can find tables giving details of PAYE and NIC rates and limits for the current tax year, for every conceivable category, at the HM Revenue and Customs website (www.hmrc.gov.uk/employers/).

Taxing everything you can put your hands on: Property taxes

Businesses and other occupiers of non-domestic properties pay Non-Domestic Rates (also known as Business Rates) to directly contribute towards the costs of local authority services. Non-domestic properties are business properties such as shops, offices, warehouses and factories, and any other property that is not classed as domestic property. In some cases, properties may be used for both domestic and non-domestic purposes (for example, a shop with a flat above it), in which case both council tax, the tax charged on personal properties, and Business Rates will be charged.

Apart from the few lucky properties such as churches, agricultural land, sewers, public parks, certain property used for disabled people, and swinging moorings for boats, which are all exempt from Business Rates, each non-domestic property has a rateable value. The valuation officers of the Valuation Office Agency (VOA) set the rateable values. The VOA is a part of HM Revenue and Customs. It draws up and maintains a full list of all rateable values.

The Valuation Office Agency carries out a revaluation every five years so that the values in the rating lists can be kept up-to-date. The total amount of Business Rates collected does not change except to reflect inflation, but revaluations make sure that this is spread fairly between ratepayers. The most recent revaluation took place in April 2005.

The rateable value broadly represents the yearly rent the property could have been let for on the open market on a particular date. Your local council works out your Business Rates bill by multiplying your rateable value by the multiplier or 'poundage' which the Government sets from 1 April each year for the whole of England. For example, if the multiplier (which is often called the uniform business rate or UBR) was set at 43.3p (43.7 in Central London) and your rateable value was £10,000, the local authority would multiply this by 43.3p and your 'property tax' bill for the year would be £4,330.

Your property may qualify for exemption under various national and local regulations or may be eligible for special reductions.

You may be able to get relief if one of the following applies to you:

✔ **Your business is small.** A UBR of 42.6p applies to certain businesses with rateable values below £6,000. The rules are complex and operate on a sliding scale.

✔ **Your property is empty and unused.** For the first three months that a business property is empty, councils don't charge Business Rates for the property. For industrial and warehouse property the rate-free period is six months. After this, a 100 per cent business rate charge usually applies.

✔ **Your business is in a rural village with a population below 3,000.** The types of business that qualify for this relief are:

- The only village general store or post office as long as it has a rateable value of up to £8,500.

- A food shop with a rateable value of up to £8,500.

- The only village pub and the only petrol station as long as it has a rateable value of up to £12,500.

These premises are entitled to a 50 per cent reduction in the Business Rates bill, or more if the council believes you need it.

If you are a business in a qualifying rural village with a rateable value of up to £16,500, your local council may decide to give you up to 100 per cent relief, as long as your business is of benefit to the community.

✔ **You are suffering severe hardship and cannot pay your Business Rates bill.** Your local council may decide to give you up to 100 per cent relief – the decision is up to them. They normally only do this in extreme cases of hardship and for businesses that are particularly important to the local community. This takes account of the fact that local council tax payers will cover part of the cost of the relief.

If you think you may qualify for any of these types of relief, you should contact the Business Rates section of your local council for more information and advice on how to apply.

Working from home

If you work from home, your local council may charge Business Rates for the part of the property used for work, and you will have to pay council tax for the rest of the property (although your property's valuation band may change). It will depend on the circumstances of each case and you should ask your local office of the Valuation Office Agency for advice.

Property taxes can take a big chunk out of a business's profit. In large organisations, an in-house accountant who deals with property taxes and knows the tax law language and methods is responsible for developing strategies to minimise property taxes. Small-business owners may want to consult a rating adviser. Members of the Royal Institution of Chartered Surveyors (RICS) and the Institute of Revenues Rating and Valuation (IRRV) are qualified and are regulated by rules of professional conduct designed to protect the public from misconduct.

You can find details of these organisations and their members on their websites:

- RICS – www.rics.org
- IRRV – www.irrv.org.uk

You can find the latest information on business rates on the official Government website at www.businesslink.gov.uk.

Before you employ a rating adviser, you should check that they have the necessary knowledge and expertise, as well as appropriate indemnity insurance. You should also be wary of false or misleading claims.

Getting to Grips with Value Added Tax

Most governments, and the UK Government is no exception, levy *sales taxes* on certain products and services sold within their jurisdictions. In the UK this tax is known as the Value Added Tax (VAT). The final consumer of the product or service pays the VAT – in other words the tax is tacked onto the product's price tag at the very end of the economic chain. The business that is selling the product or service collects the VAT and remits it to the appropriate tax agency (HM Revenue and Customs in the UK). Businesses that operate earlier in the economic chain (that is, those that sell products to other businesses that in turn resell the products) generally do not end up paying VAT but simply collect it and pass it on.

For example, when you run to your local chemist for some headache pills after all this tax business, you pay the chemist the cost of the pills plus VAT. But the chemist can reclaim the VAT it paid to the wholesaler (and so on, back along the retail chain). Only you, the final consumer, pays the VAT. (Lucky you!)

VAT is a complicated tax. Currently, you must register if your taxable turnover, that is, sales (not profit), exceeds £73,000 in any 12-month period, or looks as though it might reasonably be expected to do so. This rate is reviewed each year in the budget and is frequently changed. (The UK is significantly out of line with many other countries in Europe, where VAT entry rates are much lower.) The general rule is that all supplies of goods and services are taxable at the standard rate (20 per cent) unless they are specifically stated by the law to be zero-rated or exempt. In deciding whether your turnover exceeds the limit you have to include the zero-rated sales (things like most foods, books and children's clothing), as they are technically taxable; it's just that the rate of tax is 0 per cent. You leave out exempt items. As a designated tax collector, the business does not pay VAT on goods and services it buys from other VAT registered businesses that are destined to be sold to its customers.

If you are a small business owner/manager, be aware that if you overlook this role imposed on the business by the government, you're still responsible for paying the tax over to the government. Suppose you make a sale for £100 but don't add the £20.00 VAT, which is the rate currently applying in the UK. Big Brother says you did collect the VAT, whether you think you did or not. So you still have to pay the government the VAT element in the £100 (£16.67), which leaves you with only £83.33 in sales revenue.

There are three free booklets issued by HM Revenue and Customs: a simple introductory booklet called *Should you be registered for VAT?* and two more detailed booklets called *General Guide* and *Scope and Coverage*. If in doubt (and the language is not easy to understand) ask your accountant or the local branch of HM Revenue and Customs; after all, they would rather help you to get it right in the first place than have to sort it out later when you have made a mess of it.

Each quarter, you have to complete a return, which shows your purchases and the VAT you paid on them, and your sales and the VAT you collected on them. The VAT paid and collected are offset against each other and the balance sent to HM Revenue and Customs. If you have paid more VAT in any quarter than you have collected, you will get a refund. For this reason it sometimes pays to register if you don't have to – if you're selling mostly zero-rated items for example; also, being registered for VAT may make your business look more professional and less amateurish to your potential customers.

Tracking and recording Value Added Tax is a big responsibility for many businesses, especially if the business operates across several European countries. Having well-trained accounting staff manage this side of the business is well worth the cost. You can check the HM Revenue and Customs website for the latest rules (go to www.hmrc.gov.uk and click on 'VAT').

You can find a useful VAT calculator on the small business portal www.bytestart.co.uk. Click on 'Tax and Accounting' and then on 'VAT Calculator'.

Taxing Your Bottom Line: Company Taxes

This chapter focuses on the tax dimensions of business entities. Chapter 4 presents a basic income tax model for individuals (see the section 'The Accounting Vice You Can't Escape').

Every business must determine its annual *taxable income*, which is the amount of profit subject to corporate tax or income tax if the business is not a limited company. To determine annual *taxable income*, you deduct certain allowed expenses from gross income. Corporation tax law rests very roughly on the premise that all income is taxable unless expressly exempted, and nothing can be deducted unless expressly allowed.

When you read a profit-and-loss account that summarises a business's sales revenue and expenses for a period and ends with bottom-line profit, keep in mind that the accrual basis of accounting has been used to record sales revenue and expenses. The accrual basis gives a more trustworthy and meaningful profit number. But accrual-based sales revenue and expense numbers are not cash inflows and outflows during the period. So the bottom-line profit does not tell you the impact on cash from the profit-making activities of the business. You have to convert the revenue and expense amounts reported in the profit-and-loss account to a cash basis in order to determine the net cash increase or decrease. Well, actually, you don't have to do this – the cash flow statement does this for you, as Chapter 7 explains.

Although you determine your business's taxable income as an annual amount, you don't wait until you file your tax return to make that calculation and payment. Instead, corporation tax law requires you to estimate your corporation income tax for the year and, based on your estimate, to make two half-yearly instalment payments on your corporation tax during the year, one at the end of January and one at the end of July. Rather than calculating the tax due yourself, you can rely on HM Revenue and Customs to do the sums for you if you send in a completed tax return before the 30 September for the year in question. When you file the final tax return – with the official, rather than the estimated, taxable income amount – after the close of the year, you pay any remaining amount of tax you owe or claim a refund if you have over-paid your corporation tax during the year. If you grossly underestimate your taxable income for the year and thus end up having to pay a large amount of tax after the end of the year, you probably will owe a late payment penalty. After your first year in business, the tax you have to pay will be based on your profits for the previous tax year. A tax year runs from 6 April to 5 April.

A word on cash basis accounting for Value Added Tax

Cash basis accounting (also known as *cheque-book accounting*) isn't generally acceptable in the world of business, but is permitted by Value Added Tax law for some businesses. To use cash basis VAT accounting, a business must keep these factors in mind:

✔ Cash accounting is open to you if you are a registered trader with an expected turnover not exceeding **£1,350,000** in the next 12 months. There is a 25 per cent tolerance built into the scheme. This means that once you are using cash accounting, you can normally continue to use it until the annual value of your taxable supplies reaches **£1,600,000**.

✔ The main accounting record you must keep will be a cash book summarising all payments made and received, with a separate column for the relevant VAT. You will also need to keep the corresponding tax invoices and ensure that there is a satisfactory system of cross-referencing.

✔ These VAT records must be kept for six years, unless you have agreed upon a shorter period with your local VAT office.

✔ The longer the time lag between your issuing sales invoices and receiving payment from your customers, the more benefit cash accounting is likely to be to you. If you are usually paid as soon as you make a sale (e.g. if you use a retail scheme) you will normally be worse off under cash accounting.

The same applies to the situation where you regularly receive re-payments of VAT (e.g. because you make zero-rated supplies).

✔ One major advantage of the scheme is that it simplifies your bookkeeping requirements, and many businesses can be controlled simply by using an appropriately analysed cash book.

For the great majority of businesses, cash basis accounting is not acceptable, either for reporting to HM Revenue and Customs or for preparing financial statements. So this last advantage of cash-based VAT accounting is illusory. This method falls short of the information needed for even a relatively small business. Accrual basis accounting, described in Chapters 5 and 6, is the only real option for most businesses. Even small businesses that don't sell products should carefully consider whether cash basis is adequate for:

✔ Preparing external financial statements for borrowing money and reporting to owners.

✔ Dividing profit among owners.

For all practical purposes, only sole proprietorships (one-owner businesses) that sell just services and no products can use cash basis VAT accounting. Other businesses must use the accrual basis – which provides a much better income statement for management control and decision-making, and a much more complete picture of the business's financial condition.

WARNING! You must keep adequate accounting records to determine your business's annual taxable income. If you report the wrong taxable income amount, you can't plead that the bookkeeper was incompetent or that your accounting records were inadequate or poorly organised – in fact, the good old tax man may decide that your poor accounting was intentional and is evidence of income tax evasion. If you under-report your taxable income by too much, you may have to pay interest and penalties in addition to the tax that you owe.

When we talk about adequate accounting records, we're not talking about the accounting *methods* that you select to determine annual taxable income – Chapter 13 discusses choosing among alternative accounting methods for certain expenses. After you've selected which accounting methods you'll use for these expenses, your bookkeeping procedures must follow these methods faithfully. Choose the accounting methods that minimise your current year's taxable income – but make sure that your bookkeeping is done accurately and on time and that your accounting records are complete. If your business's income tax return is audited, HM Revenue and Customs agents first look at your accounting records and bookkeeping system.

Furthermore, you must stand ready to present evidence for expense deductions. Be sure to hold on to receipts and other relevant documents. In an HM Revenue and Customs audit, the burden of proof is on *you*. HM Revenue and Customs don't have to disprove a deduction; you have to prove that you were entitled to the deduction. *No evidence, no deduction* is the rule to keep in mind.

The following sections paint a rough sketch of the main topics of business income taxation. (We *don't* go into the many technical details of determining taxable income, however.)

Different tax rates on different levels of business taxable income

Personal taxes, which apply to sole traders and partnerships, come on a sliding scale up to a maximum of 40 per cent. When trading as a company a business's annual taxable income isn't taxed at a flat rate either. In writing the income tax law, the government gave the little guy a break. As of 2011, the corporate income tax rate starts at 20 per cent on the first £300,000 of taxable income, then quickly moves up to a 26 per cent rate on taxable income in the range of £300,001 to £1,500,000, after which it drops back to 20 per cent. Simple it ain't! The income tax on the taxable income for the year is calculated using these tax rates.

In years past, corporate income tax rates were considerably higher, and the rates could go up in the future – although most experts don't predict any increase. The Chancellor of the Exchequer looks at the income tax law every year and makes some changes virtually every year. Many changes have to do with the accounting methods allowed to determine annual taxable income.

For instance, the methods for computing annual *writing down expense*, which recognises the wear and tear on a business's long-lived operating assets, have been changed back and forth by chancellors over the years. You can check with HM Revenue and Customs for the latest rules at www.hmrc.gov.uk by simply clicking on 'Corporation Tax'.

Businesses pay tax on income at different rates depending on their size. But any capital gains (made, for example, when part of a business is sold or when owners cash in) used to be taxed at 10 per cent (if the asset concerned had been owned for two years or more) and then on a sliding scale up to 40 per cent for some assets and some time periods. However, some fiendishly complicated 'taper reliefs' existed that made understanding the true tax position very difficult. So, from 2008, all capital gains are now taxed at a single rate of 18 per cent. The simplification does mean that some taxpayers (in particular, any entrepreneurs selling up) face a tax hike of 80 per cent (from 10 per cent up to 18 per cent).

Profit accounting and taxable income accounting

You're probably thinking that this section of the chapter is about how a business's bottom-line profit – its net income – drives its taxable income amount. Actually, we want to show you the exact opposite: how income tax law drives a business's profit accounting. That's right: Tax law plays a large role in how a business determines its profit figure, or more precisely the accounting methods used to record revenue and expenses.

Before you explore that paradox, you need to understand something about the accounting methods for recording profit. For measuring and recording many expenses (and some types of revenue), no single accounting method emerges as the one and only dominant method. Accountants have a certain amount of legitimate leeway in measuring and reporting the revenue and expenses that drive the profit figure. (See Chapter 13 for further discussion of alternative accounting methods.) Therefore, two different accountants, recording the same profit-making activities for the same period, would most likely come up with two different profit figures – the numbers would be off by at least a little, and perhaps by a lot.

And that inconsistency is fine – as long as the differences are due to legitimate reasons. We'd like to be able to report to you that in measuring profit, accountants always aim right at the bull's-eye, the dead centre of the profit target. One commandment in the accountants' bible is that annual profit should be as close to the truth as can be measured; accounting methods should be objective and fair. But in the real world, profit accounting doesn't quite live up to this ideal.

Be aware that a business may be tempted to deliberately *overstate* or *understate* its profit. When a business overstates its profit in its profit and loss account, some amount of its sales revenue has been recorded too soon and/or some amount of its expenses has not yet been recorded (but will be later). Overstating profit is a dangerous game to play because it deceives investors and other interested parties into thinking that the business is doing better than it really is. Audits of financial reports by chartered accountants (as discussed in Chapter 15) keep such financial reporting fraud to a minimum but don't necessarily catch every case.

More to the point of this chapter is the fact that most businesses are under some pressure to *understate* the profit reported in their annual income statements. Businesses generally record sales revenue correctly (with some notable exceptions), but they may record some expenses sooner than these costs should be deducted from sales revenue. Why? Businesses are preoccupied with minimising income tax, which means minimising *taxable income.* To minimise taxable income, a business chooses accounting methods that record expenses as soon as possible. Keeping two sets of books (accounting records) – one for tax returns and one for internal profit accounting reports to managers – is not very practical, so the business uses the accounting methods kept for tax purposes for other purposes as well. And that's why tax concerns can drive down a business's profit figure.

In short, the income tax law permits fairly conservative expense accounting methods – expense amounts can be *front-loaded*, or deducted sooner rather than later. The reason is to give a business the option to minimise its current taxable income (even though this course has a reverse effect in later years). Many businesses select these conservative expense methods – both for their income tax returns and for their financial statements reported to managers and to outside investors and lenders. Thus financial statements of many businesses tilt to the conservative, or understated, side.

Of course, a business should report an accurate figure as its net profit, with no deliberate fudging. If you can't trust that figure, who knows for sure exactly how the company is doing? Not the owners, the value of whose investment in the business depends mostly on profit performance, and not even the business's managers, whose business decisions depend on recorded profit performance. Every business needs a reliable profit compass to navigate its way through the competitive environment of the business world – that's just common sense and doesn't even begin to address ethical issues.

Other reasons for understating profit

Minimising taxable income is a strong motive for understating profit, but businesses have other reasons as well. Imagine for the moment that business profit isn't subject to income tax (you wish!). Even in this hypothetical, no-tax world, many businesses probably would select accounting methods that measure their profit on the low side rather than the high side. Two possible reasons are behind this decision:

✔ **Don't count your chickens before they hatch philosophy:** Many business managers and owners tend to be financially conservative; they prefer to err on the low side of profit measurement rather than on the high side.

✔ **Save for a rainy day philosophy:** A business may want to keep some profit in reserve so that during a future downturn, it has a profit cushion to soften the blow.

The people who think this way tend to view *overstating profit* as a form of defrauding investors but view *understating profit* as simply being prudent. Frankly, we think that putting your thumb on either side of the profit scale (revenue being one side and expenses the other) is not a good idea. *Let the chips fall where they may* is our philosophy. Adopt the accounting methods that you think best reflect how you operate the business. The income tax law has put too much downward pressure on profit measurement, in our opinion.

We should say that many businesses do report their annual profit correctly – sales revenue and expenses are recorded properly and without any attempt to manipulate either side of the profit equation.

Refer to Chapter 13 for more about how choosing one expense accounting method over another method impacts profit. (*Note:* The following sections, which discuss expenses and income that are not deductible or are only partially deductible, have nothing to do with choosing accounting methods.)

Deductible expenses

What expenses can you claim when you are self-employed? Expenditure can be split into two main categories, 'Capital' and 'Revenue'.

✔ **Capital Expenditure:** Capital expenditure is expenditure on such items as the purchase or alteration of business premises, purchase of plant, machinery and vehicles, or the initial cost of tools. You cannot deduct 'capital expenditure' in working out your taxable profits, but some relief may be due on this type of expenditure in the form of capital allowances. Your Tax Office can give further advice on these allowances.

✔ **Revenue Expenditure:** Listing all the expenses that can be deducted is impossible but, generally speaking, allowable expenditure relates to day-to-day running costs of your business. It includes such items as wages, rent, lighting and heating of business premises, running costs of vehicles used in the business, purchase of goods for resale and the cost of replacing tools used in the business.

Non-deductible expenses

To be deductible, business expenses must be *ordinary and necessary* – that is, regular, routine stuff that you need to do to run your business. You're probably thinking that you can make an argument that *any* of your expenses meet the ordinary and necessary test. And you're mostly right – almost all business expenses meet this twofold test.

However, HM Revenue and Customs consider certain business expenses to be anything but ordinary and necessary; you can argue about them until you're blue in the face, and it won't make any difference. Examples of non-allowable expenditure are your own wages, premiums on personal insurance policies, and income tax and National Insurance contributions. Where expenditure relates to both business and private use, only the part that relates to the business will be allowed; examples are lighting, heating and telephone expenditure. If a vehicle is used for both business and private purposes, then the capital allowances and the total running expenses will be split in proportion to the business and private mileage. You will need to keep records of your total mileage and the number of miles travelled on business to calculate the correct split.

Here's a list of expenses that are *not* deductible or are only partially deductible when determining annual taxable income:

✔ **Customer entertainment expenses:** Definitely a no go area. For a while entertaining overseas customers was an allowable tax expense until the Revenue became suspicious of the amazing number of people being entertained by businesses with no export activity whatsoever.

✔ **Bribes, kickbacks, fines and penalties:** Oh, come on, did you really think that you could get rewarded for doing stuff that's illegal or, at best, undesirable? If you were allowed to deduct these costs, that would be tantamount to the Revenue encouraging such behaviour – a policy that wouldn't sit too well with the general public.

✔ **Lobbying costs:** You can't deduct payments made to influence legislation. Sorry, but you can't deduct the expenses you ran up to persuade Minister Hardnose to give your bicycle business special tax credits because riding bicycles is good exercise for people.

✔ **Start-up costs:** You can't just deduct the cost of everything needed to start a business in year one. Some assets, such as cars and equipment or machinery, have to be written down over a number of future years. This area of the tax law can get a little hairy. If you have just started a new business, you may be wise to consult a tax professional on this question, especially if your start-up costs are rather large.

✔ **Working from home:** If you use part of your home for work, you need to keep sufficient records to back up the proportion of heating and lighting costs that relate to your business and your private use. Sometimes you may not get evidence, such as a receipt, for cash expenses, especially where the amounts are small. If this happens, make a brief note as soon as you can of the amount you spent, when you spent it, and what it was for. HM Revenue and Customs don't expect you to keep photocopies of bills, although you may find them useful.

✔ **Life insurance premiums:** A business may buy life insurance coverage on key officers and executives, but if the business is the beneficiary, the premiums are not deductible. The proceeds from a life insurance policy are not taxable income to the business if the insured person dies, because the cost of the premiums was not deductible. In short, premiums are not deductible, and proceeds upon death are excluded from taxable income.

✔ **Travel and convention attendance expenses:** Some businesses pay for rather lavish conventions for their managers and spend rather freely for special meetings at attractive locations that their customers attend for free. The Revenue takes a dim view of such extravagant expenditures and may not allow a full deduction for these types of expenses. HM Revenue and Customs holds that such conventions and meetings could have been just as effective for a much more reasonable cost. In short, a business may not get a 100 per cent deduction for its travel and convention expenses if the Revenue audits these expenditures.

✔ **Transactions with related parties:** Income tax law takes a special interest in transactions where the two parties are related in some way. For example, a business may rent space in a building owned by the same people who have money invested in the business; the rent may be artificially high or low in an attempt to shift income and expenses between the two tax entities or individuals. In other words, these transactions may not be based on what's known as *arm's-length bargaining*. A business that deals with a related party must be ready to show that the price paid or received is consistent with what the price would be for an unrelated party.

You can find a useful guide to business expenses on the `www.bytestart.co.uk` small business portal. Just click on 'Tax and Accounting' and 'Business Expenses Guide'.

Equity capital disguised as debt

The general term *debt* refers to money borrowed from lenders who require that the money be paid back by a certain date, and who require that interest be paid on the debt until it is repaid. *Equity* is money invested by owners (such as shareholders) in a business in return for hoped-for, but not guaranteed, profit returns. Interest is deductible, but cash dividends paid to shareholders are not – which gives debt capital a big edge over equity capital at tax time.

Not surprisingly, some businesses try to pass off equity capital as debt on their tax returns so that they can deduct the payments to the equity sources as interest expense to determine taxable income. Don't think that HM Revenue and Customs are ignorant of these tactics: Everything that you declare as interest on debt may be examined carefully, and if the Revenue determines that what you're calling debt is really equity capital, it disallows the interest deduction. The business can make payments to its sources of capital that it calls and treats as interest – but this does not mean that HM Revenue and Customs will automatically believe that the payments are in fact interest. The Revenue follows the general principle of substance over form. If the so-called debt has too many characteristics of equity capital, HM Revenue and Customs treat the payments not as interest but rather as dividend distributions from profit to the equity sources of capital.

In summary, debt must really be debt and must have few or none of the characteristics of equity. Drawing a clear-cut line between debt and equity has been a vexing problem for HM Revenue and Customs, and the rules are complex. You'll probably have to consult a tax professional if you have a question about this issue. Be warned that if you attempt to disguise equity capital as debt, your charade may not work – and the Revenue may disallow any 'interest' payments you have made.

Chapter 4

Accounting and Your Personal Finances

*I*n this chapter, we look at you as an *individual*. We look over your financial shoulder at four different roles in which some accounting tips can help you – as a taxpayer, as a borrower, as an investor and as a retirement planner. Income tax regulations require self-employed individuals and those earning over a certain amount to do some accounting once a year to determine their taxable income and income tax. You may decide to farm out your income tax return preparation to a tax professional. Even so, you should keep in mind the income tax consequences of earning and spending your income.

The Accounting Vice You Can't Escape

All of us have to earn income, right? Therefore, we're all subject to the income tax regulations, whether we like it or not. These regulations are written in the complex and frustrating language of accounting and so they provide employment for a large number of accountants who are hired to prepare the annual tax returns of individuals and businesses. The alternative to using an accountant is to grit your teeth and do your own taxes. Either way, we strongly suggest that you see the forest and not get lost in all the trees. A thumbnail-sized model of how income tax works will help you in making many important financial decisions and is very useful for mapping your overall financial strategy.

The basic income tax model is also useful for testing investment opportunities that seem too good to be true. We have seen too many people get suckered into questionable investments because of alleged income tax advantages. We're sure you've heard the saying, 'There's one born every minute.'

Don't let the extraordinary complexity of income tax stop you from trying to understand how it works. Here's a basic income tax model for an average taxpayer that's very useful, even though just four factors (numbered 1 to 4) affect the amount of the income tax in this example.

Basic Income Tax Accounting Model

(1)	Annual Income	£62,700
(2)	Less Personal Allowances	£7,475
(3)	Less Deduction for a Stakeholder Pension	£3,600
	Equals Taxable Income	£51,625
(4)	Times the Tax Rates (20% on first £35,001 and 40% on excess)	
	Equals Amount of Income Tax	£14,318

Note: Some sources of income are not taxable or are subject to more favourable tax treatment. Some personal expenditure is deductible, and some is not. Persons who are over 65 or blind get . . . Hold on! Once you start getting into technical details, you're on a slippery slope, and there's no turning back. Our purpose here is not to provide a detailed tax guide but to provide a simple, hands-on income model to show the basic income tax effects of your financial decisions. Several good tax guides are available, including *Tolley's Tax Guides*, published by Butterworths. Websites such as the *Daily Mail*'s www.thisismoney.co.uk/tax provide the latest tax tables for every category of taxpayer.

Following is a brief – and we do mean *brief* – explanation of each factor in the basic income tax model:

- ✔ **(1) Income:** Money flowing in your direction from working or owning assets is subject to income tax – unless income tax regulations specifically make the inflow not subject to income tax. (An example is interest income on Tax Exempt savings such as ISAs.)

- ✔ **(2) Personal Allowances:** Income tax regulations give every individual a so-called *personal allowance*. The term *allowance* means that a certain amount of income is excused from income tax. For 20011/12 (the amount changes from year to year), the personal allowance was £7,475 or £9,940 for people over 65 but under 74. Over 75 and the figure goes up again to £10,090.

✔ **(3) Deductions:** The Government allows certain deductions but not others in arriving at taxable income. For example, payments up to a certain level are allowed into pension schemes.

✔ **Taxable Income:** The first £11,075 of income earned by the example in the basic income tax model shown is *not* subject to income tax – equal to the personal exemption of £7,475 plus deduction of £3,600 for contributions to a stakeholder pension (The amount you can contribute into a pension and get tax relief varies from year to year at rates announced in the budget). Income above this amount is taxable. The taxable income in this example is £51,625 because the £11,075 of income is offset by allowances and deductions. You multiply the taxable income by the tax rates – one rate for the first layer of taxable income and a higher rate for the next layer – to determine the income tax amount.

✔ **(4) Tax Rates:** UK income tax is based on the *progressive taxation* philosophy – as your income progresses, your tax rate progresses. Taxable income is subdivided into *brackets* or *layers;* each higher one is subject to a higher income tax rate. The lowest rate is 20 per cent; the top rate is 40 per cent on taxable income in excess of £35,001. The brackets and rates can change from year to year, but don't worry – the chancellor keeps you informed in the booklet that comes with your annual income tax forms.

✔ **Income Tax Amount:** In 2011/12, the tax rate on £51,625 taxable income was 20 per cent on the first £35,001. The rate then doubles to 40 per cent on all further income. As you can see in the example, the income tax on the £51,625 taxable income is £13,649.80.

In this example, the income tax of £13,649.80 is 26.44 per cent of the £51,625 taxable income and 22.77 per cent of the £62,700 gross income. However, the *marginal tax rate* gets the most attention. The marginal tax rate is the rate that applies to the margin, or highest layer of taxable income. The margin in this example is the taxable income in excess of £35,001. For each additional £1,000 of income over this amount, the person in this example pays £400 of income tax. They are in the 40 per cent marginal income tax bracket.

The marginal tax rate starts at 20 per cent on the first pound of *taxable* income. Remember that you do not have any taxable income until your annual income exceeds the total of your personal exemptions plus the standard deduction. In this example, the first £11,075 of income is not taxable because the total of personal allowances and deduction equals this amount. The remainder is taxed at 40 per cent.

We find that using a *marginal* income tax rate of 33 per cent is generally accurate and computationally convenient. This number may be too high or too low for a specific individual or married couple, but it's reasonably accurate for a broad range of taxpayers. (If you're a multimillionaire, you probably should shift up to a 39.5 per cent marginal tax rate.) In other words, most of the readers of this book can assume that if they receive a £1,000 raise, about 33 per cent of that will be lost to taxes. Or, if you'd like to buy a new pair of trainers that cost £67 at the sports shop, you need £100 of income before taxes to have £67 left over, after taxes, for the shoes.

The Ins and Outs of Figuring Interest and Return on Investment (ROI)

In addition to understanding the basic model of income tax accounting, you should have a good grip on the calculation of periodic interest and how return on investment is measured. Interest rates and return on investment (ROI) rates are tossed around freely as if everyone were intimately familiar with how these important ratios are calculated. In fact, many people do not understand these key accounting calculations. In our experience, most people get sweaty palms when they have to think about how interest is actually calculated and how investment performance is measured. The following sections should reduce your anxiety about these matters, which have a big impact on your personal financial affairs.

Individuals as borrowers

Everyone borrows money – as car loans, as mortgages, as unpaid credit card balances and so on. When you borrow money, you agree to a method of interest accounting, whether you understand the method or not. You should be clear on the following points:

✔ If you make more than one loan payment per year, divide the annual interest rate by the number of loan payments to determine the interest rate per period, which usually is a month or a quarter. In other words, the quoted annual rate is simply the number to divide into to get the real interest rate per month or per quarter.

✔ When you make two or more loan payments, each payment goes first to the interest amount; the remainder is deducted from the loan balance, called the *capital*. The amount of the capital repaid each period is referred to as the *amortisation* of the loan. The total amount borrowed has to be amortised, or paid back to the lender, over the life of the loan.

✔ Shortening the term of a very long-term loan, say from 30 years to 15 years, results in a dramatic decrease in the total interest paid over the life of the loan, but a relatively small increase in the monthly loan payment amount.

> ✔ A monthly interest rate should not be multiplied by 12 to determine the *effective annual interest rate*; likewise, a quarterly interest rate should not be multiplied by 4 to determine the effective annual interest rate. Annual effective rates assume the *compounding* of interest during the year. Compounding means paying interest on interest; it is an extremely important building block for understanding financial matters.

A good example to illustrate several of these points is a typical home mortgage loan.

Home mortgage example

The biggest loan in most individuals' financial lives is a home mortgage. Compared with a short-term car loan, a home mortgage loan can run up to 30 years, and the amount borrowed is usually much larger than for a car (unless you buy a Ferrari).

Suppose that you buy a second home and secure a £180,000 mortgage loan for 30 years at a 9 per cent annual interest rate. The loan requires equal monthly payments, so you divide the annual interest rate by 12 to determine the monthly rate, which is 0.75 per cent (or ¾ of 1 per cent) per month. How much will each of your 360 loan payments be? How do you determine this amount? You probably assume that the lender's quoted amount is correct – and you'd be pretty safe in this assumption. But how can you be sure?

Relatively inexpensive hand-held business/financial calculators are available to quickly determine monthly loan payments. These handy tools have special keys for entering each of the variables of a loan. To determine the monthly payment in this example, we pulled out a calculator and punched in the following numbers for each variable:

> ✔ **N** = number of periods – 360 months in this example.

> ✔ **INT** = interest rate per period – 0.75 per cent per month in this example (these calculators expect that the interest is given in a percentage, so we typed 0.75, not 0.0075).

> ✔ **PV** = present value, or amount borrowed today (the present time) – £180,000 in this example.

> ✔ **FV** = future value, or capital amount owed after the final monthly loan payment is made – £0 in this example (which means that the loan is fully amortised and paid off after the last monthly loan payment; otherwise, there would be a *balloon* payment due at the end of the loan).

> ✔ **PMT** = payment per period based on the four numbers just entered – £1,448.32 in this example (which appears as a negative number, meaning that you have to pay this amount per month).

The big advantage of a business/financial hand-held calculator is that you can enter the known numbers (the first four) and then simply hit the button for the unknown number, which appears instantly. Another big advantage is that you can keep all these numbers in the calculator and make 'what if' changes very, very quickly. For example, what if the annual interest rate was 8.4 per cent? Just re-enter the new interest rate (0.7 per cent per month) and then call up the new monthly payment amount, which is £1,371.31. The monthly payment difference multiplied by 360 payments is £27,725 less interest over the life of the loan. So you might decide to shop around for a lower rate.

The Financial Times Mortgage Calculator (go to www.ft.com/personal-finance/tools and click on Mortgage Calculator) works out your mortgage repayments at any rate of interest, over any time period, and with variable amounts of deposit.

Now, here's a short test to see if you've been paying attention. Suppose the lender did not charge interest – in other words, the interest rate was zero. What would your monthly payments be in the example we just used? The monthly payments would be simply £180,000 divided by 360 months, or only £500 per month. At a 9 per cent annual interest rate, you have to pay £1,448.32 per month. This does not mean that the extra £948.32 more per month, or £11,379.85 per year, is for interest. Interest is accounted for differently, and just how interest is accounted for makes a big difference to you.

Each mortgage payment is divided between interest and capital amortisation (capital repayment). For the first month, the interest amount is £1,350 (£180,000 loan balance × 0.75 per cent monthly interest rate = £1,350). Therefore, the first month's repayment of the capital is only £98.32. Right off, you can see that the loan's capital balance will go down very slowly – and that a 30-year mortgage loan involves a lot of interest. Lenders provide you with a loan repayment (amortisation) schedule. We encourage you to take a look – although trying to follow down a table of 360 rows of monthly payments is tough going.

Figure 4-1 presents the annual amounts of interest cost and capital reduction for this mortgage loan example. (We generated this data from a Microsoft Excel spreadsheet repayment schedule for the loan.) Note that the annual capital amortisation doesn't overcome annual interest cost until the *23rd year*. In other words, you pay mostly interest during the first 22 years! The right column in the figure shows how slowly the loan balance goes down.

One alternative that you should definitely consider when taking out a home mortgage is a 15-year loan instead of a 30-year loan. For this home mortgage example, the monthly payment on a 15-year loan is £1,825.68, which is an additional £377.36 per month. The total interest over the life of the 15-year loan is about £149,000, compared with £341,000 on the 30-year loan. The 15-year loan saves you about £192,000 in total interest over the life of the mortgage, and you own your home free and clear 15 years sooner. Of course, you have to come up with £377.36 more per month, which may not be possible in the short run. But after a few years of paying the 30-year amount, you can step up the amount you pay each month and pay off your mortgage sooner. Figure 4-1A (A is for *alternative*) shows the annual interest and capital payments for the 15-year mortgage.

Year	Payments	Annual Interest Cost	Annual Amortisation, or Reduction of Principal
1	£17,379.85	£16,150.09	£1,229.75
2	£17,379.85	£16,034.73	£1,345.11
3	£17,379.85	£15,908.55	£1,471.30
4	£17,379.85	£15,770.54	£1,609.31
5	£17,379.85	£15,619.57	£1,760.28
6	£17,379.85	£15,454.44	£1,925.40
7	£17,379.85	£15,273.83	£2,106.02
8	£17,379.85	£15,076.27	£2,303.58
9	£17,379.85	£14,860.18	£2,519.67
10	£17,379.85	£14,623.82	£2,756.03
11	£17,379.85	£14,365.28	£3,014.57
12	£17,379.85	£14,082.49	£3,297.36
13	£17,379.85	£13,773.18	£3,606.67
14	£17,379.85	£13,434.85	£3,945.00
15	£17,379.85	£13,064.78	£4,315.07
16	£17,379.85	£12,660.00	£4,719.85
17	£17,379.85	£12,217.24	£5,162.61
18	£17,379.85	£11,732.95	£5,646.89
19	£17,379.85	£11,203.24	£6,176.61
20	£17,379.85	£10,623.83	£6,756.02
21	£17,379.85	£9,990.07	£7,389.78
22	£17,379.85	£9,296.85	£8,083.00
23	£17,379.85	£8,538.61	£8,841.24
24	£17,379.85	£7,709.24	£9,670.61
25	£17,379.85	£6,802.07	£10,577.77
26	£17,379.85	£5,809.81	£11,570.04
27	£17,379.85	£4,724.46	£12,655.39
28	£17,379.85	£3,537.29	£13,842.56
29	£17,379.85	£2,238.77	£15,141.08
30	£17,379.85	£818.43	£16,561.42
Totals	£521,395.46	£341,395.46	£180,000.00

Figure 4-1: Annual summary for a 30-year home mortgage repayment schedule.

Year	Payments	Annual Interest Cost	Annual Amortisation, or Reduction of Principal	Loan Balance At End of Year
1	£21,908.16	£15,958.55	£5,949.61	£174,050.39
2	£21,908.16	£15,400.44	£6,507.72	£167,542.67
3	£21,908.16	£14,789.97	£7,118.19	£160,424.48
4	£21,908.16	£14,122.23	£7,785.93	£152,638.56
5	£21,908.16	£13,391.86	£8,516.30	£144,122.26
6	£21,908.16	£12,592.97	£9,315.19	£134,807.07
7	£21,908.16	£11,719.14	£10,189.02	£124,618.06
8	£21,908.16	£10,763.34	£11,144.82	£113,473.24
9	£21,908.16	£9,717.88	£12,190.28	£101,282.97
10	£21,908.16	£8,574.35	£13,333.81	£87,949.16
11	£21,908.16	£7,323.55	£14,584.61	£73,364.55
12	£21,908.16	£5,955.41	£15,952.75	£57,411.80
13	£21,908.16	£4,458.93	£17,449.23	£39,962.57
14	£21,908.16	£2,822.07	£19,086.08	£20,876.49
15	£21,908.16	£1,031.67	£20,876.49	£0.00
Totals	£328,622.37	£148,622	£180,000	

Figure 4-1A: Annual summary for a 15-year home mortgage repayment schedule.

You may be tempted to focus on the amount of the monthly payment and how this amount fits into your personal budget. But you should also look closely at the pattern of interest versus capital payments over the life of the loan. In our experience, overlooking interest versus capital payments is the biggest mistake borrowers make. You should always know how fast you're paying off capital, and you should keep track of your loan balance.

Tools of the trade

We advise everyone to invest the time and effort (plus a relatively small cost) in learning how to use one of two indispensable tools of the trade for analysing savings and investments: a hand-held business/financial calculator and a computer spreadsheet program, such as Excel, Quattro Pro or Lotus 1–2–3.

A powerful business/financial hand-held calculator costs under £50. You have to take some time and go through a few examples to learn how to operate the thing, but we think the time is well spent. The owner's manuals for the Hewlett Packard business/financial calculators are very well written and have good practical examples.

If you already use a computer spreadsheet program, take advantage of its financial functions. For example, you can easily print out loan repayment schedules, savings plans, pension fund accumulations, estimated retirement income and many other useful tables and schedules and convert these into charts for easier viewing. The spreadsheet owner's manuals are terrible, we know. We suggest buying the *For Dummies* book for the spreadsheet program you use.

Individuals as savers

Ben Franklin said, 'A penny saved is a penny earned.' His point is that one penny not spent today is a penny kept for another day. Until that later day arrives, the penny saved can earn interest income. These days, 100 pennies saved for one year earn about 6 pennies in interest income, or 6 per cent per year.

Saving is done for income and safety of capital and not for market value appreciation. Suppose you save £10,000 for one year. You expect to earn the going interest rate, *and* you expect to have little or no risk of losing any of your money during the year. You do not expect your savings to appreciate in value other than from interest income. Assuming that the going interest rate is 6 per cent, you expect that your savings will grow to £10,600 by the end of the year – the £10,000 you started with plus 6 per cent interest (or £6 per £100) earned on that money. The interest income increases your taxable income by the same amount, so keep in mind the marginal income tax rate that takes a bite out of your £600 in interest income.

The power of compounding (which means not spending your interest income)

Suppose you have some money that you want to save. You can deposit your money in a savings account at a building society or a bank. Or you can buy a government gilt stock, which is the way governments finance their borrowings. Or you can put your money in a money market fund. You can save money through many different types of vehicles and instruments, which are explained in Eric Tyson's excellent book *Personal Finance For Dummies* (Wiley). Our purpose is to demonstrate how your savings grow, or do not grow, depending on what you do with the interest income each period.

Suppose you have £100,000 in savings. (Larger amounts of money are more interesting than smaller amounts.) You leave the money alone for one year, and at the end of the year your savings balance has grown to £106,000. Therefore, you earned a 6 per cent annual interest income:

£6,000 increase in savings balance ÷ £100,000 balance at start of year = 6%

Now you have a critical choice to make: Should you withdraw the £6,000 income and spend the money, or should you leave the £6,000 in savings? Many people depend on income from their savings for living expenses. Others want to build up their money over time. Suppose you're in the second group; you leave the first year's interest income in your savings account for a second year.

At the end of the second year your savings amount is £112,360 – £6,360 more than at the start of the year. Therefore, for the second year, you also earned a 6 per cent annual interest rate:

£6,360 increase in savings balance ÷ £106,000 balance at start of year = 6%

You earned more interest income in the second year because you had more in savings at the start of the year. Notice that at the end of the second year you have two years of interest income accumulated: £6,000 from year one and £6,360 from year two, making a total increase of £12,360 in your savings amount.

If you continue to plough back annual earnings for 12 years, how much would you have at the end of the 12 years – starting with £100,000, earning 6 per cent per year, and resaving interest income every year? Without touching a calculator, we know that your savings balance after 12 years would about double, or would be £200,000. This quick-and-dirty method is based on the *rule of 72* (see the sidebar 'The rule of 72'). To be more precise, your savings balance at the end of 12 years would be £201,220. We did this computation with a calculator. (If you use Microsoft Excel, you might double-check this amount by using the FV financial function; or you can go to a website that has a financial calculator.)

Note: We use the terms *plough back* and *resaving* in order to avoid the term *reinvesting*. Reinvesting implies an investment, which, strictly speaking, involves market value fluctuation risk. Saving does not involve this risk. (We should warn you that there is always a small risk that part of the money in a savings account or fund will be lost or will be delayed in being returned to you – witness the recent Equitable Life situation in which pension funds lost considerable value.)

Figure 4-2 illustrates how your savings balance would grow year by year, assuming a 6 per cent annual interest rate for all 12 years. This growth comes at a price – you can't take out annual earnings. Not withdrawing annual earnings is called *compounding*; the term *compound interest* refers to not withdrawing interest income. Compounding means that you save more and more each year. To emphasise this important point, notice in Figure 4-2 that we include a column for the amount of interest income withdrawn each year (which is zero every year in this example).

Furthermore, the entire interest income each year is subject to individual income tax – unless the money is invested in a tax-efficient pension fund. For instance, in year 4 your interest income is £7,146 (see Figure 4-2). At the higher 40 per cent tax rate you would owe £2,858 income tax on your interest income.

Year	Savings Balance at Start of Year	Annual Interest Rate	Interest Income on Savings Balance	Amount of Interest Income Withdrawn	Savings Balance at End of Year
1	£100,000	x 6% =	£6,000	£0	£106,000
2	£106,000	x 6% =	£6,360	£0	£112,360
3	£112,360	x 6% =	£6,742	£0	£119,102
4	£119,102	x 6% =	£7,146	£0	£126,248
5	£126,248	x 6% =	£7,575	£0	£133,823
6	£133,823	x 6% =	£8,029	£0	£141,852
7	£141,852	x 6% =	£8,511	£0	£150,363
8	£150,363	x 6% =	£9,022	£0	£159,385
9	£159,385	x 6% =	£9,563	£0	£168,948
10	£168,948	x 6% =	£10,137	£0	£179,085
11	£179,085	x 6% =	£10,745	£0	£189,830
12	£189,830	x 6% =	£11,390	£0	£201,220

Figure 4-2: Growth in savings balance assuming no withdrawals and full compounding of annual interest income.

Unfortunately, compounding of earnings is often touted as a sort of magical way to build wealth over time or to make your money double. Don't be suckered by this claim. You sacrifice 12 years of earnings to make your money grow; you don't get to spend the interest income on your savings for 12 years. We don't call this magic, we call it *frugal*. Compounding is not magical – it's a conservative way to build wealth that requires you to forgo a lot of spending along the way.

The rule of 72

A handy trick of the trade is called the rule of 72. In Figure 4-2, at the end of the 12th year, notice that your savings balance is about £200,000 (rounded off) – exactly twice what you started with. This is a good example of the rule of 72. The rule states that if you take the periodic earnings rate as a whole number and divide it into 72, the answer is the number of periods it takes to double what you started with. Sure enough: 72 ÷ 6 = 12. Doubling your money at 6 per cent per year takes 12 years.

The rule of 72 assumes compounding of earnings. It's amazingly accurate over a broad range of earnings rates and number of periods. For example, how long does it take to double your money at an 8 per cent annual earnings rate? It takes nine years (72 ÷ 8 = 9). If you earn 18 per cent per year, you double your money in just four years.

One caution: For very low and very high earnings rates, the rule is not accurate and should not be used.

Individuals as investors

The last two decades have seen a remarkable explosion in the number of individuals who invest in the stock market – either directly by buying and selling stocks and shares or indirectly by putting their money in shares of mutual funds (open-end investment companies that act as intermediaries for individuals). Also during this time span, a sea change has occurred in the arena of retirement pension planning, mainly a fundamental shift away from traditional *defined-benefit* pension plans (which are based on years of service to an employer and salaries during the final years of employment) to *defined-contribution* plans (which are based on how much money has been put into individual retirement investment accounts and the earnings performance of the investments).

National Insurance is the government-sponsored defined-benefit retirement plan. Your monthly retirement benefit depends on how many years you have worked and paid the required amount of National Insurance. In the private sector, a large percentage of retired employees still depend on traditional defined-benefit pension plans. However, the growth of defined-contribution plans has been phenomenal – although we think most individuals don't realise that this type of retirement plan puts much more of a burden on them to understand investment performance accounting.

The twofold nature of return on investment

Putting money into savings, such as a savings account or a government bond, is low risk. In contrast, putting money into an *investment*, such as company shares and bonds or property, means that you are taking on more risk – that you may lose part of the amount of money you invest and that the earnings from your investment may fluctuate from year to year. There's no such thing as a free lunch. If you want the higher earnings, you must take greater risk.

Earnings from *investing* capital are generally not referred to as earnings on investment, but rather as *return on investment* (ROI). ROI consists of two parts: (1) *cash income* (if in fact there is cash income) and (2) *market value appreciation or depreciation*. When you invest, you put your money in stocks and bonds (which are called *securities*), or mutual funds, or property, or whatever. The range of possible investments is diverse, to say the least. We recommend Tony Levene's *Investing For Dummies* (Wiley). He explains the wide range of investments open to individuals, from mutual funds to property and most things in between. Investors should understand how return on investment is accounted for no matter which type of investment they choose.

The return on investment, or ROI, for a period is computed as follows, and is usually expressed as a percentage:

Return for Period ÷ Amount Invested at Start of Period = Rate of Return on Investment (ROI)

Suppose, for example, that your £100,000 investment at the start of the year provided £2,500 cash flow income during the year, and the market value of your investment asset increased £7,500 during the year. Your total return is £10,000 for the year, and your ROI is 10 per cent for the year: £10,000 return ÷ £100,000 invested = 10 per cent ROI.

Often, people use the term *ROI* when they really mean *rate*, or *percentage*, of ROI. Like some words that have a silent character, ROI is frequently used without rate or percentage. Anytime you see the % symbol, you know that the *rate* of ROI is meant. In any case, the ROI rate is not a totally satisfactory measure. For instance, suppose you tell us that your investments earned 18 per cent ROI last year. We know your wealth, or capital, increased 18 per cent – although we don't know how much of this return you received in cash income and how much was an increase in the market value of your investment, and we don't know whether you spent your cash income or reinvested it.

Individuals, financial institutions and businesses always account for the cash income component of investment return. However, the market value gain or loss during the period may or may not be recorded. Most individuals who invest in property, stocks, bonds and so on, do not record the gain or loss in the market value of their investments during the period. So they do not have a full and complete accounting of ROI for the period.

The investment accounting that most individuals do is governed largely by what's required for income tax purposes. Unrealised market value gains are not taxed, so most investors do not record market value gains. Nevertheless, they keep an eye on market value ups and downs, in addition to their cash income. For example, property investors generally do not measure and record market value changes each year, although they keep an eye on the prices of comparable properties.

In contrast, financial institutions, including banks, mutual funds, insurance companies and pension funds, are governed by generally accepted accounting principles (GAAP). They invest in marketable securities that are held for sale or trading or that are available for sale. GAAP requires that changes in market value of these investments be recognised. On the other hand, GAAP does not require the recording of market value gains and losses for their investments in fixed-income debt securities (for example, bonds and notes) that are held until maturity.

The main point of this discussion is that you should be very clear about what's included and not included in ROI. As just discussed, many individuals do not capture market value changes during the year in accounting for the return, or earnings on their investments – they account for only the cash income part, which gives an incomplete measure of ROI. On the other hand, when a mutual fund advertises that its annual ROI was 18 per cent last year you can be sure that it *does* include the market value gains in this rate (as well as cash income, of course).

A real-world example of ROI accounting

Suppose you invest £94,757.86 today in a UK Gilt (Government borrowing instrument) that has three years to go until its maturity date. The face, or par, value of this debt security is £100,000, which is its maturity value three years hence and which is also the basis on which interest is computed. This gilt-edged stock pays 6 per cent annual interest, which is paid twice a year. The 6 per cent rate is sometimes called the *coupon rate* because in the good old days (before direct deposit by electronic funds transfer) investors in debt securities had to clip one of the interest coupons attached to the debt certificate as it came due and mail the coupon for payment of the interest.

Every six months, the UK Treasury Department sends you £3,000 (depositing the amount directly in your bank account). Assume that you spend the £3,000 twice-yearly interest income. So far, so good. But now comes a tough question: What's your ROI rate on this investment?

By paying £94,757.86, you buy the Gilt at a *discount* from its £100,000 maturity value. The discount provides part of your return on investment in addition to your cash-flow interest income. Most of your ROI consists of cash income every six months. But part consists of *market value appreciation* as the note moves closer to its maturity date. This second component does not provide cash flow until the maturity date is reached. Taking both parts into account, your ROI rate is more than the 6 per cent annual interest rate based on the par value of the note.

Tell you what. Guess that the correct ROI rate is 4 per cent per period (every six months), and see whether this rate is correct. We'll walk you quickly through the accounting in this example to test out the 4 per cent ROI rate. Figure 4-3 demonstrates that in each period, the return on the investment indeed equals 4 per cent of the amount invested at the start of the period. The investor receives only £3,000 per period of cash income. The increase in the value of the note each period as it moves toward its maturity value provides the remainder of the return each period. The total increase in value over the three years is not received until the maturity date, at which time the investment is cashed out. At this time, the individual has to find another investment to put his or her £100,000 into.

An important note regarding annualised ROI rates

In the investment example in Figure 4-3, the increase in value each period is not received in cash. Therefore, it is 'automatically' reinvested, or compounded. Due to this compounding, the amount invested increases period to period – see the left column. As a result, the increase in the value amount is larger from period to period.

Period	Investment at Start of Period	Total Return (ROI = 4.0% on Starting Amount)	Two Components of Return			Investment at End of Period
			Cash Income		Increase in Value	
1	£94,757.86	£3,790.31	£3,000.00	+	£790.31	£95,548.18
2	£95,548.18	£3,821.93	£3,000.00	+	£821.93	£96,370.10
3	£96,370.10	£3,854.80	£3,000.00	+	£854.80	£97,224.91
4	£97,224.91	£3,889.00	£3,000.00	+	£889.00	£98,113.91
5	£98,113.91	£3,924.56	£3,000.00	+	£924.56	£99,038.46
6	£99,038.46	£3,961.54	£3,000.00	+	£961.54	£100,000.00
	Totals =	£23,242.14	£18,000.00		£5,242.14	

Figure 4-3: Investing in a UK Gilt at a discount from its maturity value to illustrate a higher ROI rate than just the periodic interest rate paid on the investment.

Please Note: Only the increase in value is compounded, or reinvested each period. The £3,000 cash income each period is not compounded but is, instead, withdrawn from the investment. The amount invested grows period to period only by the increase in value. The total return each period equals 4.0% of the amount invested at the start of the period.

Seems odd, doesn't it? A 4 per cent ROI earned each half-year is treated as equivalent to 8.16 per cent ROI earned for the whole year. The purpose is to put all investments on the same footing, as it were – so that annual ROI rates can be compared among different investments. The standard practice in the world of finance is to express ROI rates on the basis of a one-year period – even though the investment may be for a shorter period of time. When a less-than-one-year ROI rate (or interest rate) is converted into an equivalent full-year rate, the shorter-term rate is *annualised*. Usually the word *annualised* is not included; it is assumed that you understand that shorter-term rates have been converted into an equivalent annual rate. Any investment income received during the year is assumed to be compounded (reinvested) for the rest of the year to determine the annualised ROI rate, or we should say just the ROI rate.

Suppose you have held an investment for some time – say, 5, 10 or 20 years. Your ROI rate probably has fluctuated from year to year, high in some years and low in others. Now, suppose we ask how you have done on this investment over the years. You could give us the yearly ROI rates. But the more common practice in the investment world is to calculate the *average* ROI – the equivalent constant, or flat rate that would have resulted in the same ending value of your investment.

Average ROI rates are commonly used to summarise the historical investment performance of a mutual fund. You see this measure in several other places as well – for example, in the reporting of investment performance to individuals by their retirement fund managers. Be very careful about using these ROI rates. Keep in mind that the average ROI rate masks the actual year-by-year volatility in investment performance.

For example, suppose that five years ago you put £100,000 in an investment that paid no cash income any year; all the return was in annual changes in the value of the investment. Figure 4-4 summarises the yearly performance of your investment. Your £100,000 original investment five years ago is now worth £248,832. But the annual returns fluctuated widely; you had some good ROI years and some bad years. (Many investors would not tolerate the annual ROI volatility of this type of investment.) What is the average annual ROI for your investment?

Figure 4-4:	Year	Investment Value at Start of Year	Market Value Change During Year	Investment Value at End of Year	ROI For Year
Yearly	1	£100,000	£70,000	£170,000	70%
investment	2	£170,000	£70,418	£240,418	41%
perfor-	3	£240,418	£0	£240,418	0%
mance over	4	£240,418	(£24,042)	£216,376	-10%
five years.	5	£216,376	£32,456	£248,832	15%

Believe it or not, the average ROI for this investment is 20 per cent. You may ask: How can this be correct? Well, 20 per cent is indeed correct. The average annual ROI rate is the uniform rate that would make the investment grow from the original amount invested (£100,000 in this example) to the final value at the end of the investment (£248,832 in this example). You may not be convinced that the average annual ROI rate is 20 per cent unless you actually walk through what would have happened if your investment had increased 20 per cent in value each year.

Figure 4-5 shows this imaginary year-by-year investment value growth. Note that the investment value at the end of the fifth year is exactly £248,832. Of course, you didn't actually earn 20 per cent ROI each year, as a comparison with the actual investment performance in Figure 4-4 reveals. But advertising that the average annual ROI for this investment is 20 per cent is legal and even accurate. Let the investor beware!

Figure 4-5:	Year	Investment Value at Start of Year	Imputed 20% ROI For Year	Investment Value at End of Year
Proof that	1	£100,000	£20,000	£120,000
the average	2	£120,000	£24,000	£144,000
annual ROI	3	£144,000	£28,800	£172,800
rate for the	4	£172,800	£34,560	£207,360
five-year investment is 20 per cent.	5	£207,360	£41,472	£248,832

The Move Channel has a sophisticated online ROI calculator that you can find at www.themovechannel.com/calculators/roi.asp. The calculator is designed with property investors in mind, but works equally as well with all types of investment. Just substitute their terms, rent, refurbishment costs and so forth, with your own.

An Accounting Template for Retirement Planning

The main financial concern of most people as they approach retirement is whether they will have enough retirement income in addition to what they will receive from the state pension. How much retirement income do you need? How should you take money out of your retirement account, assuming that you have choices? What are the income tax effects of withdrawals from your tax-deferred retirement funds?

We can't begin to answer these questions here. But we can offer a basic template to get you going and to help you negotiate the first steps in financial retirement planning. Figure 4-6 illustrates how to calculate your *replacement ratio,* which you compute by dividing retirement income by pre-retirement income. The point is that your retirement income replaces your wage, or salary, or other earned income, and that it's very important to calibrate your retirement income as a percentage of your pre-retirement income. Most financial advisers recommend that your replacement ratio should be at least 70 per cent, in order to maintain your standard of living at a reasonably comparable level.

Monthly Income and Deductions	Before retirement £	After retirement £
Gross income before deductions	6,000	3,960
National Insurance at 11%	(660)	
Employees pension contribution (at 7%)	(420)	
Additional Personal Tax allowance for the over 65s		28
Take home pay before tax	4,920	3,988
REPLACEMENT RATIO 81%		

Figure 4-6: Accounting template for figuring retirement income replacement ratio.

For this example, we used numbers based on reasonable assumptions and typical conditions. Prior to retirement, Pat (as we call the person in this example) was earning £6,000 per month. Upon retirement, this regular pay cheque stops coming. Pat has to depend on either the company's pension plan (in a defined-benefit retirement plan) or on the accumulated investment amount (in a defined-contribution plan). Without going into details, assume that Pat's monthly retirement income will be £3,960 per month, which is two thirds of Pat's pre-retirement income. But hold on; you have to consider several other important factors.

In 2011/12, an employee has to pay 12 per cent National Insurance tax on the first £43,875 (approx) of annual earned income. Once retired, Pat doesn't have to pay the tax; instead Pat starts receiving state pension income, which is about £520 per month for a married man (This whole state pension arena is up for grabs right now, so goodness knows what this figure will actually be when you come to retire). Pat also stops making pension contributions. The bottom line is that Pat's take-home monthly income, before income tax, is £3,988 after retirement and £4,920 before retirement – which is a replacement ratio of 81 per cent. Most financial advisers consider this ratio adequate, although it would be better, of course, if Pat's retirement nest egg had been bigger to provide more income during the golden years. The template shown in Figure 4-6 allows you to start with a replacement ratio goal, say 85 per cent, and then work back to how much your retirement income would have to be. Good luck on accumulating enough in your retirement fund to provide the income you need.

To help you work out how much retirement income you might receive from saving into personal, stakeholder or company pensions, use the pension calculator at www.pensioncalculator.org.uk.

Part II
Getting a Grip on Financial Statements

'Look, Mr Brinkley, you don't fool me —
you don't have a proper accountant in
this company do you?'

In this part . . .

Financial statements are like the tip of an iceberg – they only show the visible part, underneath which are a lot of record-keeping, accounting methods, and reporting decisions. The managers of a business, the investors in a business, and the lenders to a business need a firm grasp on these accounting communications. They need to know which handles to grab hold of and how to find both the good and bad signals in financial statements – and, ugh, this includes the small-print footnotes that go with financial statements.

Accountants prepare three primary financial statements. The *profit and loss account* reports the profit-making activities of the business and how much profit or loss the business made. (Sounds odd, doesn't it, to say a business *made a loss*? But to make profit, a business has to take the risk that it may suffer a loss.) The *balance sheet* reports the financial situation and position of the business at a point in time – usually the last day of the profit period. The *cash flow statement* reports how much cash was actually realised from profit and other sources of cash, and what the business did with this money. In short, the financial life of a business and its prospects for success or potential danger of failing is all revealed in its financial statements, as this part of the book exposes.

But, as with much in accounting, not everything is quite as it appears. Changing a single letter (FIFO to LIFO) in the footnotes to the accounts can add (or subtract) a small fortune from the reported profit, as you'll see in Chapter 8.

Chapter 5

Profit Mechanics

*I*n this chapter we lift up the bonnet and investigate how the profit engine runs. At first glance, making profit may seem fairly simple – sell stuff and control expenses. Bring in more pounds from sales revenue than the pounds paid out for expenses. The excess of revenue over expenses is profit. What's the big deal?

Well, making a profit and determining its amount isn't nearly as simple as you may think. This chapter starts with a simple case in which the increase in cash is equal to profit – the business collects cash for all of its sales during the period and pays out cash for all of its expenses, and profit equals the cash left over. But alas, the business world is not so simple. So the chapter continues one step at a time to build a realistic profit model. Walking through this example lets you answer one very important question: At the end of the day, where exactly is the profit that you worked so hard to earn?

Swooping Profit into One Basic Equation

For a business that sells products, its profit equation is simply sales revenue – expenses = profit, which almost always is reported in a vertical format like this:

Basic Profit Equation		
Sales Revenue		£1,000,000
Less Expenses	£940,000	
Equals Profit		£60,000

Profit, in short, equals what's left over from sales revenue after you deduct all expenses. (You never see the term *net sales revenue* instead of *profit*.) This business earned £60,000 on £1,000,000 total sales revenue for the period, which is 6 per cent. Expenses used up 94 per cent of sales revenue. Although it may seem rather thin, a 6 per cent profit margin on sales is typical for many businesses – although some businesses consistently make a bottom-line profit of 10–20 per cent of sales, and others are satisfied with a 1 or 2 per cent profit margin on sales revenue. Normal profit ratios vary widely from industry to industry.

Businesses that sell services instead of products also use the term *sales revenue* for *gross income* (total income before deducting expenses) from sales of their services – but you also see variations on this term. Businesses that don't sell anything as such – financial institutions that earn investment income, for example – use other terms for their gross income.

Notice the following points about the basic profit equation:

✔ Even though you're deducting expenses from sales revenue, you generally don't use a minus sign or parentheses to indicate that the expense amount is a negative number (although some people do).

✔ Using a double underline under the profit number is common practice but not universal. Some people use bold type. You generally don't see anything as garish as a fat arrow pointing to the profit number or a big smiley encircling the profit number – but again, tastes vary.

✔ Profit isn't always called *profit*. It's often called *net income* or the *bottom line* or – particularly on financial reports intended for people outside the business – *net earnings*. (Can't accountants agree on *anything*?) Throughout this book we use the terms *net income* and *profit* pretty much interchangeably.

✔ *Sales revenue* is the total amount of money or other assets received from sales of the company's products for the entire year. The number used in the profit equation represents all sales – you can't tell how many different sales were made, how many different customers the company sold products to or how the sales were distributed over the 12 months of the year.

Sales revenue is strictly what belongs to the business and doesn't include money that anyone else can claim (for example, VAT that the business collects from customers and then remits to the government).

Note: A business may have other sources of income in addition to the sales revenue from its products. One common alternative source of income is interest or other return earned on investments the company makes. In the profit report, investment income goes on a separate line and is not included with sales revenue – to make clear that this source of income is secondary to the mainstream sales revenue of the business.

✔ *Expenses* consist of a wide variety of costs of operating the business and making sales, starting with the cost of the goods (products) sold to the customers and including many other costs of operating the business:

- Payroll costs (wages, salaries and benefits paid to employees).

- Insurance costs.

- Property taxes on buildings and land.

- Cost of gas and electric utilities.

- Telephone and Internet charges.

- Depreciation of operating assets that last more than one year (such as buildings, cars and trucks, computers, office furniture, tools and machinery, and shelving).

- Website maintenance, advertising and sales promotion costs.

- Office supplies.

- Legal and audit costs.

- Interest paid on loans.

- Income taxes.

As is the case with sales revenue, you can't tell from the amount reported as an expense how much was spent on each component making up the total. For example, the total depreciation expense amount doesn't tell you how much was for buildings and how much was for vehicles.

By the way, notice that only one total is shown for all the business's expenses – to keep the profit equation as short as possible. However, when preparing a formal profit report – which is called a *profit and loss account* – expenses are broken down into several basic categories. (See 'Reporting Profit to Managers and Investors: The Profit and Loss Account' at the end of the chapter.)

Measuring the Financial Effects of Profit-Making Activities

In the basic profit equation example introduced earlier in this chapter, a business earned £60,000 net income for the year. That means it's £60,000 richer now, right? Well, that could happen in a make-believe world, and we start this section with a hypothetical profit example in which the business checking account *does* increase by £60,000 – but this example is extremely oversimplified. In the real world, nothing is that simple.

The financial effects of making profit go far beyond a fatter bank account. To get a clear picture, a balance sheet equation is handy to sort out the various effects. The general format of the balance sheet equation (also called the *accounting equation*) is as follows:

Assets = liabilities + owners' equity

See Chapter 2 for more information about this equation.

Making a profit increases the assets of a business. Assets also increase when the owners invest money in the business and when the business borrows money. These two types of increases in assets are not profit. Profit is the net increase of assets from sales revenue less expenses, not from borrowing and not from its owners investing capital in the business.

Most businesses do not distribute all of their annual profit to their owners; they could, but they don't. Instead, the increase in assets from making profit is used to expand the resource base of the business. Profit not distributed is called reserves or *retained earnings*. The nature of retained earnings is shown in the following rearrangement of the balance sheet equation:

Assets – liabilities – invested capital = retained earnings

The key idea here is that if you start with total assets and then take away how much of the assets came from liabilities and how much was invested by the owners, the remainder must have come from retained earnings. For example, if a business has £6 million in assets, £2 million in liabilities and £3 million in invested capital, the remaining £1 million must be due to retained earnings.

The retained earnings account is *not* – we repeat, *not* – an asset, even though its name may suggest otherwise. It is a *source*-of-assets account, not an asset account. See the 'So why is it called retained earnings?' sidebar for more information about the retained earnings account.

So why is it called retained earnings?

The retained earnings account, like all balance sheet accounts, reports the net balance in the account after recording both the increases *and the decreases* in the account through the end of the period. The retained earnings account increases when the business makes a profit and then decreases when the business distributes some of the profit to the owners. That is, the total amount of profit paid out to the owners is recorded as a decrease in the retained earnings account. (Exactly how the profit is divided among the owners depends on the ownership structure of the business – see Chapter 11.)

The profit-making activities of a business affect several assets and also some liabilities – not the kind recorded when borrowing money (interest-bearing debt), but the kind recorded for expenses that have not been paid immediately. The accounts used to record unpaid expenses are referred to as *operating liabilities*. Interest is paid on debt (borrowed money), but not on operating liabilities. The term *operating* simply refers to the sales and expense operations of a business that are necessary for making profit.

An example: During a period, a business records the full cost of all wages and benefits that its employees earn. The full cost is the correct amount of expense to record in the period to measure profit for the period. But at the end of the period, some part of this total cost has not been paid. The unpaid balance of the total cost is recorded in an operating liability account.

Preparing the balance sheet equation

Each asset of a business is different from the others, but cash is in a class by itself. Furthermore, the cash flow aspects of profit are receiving a great deal of attention these days with survival being as much of a concern as profit itself. So separating assets into cash and non-cash assets is useful. Moreover, separating liabilities into operating liabilities and borrowed money (generally referred to as *debt*) is useful, and separating owners' equity into invested capital and retained earnings is useful. This six-fold subdivision of the balance sheet equation looks like this:

Cash + non-cash assets = operating liabilities + debt + invested capital + retained earnings

On the one hand, this expansion of the balance sheet equation helps clarify the different types of assets, liabilities and owners' equity. On the other hand, for exploring the profit-making process, debt and invested capital are not needed because revenue and expenses do not involve these two types of accounts. Debt and invested capital are excess baggage for the following journey through the profit-making process of a business. So to simplify the equation assume that the business has no debt and no invested capital (not realistic, but very convenient here). Thus the balance sheet equation that we use in the following sections is as follows:

Cash + Non-cash Assets = Operating Liabilities + Retained Earnings

A simple, all-cash example to start things off: Suppose your business collected all sales revenue for the year immediately in cash and paid all expenses for the year immediately in cash. Your profit for the year was £60,000. Here's how that profit affects the financial condition of your business (to simplify, pound signs are not used):

Cash	**+ Non-cash Assets**	**= Operating Liabilities**	**+ Retained Earnings**
+60,000			+60,000

The cash asset account increases by £60,000, which is the net difference between sales revenue and expenses – your business bank account balance is £60,000 higher at the end of the year than at the beginning of the year. (If you had distributed some of the profit, the balance of the retained earnings account would be the amount you distributed subtracted from £60,000, and your cash would be lower by the same amount.)

Exploring the Profit-Making Process One Step at a Time

We don't mean to scare you off, but the profit picture gets more complex than the simple all-cash example just discussed. Many businesses sell their products on credit rather than cash, for example, and usually don't collect all their sales revenue by the end of the year. In other words some of the expenses for the year aren't paid by the end of the year. Each of the following steps adds a layer of reality, one at a time, to make the profit picture more realistic. The following sections start with the all-cash scenario as the point of departure and then make one change at a time to show you how the additional factor affects the balance sheet equation.

Making sales on credit

If your business allows customers to buy its products or services on credit, you need to add an asset account called *debtors* or *accounts receivable* (also terms we will use interchangeably) that records the total amount owed to the business by its customers who made purchases unofficially and haven't paid up yet. You probably wouldn't have collected all your receivables by the end of the year, especially for credit sales that occurred in the last weeks of the year. However, you still record the sales revenue and the cost-of-goods-sold expense for these sales in the year in which the sales occurred. The initial scenario in which all sales were collected in cash and all expenses were paid in cash is used as the point of reference in the following steps.

Your business had sales revenue of £1 million and total expenses of £940,000, all of which were paid by year-end, making for a bottom-line profit of £60,000. Now assume that £80,000 of the sales revenue came from credit sales that haven't yet been collected at the end of the year. Here's what the financial effects look like (for convenience, pound signs in the balance sheet equation are not used):

Cash	+	Non-cash Assets	=	Operating Liabilities	+	Retained Earnings
+60,000						+60,000
Accounts receivable						
–80,000						+80,000

Note that the first line in the balance sheet equation (which is underlined) is from the initial all-cash scenario and serves as the point of reference. Everything in the new scenario is the same as in the all-cash scenario except for the changes shown below the line. Also note that the name of the specific non-cash asset – in this case, accounts receivable – is entered in the balance sheet equation column. When a change in a non-cash asset is entered in the balance sheet equation, the corresponding effect on cash is shown in the cash column.

The £80,000 of uncollected sales revenue at year-end has the effect of decreasing the cash you have by £80,000. Accounts receivable represents cash waiting in the wings to be collected in the near future (assuming that all your customers will pay their accounts receivable to you on time). But until the money is actually received, your business is without the £80,000 cash inflow. This situation may appear to be pretty serious. But hang on; there are several more steps to go.

Whether collected entirely in cash or not, the entire £1 million in sales revenue for the year is recorded and used to calculate profit. So bottom-line profit is £60,000 – the same as in the all-cash scenario. But the cash effects between the two scenarios are quite different. When making sales on credit, you count the sales in calculating your profit, even though the cash is not collected from customers until sometime later. This is one feature of the *accrual basis of accounting*, which is explained in Chapter 3. The accrual basis of accounting records revenue when sales are made and records expenses when these costs are incurred. When sales are made on credit, the accounts receivable asset account is increased; later, when cash is received from the customer, cash is increased and the accounts receivable account is decreased.

Depreciation expense

Depreciation expense accounting is the method of spreading out the cost of a fixed asset instead of charging the entire cost to the year of purchase. That way, each year of use bears a share of the total cost. *Fixed assets* are long-lived operating assets – buildings, machinery, office equipment, vehicles, computers and data-processing equipment, shelving and cabinets, and so on.

For example, cars and light trucks may be depreciated over five years. (Businesses apply the five-year rule to other kinds of assets as well.) The basic idea of depreciation is to charge a fraction of the total cost to depreciation expense for each of the five years. (The actual fraction each year depends on which method of depreciation you choose, which is explained in Chapter 13.)

Suppose your £940,000 total of expenses for the year includes £25,000 depreciation for fixed assets. (You bought these assets for £125,000 and are charging one-fifth of the cost each year for five years.) But you didn't actually pay anything for the fixed assets this year – you bought the assets in previous years. Depreciation is a real expense, but not a *cash outlay* expense after the fixed assets are already bought and paid for. (See the 'Appreciating the positive impact of depreciation on cash flow' sidebar if you're confused about this point.)

Here's what the financial effects of depreciation expense look like:

Cash	**+**	**Non-cash Assets**	**=**	**Operating Liabilities**	**+**	**Retained Earnings**
+60,000						+60,000
+25,000				Fixed assets –25,000		

Appreciating the positive impact of depreciation on cash flow

While making sales on credit does not generate immediate cash inflow and thus has a temporarily negative impact on your cash flow, depreciation is good news for cash flow. This concept gets a little complex, so stay with us here.

Fundamentally, a business sets its sales prices high enough to recover its expenses plus provide a profit. In a real sense, the business is passing on the cost of its fixed assets to its customers and recovering some of the cost of the fixed assets each year through sales revenue. A good example to illustrate this critical point is a taxicab driver who owns his cab. He sets his fares high enough to pay for his time; to pay for the insurance, licence, petrol and oil; and to recover the cost of the cab. Included in each fare is a tiny fraction of the cost of the cab, which over the course of the year adds

up to the depreciation expense that he passed on to his passengers and collected in fares. At the end of the year, he has collected a certain amount of money that pays him back for part of the cost of the cab.

In short, fixed assets are gradually *liquidated*, or turned back into cash, each year. Part of sales revenue recovers a fraction of the cost of fixed assets, which is why the decrease in the fixed assets account to record depreciation expense has the effect of increasing cash (assuming your sales revenue was collected in cash during the year). What the company does with this cash recovery is another matter. Sooner or later, you need to replace the fixed assets to continue in business. In this chapter, we do not look beyond the cash recovery of part of the original cost invested in the fixed asset.

Compared with the cash flow effects of accounts receivable, depreciation is good news. Let us put it this way: If all sales revenue had been collected and all expenses except depreciation had been paid during the year, your cash would have increased by £85,000. The company would have realised £60,000 from your profit-making activities plus the £25,000 depreciation recovery during the year. The positive impact of depreciation on cash is just the prelude. Next in line are the favourable cash flow effects of unpaid expenses.

Unpaid expenses

A typical business pays many expenses after the period benefited by the expense. For example, suppose that your business hires a law firm that does a lot of legal work for the company during the year but you don't pay the bill until the following year. Your business may match retirement contributions made by employees but you may not pay your share until the following year. Or your business may have unpaid bills for telephone, gas, electricity and water that it has used during the year.

Accountants use three different types of operating liability accounts to record a business's unpaid expenses:

- ✔ **Accounts payable, or creditors:** For items that the business buys on credit and for which it receives an invoice (a bill).

- ✔ **Accrued expenses payable:** For unpaid costs that a business generally has to estimate because it doesn't receive an invoice for them. An example of accrued expenses is unused holiday that your employees carry over to the following year, which you will have to pay for in the coming year.

- ✔ **Income tax payable:** For income taxes, or corporation tax, that a business still owes to HM Revenue and Customs.

Your business has each of the three operating liabilities we just listed. Some of your total expenses for the year are unpaid at year-end – part in the accounts payable account, part in the accrued expenses payable account and part in the income tax payable account. Here's what the financial effects of your unpaid expenses look like in the balance sheet equation:

Cash	**+ Non-cash Assets**	**=**	**Operating Liabilities**	**+ Retained Earnings**
+60,000				+60,000
+30,000			Accounts payable +30,000	
+35,000			Accrued expenses payable +35,000	
+5,000			Income tax payable +5,000	

The total of these three unpaid operating liabilities is £70,000 (£30,000 accounts payable + £35,000 accrued expenses payable + £5,000 income tax payable). Your balance sheet would report these liabilities because they are claims against the business. You may think that liabilities are bad, but for cash flow, liabilities are good. Your business has not yet paid £70,000 of the expenses for the year, and your cash balance is higher by this amount – you get to hang on to the cash until you pay the liabilities. Of course, you have to pay these liabilities next year, but isn't it nice to have your balance sheet show a big, fat cash increase for this year even though you have to show the liabilities as well?

Prepaid expenses

Prepaid expenses are the opposite of unpaid expenses. For example, a business buys fire insurance and general liability insurance (in case a customer who slips on a wet floor sues the business). You pay insurance premiums ahead of time, before the period in which you're covered, but you charge that expense to the actual period benefited. At the end of the year, the business may be only halfway through the insurance coverage period, so it charges off only half the premium cost as an expense (for a six-month policy, you charge one-sixth of the premium cost to each of the six months covered). So at the time you pay the premium, you charge the entire amount to the prepaid expenses asset account, and for each month of coverage, you transfer the appropriate fraction of the cost to the insurance expense account.

Here's what the financial effects of your prepaid expenses look like in the balance sheet equation:

Cash	**+**	**Non-cash Assets**	**=**	**Operating Liabilities**	**+**	**Retained Earnings**
+60,000						+60,000
–15,000		Prepaid expenses +15,000				

The build-up of prepaid expenses has a negative impact on the business's cash. In other words you had to write cheques for the prepaid expenses so your cash balance is smaller. The prepayment of these expenses lays the groundwork for continuing your operations seamlessly into next year. What it comes down to is that certain costs of your profit-making operations must be paid in advance – you don't have a choice. Remember that although your business is £15,000 cash poorer, profit remains the same (£60,000) as it was in all the previous scenarios.

Stock (or Inventory) and cost of goods sold expense

Cost of goods sold is one of the primary expenses of businesses that sell products. It's just what its name implies: the cost that a business paid for the products it sells to customers. A business makes profit by setting its sales prices high enough to cover the actual costs of products sold, the costs of operating the business, interest on borrowed money, and income taxes (assuming that the business pays income tax), with something left over for profit.

When the business acquires a product, the cost of the product goes into a *stock asset account* (and, of course, the cost is either deducted from the cash account or added to the accounts payable liability account, depending on whether the business paid with cash or bought on credit). When a customer buys that product, the business transfers the cost of the product from the stock asset account to the cost-of-goods-sold expense account because the product is no longer in the business's stock; the product has been delivered to the customer.

The first step in determining profit for the period is deducting the cost-of-goods-sold expense from the sales revenue for the goods sold. Most profit and loss accounts report the cost of goods sold as a separate expense (refer to 'Reporting Profit to Managers and Investors: The Profit and Loss Account,' later in this chapter).

So assume that your business did, in fact, start the year with a sizable stock of products whose cost is recorded in the stock asset account. As your business sold the products early in the year, the cost of the goods sold was removed from the stock account, and that cost was charged to expense.

Your business sells products so you need to have a stock of products on hand to sell to your customers. This stockpile of goods on the shelves waiting to be sold (or in storage space in the back room) is called *stock*. When you drive by a car dealer and see all the cars waiting to be sold, remember that these products are called stock. The cost of unsold products (goods held in stock) is not charged to expense until the products are actually sold. In this way, the cost-of-goods-sold expense is correctly matched against the sales revenue from the goods sold.

During the year you increased the number of products offered for sale. Therefore, your total purchases of products during the year was £55,000 more than your total cost of goods sold. In other words, you increased the size of your stock by £55,000 cost. The financial effects of your ending stock increase in the balance sheet equation are as follows:

Cash +	Non-cash Assets =	Operating Liabilities +	Retained Earnings
+60,000			+60,000
−55,000	Stock +55,000		

You not only replaced the products sold to customers during the year, but you also bought additional products that cost £55,000. This stock build-up requires cash – notice the £55,000 drain on cash. Your increase in stock may be a smart move but it did use £55,000 in cash.

An increase in the accounts payable liability account may provide part of the stock increase because businesses that have established good credit histories can buy their stock on credit. However, we didn't want to add another change in the accounts payable account and in most situations, a good part of the stock increase would have to be paid for by the end of the year.

So Where's Your Hard-Earned Profit?

As a business manager, not only should you make profit, but you should also understand and manage the financial effects of profit. In particular, understand that profit does not simply mean an increase in cash. Sales revenue and expenses, the two factors of profit, affect many assets and operating liabilities – making sales on credit affects accounts receivable, expenses paid in advance affect prepaid assets, unpaid expenses affect operating liabilities and so on. You simply can't have expenses without a variety of changes in assets and operating liabilities.

Knowing how much profit your business made isn't enough. You need to take another step and ask, 'Did the profit generate an increase in cash equal to the profit?' and, because it hardly ever does, 'Where is the rest of the profit?'

So far, we've looked at each step along the reality road separately, as if it were the only change from the simple cash-basis example. Now we assemble all the steps together that we've analysed since starting with the simple all-cash example. In reading the following summary remember that increases in assets hurt your cash balance but that increases in operating liabilities help your cash balance:

**Summary of Changes during Year in Non-cash
Assets and Operating Liabilities**

Changes in Non-cash Assets:		
Accounts receivable	*+80,000*	
Stock	*+55,000*	
Prepaid expenses	*+15,000*	
Fixed assets	*–25,000*	
Net increase in non-cash assets		*£125,000*
Changes in Operating Liabilities:		
Creditors (accounts payable)	*+30,000*	
Accrued expenses payable	*+35,000*	
Income tax payable	*+5,000*	
Increase of operating liabilities	*£70,000*	
Net decrease in cash balance during year		*£55,000*

Our purpose right now is simply to explain that £55,000 of your profit for the year is not found in an increase in cash but rather consists of the changes in non-cash assets and operating liabilities. Profit is a mixture of changes in the assets and operating liabilities that are an integral part of the profit-making process.

If it isn't in cash, where is it? The following schedule summarises the changes in your non-cash assets and operating liabilities caused by the profit-making steps we showed you earlier in this chapter:

Changes in Non-cash Assets		
Accounts receivable	+80,000	
Stock	+55,000	
Prepaid expenses	+15,000	
Fixed assets	–25,000	
Net increase of assets		+£125,000
Changes in Operating Liabilities		
Creditors (accounts payable)	+30,000	
Accrued expenses payable	+35,000	
Income tax payable	+5,000	
Less increase of operating liabilities		–£70,000
Non-cash components of profit		+£55,000

Note: The amounts shown in this summary are the *changes* – the increases and decreases – in the accounts caused by the sales revenue and expense transactions of your business during the year.

And there you have the story of the £60,000 profit – equal to the £5,000 increase of cash plus the £125,000 increase of non-cash assets minus the £70,000 increase in operating liabilities. Probably your biggest surprise here is that, even though your business earned £60,000 in profit for the year, your cash balance increased only £5,000. In managing your profit-making activities (sales revenue and expenses) during the year, you caused cash and three other assets to increase, one asset to decrease and three operating liabilities to increase. Notice that we've put the onus on you, the owner or manager of the business. The point is that these increases and decreases don't happen automatically – they are the result of management decisions.

By the by, you may not like referring to expenses as profit-making activity but they are! The main point is that expenses should generate sales revenue.

Advertising expense creates the incentive in customers to buy products sold by the business. Buying products at £60 cost per unit and selling them for £100 per unit generates £40 profit before other expenses are considered – even though the business has £60 of expense (cost of goods sold). Much of business profit-making is built on the model of incurring, say, £90 in expenses to generate, say, £100 in sales revenue.

Other transactions also change the assets, debt and owners' equity accounts of a business – such as borrowing money and buying new fixed assets. The balance sheet, in other words, is changed by all the business's transactions. The profit-making transactions (sales and expenses) are the main transactions changing the balance sheet, but many other transactions are recorded in the asset, liability and owners' equity accounts. Therefore, a separate summary of the profit-making transactions – limited to sales revenue and expenses – that ends with the profit for the period is a standard part of a complete financial report. This separate profit report is called the *profit and loss account.*

Reporting Profit to Managers and Investors: The Profit and Loss Account

At the end of each period, the accountant prepares a profit report called a *profit and loss account.* You may think that the report would be called the *net profit and loss account* because the bottom-line profit term preferred by accountants is *net income* – but the word *net* is dropped off the title. Other variations of the term are also used, such as *statement of operating results* and *statement of earnings.* Traditionally, the profit and loss account has been called the *profit and loss statement,* or simply the *P&L,* although in external financial reports, businesses and accountants often use the term *income statement.*

The profit and loss account reports the business's sales and expense transactions for the period, with the final profit result on the bottom line. These transactions are *inflows* and *outflows*: Sales revenue is an inflow, and expenses are outflows. Profit, the bottom line, is the *net* inflow. Please note that we didn't say *cash* flow. Making profit involves the inflows and outflows of many assets other than cash, as demonstrated in the steps in the profit-making process examined earlier in the chapter. In the business example earlier in the chapter, the earning of profit involved cash and four other asset accounts as well as three operating liabilities.

The annual profit and loss account included in an external financial report that circulates outside a business has two basic sections (or *layers*):

- ✔ The first section presents the usual, ordinary, continuing sales and expense operations of the business for the year.

- ✔ The second section presents any unusual, extraordinary, and non-recurring gains and losses that the business recorded in the year.

However, a business that didn't experience any extraordinary gains or losses wouldn't include that second section in its profit and loss account – its profit and loss account would consist simply of the first section.

Reporting normal, ongoing profit-making operations

The top section of a profit and loss account (which is the only section of the profit and loss account if the business doesn't have extraordinary gains or losses to report) typically breaks down total expenses for the year into at least four basic classes. (Refer to the sample profit and loss account at the end of this section for an example.)

- ✔ **Cost-of-goods-sold expense:** The cost of the products sold to customers for which the company received the sales revenue reported on the first line of the profit and loss account. The profit line following the deduction of this expense from sales revenue is called *gross margin* (or *gross profit*) – that's your profit before you factor in the other expenses.

   Note: Companies that sell services rather than products (airlines, cinemas, accountancy firms and so on) often do not have a cost-of-goods-sold expense line in their profit and loss accounts.

- ✔ **Sales, administrative and general expenses:** A broad, catch-all category for all expenses except those reported on the other lines in the profit and loss account. This expense combines such things as legal fees, the boss's salary, advertising costs, travel and entertainment costs, and much more – probably including some of the company's dirty laundry buried deep within.

   The next profit line, which is generally called *earnings before interest and tax* and abbreviated EBIT, is the result after deducting the sales, administrative and general expenses from gross margin.

✔ **Interest expense:** Interest paid on borrowed money (applies only to businesses that have borrowed money, obviously). This expense is usually reported on a separate line even though it may be relatively small. The profit line after deducting interest expense from earnings before interest and tax is typically called *earnings before income tax* or something similar. (Unfortunately, accounting terminology is not entirely uniform and standardised; you see variations from business to business.)

✔ **Income tax expense:** Income taxes paid by the business, *not* including property and employer payroll taxes, which are included in the sales, administrative, and general expenses line. Income tax expense is always reported on a separate line. The final profit line, the bottom line after you deduct income tax, is called *net income* – the bottom-line profit figure, unless the business has extraordinary gains and losses to report. If so, the non-recurring gains and losses are included to get down to the bottom line.

To close the business example that we've been using throughout this chapter, here is your annual profit and loss account:

Annual Profit and Loss Account for the Example

Sales revenue	*+1,000,000*
Cost of goods sold expense	*–600,000*
Gross margin	*+400,000*
Sales, administrative and general expenses	*–285,000*
Earnings before interest and tax (EBIT)	*+115,000*
Interest expense	*–25,000*
Earnings before income tax	*+90,000*
Income tax expense	*–30,000*
Net income	*+60,000*

Here are two key points to keep in mind about profit and loss accounts:

✔ The profit and loss account format that we discuss here is what you find in *external* reports released outside the business that are directed to its absentee owners who do not participate in the day-to-day management of the business. The external profit and loss account does not provide the level of detail about sales revenue and expenses needed for management purposes. Managers must have reports that drill down to the relevant detail they need to make specific decisions and for control purposes. The external profit and loss account is a fairly condensed summary.

✔ The profit and loss account does not report the financial effects of sales revenue and expenses – the increases and decreases in the assets and operating liabilities that revenue and expenses cause. Readers of the profit report have to look at the balance sheet to see the assets and liabilities of the business. Actually, the cash flow statement that Chapter 7 explains is the link between the profit and loss account and the balance sheet. In short, the profit and loss account is not really a stand-alone financial statement; you have to put it into the financial context of the business's other two primary financial statements: the balance sheet and the cash flow statement.

The website www.score.org offers a downloadable Excel spreadsheet that enables you to tailor a profit and loss account to your own needs. Scope exists for 7 categories of revenue, 7 cost of sales categories and 20 items of expense. You can find the spreadsheet by going to the SCORE homepage and clicking on 'Templates & Tools' where you will find an extensive selection of templates and calculators.

Reporting unusual gains and losses

The road to profit is anything but smooth and straight. Every business experiences an occasional *discontinuity* – a serious disruption that comes out of the blue, doesn't happen regularly or often, and can dramatically affect bottom-line profit. In other words, a discontinuity is something that disturbs the basic continuity of business operations – the regular flow of profit-making activities.

Here are some examples of discontinuities:

✔ Downsizing and restructuring the business.

✔ Abandoning product lines.

✔ Settling lawsuits and other legal actions.

✔ Writing down (also called *writing off*) damaged and impaired assets.

✔ Changing accounting methods.

✔ Correcting errors from previous financial reports.

With all these extraordinary losses and gains, how can you distinguish the profit that a business earned from its normal revenue and expense activities from profit caused by other forces entirely? This is one case where accounting rules are actually working *for you,* the non-accountant reader of financial reports.

According to financial reporting standards a business must make these one-time losses and gains very visible in the profit and loss account. So in addition to the normal part of the profit and loss account, which reports normal profit activities, a business with unusual, extraordinary losses or gains must add a second layer to the profit and loss account to report on *these* happenings.

If a business has no unusual gains or losses in the year, its profit and loss account ends with one bottom line, usually called *net income* or *profit/loss for the period*. When a profit and loss account includes a second layer, that line becomes *net income from continuing operations before unusual gains and losses*. Below this line, those unusual gains and losses appear for each significant, non-recurring gain or loss.

Say that a business suffered a relatively minor loss from quitting a product line and a very large loss from adopting a new accounting standard. Here's what the second layer of this business's profit and loss account looks like:

Net income from continuing operations	*+267,000,000*
Discontinued operations, net of applicable income taxes	*−20,000,000*
Earnings before cumulative effect of changes in accounting principles	*+247,000,000*
Cumulative effect of changes in accounting principles, net of applicable income taxes	*−456,000,000*
Net earnings (loss)	*−209,000,000*

What new accounting standards could possibly cause a £456 million charge? A very likely scenario could be that this charge is the result of the Accounting Standards Board (ASB) changing the way a business records benefits to retired employees. This business probably hadn't been recording those benefits all along, while the employees were still working (see Chapter 13 for more about recording these kinds of future expenses). For a mature business with many retired employees, the accumulated cost for those benefits could quite conceivably reach that high.

The gains and losses reported in the second layer of the external profit and loss account are generally complex and are not always fully explained in the financial report. So where does that leave you? As we advise in Chapter 14, your best bet is to seek the counsel of expert financial report readers – financial reports are, for all practical purposes, designed for an audience of stockbrokers, sophisticated readers of *The Financial Times* and the like, so don't feel bad that you can't understand a report without a degree in accounting-ese.

Even if you have someone else analyse a two-layer profit and loss account for you, you should be aware of controversial issues that extraordinary losses or gains raise. To really get some respect from your stockbroker or from Joe in Accounting, ask these questions about an unusual loss that a business reports:

✔ Were the annual profits reported in prior years overstated?

✔ Why wasn't the loss recorded on a more piecemeal and gradual year-by-year basis instead of as a one-time charge?

✔ Was the loss really a surprising and sudden event that could not have been anticipated?

✔ Will such a loss occur again in the future?

Every company that stays in business for more than a couple of years experiences a discontinuity of one sort or another. But beware of a business that takes advantage of discontinuities in either of the following ways:

✔ **Discontinuities become 'continuities':** This business makes an extraordinary loss or gain a regular feature on its profit and loss account. Every year or so, the business loses a major lawsuit, abandons product lines, or restructures itself. It reports 'non-recurring' gains or losses from the same source on a recurring basis every year.

✔ **A discontinuity becomes an opportunity to dump all sorts of write-downs and losses:** When recording an unusual loss (such as settling a lawsuit), the business opts to record other losses at the same time – everything but the kitchen sink (and sometimes that, too) gets written off. This *big-bath theory* says that you may as well take a big bath now in order to avoid taking little showers in the future.

Putting the profit and loss account in perspective

The profit and loss account occupies centre stage; the bright spotlight is on this financial statement because it reports profit or loss for the period. But think of the three primary financial statements – the other two being the balance sheet and the cash flow statement – as a three-ring circus. The profit and loss account may draw the most attention but you have to watch what's going on in all three places. As important as profit is to the financial success of a business, the profit and loss account is not an island unto itself. To understand and manage profit, managers have to follow through to the financial effects of revenue and expenses on the assets and liabilities of the business and pay particular attention to cash flow, which Chapter 7 explores.

The term *financial report,* or *package of accounts,* is the umbrella term referring to a complete set of financial statements. Financial statements are supplemented with footnotes and other commentary from a business's managers. If the financial statements have been audited, the accounting firm includes a short report stating whether the financial statements follow generally accepted accounting principles. Most financial reports, even by small businesses, are bound between two covers. A financial report can be anywhere from 5 pages to more than 50 pages to even 100 pages for very large, publicly owned business corporations. More and more public corporations make their annual financial reports available on their websites, and Yahoo provides direct links to most public companies' reports and accounts online (go to http://uk.finance.yahoo.com and click on 'Free annual reports').

The term *financial statement* refers to one of the following three key summaries prepared periodically by every business:

- **Profit and loss account:** Summarises sales revenue and expenses and ends with the net income (profit) earned for the period or the loss suffered for the period.

- **Balance sheet:** Summarises the balances in the business's assets, liabilities and owners' equity accounts at the close of the period.

- **Cash flow statement:** Summarises the sources and uses of cash during the period.

The annual financial report of a business must include all three of these financial statements. Some businesses also prepare other schedules and summaries of a more limited focus that may also be called a financial statement – but in this book the term *financial statement* refers only to the three primary financial statements that we just listed.

In response to contractual or regulatory requirements some businesses issue special financial reports that do not include a complete set of financial statements with all footnote disclosures, or they may not adopt generally accepted accounting principles for certain matters. The distribution of these special financial reports is limited to specific parties. These special reports should be distinguished from the *general-purpose* financial reports that are distributed to the owners and creditors of the business based on generally accepted accounting principles

Chapter 6

The Balance Sheet from the Profit and Loss Account Viewpoint

In This Chapter

▶ Coupling the profit and loss account with the balance sheet

▶ Seeing how sales revenue and expenses drive assets and liabilities

▶ Sizing up assets and liabilities

▶ Drawing the line between debt and owners' equity

▶ Grouping short-term assets and liabilities to determine solvency

▶ Understanding costs and other balance sheet values

*T*his chapter explores one of the three primary financial statements reported by businesses – the *balance sheet*, or, to be more formal, the *statement of financial condition*. This key financial statement may seem to stand alone – like an island to itself – because it's presented on a separate page in a financial report. In fact, the assets and liabilities reported in a balance sheet are driven mainly by the transactions the business engages in to make profit. These sale and expense transactions of a business are summarised for a period in its *profit and loss account,* which is explained in Chapter 5.

You've probably heard the expression that it takes money to make money. For a business it takes *assets* to make profit. This chapter identifies the particular assets needed to make profit. Also, the chapter points out the particular liabilities involved in the pursuit of profit.

In brief, a business needs a lot of assets to open its doors and to carry on its profit-making activities – making sales and operating the business from day to day. For example, companies that sell products need to carry a *stock* of products that are available for delivery to customers when sales are made. A business can purchase products for its stock on credit, and delay payment for the purchase (assuming it has a good credit rating). In most cases, however, the business has to pay for these purchases before all the products have been sold – the stock-holding period is considerably longer than the credit period. The business needs cash to pay for its stock purchases. Where does the cash come from?

In fact a business needs many more assets than just stock. Where does the money for these assets come from? Assets are the first act of a two-act play. The second act looks at where the money comes from, or the *sources of capital* for businesses. As Chapter 1 explains, the *balance sheet* of a business is the financial statement that reports its assets on one side and the sources of capital on the other side.

Of course, as we repeat throughout this book, you need to use all three primary financial statements to paint a business's complete financial picture. The *profit and loss account* details sales revenue and expenses, which directly determine the amounts of assets (and two or three of the liabilities) that are summarised in the *balance sheet.* The *cash flow statement* answers the important question of how much of the profit has been converted to cash, and the company's other sources and uses of cash during the period.

This chapter connects sales revenue and expenses, which are reported in the profit and loss account, with their corresponding assets and liabilities in the balance sheet. The chapter also explains the sources of capital that provide the money a business uses to invest in its assets.

Coupling the Profit and Loss Account with the Balance Sheet

Sales revenue generates the inflow of assets and expenses cause the outflow of assets. These increases and decreases in assets have to be recorded. Also, some expenses spawn short-term liabilities that have to be recorded. In short, accounting for profit involves much more than keeping track of cash inflows and outflows. Which specific assets and liabilities are directly involved in recording the sales revenue and expenses of a business? And how are these assets and liabilities reported in a business's balance sheet at the end of the profit period? These are the two main questions that this chapter answers.

This chapter explains how the profit-making transactions reported in the profit and loss account connect with the assets (and some operating liabilities) reported in the balance sheet. We stress the dovetail fit between these two primary financial statements (the profit and loss account and the balance sheet). And don't forget that business accounting also keeps track of where the money for the assets comes from – to invest in its assets, a business needs to raise money by borrowing and persuading owners to put money in the business. You shouldn't look at assets without also looking at where the money (the capital) for the assets comes from.

The *balance sheet*, or statement of financial condition, summarises a business's assets, liabilities and owners' equity at a point in time and, as shown in Chapter 5, can be summarised in the following equation:

Assets	**Liabilities**	**Owners' Equity**
Cash + Non-cash Assets =	Operating Liabilities + Debt +	Invested Capital + Retained Earnings

Figure 6-1 shows a balance sheet for a fictitious company – not from left to right as shown in the accounting equation just above, but rather from top to bottom, which is a vertical expression of the accounting equation. This balance sheet is stripped down to the bare-bone essentials – please note that it would need a little tidying up before you'd want to show it off to the world in an external financial report (see Chapter 8).

Assets

Cash		£ 2,000,000
Debtors		£ 2,500,000
Stock		£ 3,575,000
Prepaid Expenses		£ 480,000
Fixed Assets (at Original cost)	£ 11,305,000	
Accumulated Depreciation	£ (5,780,000)	£ 5,525,000
Total		£ 14,080,000

Liabilities and Owners' Equity

Creditors	£ 800,000	
Accrued Expenses Payable	£ 1,200,000	
Income Tax Payable	£ 80,000	
Total Operating Liabilities		£ 2,080,000
Notes Payable (Interest-bearing debt)		£ 5,000,000
Owners' Invested Capital		£ 2,000,000
Retained Earnings		£ 5,000,000
Total		£ 14,080,000

Figure 6-1: A balance sheet example showing a business's various assets, liabilities and owners' equity.

A balance sheet doesn't have a punch line like the profit and loss account does – the profit and loss account's punch line being the net income line (which is rarely humorous to the business itself, but can cause some sniggers among analysts). You can't look at just one item on the balance sheet, murmur an appreciative 'ah-hah,' and rush home to watch the footy game. You have to read the whole thing (sigh) and make comparisons among the items. See Chapters 8 and 14 for more information on interpreting financial statements.

At the most basic level, the best way to understand a balance sheet (most of it, anyway) is to focus on the assets that are generated by the company's profit-making activities – in other words, the cause-and-effect relationship between an item that's reported in the profit and loss account and an item that's reported in the balance sheet.

Figure 6-2 lays out the vital links between sales revenue and expenses and the assets and liabilities that are driven by these profit-seeking activities. You can refer back to each connection as sales revenue and expenses are discussed below. The format of the profit and loss account is virtually the same as the format introduced in Chapter 5, except that depreciation expense is reported on a separate line (in Chapter 5, depreciation is buried in the sales, administrative and general expenses account).

INCOME STATEMENT (in thousands)		BALANCE SHEET (in thousands)	
Sales Revenue	£ 25,000	**Assets**	
Cost of Goods Sold Expense	15,000	Cash	£ 2,000
Gross Margin	£ 10,000	Debtors	2,500
Sales, Administrative, and General Expenses	6,000	Stock	3,575
Depreciation Expense	1,200	Prepaid Expenses	480
Earnings Before Interest and Income Tax	£ 2,800	Fixed Assets	11,305
Interest Expense	400	Accumulated Depreciation	(5,780)
Earnings Before Income Tax	£ 2,400	Total	£ 14,080
Income Tax Expense	800	**Liabilities & Owners' Equity**	
Net Income (Net Profit)	£ 1,600	Creditors	£ 800
		Accrued Expenses Payable	1,200
		Income Tax Payable	80
		Bank Loan	5,000
		Owners' Invested Capital	2,000
		Retained Earnings	5,000
		Total	£ 14,080

Figure 6-2: Connections between the assets and operating liabilities of a business and its sales revenue and expenses.

The amounts reported in the profit and loss account are the cumulative totals for the whole year (or other time period). In contrast, the amounts reported in the balance sheet are the *balances* at the end of the year – the net amount, starting with the balance at the start of the year, adjusted for increases and decreases that occur during the year. For example, the total cash inflows and outflows over the course of the entire year were much more than the £2 million ending balance for cash.

The purpose of Figure 6-2 is to highlight the connections between the particular assets and operating liabilities that are tightly interwoven with sales revenue and expenses. Business managers need a good grip on these connections to control assets and liabilities. And outside investors need to understand these connections to interpret the financial statements of a business (see Chapter 14).

Most people intuitively understand that sooner or later sales revenue increases cash and expenses decrease cash. (The exception is depreciation expense, as explained in Chapters 5 and 7.) It's the 'sooner or later' that gives rise to the assets and liabilities involved in making profit.

The assets and liabilities driven by sales revenue and expenses are as follows:

✔ Sales revenue derives from selling products and services to customers.

✔ The cost of goods sold expense is what the business paid for the products that it sells to its customers. You can't charge the cost of products to this expense account until you actually sell the goods, so that cost goes into the *stock* asset account until the goods are sold.

✔ The sales, administrative and general expenses (SA&G) category covers many different operating expenses (such as advertising, travel and telephone costs). SA&G expenses drive the following items on the balance sheet:

  • The *prepaid expenses* asset account holds the total amount of cash payments for future expenses (for example, you pay insurance premiums before the policy goes into effect, so you charge those premiums to the months covered by the policy).

  • The *creditor* liability account is the total amount of expenses that haven't been paid yet but that affect the current period. For example, you receive a bill for electricity that you used the month before, so you charge that bill to the month benefited by the electricity – thanks to the accrual basis of accounting.

  • The *accrued expenses payable* account is the opposite of the prepaid expenses asset account: this liability account holds costs that are paid after the cost is recorded as an expense. An example is the accumulated holiday pay that the company's employees have earned by the end of the year; when the employees take their holidays next year the company pays this liability.

✔ The purpose of depreciation is to spread out the original cost of a *fixed asset* over the course of the asset's life. If you buy a vehicle that's going to serve you for five years, you charge one-fifth of the cost to depreciation expense each of the five years. (Instead of charging this straight line, or level amount to each year, a business can choose an accelerated depreciation method, as explained in Chapter 13.) Rather than decreasing the fixed assets account directly (which would make some sense), accountants put depreciation expense in an offset account called *accumulated depreciation*, the balance of which is deducted from the original cost of fixed assets. Thus, both the original cost and the amount by which the original cost has been depreciated to date are available in separate accounts – both items of information are reported in the balance sheet.

✔ Interest expense depends on the amount of money that the business borrows and the interest rate that the lender charges. *Debt* is the generic term for borrowed money; and debt bears interest. *Loans* and *overdrafts* are the most common terms you see for most debt because the borrower (the business) signs a legal instrument called a *note*. Normally, the total interest expense for a period hasn't been paid by the end of the period so the unpaid part is recorded in *accrued expenses payable* (or in a more specific account of this type called *accrued interest payable*).

✔ A small part of the total income tax owed on the company's taxable income for the year probably will not be paid by the end of the year, and the unpaid part is recorded in the *income tax payable* account.

✔ A final note: The bottom-line profit (net income) for the year increases the reserves or, as it is also known, the *retained earnings* account, which is one of the two owners' equity accounts.

Sizing Up Assets and Liabilities

Although the business example shown in Figure 6–2 is hypothetical, we didn't make up the numbers at random – not at all. We use a medium-sized business that has £25 million in annual sales revenue as the example. (Your business may be a lot smaller or larger than one with £25 million annual sales revenue, of course.) All the other numbers in both the profit and loss account and the balance sheet of the business are realistic relative to each other. We assume the business earns 40 per cent gross margin (£10 million gross margin ÷ £25 million sales revenue = 40 per cent), which means its cost of goods sold expense is 60 per cent of sales revenue. The sizes of particular assets and liabilities compared with their relevant profit and loss account numbers vary from industry to industry, and even from business to business in the same industry.

Based on its history and policies, the managers of a business can estimate what the size of each asset and liability should be – and these estimates provide very useful *control benchmarks*, or yardsticks, against which the actual balances of the assets and liabilities are compared to spot any serious deviations. In other words, assets (and liabilities, too) can be too high or too low in relation to the sales revenue and expenses that drive them, and these deviations can cause problems that managers should try to correct as soon as possible.

Turning over assets

Assets should be *turned over,* or put to use by making sales. The higher the turnover (the more times the assets are used and then replaced), the better. The more sales, the better – because every sale is a profit-making opportunity. The *asset turnover ratio* compares annual sales revenue with total assets:

Annual sales revenue ÷ total assets = asset turnover ratio

The asset turnover ratio is interesting as far as it goes, but it unfortunately doesn't go very far. This ratio looks only at total assets as an aggregate total. And the ratio looks only at sales revenue. The expenses of the business for the year are not considered – even though expenses are responsible for most of the assets of a business.

Note: The asset turnover ratio is a quick-and-dirty test of how well a business is using its assets to generate sales. The ratio does not evaluate profitability; profit is not in the calculation. Basically, the ratio indicates how well assets are being used to generate sales – nothing more.

For example, based on the credit terms extended to customers and the company's actual policies regarding how aggressive the business is in collecting past-due receivables, a manager can determine the range for how much a proper, or within-the-boundaries, balance of accounts receivable should be. This figure would be the control benchmark. If the actual balance is reasonably close to this control benchmark, the debtors' level is under control. If not, the manager should investigate why the debtors' level is higher or lower than it should be.

The following sections discuss the relative sizes of the assets and liabilities in the balance sheet that result from sales and expenses. The sales and expenses are the *drivers*, or causes, of the assets and liabilities. If a business earned profit simply by investing in stocks and bonds, for example, it would not need all the various assets and liabilities explained in this chapter. Such a business – a mutual fund, for example – would have just one income-producing asset: investments in securities. But this chapter focuses on businesses that sell products to make profit.

Sales revenue and debtors

In Figure 6-2 the annual sales revenue is £25 million. Debtors represent one-tenth of this, or £2.5 million. In rough terms, the average customer's credit period is about 36 days – 365 days in the year multiplied by the 10 per cent ratio of ending debtors balance to annual sales revenue. Of course, some customers' balances owed to the business may be past 36 days and some quite new. It's the overall average that you should focus on. The key question is whether or not a customer-credit period averaging 36 days is reasonable or not.

Cost of goods sold expense and stock

In Figure 6-2 the annual cost of goods sold expense is £15 million. The stock is £3,575,000, or about 24 per cent. In rough terms, the average product's stock-holding period is 87 days – 365 days in the year multiplied by the 24 per cent ratio of ending stock to annual cost of goods sold. Of course, some products may remain in stock longer than the 87-day average and some products may sell in a much shorter period than 87 days. It's the overall average that you should focus on. Is an 87-day average stock-holding period reasonable?

The 'correct' average stock-holding period varies from industry to industry. In some industries, the stock-holding period is very long, three months or longer, especially for manufacturers of heavy equipment and high-tech products. The opposite is true for high-volume retailers such as retail supermarkets who depend on getting products off the shelves as quickly as possible. The 87-day average holding period in the example is reasonable for many businesses, but would be far too high for many other businesses.

SA&G expenses and the four balance sheet accounts that are connected with the expenses

Note that in Figure 6-2 sales, administrative and general (SA&G) expenses connect with four balance sheet accounts – cash, prepaid expenses, creditors and accrued expenses payable. The broad SA&G expense category includes many different types of expenses that are involved in making sales and operating the business. (Separate expense accounts are maintained for specific expenses; depending on the size of the business and the needs of its various managers, hundreds or thousands of specific expense accounts are established.)

Cash is paid when recording payroll, mailing and some other expenses. In contrast, insurance and office supplies costs are prepaid, and then released to expense gradually over time. So, cash is paid before the recording of the expense. Some of these expenses are not paid until weeks after being recorded; to recognise the delayed payment the amounts owed are recorded in an accounts payable or an accrued expenses payable liability account.

One point we would like to repeat is that the company's managers should adopt benchmarks for each of these accounts that are connected with the operating expenses of the business. For example, the £1.2 million ending balance of accrued expenses payable is 20 per cent of the £6 million SA&G for the year. Is this ratio within control limits? Is it too high? Managers should ask and answer questions like these for every asset and liability connected with the expenses of the business.

Fixed assets and depreciation expense

As explained in Chapter 5, depreciation is a truly unique expense. Depreciation is like other expenses in that, like all other expenses, it is deducted from sales revenue to determine profit. Other than this, however, depreciation is very different. None of the depreciation expense recorded to the period requires cash outlay during the period. Rather, depreciation expense for the period is that portion of the total cost of a business's fixed assets that is allocated to the period to record an amount of expense for using the assets during the period. Depreciation is an imputed cost, based on what fraction of the total cost of fixed assets is assigned to the period.

The higher the total cost of its fixed assets, the higher a business's depreciation expense. However, there is no standard ratio of depreciation expense to the total cost of fixed assets. The amount of depreciation expense depends on the useful lives of the company's fixed assets and which depreciation method the business selects. (How to choose depreciation methods is explained in Chapter 13.) The annual depreciation expense of a business is seldom more than 10–15 per cent of the total cost of its fixed assets. The depreciation expense for the year is either reported as a separate expense in the profit and loss account (as in Figure 6–2) or the amount is disclosed in a footnote.

Because depreciation is based on the cost of fixed assets, the balance sheet reports not one but two numbers – the original cost of the fixed assets and the *accumulated depreciation* amount (the amount of depreciation that has been charged as an expense from the time of acquiring the fixed asset to the current balance sheet date).

The point isn't to confuse you by giving you even more numbers to deal with. Seeing both numbers gives you an idea of how old the fixed assets are and also tells you how much these fixed assets originally cost.

What about cash?

A business's cash account consists of the money it has in its bank accounts plus the money that it keeps on hand to provide change for its customers. Cash is the essential lubricant of business activity. Sooner or later, virtually everything passes through the cash account.

How much of a cash balance should a business maintain? This question has no right answer. A business needs to determine how large a cash safety reserve it's comfortable with to meet unexpected demands on cash while keeping the following wisdom in mind:

✔ Excess cash balances are non-productive and don't earn any profit for the business.

✔ Insufficient cash balances can cause the business to miss taking advantage of opportunities that require quick action and large amounts of cash – such as snatching up a prized piece of property that just came on the market and that the business has had its eye on for some time, or buying out a competitor when the business comes up for sale.

The cash balance of the business whose balance sheet is presented in Figure 6–2 is £2,000,000 – which would be too large for some other businesses and too small for others.

In the example, the business has, over several years, invested £11,305,000 in its fixed assets (that it still owns and uses), and it has already charged off depreciation of £4,580,000 in previous years. In this year, the business records £1,200,000 depreciation expense (you can't tell from the balance sheet how much depreciation was charged this year; you have to look at the profit and loss account in Figure 6–2). The remaining non-depreciated cost of this business's fixed assets at the end of the year is £5,525,000. So the fixed assets part of this year's balance sheet looks like this:

Fixed assets	£11,305,000
Accumulated depreciation	(5,780,000)
Net amount included in total assets	£5,525,000

You can tell that the collection of fixed assets includes both old and new assets because the company has recorded £5,780,000 total depreciation since the assets were bought, which is a fairly sizable percentage of original cost (more than half). But many businesses use accelerated depreciation methods, which pile up a lot of the depreciation expense in the early years and less in the back years (see Chapter 13 for more details) so it's hard to estimate the average age of the assets.

Debt and interest expense

The business example whose balance sheet and profit and loss accounts are presented in Figure 6–2 has borrowed £5 million on loans, which, at an 8 per cent annual interest rate, is £400,000 in interest expense for the year. (The business may have had more or less borrowed at certain times during the year, of course, and the actual interest expense depends on the debt levels from month to month.)

For most businesses, a small part of their total annual interest is unpaid at year-end; the unpaid part is recorded to bring the expense up to the correct total amount for the year. In Figure 6–2, the accrued amount of interest is included in the more inclusive accrued expenses payable liability account. You seldom see accrued interest payable reported on a separate line in a balance sheet unless it happens to be a rather large amount or if the business is seriously behind in paying interest on its debt.

Income tax expense

In Figure 6-2, earnings before income tax – after deducting interest and all other expenses from sales revenue – is £2,400,000. (The actual taxable income of the business for the year probably would be somewhat more or less than this amount because of the many complexities in the income tax law, which are beyond the scope of this book.) In the example we use a tax rate of one-third for convenience, so the income tax expense is £800,000 of the pre-tax income of £2,400,000. Most of the income tax for the year must be paid over to HM Revenue and Customs before the end of the year. But a small part is usually still owed at the end of the year. The unpaid part is recorded in the *income tax payable* liability account – as you see in Figure 6–2. In the example, the unpaid part is £80,000 of the total £800,000 income tax for the year – but we don't mean to suggest that this ratio is typical. Generally, the unpaid income tax at the end of the year is fairly small, but just how small depends on several technical factors. You may want to check with your tax professional to make sure you have paid over enough of the annual income tax by the end of the year to avoid a penalty for late payment.

The bottom line: net profit (net income) and cash dividends (if any)

A business may have other sources of income during the year, such as interest income on investments. In this example, however, the business has only sales revenue, which is gross income from the sale of products and services. All expenses, starting with cost of goods sold, down to and including income tax, are deducted from sales revenue to arrive at the last, or bottom line, of the profit and loss account. The preferred term for bottom-line profit is *net income*, as you see in Figure 6–2.

The £1,600,000 net income for the year increases *retained earnings* by the same amount, hence the line of connection from net income and retained earnings in Figure 6-2. The £1,600,000 profit (here we go again using the term profit instead of net income) either stays in the business, or some of it is paid out and divided among the owners of the business. If the business paid out cash dividends from profit during the year, these cash payments to its owners (shareholders) are deducted from retained earnings. You can't tell from the profit and loss account or the balance sheet whether any cash dividends were paid. You have to look in the cash flow statement for this information – which is explained in Chapter 7.

Financing a Business: Owners' Equity and Debt

You may have noticed in Figure 6-2 that there are two balance sheet accounts that have no lines of connection from the profit and loss account – loans and owners' invested capital. Revenue and expenses do not affect these two key balance sheet accounts (nor the fixed assets account for that matter, which is explained in Chapter 7). However, both debt and owners' invested capital are extremely important for making profit.

To run a business you need financial backing, otherwise known as *capital*. Capital is all incoming funds that are not derived from sales revenue (or from selling off assets). A business raises capital by borrowing money, getting owners to invest money in the business, and making profit that is retained in the business. Borrowed money is known as *debt*; invested money and retained profits are the two sources of *owners' equity*. Those two sources need to be kept separate according to the rules of accounting. See Chapters 5 and 9 for more about profit.

How much capital does the business shown in Figure 6-2 have? Its total assets are £14,080,000, but this is not quite the answer. The company's profit-making activities generated three operating liabilities – creditors, accrued expenses payable and income tax payable – and in total these three liabilities provided £2,080,000 of the total assets of the business. So, deducting this amount from total assets gives the answer: The business has £12 million in capital. Where did this capital come from? Debt provided £5 million and the two sources of owners' equity provided the other £7 million (see Figure 6-1 or 6-2 to check these numbers).

Creditors, accrued expenses payable and income tax payable are short-term, non-interest-bearing liabilities that are sometimes called *current liabilities* because they arise directly from a business's expense activities – they aren't the result of borrowing money but rather are the result of buying things on credit or delaying payment of certain expenses.

This particular business has decided to finance itself through debt and equity in the following mix:

Debt	£5,000,000
Owners' equity	7,000,000
Total sources of capital	£12,000,000

Deciding how to divide your sources of capital can be tricky. In a very real sense, the debt-versus-equity question never has a final answer; it's always under review and reconsideration by most businesses. Some companies, just like some individuals, are strongly anti-debt, but even they may find that they need to take on debt eventually to keep up with changing times.

Debt is both good and bad, and in extreme situations it can get very ugly. The advantages of debt are:

- Most businesses can't raise all the capital they need from owners' equity and debt offers another source of capital (though, of course, many lenders may provide only half or less of the capital that a business needs).

- Interest rates charged by lenders are lower than rates of return expected by owners. Owners expect a higher rate of return because they're taking a greater risk with their money – the business is not required to pay them back the same way that it's required to pay back a lender. For example, a business may pay 8 per cent interest on its debt and have to earn a 13 per cent rate of return on its owners' equity. (See Chapter 14 for more on earning profit for owners.)

The disadvantages of debt are:

- ✔ A business must pay the fixed rate of interest for the period even if it suffers a loss for the period.

- ✔ A business must be ready to pay back the debt on the specified due date, which can cause some pressure on the business to come up with the money on time. (Of course, a business may be able to *roll over* its debt, meaning that it replaces its old debt with an equivalent amount of new debt, but the lender has the right to demand that the old debt be paid and not rolled over.)

If you default on your debt contract – you don't pay the interest on time, or you don't pay back the debt on the due date – you face some major unpleasantries. In extreme cases, a lender can force you to shut down and liquidate your assets (that is, sell off everything you own for cash) to pay off the debt and unpaid interest. Just as you can lose your home if you don't pay your home mortgage, your business can be forced into involuntary bankruptcy if you don't pay your business debts.

A lender may allow the business to try to work out its financial crisis through bankruptcy procedures, but bankruptcy is a nasty business that invariably causes many problems and can really cripple a business.

Reporting Financial Condition: The Classified Balance Sheet

The assets, liabilities and owners' equity of a business are reported in its *balance sheet,* which is prepared at the end of the profit and loss account period.

The balance sheet is not a flow statement but a *position* statement which reports the financial condition of a company at a precise moment in time – unlike the income and cash flow statements which report inflows and outflows. The balance sheet presents a company's assets, liabilities and owners' equity that exist at the time the report is prepared.

An accountant can prepare a balance sheet at any time that a manager wants to know how things stand financially. However, balance sheets are usually prepared only at the end of each month, quarter and year. A balance sheet is always prepared at the close of business on the last day of the profit period so that the financial effects of sales and expenses (reported in the profit and loss account) also appear in the assets, liabilities and owners' equity sections of the balance sheet.

Trading on the equity: Taking a chance on debt

The large majority of businesses borrow money to provide part of the total capital needed for their assets. The main reason for debt, by and large, is to close the gap between how much capital the owners can come up with and the amount the business needs. Lenders are willing to provide the capital because they have a senior claim on the assets of the business. Debt has to be paid back before the owners can get their money out of the business. The owners' equity provides the permanent base of capital and gives the lenders a cushion of protection.

The owners use their capital invested in the business as the basis to borrow. For example, for every two pounds the owners have in the business, lenders may be willing to add another pound (or even more). Thus, for every two pounds of owners' equity the business can get three pounds total capital to work with. Using owners' equity as the basis for borrowing is called *trading on the equity.* It is also referred to as *financial leverage,* because the equity is the lever for increasing the total capital of the business.

These terms also refer to the potential gain a business can realise from making more EBIT (earnings before interest and tax) on the amount borrowed than the interest on the debt. For a simple example, assume that debt supplies one-third of the total capital of a business (and owners' equity two-thirds, of course), and the business's EBIT for the year just ended is a nice, round £3,000,000. Fair is fair, so you could argue that the lenders who put up one-third of the money should get one-third or £1,000,000 of the profit. This is not how it works. The lenders (investors) get only the interest amount on their loans (their investments). Suppose this total interest is £750,000. The financial leverage gain, therefore, is £250,000. The owners would get their two-thirds share of EBIT plus the £250,000 pre-tax financial leverage gain.

Trading on the equity may backfire. Instead of a gain, the business may realise a financial leverage loss – one-third of its EBIT may be *less* than the interest due on its debt. That interest has to be paid no matter what amount of EBIT the business earns. Suppose the business just breaks even, which means its EBIT equals zero for the year. Nevertheless, it must pay the interest on its debt. So, the business would have a bottom-line loss for the year.

We haven't said much about the situation in which a business has a loss for the year, instead of a profit. A loss has the effect of decreasing the assets of a business (whereas a profit increases its assets). To keep it simple, assume cash is the only asset decreased by the loss (although other assets could also decrease as a result of the loss). Basically, cash goes down by the amount of the loss; and, on the other side of the balance sheet, the retained earnings account goes down the same amount. The owners do not have to invest additional money in the business to cover the loss. The impact on the owners is that their total equity (the recorded value of their ownership in the business) takes a hit equal to the amount of the loss.

The balance sheet shown in Figure 6-1 is a bare-bones statement of financial condition. Yes, the basic assets, liabilities and owners' equity accounts are presented but for both internal management reporting and for external reporting to investors and lenders, the balance sheet must be dressed up rather more than the one shown in Figure 6-1.

For internal reporting to managers, balance sheets include much more detail either in the body of the financial statement itself or, more likely, in supporting schedules. For example, only one cash account is shown in Figure 6-1 but the chief financial officer of a business needs to see the balances in each of the business's bank accounts.

As another example, the balance sheet shown in Figure 6-1 includes just one total amount for debtors but managers need details on which customers owe money and whether any major amounts are past their due date. Therefore, the assets and liabilities of a business are reported to its managers in greater detail, which allows for better control, analysis and decision-making. Management control is very detail-oriented: Internal balance sheets and their supporting schedules should provide all the detail that managers need to make good business decisions.

In contrast, balance sheets presented in *external* financial reports (which go out to investors and lenders) do not include much more detail than the balance sheet shown in Figure 6-1. However, external balance sheets must classify (or group together) short-term assets and liabilities. For this reason, external balance sheets are referred to as *classified balance sheets*. This classification is not mandatory for internal reporting to managers, although separating short-term assets and liabilities is also useful for managers.

Business balance sheets are not vetted by the accountant to make sure no secrets are being disclosed that would harm national security. The term 'classified' applied to a balance sheet does not mean restricted or top secret; rather, the term means that assets and liabilities are sorted into basic classes, or groups, for external reporting. Classifying certain assets and liabilities into current categories is done mainly to help readers of the balance sheet more easily compare total current assets with total current liabilities for the purpose of judging the short-term solvency of the business.

Solvency refers to the ability of a business to pay its liabilities on time. Delays in paying liabilities on time can cause very serious problems for a business. In extreme cases, a business could be thrown into *bankruptcy* – even the threat of bankruptcy can cause serious disruptions in the normal operations of a business, and profit performance is bound to suffer. If current liabilities become too high relative to current assets – which are the first line of defence for paying those current liabilities – managers should move quickly to raise additional cash to reduce one or more of the current liabilities. Otherwise, a low current ratio will raise alarms in the minds of the outside readers of the business's financial report.

Figure 6-3 presents the *classified* balance sheet for the same company. What's new? Not the assets, liabilities and owners' equity accounts and their balances. These numbers are the same ones shown in Figure 6-1. The classified balance sheet shown in Figure 6-3 includes the following new items of information:

✔ The first four asset accounts (cash, debtors, stock and prepaid expenses) are added to give the £8,555,000 subtotal for *current assets*.

✔ The £5,000,000 total debt of the business is divided between £2,000,000 short-term notes payable and £3,000,000 long-term notes payable.

✔ The first four liability accounts (accounts payable, accrued expenses payable, income tax payable and short-term notes payable) are added to give the £4,080,000 subtotal for *current liabilities*.

Assets		
Cash		£ 2,000,000
Debtors		£ 2,500,000
Stock		£ 3,575,000
Prepaid Expenses		£ 480,000
Current Assets		£ 8,555,000
Fixed Assets (at original cost)	£ 11,305,000	
Accumulated Depreciation	£ (5,780,000)	£ 5,525,000
Total Assets		£ 14,080,000
Liabilities and Owners' Equity		
Creditors		£ 800,000
Accrued Expenses Payable		£ 1,200,000
Income Tax Payable		£ 80,000
Overdraft		£ 2,000,000
Current Liabilities		£ 4,080,000
Loans		£ 3,000,000
Owners' Invested Capital	£ 2,000,000	
Retained Earnings	£ 5,000,000	£ 7,000,000
Total Liabilities and Owners' Equity		£ 14,080,000

Figure 6-3: Example of an external (classified) balance sheet for a business.

Current (short-term) assets

Short-term, or *current*, assets are:

- Cash
- Marketable securities that can be immediately converted into cash
- Operating assets that are converted into cash within one *operating cycle*

Operating cycle refers to the process of putting cash into stock, selling products on credit (which generates debtors) and then collecting the receivables in cash. In other words, the operating cycle is the 'from cash – through stock and debtors – back to cash' sequence. The term *operating* refers to those assets that are directly part of making sales and directly involved in the expenses of the company.

Current (short-term) liabilities

Short-term, or *current*, liabilities are those non-interest-bearing liabilities that arise from the operating activities of the business, as well as interest-bearing overdrafts that have a maturity date one year or less from the balance sheet date. Current liabilities also include any other liabilities that must be paid within the upcoming financial period.

Current liabilities are generally paid out of current assets. That is, current assets are the first source of money to pay the current liabilities when those liabilities come due. Thus, total current assets are compared against total current liabilities in order to compute the *current ratio*. For the balance sheet shown in the preceding section, you can compute the current ratio as follows:

£8,555,000 current assets ÷ £4,080,000 current liabilities = 2.1 current ratio

The general rule is that a company's current ratio should be 1.5 or higher. However, business managers know that the current ratio depends a great deal on how the business's short-term operating assets are financed from current liabilities. Some businesses do quite well with a current ratio less than 1.5. Therefore, take the 1.5 current ratio rule with a grain of salt. A lower current ratio does not necessarily mean that the business won't be able to pay its short-term (current) liabilities on time. Chapters 14 and 17 explain current ratios in more detail.

Costs and Other Balance Sheet Values

The balance sheet summarises the financial condition for a business at a point in time. Business managers and investors should clearly understand the values reported in this primary financial statement. In our experience, understanding balance sheet values can be a source of confusion for both business managers and investors who tend to put all pound amounts on the same value basis. In their minds, a pound is a pound, whether it's in the debtors, stock, fixed assets, or accounts payable. Assigning the same value to every account value tends to gloss over some important differences and can lead to serious misinterpretation of the balance sheet.

A balance sheet mixes together several different types of accounting values:

- **Cash:** Amounts of money on hand in coin and currency; money on deposit in bank accounts

- **Debtors:** Amounts not yet collected from credit sales to customers

- **Stock:** Amounts of purchase costs or production costs for products that haven't sold yet

- **Fixed assets (or Property, plant, and equipment):** Amounts of costs invested in long-life, tangible, productive operating assets

- **Creditors and accrued liabilities:** Amounts for the costs of unpaid expenses

- **Overdrafts and loans:** Amounts borrowed on interest-bearing liabilities

- **Capital stock:** Amounts of capital invested in the business by owners (shareholders). This can be either by way of the initial capital introduced or profits left in the business after trading gets under way

- **Retained earnings (or reserves):** Amounts remaining in the owners' equity account

In short, a balance sheet represents a diversity, or a rainbow, of values – not just one colour. This is the nature of the generally accepted accounting principles – the accounting methods used to prepare financial statements.

Book values are the amounts recorded in the accounting process and reported in financial statements. Do not assume that the book values reported in a balance sheet necessarily equal the current *market values*. Book values are based on the accounting methods used by a business. Generally speaking – and we really mean *generally* here because we're sure that you can find exceptions to this rule – cash, debtors, and liabilities are recorded at close to their market or settlement values. These receivables will be turned into cash (at the same amount recorded on the balance sheet) and liabilities will be paid off at the amounts reported in the balance sheet. It's the book values of stock and fixed assets that most likely are lower than current market values, as well as any other non-operating assets in which the business invested some time ago.

A business can use alternative accounting methods to determine the cost of stock and the cost of goods sold, and to determine how much of a fixed asset's cost is allocated to depreciation expense each year. A business is free to use very conservative accounting methods – with the result that its stock cost value and the non-depreciated cost of its fixed assets may be much lower than the current replacement cost values of these assets. Chapter 13 explains more about choosing different accounting methods.

Growing Up

In the layout in Figure 6-4 we start with the fixed assets rather than liquid assets such as cash and work our way down. After the fixed asset sum has been determined to arrive at the residual unwritten down 'value' of those assets, in this case £5,525,000, we work our way down the current assets in the reverse order of their ability to be turned into cash. The total of the current assets comes to £8,555,000.

Next we get the current liabilities, which come to a total of £4,080,000, and subtract that from the current asset total of £8,555,000 to arrive at a figure of £4,475,000. This is often referred to as the *working capital*, as it represents the money circulating through the business day to day.

By adding the net current assets (working capital) of £4,475,000 to the net book value of the fixed assets, £5,525,000, bingo! We can see we have £10,000,000 tied up in net total assets. Deduct the money we owe long term, the creditors due over one year (a fancy way of describing bank and other debt other than overdraft), and we arrive at the net total assets. Net, by the way, is accountant-speak for deduction of one number from another, often adding a four-figure sum to the bill for doing so.

The net total assets figure of £7,000,000 bears an uncanny similarity to the total of the money put in by the owners of the business when they started out, £2,000,000, and the sum they have left in by way of profits undistributed over the years, £5,000,000. So the balance sheet balances, but with a very different total from that of Figure 6-3.

You can find a blank balance sheet and profit and loss accounts in Excel format, as well as a tutored exercise and supporting notes, at www.bized. co.uk/learn/sheets/tasker.xls.

	£	£	£
Fixed Assets	11,305,000		
Less Accumulated Depreciation	5,780,000		
Net Book Value			5,525,000
Current Assets			
Prepaid Expenses	480,000		
Stock	3,575,000		
Debtors	2,500,000		
Cash	2,000,000		
Total Current Assets		8,555,000	
Less Current Liabilities			
Overdraft	2,000,000		
Income Tax Payable	80,000		
Accrued Expenses	1,200,000		
Creditors	800,000		
Total Current Liabilities		4,080,000	
Net Current Assets			4,475,000
Total Assets			10,000,000
Less Creditors, amounts falling due in over one year			3,000,000
Net Total Assets			7,000,000
Financed By:			
Owners' Capital Introduced		2,000,000	
Reserves (Accumulated Profits)		5,000,000	7,000,000

Figure 6-4: A balance sheet.

Chapter 7

Cash Flows and the Cash Flow Statement

In This Chapter

▶ Separating the three types of cash flows

▶ Figuring out how much actual cash increase was generated by profit

▶ Looking at a business's other sources and uses of cash

▶ Being careful about free cash flow

▶ Evaluating managers' decisions by scrutinising the cash flow statement

his chapter talks about *cash flows* – which in general refers to cash inflows and outflows over a period of time. Suppose you tell us that last year you had total cash inflows of £145,000 and total cash outflows of £140,000. We know that your cash balance increased £5,000. But we don't know where your £145,000 cash inflows came from. Did you earn this much in salary? Did you receive an inheritance from your rich uncle? Likewise, we don't know what you used your £140,000 cash outflow for. Did you make large payments on your credit cards? Did you lose a lot of money at the races? In short, cash flows have to be sorted into different sources and uses to make much sense.

The Three Types of Cash Flow

Accountants categorise the cash flows of a business into three types:

✔ Cash inflows from making sales and cash outflows for expenses – sales and expense transactions – are called the *operating activities* of a business (although they could be called profit activities just as well, because their purpose is to make profit).

✔ Cash outflows for making investments in new assets (buildings, machinery, tools and so on) and cash inflows from liquidating old investments (assets no longer needed that are sold off); these transactions are called *investment activities*.

✔ Cash inflows from borrowing money and from the additional investment of money in the business by its owners, and cash outflows for paying off debt, returning capital that the business no longer needs to owners and making cash distributions of profit to its owners; these transactions are called *financing activities*.

The cash flow statement (or *statement of cash flows*) summarises the cash flows of a business for a period according to this three-way classification. Generally accepted accounting principles require that whenever a business reports its income statement, it must also report its cash flow statement for the same period – a business shouldn't report one without the other. A good reason exists for this dual financial statement requirement.

The income statement is based on the *accrual basis of accounting* that records sales when made, whether or not cash is received at that time, and records expenses when incurred, whether or not the expenses are paid at that time. (Chapter 3 explains accrual basis accounting.) Because accrual basis accounting is used to record profit, you can't equate bottom-line profit with an increase in cash. Suppose a business's annual income statement reports that it earned £1.6 million net income for the year. This does not mean that its cash balance increased £1.6 million during the period. You have to look in the cash flow statement to find out how much its cash balance increased (or, possibly, decreased!) from its operating activities (sales revenue and expenses) during the period.

In the chapter, we refer to the net increase (or decrease) in the business's cash balance that results from collecting sales revenue and paying expenses as *cash flow from profit* (the alternative term for *cash flow from operating activities*). Cash flow from profit seems more user-friendly than cash flow from operating activities, and in fact the term is used widely. In any case, do not confuse cash flow from profit with the other two types of cash flow – from the business's investing activities and financing activities during the period.

Before moving on, here's a short problem for you to solve. This summary of the business's net cash flows (in thousands) for the year just ended, which uses the three-way classification of cash flows explained earlier, has one amount missing:

(1) From profit (operating activities)	?
(2) From investing activities	– £1,275
(3) From financing activities	+ £160
Decrease in cash balance during year	– £15

Note that the business's cash balance from all sources and uses decreased £15,000 during the year. The amounts of net cash flows from the company's investing and financing activities are given. So you can determine that the net cash flow from profit was £1,100,000 for the year. Understanding cash flows from investing activities and financing activities is fairly straightforward. Understanding the net cash flow from profit, in contrast, is more challenging – but business managers and investors should have a good grip on this very important number.

Setting the Stage: Changes in Balance Sheet Accounts

The first step in understanding the amounts reported by a business in its cash flow statement is to focus on the *changes* in the business's assets, liabilities and owners' equity accounts during the period – the increases or decreases of each account from the start of the period to the end of the period. These changes are found in the comparative two-year balance sheet reported by a business. Figure 7-1 presents the increases and decreases during the year in the assets, liabilities and owners' equity accounts for a business example. Figure 7-1 is not a balance sheet but only a summary of *changes* in account balances. We do not want to burden you with an entire balance sheet, which has much more detail than is needed here.

Take a moment to scan Figure 7-1. Note that the business's cash balance decreased £15,000 during the year. (An increase is not necessarily a good thing, and a decrease is not necessarily a bad thing; it depends on the overall financial situation of the business.) One purpose of reporting the cash flow statement is to summarise the main reasons for the change in cash – according to the three-way classification of cash flows explained earlier. One question on everyone's mind is this: How much cash did the profit for the year generate for the business? The cash flow statement begins by answering this question.

Assets	
Cash	(15)
Debtors	800
Stock	975
Prepaid Expenses	145
Fixed Assets	1,275
Accumulated Depreciation*	(1,200)
Total	1,980
Liabilities & Owners' Equity	
Creditors	80
Accrued Expenses Payable	1,20
Income Tax Payable	20
Overdraft	200
Long-term Loans	300
Owners' Invested Capital	60
Retained Earnings	1,200
Total	1,980

* Accumulated Depreciation is a negative asset account which is deducted from Fixed Assets. The negative £1,200 change increases the negative balance of the account.

Figure 7-1:
Changes in balance sheet assets and operating liabilities that affect cash flow from profit.

Getting at the Cash Increase from Profit

Although all amounts reported on the cash flow statement are important, the one that usually gets the most attention is *cash flow from operating activities*, or *cash flow from profit* as we prefer to call it. This is the increase in cash generated by a business's profit-making operations during the year exclusive of its other sources of cash during the year (such as borrowed money, sold-off fixed assets and additional owners' investments in the business). *Cash flow from profit* indicates a business's ability to turn profit into available cash – cash in the bank that can be used for the needs of business. Cash flow from profit gets just as much attention as net income (the bottom-line profit number in the income statement).

Before presenting the cash flow statement – which is a rather formidable, three-part accounting report – in all its glory, in the following sections we build on the summary of changes in the business's assets, liabilities and owners' equities shown in Figure 7-1 to explain the components of the £1,100,000 increase in cash from the business's profit activities during the year. (The £1,100,000 amount of cash flow from profit was determined earlier in the chapter by solving the unknown factor.)

The business in the example experienced a rather strong growth year. Its accounts receivable and stock increased by relatively large amounts. In fact, all the relevant accounts increased; their ending balances are larger than their beginning balances (which are the amounts carried forward from the end of the preceding year). At this point, we need to provide some additional information. The £1.2 million increase in retained earnings is the net difference of two quite different things.

The £1.6 million net income earned by the business increased retained earnings by this amount. As you see in Figure 7-1, the account increased only £1.2 million. Thus there must have been a £400,000 decrease in retained earnings during the year. The business paid £400,000 cash dividends from profit to its owners (the shareholders) during the year, which is recorded as a decrease in retained earnings. The amount of cash dividends is reported in the *financing activities* section of the cash flow statement. The entire amount of net income is reported in the *operating activities* section of the cash flow statement.

Computing cash flow from profit

Here's how to compute cash flow from profit based on the changes in the company's balance sheet accounts presented in Figure 7–1:

Computation of Cash Flow from Profit (in thousands of pounds)

	Negative Cash Flow Effects	Positive Cash Flow Effects
Net income for the year		£1,600
Debtors increase	£800	
Stock increase	£975	
Prepaid expenses increase	£145	
Depreciation expense		£1,200
Creditors increase		£80
Accrued expenses payable increase		£120
Income tax payable increase		£20
Totals	£1,920	£3,020
Cash flow from profit (£3,020 positive increases minus £1,920 negative increases)	£1,100	

Note that net income (profit) for the year – which is the correct amount of profit based on the accrual basis of accounting – is listed in the positive cash flow column. This is only the starting point. Think of this the following way: If the business had collected all its sales revenue for the year in cash, and if it had made cash payments for its expenses exactly equal to the amounts recorded for the expenses, then the net income amount would equal the increase in cash. These two conditions are virtually never true, and they are not true in this example. So the net income figure is just the jumping-off point for determining the amount of cash generated by the business's profit activities during the year.

We'll let you in on a little secret here. The analysis of cash flow from profit asks what amount of profit would have been recorded if the business had been on the cash basis of accounting instead of the accrual basis. This can be confusing and exasperating, because it seems that two different profit measures are provided in a business's financial report – the true economic profit number, which is the bottom line in the income statement (usually called *net income*), and a second profit number called *cash flow from operating activities* in the cash flow statement.

When the cash flow statement was made mandatory, many accountants worried about this problem, but the majority opinion was that the amount of cash increase (or decrease) generated from the profit activities of a business is very important to disclose in financial reports. For reading the income statement you have to wear your accrual basis accounting lenses, and for the cash flow statement you have to put on your cash basis lenses. Who says accountants can't see two sides of something?

The following sections explain the effects on cash flow that each balance sheet account change causes (refer to Figure 7-1).

Getting specific about changes in assets and liabilities

As a business manager, you should keep a close watch on each of your assets and liabilities and understand the cash flow effects of increases (or decreases) caused by these changes. Investors should focus on the business's ability to generate a healthy cash flow from profit, so investors should be equally concerned about these changes.

Debtors increase

Remember that the *debtors* asset shows how much money customers who bought products on credit still owe the business; this asset is a promise of cash that the business will receive. Basically, *debtors* is the amount of uncollected sales revenue at the end of the period. Cash does not increase until the business collects money from its customers.

But the amount in debtors *is* included in the total sales revenue of the period – after all, you did make the sales, even if you haven't been paid yet. Obviously, then, you can't look at sales revenue as being equal to the amount of cash that the business received during the period.

To calculate the actual cash flow from sales, you need to subtract from sales revenue the amount of credit sales that you did not collect in cash over the period – but you add in the amount of cash that you collected during the period just ended for credit sales that you made in the *preceding* period. Take a look at the following equation for the business example, which is first introduced in Chapter 6 – the income statement figures used here are given in Figure 6–2 and the asset and liability changes are shown in Figure 7–1. (No need to look back to Figure 6–2 unless you want to review the income statement.)

£25 million sales revenue – £0.8 million increase in debtors = £24.2 million cash collected from customers during the year

The business started the year with £1.7 million in debtors and ended the year with £2.5 million in debtors. The beginning balance was collected during the year but at the end of the year the ending balance had not been collected. Thus the *net* effect is a shortfall in cash inflow of £800,000, which is why it's called a negative cash flow factor. The key point is that you need to keep an eye on the increase or decrease in debtors from the beginning of the period to the end of the period.

✔ If the amount of credit sales you made during the period is greater than the amount collected from customers during the same period, your debtors *increased* over the period. Therefore you need to *subtract* from sales revenue that difference between start-of-period debtors and end-of-period debtors. In short, an increase in debtors hurts cash flow by the amount of the increase.

✔ If the amount you collected from customers during the period is greater than the credit sales you made during the period, your debtors *decreased* over the period. In this case you need to *add* to sales revenue that difference between start-of-period debtors and end-of-period debtors. In short, a decrease in debtors helps cash flow by the amount of the decrease.

In the example we've been using, debtors increased £800,000. Cash collections from sales were £800,000 less than sales revenue. Ouch! The business increased its sales substantially over last period, so you shouldn't be surprised that its debtors increased. The higher sales revenue was good for profit but bad for cash flow from profit.

An occasional hiccup in cash flow is the price of growth – managers and investors need to understand this point. Increasing sales without increasing debtors is a happy situation for cash flow, but in the real world you can't have one increase without the other (except in very unusual circumstances).

Stock increase

Stock is the next asset in Figure 7-1 – and usually the largest short-term, or *current,* asset for businesses that sell products. If the stock account is greater at the end of the period than at the start of the period – because either unit costs increased or the quantity of products increased – what the business actually paid out in cash for stock purchases (or manufacturing products) is more than the business recorded as its cost-of-goods-sold expense in the period. Therefore, you need to deduct the stock increase from net income when determining cash flow from profit.

In the example, stock increased £975,000 from start-of-period to end-of-period. In other words, this business replaced the products that it sold during the period *and* increased its stock by £975,000. The easiest way to understand the effect of this increase on cash flow is to pretend that the business paid for all its stock purchases in cash immediately upon receiving them. The stock on hand at the start of the period had already been paid for *last* period, so that cost does not affect this period's cash flow. Those products were sold during the period and involved no further cash payment by the business. But the business did pay cash *this* period for the products that were in stock at the end of the period.

In other words, if the business had bought just enough new stock (at the same cost that it paid out last period) to replace the stock that it sold during the period, the actual cash outlay for its purchases would equal the cost-of-goods-sold expense reported in its income statement. Ending stock would equal the beginning stock; the two stock costs would cancel each other out and thus would have no effect on cash flow. But this hypothetical scenario doesn't fit the example because the company increased its sales substantially over the last period.

To support the higher sales level, the business needed to increase its stock level. So the business bought £975,000 more in products than it sold during the period – and it had to come up with the cash to pay for this stock increase. Basically, the business wrote cheques amounting to £975,000 more than its cost-of-goods-sold expense for the period. This step-up in its stock level was necessary to support the higher sales level, which increased profit – even though cash flow took a hit.

It's that accrual basis accounting thing again: The cost that a business pays *this* period for *next* period's stock is reflected in this period's cash flow but isn't recorded until next period's income statement (when the products are actually sold). So if a business paid more *this* period for *next* period's stock than it paid *last* period for *this* period's stock, you can see how the additional expense would adversely affect cash flow but would not be reflected in the bottom-line net income figure. This cash flow analysis stuff gets a little complicated, we know, but hang in there. The cash flow statement, presented later in the chapter, makes a lot more sense after you go through this background briefing.

Prepaid expenses increase

The next asset, after stock, is prepaid expenses (refer to Figure 7-1). A change in this account works the same way as a change in stock and debtors, although changes in prepaid expenses are usually much smaller than changes in those other two asset accounts.

Again, the beginning balance of prepaid expenses is recorded as an expense this period but the cash was actually paid out last period, not this period. This period, a business pays cash for next period's prepaid expenses – which affects this period's cash flow but doesn't affect net income until next period. So the £145,000 increase in prepaid expenses from start-of-period to end-of-period in this example has a negative cash flow effect.

As it grows, a business needs to increase its prepaid expenses for such things as fire insurance (premiums have to be paid in advance of the insurance coverage) and its stocks of office and data processing supplies. Increases in debtors, stock and prepaid expenses are the price a business has to pay for growth. Rarely do you find a business that can increase its sales revenue without increasing these assets.

The simple but troublesome depreciation factor

Depreciation expense recorded in the period is both the simplest cash flow effect to understand and, at the same time, one of the most misunderstood elements in calculating cash flow from profit. (Refer to Chapters 5 and 6 for more about depreciation.) To start with, depreciation is not a cash outlay during the period. The amount of depreciation expense recorded in the period is simply a fraction of the original cost of the business's fixed assets that were bought and paid for years ago. (Well, if you want to nit-pick here, some of the fixed assets may have been bought during this period, and their cost is reported in the investing activities section of the cash flow statement.) Because the depreciation expense is not a cash outlay this period, the amount is added back to net income in the calculation of cash flow from profit – so far so good.

When measuring profit on the accrual basis of accounting you count depreciation as an expense. The fixed assets of a business are on an irreversible journey to the junk heap. Fixed assets have a limited life of usefulness to a business (except for land); depreciation is the accounting method that allocates the total cost of fixed assets to each year of their use in helping the business generate sales revenue. Part of the total sales revenue of a business constitutes *recovery of cost invested in its fixed assets*. In a real sense, a business 'sells' some of its fixed assets each period to its customers – it factors the cost of fixed assets into the sales prices that it charges its customers. For example, when you go to a supermarket, a very small slice of the price you pay for that box of cereal goes toward the cost of the building, the shelves, the refrigeration equipment and so on. (No wonder they charge so much for a box of cornflakes!)

Each period, a business recoups part of the cost invested in its fixed assets. In other words, £1.2 million of sales revenue (in the example) went toward reimbursing the business for the use of its fixed assets during the year. The problem regarding depreciation in cash flow analysis is that many people simply add back depreciation for the year to bottom-line profit and then stop, as if this is the proper number for cash flow from profit. It ain't so. The changes in other assets as well as the changes in liabilities also affect cash flow from profit. You should factor in *all* the changes that determine cash flow from profit, as explained in the following section.

Adding net income and depreciation to determine cash flow from profit is mixing apples and oranges. The business did not realise £1,600,000 cash increase from its £1,600,000 net income. The total of the increases of its debtors, stock and prepaid expenses is £1,920,000 (refer to Figure 7-1), which wipes out the net income amount and leaves the business with a cash balance hole of £320,000. This cash deficit is offset by the £220,000 increase in liabilities (explained later), leaving a £100,000 net income *deficit* as far as cash flow is concerned. Depreciation recovery increased cash flow £1.2 million. So the final cash flow from profit equals £1.1 million. But you'd never know this if you simply added depreciation expense to net income for the period.

The managers did not have to go outside the business for the £1.1 million cash increase generated from its profit for the year. Cash flow from profit is an *internal* source of money generated by the business itself, in contrast to *external* money that the business raises from lenders and owners. A business does not have to find sources of external money if its internal cash flow from profit is sufficient to provide for its growth.

Net income + depreciation expense doesn't equal cash flow from profit!

The business in our example earned £1.6 million in net income for the year, plus it received £1.2 million cash flow because of the depreciation expense built into its sales revenue for the year. The sum of these figures is £2.8 million. Is £2.8 million the amount of cash flow from profit for the period? The knee-jerk answer of many investors and managers is 'yes'. But if net income + depreciation truly equals cash flow, then *both* factors in the brackets – both net income and depreciation – must be fully realised in cash. Depreciation is, but the net income amount is not fully realised in cash because the company's debtors, stock and prepaid expenses increased during the year, and these increases have negative impacts on cash flow.

In passing, we should mention that a business could have a negative cash flow from profit for a year – meaning that despite posting a net income for the period, the changes in the company's assets and liabilities caused its cash balance to decrease. In reverse, a business could report a bottom line *loss* in its income statement yet have a *positive* cash flow from its operating activities: The positive contribution from depreciation expense plus decreases in its debtors and stock could amount to more than the amount of loss. More commonly, a loss leads to negative cash flow or very little positive cash flow.

Operating liabilities increases

The business in the example, like almost all businesses, has three basic liabilities that are inextricably intertwined with its expenses: creditors, accrued expenses payable and income tax payable. When the beginning balance of one of these liability accounts is the same as the ending balance of the same account (not too likely, of course), the business breaks even on cash flow for that account. When the end-of-period balance is higher than the start-of-period balance, the business did not pay out as much money as was actually recorded as an expense on the period's income statement.

In the example we've been using, the business disbursed £720,000 to pay off last period's creditors balance. (This £720,000 was reported as the creditors balance on last period's ending balance sheet.) Its cash flow this period decreased by £720,000 because of these payments. But this period's ending balance sheet shows the amount of creditors that the business will need to pay next period – £800,000. The business actually paid off £720,000 and recorded £800,000 of expenses to the year, so this time cash flow is *richer* than what's reflected in the business's net income figure by £80,000 – in other words, the increase in creditors has a positive cash flow effect. The increases in accrued expenses payable and income tax payable work the same way.

Therefore, liability increases are favourable to cash flow – in a sense the business borrowed more than it paid off. Such an increase means that the business delayed paying cash for certain things until next year. So you need to add the increases in the three liabilities to net income to determine cash flow from profit, following the same logic as adding back depreciation to net income. The business did not have cash outlays to the extent of increases in these three liabilities.

The analysis of the changes in assets and liabilities of the business that affect cash flow from profit is complete for the business example. The final result is that the company's cash balance increased £1.1 million from profit. You could argue that cash should have increased £2.8 million – £1.6 million net income plus £1.2 million depreciation that was recovered during the year – so the business is £1.7 million behind in turning its profit into cash flow (£2.8 million less the £1.1 million cash flow from profit). This £1.7 million lag in converting profit into cash flow is caused by the £1,920,000 increase in assets less the £220,000 increase in liabilities, as shown in Figure 7–1.

Presenting the Cash Flow Statement

The cash flow statement is one of the three primary financial statements that a business must report to the outside world, according to generally accepted accounting principles (GAAP). To be technical, the rule says that whenever a business reports a profit and loss account, it should also report a cash flow statement. The *profit and loss account* summarises sales revenue and expenses and ends with the bottom-line profit for the period. The *balance sheet* summarises a business's financial condition by reporting its assets, liabilities and owners' equity. (Refer to Chapters 5 and 6 for more about these reports.)

You can probably guess what the *cash flow statement* does by its name alone: This statement tells you where a business got its cash and what the business did with its cash during the period. We prefer the name given to this statement in the old days in the US – the *Where Got, Where Gone* statement. This nickname goes straight to the purpose of the cash flow statement: asking where the business got its money and what it did with the money.

To give you a rough idea of what a cash flow statement reports, we repeat some of the questions we asked at the start of the chapter: How much money did you earn last year? Did you get all your income in cash (or did some of your wages go straight into a pension plan or did you collect a couple of IOUs)? Where did you get other money (did you take out a loan, win the lottery or receive a gift from a rich uncle)? What did you do with your money (did you buy a house, support your out-of-control Internet addiction or lose it playing bingo)?

Getting a little too personal for you? That's exactly why the cash flow statement is so important: It bares a business's financial soul to its lenders and owners. Sometimes the cash flow statement reveals questionable judgment calls that the business's managers made. At the very least, the cash flow statement reveals how well a business handles the cash increase from its profit.

As explained at the start of the chapter, the cash flow statement is divided into three sections according to the three-fold classification of cash flows for a business: operating activities (which we also call *cash flow from profit* in the chapter), investing activities and financing activities.

The cash flow statement reports a business's net cash increase or decrease based on these three groupings of the cash flow statement. Figure 7-2 shows what a cash flow statement typically looks like – in this example, for a *growing* business (which means that its assets, liabilities and owners' equity increase during the period).

The history of the cash flow statement

The cash flow statement was not required for external financial reporting until the late 1980s. Until then, the accounting profession had turned a deaf ear to calls from the investment community for cash flow statements in annual financial reports. (Accountants had presented a *funds flow statement* prior to then, but that report proved to be a disaster – the term *funds* included more assets than just cash and represented a net amount after deducting short-term liabilities from short-term, or current, assets.)

In our opinion, the reluctance to require cash flow statements came from fears that the *cash flow from profit* figure would usurp net income – people would lose confidence in the net income line.

Those fears have some justification – considering the attention given to cash flow from profit and what is called 'free cash flow' (discussed later in the chapter). Although the profit and loss account continues to get most of the fanfare (because it shows the magic bottom-line number of net income), cash flow gets a lot of emphasis these days.

Cash Flow Statement for Year (in thousands of pounds)		
Cash Flows from Operating Activities		
Net Income		£ 1,600
Debtors	£ (800)	
Stock Increase	£ (975)	
Prepaid Expenses Increase	£ (145)	
Depreciation Expense	£ 1,200	
Creditors Increase	£ 80	
Accrued Expense Increase	£ 120	
Income Tax Payable Increase	£ 20	£ (500)
Cash Flow from Operating Activities		£ 1,100
Cash Flows from Investing Activities		
Purchases of Property, Plant & Equipment		£ (1,275)
Cash Flows from Financing Activities		
Short-term Debt Borrowing Increase	£ 200	
Long-term Debt Borrowing Increase	£ 300	
Share Issue	£ 60	
Dividends Paid Stockholders	£ (400)	£ 160
Increase (Decrease) In Cash During Year		£ (15)
Beginning Cash Balance		£ 2,015
Ending Cash Balance		£ 2,000

Figure 7-2:
Cash flow statement for the business in the example.

The trick to understanding cash flow from profit is to link the sales revenue and expenses of the business with the changes in the business's assets and liabilities that are directly connected with its profit-making activities. Using this approach earlier in the chapter, we determine that the cash flow from profit is £1.1 million for the year for the sample business. This is the number you see in Figure 7-2 for cash flow from operating activities. In our experience, many business managers, lenders and investors don't fully understand these links, but the savvy ones know to keep a close eye on the relevant balance sheet changes.

What do the figures in the first section of the cash flow statement (See Figure 7-2) reveal about this business over the past period? Recall that the business experienced rapid sales growth over the last period. However, the downside of sales growth is that operating assets and liabilities also grow – the business needs more stock at the higher sales level and also has higher debtors.

The business's prepaid expenses and liabilities also increased, although not nearly as much as debtors and stock. The rapid growth of the business yielded higher profit but also caused quite a surge in its operating assets and liabilities – the result being that cash flow from profit is only £1.1 million compared with £1.6 million in net income – a £500,000 shortfall. Still, the business had £1.1 million at its disposal after allowing for the increases in assets and liabilities. What did the business do with this £1.1 million of available cash? You have to look to the remainder of the cash flow statement to answer this key question.

A very quick read through the rest of the cash flow statement (refer to Figure 7-2) goes something like this: The company used £1,275,000 to buy new fixed assets, borrowed £500,000 and distributed £400,000 of the profit to its owners. The result is that cash decreased £15,000 during the year. Shouldn't the business have increased its cash balance, given its fairly rapid growth during the period? That's a good question! Higher levels of sales generally require higher levels of operating cash balances. However, you can see in its balance sheet at the end of the year (refer back to Figure 6-2) that the company has £2 million in cash, which, compared with its £25 million annual sales revenue, is probably enough.

A better alternative for reporting cash flow from profit?

We call your attention, again, to the first section of the cash flow statement in Figure 7-2. You start with net income for the period. Next, changes in assets and liabilities are deducted or added to net income to arrive at cash flow from operating activities (the cash flow from profit) for the year. This format is called the *indirect method*. The alternative format for this section of the cash flow statement is called the *direct method* and is presented like this (using the same business example, with pound amounts in millions):

Cash inflow from sales	£24.2
Less cash outflow for expenses	£23.1
Cash flow from operating activities	£1.1

You may remember from the earlier discussion that sales revenue for the year is £25 million, but that the company's debtors increased £800,000 during the year, so cash flow from sales is £24.2 million. Likewise, the expenses for the year can be put on a cash flow basis. But we 'cheated' here – we have already determined that cash flow from profit is £1.1 million for the year, so we plugged the figure for cash outflow for expenses. We would take more time to explain the direct approach, except for one major reason.

Where to put depreciation?

Where the depreciation line goes within the first section (operating activities) of the cash flow statement is a matter of personal preference – no standard location is required. Many businesses report it in the middle or toward the bottom of the changes in assets and liabilities – perhaps to avoid giving people the idea that cash flow from profit simply requires adding back depreciation to net income.

Although the Accounting Standards Board (ASB) expresses a definite preference for the direct method, this august rule-making body does permit the indirect method to be used in external financial reports – and, in fact, the overwhelming majority of businesses use the indirect method. Unless you're an accountant, we don't think you need to know much more about the direct method.

Sailing through the Rest of the Cash Flow Statement

After you get past the first section, the rest of the cash flow statement is a breeze. The last two sections of the statement explain what the business did with its cash and where cash that didn't come from profit came from.

Investing activities

The second section of the cash flow statement reports the investment actions that a business's managers took during the year. Investments are like tea leaves, serving as indicators regarding what the future may hold for the company. Major new investments are the sure signs of expanding or modernising the production and distribution facilities and capacity of the business. Major disposals of long-term assets and the shedding of a major part of the business could be good news or bad news for the business, depending on many factors. Different investors may interpret this information differently, but all would agree that the information in this section of the cash flow statement is very important.

Certain long-lived operating assets are required for doing business – for example, Federal Express wouldn't be terribly successful if it didn't have aeroplanes and vans for delivering packages and computers for tracking deliveries. When those assets wear out, the business needs to replace them. Also, to remain competitive, a business may need to upgrade its equipment to take advantage of the latest technology or provide for growth. These investments in long-lived, tangible, productive assets, which we call *fixed assets* in this book, are critical to the future of the business and are called *capital expenditures* to stress that capital is being invested for the long term.

One of the first claims on cash flow from profit is capital expenditure. Notice in Figure 7–2 that the business spent £1,275,000 for new fixed assets, which are referred to as *property, plant and equipment* in the cash flow statement (to keep the terminology consistent with account titles used in the balance sheet, because the term *fixed assets* is rather informal).

Cash flow statements generally don't go into much detail regarding exactly what specific types of fixed assets a business purchased – how many additional square feet of space the business acquired, how many new drill presses it bought and so on. (Some businesses do leave a clearer trail of their investments, though. For example, airlines describe how many new aircraft of each kind were purchased to replace old equipment or expand their fleets.)

Note: Typically, every year a business disposes of some of its fixed assets that have reached the end of their useful lives and will no longer be used. These fixed assets are sent to the junkyard, traded in on new fixed assets, or sold for relatively small amounts of money. The value of a fixed asset at the end of its useful life is called its *salvage value*. The disposal proceeds from selling fixed assets are reported as a source of cash in the investments section of the cash flow statement. Usually, these amounts are fairly small. In contrast, a business may sell off fixed assets because it's downsizing or abandoning a major segment of its business. These cash proceeds can be fairly large.

Financing activities

Note that in the annual cash flow statement (refer to Figure 7-2) of the business example we've been using, the positive cash flow from profit is £1,100,000 and the negative cash flow from investing activities is £1,275,000. The result to this point, therefore, is a net cash outflow of £175,000 – which would have decreased the company's cash balance this much if the business did not go to outside sources of capital for additional money during the year. In fact, the business increased its short-term and long-term debt during the year, and its owners invested additional money in the business. The third section of the cash flow statement summarises these financing activities of the business over the period.

The term *financing* generally refers to a business raising capital from debt and equity sources – from borrowing money from banks and other sources willing to loan money to the business and from its owners putting additional money in the business. In addition, the term includes making payments on debt and returning capital to owners. *Financing* also refers to cash distributions (if any) from profit by the business to its owners.

Most businesses borrow money for a short term (generally defined as less than one year), as well as for longer terms (generally defined as more than one year). In other words, a typical business has both short-term and long-term debt. (Chapter 6 explains that short-term debt is presented in the current liabilities section of the balance sheet.) The business in our example has both short-term and long-term debt. Although not a hard-and-fast rule, most cash flow statements report just the *net* increase or decrease in short-term debt, not the total amount borrowed and the total payments on short-term debt during the period. In contrast, both the total amount borrowed and the total amount paid on long-term debt during the year are reported in the cash flow statement.

For the business we've been using as an example, no long-term debt was paid down during the year but short-term debt was paid off during the year and replaced with new short-term notes payable. However, only the net increase (£200,000) is reported in the cash flow statement. The business also increased its long-term debt by £300,000 (refer to Figure 7-2).

The financing section of the cash flow statement also reports on the flow of cash between the business and its owners (who are the stockholders of a corporation). Owners can be both a *source* of a business's cash (capital invested by owners) and a *use* of a business's cash (profit distributed to owners). This section of the cash flow statement reports capital raised from its owners, if any, as well as any capital returned to the owners. In the cash flow statement (Figure 7–2), note that the business did issue additional stock shares for £60,000 during the year, and it paid a total of £400,000 cash dividends (distributions) from profit to its owners.

Free Cash Flow: What on Earth Does That Mean?

A new term has emerged in the lexicon of accounting and finance – *free cash flow*. This piece of language is not – we repeat, *not* – an officially defined term by any authoritative accounting rule-making body. Furthermore, the term does *not* appear in the cash flow statements reported by businesses. Rather, free cash flow is street language, or slang, even though the term appears often in *The Financial Times* and *The Economist*. Securities brokers and investment analysts use the term freely (pun intended). Like most new words being tossed around for the first time, this one hasn't settled down into one universal meaning although the most common usage of the term pivots on cash flow from profit.

The term *free cash flow* is used to mean any of the following:

- Net income plus depreciation (plus any other expense recorded during the period that does not involve the outlay of cash but rather the allocation of the cost of a long-term asset other than property, plant and equipment – such as the intangible assets of a business).

- Cash flow from operating activities (as reported in the cash flow statement).

- Cash flow from operating activities minus some or all of the capital expenditures made during the year (such as purchases or construction of new, long-lived operating assets such as property, plant and equipment).

- Cash flow from operating activities plus interest, and depreciation, and income tax expenses, or, in other words, cash flow before these expenses are deducted.

In the strongest possible terms, we advise you to be very clear on which definition of *free cash flow* the speaker or writer is using. Unfortunately, you can't always determine what the term means in any given context. The reporter or investment professional should define the term.

One definition of free cash flow, in our view, is quite useful: cash flow from profit minus capital expenditures for the year. The idea is that a business needs to make capital expenditures in order to stay in business and thrive. And to make capital expenditures, the business needs cash. Only after paying for its capital expenditures does a business have 'free' cash flow that it can use as it likes. In our example, the free cash flow is, in fact, negative – £1,100,000 cash flow from profit minus £1,275,000 capital expenditures for new fixed assets equals a *negative* £175,000.

This is a key point. In many cases, cash flow from profit falls short of the money needed for capital expenditures. So the business has to borrow more money, persuade its owners to invest more money in the business, or dip into its cash reserve. Should a business in this situation distribute some of its profit to owners? After all, it has a cash *deficit* after paying for capital expenditures. But many companies like the business in our example do, in fact, make cash distributions from profit to their owners.

Scrutinising the Cash Flow Statement

Analysing a business's cash flow statement inevitably raises certain questions: What would I have done differently if I were running this business? Would I have borrowed more money? Would I have raised more money from the owners? Would I have distributed so much of the profit to the owners? Would I have let my cash balance drop by even such a small amount?

One purpose of the cash flow statement is to show readers what judgment calls and financial decisions the business's managers made during the period. Of course, management decisions are always subject to second-guessing and criticising, and passing judgment based on a financial statement isn't totally fair because it doesn't reveal the pressures the managers faced during the period. Maybe they made the best possible decisions given the circumstances. Maybe not.

The business in our example (refer to Figure 7-2) distributed £400,000 cash from profit to its owners – a 25 per cent *pay-out ratio* (which is the £400,000 distribution divided by £1.6 million net income). In analysing whether the pay-out ratio is too high, too low or just about right, you need to look at the broader context of the business's sources of, and needs for, cash.

First look at cash flow from profit: £1.1 million, which is not enough to cover the business's £1,275,000 capital expenditures during the year. The business increased its total debt £500,000. Given these circumstances, maybe the business should have hoarded its cash and not paid so much in cash distributions to its owners.

So does this business have enough cash to operate with? You can't answer that question just by examining the cash flow statement – or any financial statement for that matter. Every business needs a buffer of cash to protect against unexpected developments and to take advantage of unexpected opportunities, as we explain in Chapter 10 on budgeting. This particular business has a £2 million cash balance compared with £25 million annual sales revenue for the period just ended, which probably is enough. If you were the boss of this business how much working cash balance would you want? Not an easy question to answer! Don't forget that you need to look at all three primary financial statements – the profit and loss account and the balance sheet as well as the cash flow statement – to get the big picture of a business's financial health.

You probably didn't count the number of lines of information in Figure 7-2, the cash flow statement for the business example. Anyway, the financial statement has 17 lines of information. Would you like to hazard a guess regarding the average number of lines in cash flow statements of publicly owned companies? Typically, their cash flow statements have 30 to 40 lines of information by our reckoning. So it takes quite a while to read the cash flow statement – more time than the average investor probably has. (Professional stock analysts and investment managers are paid to take the time to read this financial statement meticulously.) Quite frankly, we find that many cash flow statements are not only rather long but also difficult to understand – even for an accountant. We won't get on a soapbox here but we definitely think businesses could do a better job of reporting their cash flow statements by reducing the number of lines in their financial statements and making each line clearer.

The website `www.score.org` offers a downloadable Excel spreadsheet that enables you to tailor a cash flow statement to your requirements. You can find the spreadsheet by going to the SCORE homepage and clicking on 'Templates & Tools' where you can find an extensive selection of templates and calculators. Microsoft also has a comprehensive range of templates at `http://office.microsoft.com/en-gb/Templates` followed by a search term, in this case 'cash flow'.

Chapter 8

Getting a Financial Report Ready for Prime Time

The primary financial statements of a business (as explained in Chapters 5, 6 and 7) are:

- **Profit and loss account:** Summarises sales revenue inflows and expense outflows for the period and ends with the bottom-line profit, which is the net inflow for the period (a loss is a net outflow).

- **Balance sheet:** Summarises financial condition at the end of the period, consisting of amounts for assets, liabilities and owners' equity at that instant in time.

- **Cash flow statement:** Summarises the net cash inflow (or outflow) from profit for the period plus the other sources and uses of cash during the period.

An annual financial report of a business contains more than just these three financial statements. In the 'more', the business manager plays an important role – which outside investors and lenders should understand. The manager should do certain critical things before the financial report is released to the outside world.

1. **The manager should review with a critical eye the *vital connections* between the items reported in all three financial statements** – all amounts have to fit together like the pieces of a jigsaw. The net cash increase (or decrease) reported at the end of the cash flow statement, for instance, has to tie in with the change in cash reported in the balance sheet. Abnormally high or low ratios between connected accounts should be scrutinised carefully.

2. **The manager should carefully review the *disclosures* in the financial report** (all information in addition to the financial statements) to make sure that disclosure is adequate according to financial reporting standards, and that all the disclosure elements are truthful but not damaging to the interests of the business.

   This disclosure review can be compared with the notion of *due diligence*, which is done to make certain that all relevant information is collected, that the information is accurate and reliable, and that all relevant requirements and regulations are being complied with. This step is especially important for public corporations whose securities (shares and debt instruments) are traded on national securities exchanges.

3. **The manager should consider whether the financial statement numbers need *touching up*** to smooth the jagged edges off the company's year-to-year profit gyrations or to improve the business's short-term solvency picture. Although this can be described as putting your thumb on the scale, you can also argue that sometimes the scale is a little out of balance to begin with and the manager is adjusting the financial statements to jibe better with the normal circumstances of the business.

In discussing the third step later in the chapter, we walk on thin ice. Some topics are, shall we say, rather delicate. The manager has to strike a balance between the interests of the business on the one hand and the interests of the owners (investors) and creditors of the business on the other. The best analogy we can think of is the advertising done by a business. Advertising should be truthful but, as we're sure you know, businesses have a lot of leeway in how to advertise their products and they have been known to engage in hyperbole. Managers exercise the same freedoms in putting together their financial reports.

Reviewing Vital Connections

Business managers and investors read financial reports because these reports provide information regarding how the business is doing. The top managers of a business, in reviewing the annual financial report before releasing it outside the business, should keep in mind that a financial report is designed to answer certain basic financial questions:

🖊 Is the business making a profit or suffering a loss, and how much?

🖊 How do assets stack up against liabilities?

🖊 Where did the business get its capital and is it making good use of the money?

🖊 Is profit generating cash flow?

🖊 Did the business reinvest all its profit or distribute some of the profit to owners?

🖊 Does the business have enough capital for future growth?

As a hypothetical but realistic business example, Figure 8-1 highlights some of the vital connections – the lines connect one or more balance sheet accounts with sales revenue or an expense in the profit and loss account. The savvy manager or investor checks these links to see whether everything is in order or whether some danger signals point to problems. (We should make clear that these lines of connection do not appear in actual financial reports.)

(Amounts in thousands)			
		Balance Sheet at End of Year	
		Assets	
Profit and Loss Account for Year		Cash	£ 3,500
Sales Revenue	£ 52,000	Debtors	5,000
Cost of Goods Sold Expense	31,200	Stock	7,800
Gross Margin	£ 20,800	Prepaid Expenses	900
Sales, Administration, and General Expenses	15,600	Fixed Assets	19,500
Depreciation Expense	1,650	Accumulated Depreciation	(6,825)
Earnings Before Interest and Income Tax	£ 3,550	Total Assets	£ 29,875
Interest Expense	750	Liabilities	
Earnings Before Income Tax	£ 2,800	Creditors	£ 1,500
Income Tax Expense	900	Accrued Expenses Payable	2,400
Net Income	£ 1,900	Income Tax Payable	75
		Overdraft	4,000
		Long Term Loans	6,000
		Owners' Equity	
		Share Capital	4,000
		Retained Earnings	11,900
		Liabilities and Owners' Equity	£ 29,875

Figure 8-1: Vital connections between the profit and loss account and the balance sheet.

In the following list, we briefly explain these five connections, mainly from the manager's point of view. Chapters 14 and 17 explain how investors and lenders read a financial report and compute certain ratios. (Investors and lenders are on the outside looking in; managers are on the inside looking out.)

Note: We cut right to the chase in the following brief comments and we do not illustrate the calculations behind the comments. The purpose here is to emphasise why managers should pay attention to these important ratios. (Chapters 5 and 6 provide fuller explanations of these and other connections of operating assets and liabilities with sales revenue and expenses.)

1. **Sales Revenue and Debtors:** This business's ending balance of debtors is five weeks of its annual sales revenue. The manager should compare this ratio to the normal credit terms offered to the business's customers. If the ending balance is too high, the manager should identify which customers' accounts are past due and take actions to collect these amounts, or perhaps shut off future credit to these customers. An abnormally high balance of debtors may signal that some of these customers' amounts owed to the business should be written off as uncollectable bad debts.

2. **Cost of Goods Sold Expense and Stock:** This business's ending stock is 13 weeks of its annual cost of goods sold expense. The manager should compare this ratio to the company's stock policies and objectives regarding how long stock should be held awaiting sale. If stock is too large the manager should identify which products have been in stock too long; further purchases (or manufacturing) should be curtailed. Also, the manager may want to consider sales promotions or cutting sales prices to move these products out of stock faster.

3. **Sales, Administration and General (SA&G) Expenses and Prepaid Expenses:** This business's ending balance of prepaid expenses is three weeks of the total of these annual operating expenses. The manager should know what the normal ratio of prepaid expenses should be relative to the annual SA&G operating expenses (excluding depreciation expense). If the ending balance is too high, the manager should investigate which costs have been paid too far in advance and take action to bring these prepaids back down to normal.

4. **Sales, Administration and General (SA&G) Expenses and Creditors:** This business's ending balance of creditors is five weeks of its annual operating expenses. Delaying payment of these liabilities is good from the cash flow point of view (refer to Chapter 7) but delaying too long may jeopardise the company's good credit rating with its key suppliers and vendors. If this ratio is too high, the manager should pinpoint which specific liabilities have not been paid and whether any of these are overdue and should be paid immediately. Or, the high balance may indicate that the company is in a difficult short-term solvency situation and needs to raise more money to pay the amounts owed to suppliers and vendors.

5. **Sales, Administration and General (SA&G) Expenses and Accrued Expenses Payable:** This business's ending balance of this operating liability is eight weeks of the business's annual operating expenses. This ratio may be consistent with past experience and the normal lag before paying these costs. On the other hand, the ending balance may be abnormally high. The manager should identify which of these unpaid costs are higher than they should be. As with creditors, inflated amounts of accrued liabilities may signal serious short-term solvency problems.

These five key connections are very important ones, but the manager should scan all basic connections to see whether the ratios pass the common sense test. For example, the manager should make a quick eyeball test of interest expense compared with interest-bearing debt. In Figure 8-1, interest expense is £750,000 compared with £10 million total debt, which indicates a 7.5 per cent interest rate. This seems OK. But if the interest expense were more than £1 million, the manager should investigate and determine why it's so high.

There's always the chance of errors in the accounts of a business. Reviewing the vital connections between the profit and loss account items and the balance sheet items is a very valuable final check before the financial statements are approved for inclusion in the business's financial report. After the financial report is released to the outside world, it becomes the latest chapter in the official financial history of the business. If the financial statements are wrong, the business and its top managers are responsible.

Statement of Changes in Owners' Equity and Comprehensive Income

In many situations a business needs to prepare one additional financial statement – the *statement of changes in owners' equity*. Owners' equity consists of two fundamentally different sources – capital invested in the business by the owners, and profit earned by and retained in the business. The specific accounts maintained by the business for its total owners' equity depend on the legal organisation of the business entity. One of the main types of legal organisation of business is the *company*, and its owners are *shareholders* because the company issues ownership *shares* representing portions of the business. So, the title *statement of changes in shareholders' equity* is used for companies. (Chapter 11 explains the corporation and other legal types of business entities.)

First, consider the situation in which a business does *not* need to report this statement – to make clearer why the statement is needed. Suppose a company has only one class of share and it did not buy any of its own shares during the year and it did not record any gains or losses in owners' equity during the year due to *other comprehensive income* (explained below). This business does not need a statement of changes in shareholders' equity. In reading the financial report of this business you would see in its cash flow statement (Figure 7–2 shows an example) whether the business raised additional capital from its owners during the year and how much in *cash dividends* (distributions from profit) was paid to the owners during the year. The cash flow statement contains all the changes in the owners' equity accounts during the year.

In sharp contrast, larger businesses – especially publicly traded corporations – generally have complex ownership structures consisting of two or more classes of shares; they usually buy some of their own shares and they have one or more technical types of gains or losses during the year. So, they prepare a statement of changes in stockholders' equity to collect together in one place all the changes affecting the owners' equity accounts during the year. This particular 'mini' statement (that focuses narrowly on changes in owners' equity accounts) is where you find certain gains and losses that increase or decrease owners' equity but which are *not* reported in the profit and loss account. Basically, a business has the option to bypass the profit and loss account and, instead, report these gains and losses in the statement of changes in owners' equity. In this way the gains or losses do not affect the bottom-line profit of the business reported in its profit and loss account. You have to read this financial summary of the changes in the owners' equity accounts to find out whether the business had any of these gains or losses and the amounts of the gains or losses.

The special types of gains and losses that can be reported in the statement of owners' equity (instead of the profit and loss account) have to do with foreign currency translations, unrealised gains and losses from certain types of securities investments by the business and changes in liabilities for unfunded pension fund obligations of the business. *Comprehensive income* is the term used to describe the normal content of the profit and loss account *plus* the additional layer of these special types of gains and losses. Being so technical in nature, these gains and losses fall in a 'twilight zone' as it were, in financial reporting. The gains and losses can be tacked on at the bottom of the profit and loss account or they can be put in the statement of changes in owners' equity – it's up to the business to make the choice. If you encounter these gains and losses in reading a financial report, you'll have to study the footnotes to the financial statements to learn more information about each gain and loss.

Keep on the lookout for the special types of gains and losses that are reported in the statement of changes in owners' equity. A business has the option to tack such gains and losses onto the bottom of its profit and loss account – below the net income line. But, most businesses put these income gains and losses in their statement of changes in shareholders' equity, or in a note or notes to their accounts. So, watch out for any large amounts of gains or losses that are reported in the statement of changes in owners' equity.

The general format of the statement of changes in shareholders' equity includes a column for each class of stock (ordinary shares, preference shares and so on); a column for any shares of its own that the business has purchased and not cancelled; a column for retained earnings; and one or more columns for any other separate components of the business's owners' equity. Each column starts with the beginning balance and then shows the increases or decreases in the account during the year. For example, a comprehensive gain is shown as an increase in retained earnings and a comprehensive loss as a decrease. The purchase of its own shares is shown as an increase in the relevant column and if the business reissued some of these shares (such as for stock options exercised by executives), the cost of these shares reissued is shown as a decrease in the column.

We have to admit that reading the statement of changes, or *notes to the accounts* in shareholders' equity can be heavy going. The professionals – stock analysts, money and investment managers and so on – carefully read through and dissect this statement, or at least they should. The average non-professional investor should focus on whether the business had a major increase or decrease in the number of shares during the year, whether the business changed its ownership structure by creating or eliminating a class of stock, and the impact of stock options awarded to managers of the business.

Making Sure that Disclosure Is Adequate

The primary financial statements (including the statement of changes in owners' equity, if reported) are the backbone of a financial report. In fact, a financial report is not deserving of the name if the primary financial statements are not included. But, as mentioned earlier, there's much more to a financial report than the financial statements. A financial report needs *disclosures.* Of course, the financial statements provide disclosure of the most important financial information about the business. The term disclosures, however, usually refers to additional information provided in a financial report. In a nutshell, a financial report has two basic parts: (1) the primary financial statements and (2) disclosures.

The chief officer of the business (usually the CEO of a publicly owned company, the president of a private corporation or the managing partner of a partnership) has the primary responsibility to make sure that the financial statements have been prepared according to prevailing accounting standards and that the financial report provides adequate disclosure. He or she works with the chief financial officer of the business to make sure that the financial report meets the standard of adequate disclosure. (Many smaller businesses hire an independent qualified accountant to advise them on their financial statements and other disclosures in their financial reports.)

Types of disclosures in financial reports

For a quick survey of disclosures in financial reports – that is to say, the disclosures in addition to the financial statements – the following distinctions are helpful:

- **Footnotes** that provide additional information about the basic figures included in the financial statements; virtually all financial statements need footnotes to provide additional information for the account balances in the financial statements.

- **Supplementary financial schedules and tables** that provide more details than can be included in the body of financial statements.

- A wide variety of **other information**, some of which is required if the business is a company quoted on a stock market subject to government regulations regarding financial reporting to its shareholders and other information that is voluntary and not strictly required legally or according to GAAP.

Footnotes: Nettlesome but needed

Footnotes appear at the end of the primary financial statements. Within the financial statements you see references to particular footnotes. And at the bottom of each financial statement, you find the following sentence (or words to this effect): 'The footnotes are integral to the financial statements.' You should read all footnotes for a full understanding of the financial statements.

Footnotes come in two types:

- One or more footnotes must be included to identify the **major accounting policies and methods** that the business uses. (Chapter 13 explains that a business must choose among alternative accounting methods for certain expenses, and for their corresponding operating assets and liabilities.) The business must reveal which accounting methods it uses for its major expenses. In particular, the business must identify its cost of goods sold expense (and stock) method and its depreciation methods.

✔ Other footnotes provide **additional information and details** for many assets and liabilities. Details about share option plans for key executives are the main type of footnote to the capital stock account in the owners' equity section of the balance sheet.

One problem that most investors face when reading footnotes – and, for that matter, many managers who should understand their own footnotes but find them a little dense – is that footnotes often deal with complex issues (such as lawsuits) and rather technical accounting matters. Let us offer you one footnote that brings out this latter point. This footnote is taken from the recent financial report of a well-known manufacturer that uses a very conservative accounting method for determining its cost of goods sold expense and stock cost value. We know that we have not yet talked about these accounting methods; this is deliberate on our part. (Chapter 13 explains accounting methods.) We want you to read the following footnote from the 2011 Annual Report of this manufacturer and try to make sense of it (amounts are in thousands).

> **D. Inventories***: Inventories are valued principally by the LIFO (last-in, first-out) method. If the FIFO (first-in, first-out) method had been in use, inventories would have been £2,000 million and £1,978 million higher than reported at December 31, 2010 and 2011, respectively.*

Yes, these amounts are in *millions* of pounds. The company's stock cost value at the end of 2010 would have been £2 billion higher if the FIFO method had been used. Of course, you have to have some idea of the difference between the two methods, which we explain in Chapter 13.

You may wonder how different the company's annual profits would have been if the alternative method had been in use. A manager can ask the accounting department to do this analysis. But, as an outside investor, you would have to compute these amounts. Businesses disclose which accounting methods they use but they do not have to disclose how different annual profits would have been if the alternative method had been used – and very few do.

Other disclosures in financial reports

The following discussion includes a fairly comprehensive list of the various types of disclosures found in annual financial reports of larger, publicly owned businesses – in addition to footnotes. A few caveats are in order. First, not every public company includes every one of the following items although the disclosures are fairly common. Second, the level of disclosure by private businesses – after you get beyond the financial statements and footnotes – is much less than in public companies. Third, tracking the actual disclosure practices of private businesses is difficult because their annual financial reports are circulated only to their owners and lenders. A private business may include any or all of the following disclosures but, by and large, it is not legally required to do so. The next section further explains the differences between private and public businesses regarding disclosure practices in their annual financial reports.

Warren Buffett's annual letter to shareholders

We have to call your attention to one notable exception to the generally self-serving and slanted writing found in the letter to shareholders by the chief executive officer of the business in annual financial reports. The annual letter to stockholders of Berkshire Hathaway, Inc. is written by Warren Buffett, the Chairman and CEO. Mr Buffett has become very well known – he's called the 'Oracle of Omaha'. In the annual ranking of the world's richest people by *Forbes* magazine he is near the top of the list – right behind people like Bill Gates, the co-founder of Microsoft. If you had invested £1,000 with him in 1960, your investment would be worth well over £1,000,000 today. Even in the recent financial meltdown Berkshire Hathaway stock delivered a return of nearly 80% over the period 2000–2011 compared to a negative 12% return for the S&P 500. Mr Buffett's letters are the epitome of telling it like it is; they are very frank and quite humorous.

You can go to the website of the company (www.berkshirehathaway.com) and download his most recent letter. You'll learn a lot about his investing philosophy and the letters are a delight to read.

Public corporations typically include most of the following disclosures in their annual financial reports to their shareholders:

- ✔ **Cover (or transmittal) letter:** A letter from the chief executive of the business to the shareholders.

- ✔ **Highlights table:** A short table that presents the shareholder with a financial thumbnail sketch of the business.

- ✔ **Management discussion and analysis (MD&A):** Deals with the major developments and changes during the year that affected the financial performance and situation of the business.

- ✔ **Segment information:** The sales revenue and operating profits are reported for the major divisions of the organisation or for its different markets (international versus domestic, for example).

- ✔ **Historical summaries:** Financial history that extends back beyond the years (usually three but can be up to five or six) included in the primary financial statements.

- ✔ **Graphics:** Bar charts, trend charts and pie charts representing financial conditions; photos of key people and products.

- ✔ **Promotional material:** information about the company, its products, its employees and its managers, often stressing an over-arching theme for the year.

- ✔ **Profiles:** Information about members of top management and the board of directors.

✔ **Quarterly summaries of profit performance and share prices and dividends:** Shows financial performance for all four quarters in the year and share price ranges for each quarter.

✔ **Management's responsibility statement:** A short statement that management has primary responsibility for the accounting methods used to prepare the financial statements and for providing the other disclosures in the financial report.

✔ **Independent auditor's report:** The report from the accounting firm that performed the audit, expressing an opinion on the fairness of the financial statements and accompanying disclosures. (Chapter 15 discusses the nature of audits.) Public companies are required to have audits; private businesses may or may not have their annual financial reports audited depending on their size.

✔ **Company contact information:** Information on how to contact the company, the website address of the company, how to get copies of the reports filed with the London Stock Exchange, SEC, the stock transfer agent and registrar of the company, and other information.

Managers of public corporations rely on lawyers, auditors and their financial and accounting officers to make sure that everything that should be disclosed in the business's annual financial reports is included and that the exact wording of the disclosures is not misleading, inaccurate or incomplete. This is a tall order. The field of financial reporting disclosure changes constantly. Laws, as well as authoritative accounting standards, have to be observed. Inadequate disclosure in an annual financial report is just as serious as using wrong accounting methods for measuring profit and for determining values for assets, liabilities and owners' equity. A financial report can be misleading because of improper accounting methods or because of inadequate or misleading disclosure. Both types of deficiencies can lead to nasty lawsuits against the business and its managers.

Companies House provides forms showing how the Companies Act requires balance sheets and profit and loss accounts to be laid out. To access their guidance, go to www.companieshouse.gov.uk/forms/introduction. shtml. All their statutory forms are available on request and free of charge.

Keeping It Private versus Going Public

Compared with their big brothers and sisters, privately owned businesses provide very little additional disclosures in their annual financial reports. The primary financial statements and footnotes are pretty much all you get.

The annual financial reports of publicly owned corporations include all, or nearly all, of the disclosure items listed earlier. Somewhere in the range of 3,000 companies are publicly owned, and their shares are traded on the London Stock Exchange, NASDAQ or other stock exchanges. Publicly owned companies must file annual financial reports with the Stock Exchange, which is the agency that makes and enforces the rules for trading in securities and for the financial reporting requirements of publicly owned corporations. These filings are available to the public on the London Stock Exchange's website (www.londonstockexchange.com) or for US companies on the Securities Exchange Commission's (SEC's) EDGAR database at the SEC's website – www.sec.gov/edgar/searchedgar/cik.htm.

Both privately held and publicly owned businesses are bound by the same accounting rules for measuring profit, assets, liabilities and owners' equity in annual financial reports to the owners of the business and in reports that are made available to others (such as the lenders to the business). There aren't two different sets of accounting rules – one for private companies and another one for public businesses. The accounting measurement and valuation rules are the same for all businesses. However, *disclosure* requirements and practices differ greatly between private and public companies.

Publicly owned businesses live in a fish bowl. When a company goes public with an *IPO* (initial public offering of shares), it gives up a lot of the privacy that a closely held business enjoys. Publicly owned companies whose shares are traded on national stock exchanges live in glass houses. In contrast, privately owned businesses lock their doors regarding disclosure. Whenever a privately owned business releases a financial report to its bank in seeking a loan, or to the outside non-management investors in the business, it should include its three primary financial statements and footnotes. But beyond this, they have much more leeway and do not have to include the additional disclosure items listed in the preceding section.

A private business may have its financial statements audited by a professional accounting firm. If so, the audit report is included in the business's annual financial report. The very purpose of having an audit is to reassure shareholders and potential investors in the business that the financial statements can be trusted. But as we look up and down the preceding list of disclosure items we don't see any other absolutely required disclosure item for a privately held business. The large majority of closely held businesses guard their financial information like Fort Knox.

The less information divulged in the annual financial report, the better – that's their thinking. And we don't entirely disagree. The shareholders don't have the liquidity for their shares that shareholders of publicly held corporations enjoy. The market prices of public companies are everything, so information is made publicly available so that market prices are fairly determined. The shares of privately owned businesses are rarely traded, so there is not such an urgent need for a complete package of information.

A private company could provide all the disclosures given in the preceding list – there's certainly no law against this. But usually they don't. Investors in private businesses can request confidential reports from managers at the annual shareholders' meetings, but doing so is not practical for a shareholder in a large public corporation.

Nudging the Numbers

This section discusses two accounting tricks that business managers and investors should know about. We don't endorse either technique, but you should be aware of both of them. In some situations, the financial statement numbers don't come out exactly the way the business wants. Accountants use certain tricks of the trade – some would say sleight-of-hand – to move the numbers closer to what the business prefers. One trick improves the appearance of the *short-term solvency* of the business, in particular the cash balance reported in the balance sheet at the end of the year. The other device shifts profit from one year to the next to make for a smoother trend of net income from year to year.

Not all businesses use these techniques, but the extent of their use is hard to pin down because no business would openly admit to using these manipulation methods. The evidence is fairly convincing, however, that many businesses use these techniques. We're sure you've heard the term *loopholes* applied to income tax accounting. Well, some loopholes exist in financial statement accounting as well.

Fluffing up the cash balance by 'window dressing'

Suppose you manage a business and your accountant has just submitted to you a preliminary, or first draft, of the year-end balance sheet for your review. (Chapter 6 explains the balance sheet, and Figure 6-1 shows a complete balance sheet for a business.) Your preliminary balance sheet includes the following:

Preliminary Balances, Before Window Dressing

Cash	£0	Creditors	£235,000
Debtors	£486,000	Accrued expenses payable	£187,000
Stock	£844,000	Income tax payable	£58,000
Overdraft	£200,000		
Prepaid expenses	£72,000		
Current assets	£1,402,000	Current liabilities	£680,000

You start reading the numbers when something strikes you: a zero cash balance? How can that be? Maybe your business has been having some cash flow problems and you've intended to increase your short-term borrowing and speed up collection of debtors to help the cash balance. But that plan doesn't help you right now, with this particular financial report that you must send out to your business's investors and your banker. Folks generally don't like to see a zero cash balance – it makes them kind of nervous, to put it mildly, no matter how you try to cushion it. So what do you do to avoid alarming them?

Your accountant is probably aware of a technique known as *window dressing*, a very simple method for making the cash balance look better. Suppose your financial year-end is October 31. Your accountant takes the cash receipts from customers paying their bills that are actually received on November 1, 2 and 3, and records them as if these cash collections had been received on October 31. After all, the argument can be made that the customers' cheques were in the mail – that money is yours, as far as the customers are concerned, so your reports should reflect that cash inflow.

What impact does window dressing have? It reduces the amount in debtors and increases the amount in cash by the same amount – it has absolutely no effect on the profit figure. It just makes your cash balance look a touch better. Window dressing can also be used to improve other accounts' balances, which we don't go into here. All of these techniques involve holding the books open to record certain events that take place after the end of the financial year (the ending balance sheet date) to make things look better than they actually were at the close of business on the last day of the year.

Sounds like everybody wins, doesn't it? Your investors don't panic and your job is safe. We have to warn you, though, that window dressing may be the first step on a slippery slope. A little window dressing today and tomorrow, who knows? – Maybe giving the numbers a nudge will lead to serious financial fraud. Any way you look at it, window dressing is deceptive to your investors who have every right to expect that the end of your fiscal year as stated on your financial reports is truly the end of your fiscal year. Think about it this way: If you've invested in a business that has fudged this data, how do you know what other numbers on the report are suspect?

Smoothing the rough edges off profit

Managers strive to make their numbers and to hit the milestone markers set for the business. Reporting a loss for the year, or even a dip below the profit trend line, is a red flag that investors view with alarm.

Managers can do certain things to deflate or inflate profit (the net income) recorded in the year, which are referred to as *profit-smoothing* techniques. Profit smoothing is also called *income smoothing*. Profit smoothing is not nearly as serious as *cooking the books*, or *juggling the books*, which refers to deliberate, fraudulent accounting practices such as recording sales revenue that has not happened or not recording expenses that have happened. Cooking the books is very serious; managers can go to jail for fraudulent financial statements. Profit smoothing is more like a white lie that is told for the good of the business, and perhaps for the good of managers as well. Managers know that there is always some noise in the accounting system. Profit smoothing muffles the noise.

Managers of publicly owned companies whose shares are actively traded are under intense pressure to keep profits steadily rising. Security analysts who follow a particular company make profit forecasts for the business, and their buy-hold-sell recommendations are based largely on these earnings forecasts. If a business fails to meet its own profit forecast or falls short of analysts' forecasts, the market price of its shares suffers. Share option and bonus incentive compensation plans are also strong motivations for achieving the profit goals set for the business.

The evidence is fairly strong that publicly owned businesses engage in some degree of profit smoothing. Frankly, it's much harder to know whether private businesses do so. Private businesses don't face the public scrutiny and expectations that public corporations do. On the other hand, key managers in a private business may have incentive bonus arrangements that depend on recorded profit. In any case, business investors and managers should know about profit smoothing and how it's done.

Most profit smoothing involves pushing revenue and expenses into other years than they would normally be recorded. For example, if the president of a business wants to report more profit for the year, he or she can instruct the chief accountant to accelerate the recording of some sales revenue that normally wouldn't be recorded until next year, or to delay the recording of some expenses until next year that normally would be recorded this year. The main reason for smoothing profit is to keep it closer to a projected trend line and make the line less jagged.

Chapter 13 explains that managers choose among alternative accounting methods for several important expenses. After making these key choices the managers should let the accountants do their jobs and let the chips fall where they may. If bottom-line profit for the year turns out to be a little short of the forecast or target for the period, so be it. This hands-off approach to profit accounting is the ideal way. However, managers often use a hands-on approach – they intercede (one could say interfere) and override the normal accounting for sales revenue or expenses.

Both managers who do it and investors who rely on financial statements in which profit smoothing has been done should definitely understand one thing – these techniques have robbing-Peter-to-pay-Paul effects. Accountants refer to these as *compensatory effects*. The effects on next year's statement simply offset and cancel out the effects on this year. Less expense this year is counterbalanced by more expense next year. Sales revenue recorded this year means less sales revenue recorded next year.

Two profit histories

Figure 8-2 shows, side by side, the annual profit histories of two different companies over six years. Business X shows a nice steady upward trend of profit. Business Y, in contrast, shows somewhat of a rollercoaster ride over the six years. Both businesses earned the same total profit for the six years – in this case, £1,050,449. Their total six-year profit performance is the same, down to the last pound. Which company would you be more willing to risk your money in? We suspect that you'd prefer Business X because of the steady upward slope of its profit history.

Question: Does Figure 8-2 really show two different companies – or are the two profit histories actually alternatives for the same company? The year-by-year profits for Business X could be the company's *smoothed* profit, and the annual profits for Business Y could be the *actual* profit of the same business – the profit that would have been recorded if smoothing techniques had not been applied.

For the first year in the series, 2006, no profit smoothing occurred. Actual profit is on target. For each of the next five years, the two profit numbers differ. The under-gap or over-gap of actual profit compared with smoothed profit for the year is the amount of revenue or expenses manipulation that was done in the year. For example, in 2007, actual profit would have been too high, so the company moved some expenses that normally would be recorded the following year into 2007. In contrast, in 2008, actual profit was running too low, so the business took action to put off recording some expenses until 2011.

If a business has a particularly bad year, all the profit-smoothing tricks in the world won't close the gap. But several smoothing techniques are available for filling the potholes and straightening the curves on the profit highway.

Profit-smoothing techniques

One common technique for profit smoothing is *deferred maintenance*. Many routine and recurring maintenance costs required for vehicles, machines, equipment and buildings can be put off, or deferred until later. These costs are not recorded to expense until the actual maintenance is done, so putting off the work means that no expense is recorded. Or a company can cut back on its current year's outlays for market research and product development. Keep in mind that most of these costs will be incurred next year, so the effect is to rob Peter (make next year absorb the cost) to pay Paul (let this year escape the cost).

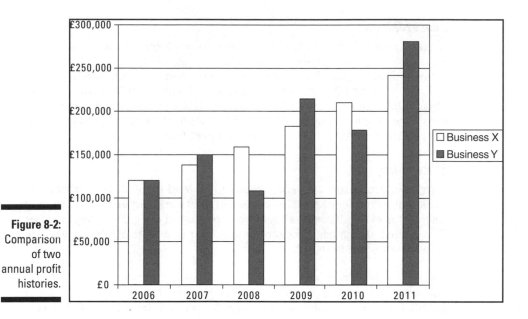

Figure 8-2:
Comparison
of two
annual profit
histories.

A business can ease up on its rules regarding when slow-paying customers are decided to be bad debts (uncollectable debtors). A business can put off recording some of its bad debts expense until next year. A fixed asset out of active use may have very little or no future value to a business. Instead of writing off the non-depreciated cost of the *impaired asset* as a loss this year, the business may delay the write-off until next year.

So, managers have control over the timing of many expenses, and they can use this discretion for profit smoothing. Some amount of expenses can be accelerated into this year or deferred to next year in order to make for a smoother profit trend. Of course, in its external financial report a business does not divulge the extent to which it has engaged in profit smoothing. Nor does the independent auditor comment on the use of profit-smoothing techniques by the business – unless the auditor thinks that the company has gone too far in massaging the numbers and that its financial statements are misleading.

Sticking to the accounting conventions

Over time, a generally accepted approach to the boundaries of acceptable number nudging has been arrived at. This hinges on the use of three conventions: conservatism, materiality and consistency.

Conservatism

Accountants are often viewed as merchants of gloom, always prone to taking a pessimistic point of view. The fact that a point of view has to be taken at all is the root of the problem. The convention of *conservatism* means that, given a choice, the accountant takes the figure that will result in a lower end profit. This might mean, for example, taking the higher of two possible expense figures. Few people are upset if the profit figure at the end of the day is higher than earlier estimates. The converse is never true.

Materiality

A strict interpretation of depreciation could lead to all sorts of trivial paperwork. For example, pencil sharpeners, staplers and paperclips, all theoretically items of fixed assets, should be depreciated over their working lives. This is obviously a useless exercise and in practice these items are written-off when they are bought.

Clearly, the level of *materiality* is not the same for all businesses. A multinational may not keep meticulous records of every item of machinery under £1,000. For a small business this may represent all the machinery it has.

Consistency

Even with the help of those concepts and conventions, there's a fair degree of latitude in how you can record and interpret financial information. You need to choose the methods that give the fairest picture of how the firm is performing and stick with them. Keeping track of events in a business that's always changing its accounting methods is very difficult. This doesn't mean that you're stuck with one method forever. Any change, however, is an important step.

Browsing versus Reading Financial Reports

Very few people have the time to carefully read all the information in an annual financial report – even if the report is relatively short.

Annual financial reports are long and dense documents – like lengthy legal contracts in many ways. Pick up a typical annual financial report of a public corporation: You would need many hours (perhaps the whole day) to thoroughly read everything in the report. You would need at least an hour or two just to read and absorb the main points in the report. How do investors in a business deal with the *information overload* of annual financial reports put out by businesses?

An annual financial report is like the Sunday edition of *The Times* or *The Telegraph.* Hardly anyone reads every sentence on every page of these Sunday papers – most people pick and choose what they want to read. Investors read annual financial reports like they read Sunday newspapers. The information is there if you really want to read it, but most readers pick and choose which information they have time to read.

Annual financial reports are designed for archival purposes, not for a quick read. Instead of addressing the needs of investors and others who want to know about the profit performance and financial condition of the business – but have only a very limited amount of time to do so – accountants produce an annual financial report that is a voluminous financial history of the business. Accountants leave it to the users of annual reports to extract the main points from an annual report. So, financial statement readers use relatively few ratios and other tests to get a feel for the financial performance and position of the business. (Chapters 14 and 17 explain how readers of financial reports get a fix on the financial performance and position of a business.)

Some businesses (and non-profit organisations in reporting to their members and other constituencies) don't furnish an annual financial report. They know that few people have the time or the technical background to read through their annual financial reports. Instead, they provide relatively brief summaries that are boiled-down versions of their official financial statements. Typically these summaries do not provide footnotes or the other disclosures that are included in annual financial reports. These *condensed financial statements*, without footnotes, are provided by several non-profit organisations – credit unions, for instance. If you really want to see the complete financial report of the organisation you can ask its headquarters to send you a copy.

You should keep in mind that annual financial reports do not report everything of interest to owners, creditors and others who have a financial interest in the business. *Annual* reports, of course, come out only once a year – usually two months or so after the end of the company's fiscal (accounting) year. You have to keep abreast of developments during the year by reading financial newspapers or through other means. Also, annual financial reports present the 'sanitised' version of events; they don't divulge scandals or other negative news about the business.

Finally, not everything you may like to know as an investor is included in the annual financial report. For example, for US companies, information about salaries and incentive compensation arrangements with the top-level managers of the business are disclosed in the *proxy statement*, not in the annual financial report of the business. A proxy statement is the means by which the corporation solicits the votes of shareholders on issues that require their approval –

one of which is compensation packages of top-level managers. In the US, proxy statements are filed with the SEC and are available on its EDGAR database, `www.sec.gov/edgar/searchedgar/cik.htm`. In the UK this information would usually appear in the body of the main report under the heading 'Report of the Directors on Remuneration'.

The quality of financial reports varies from company to company. The Investor Relations Society (go to `www.irs.org.uk` and click on 'IR Best Practice') makes an award each year to the company producing the best (in other words, 'complete' and 'clear') set of reports and accounts.

Part III
Accounting in Managing a Business

After the FIFO method and the LIFO method comes the LILO method.

In this part . . .

Business managers and owners depend on financial statements as well as other internal accounting reports to know how much profit they're making, where that profit is at the end of the period, and whether the business is in good financial shape or needs improvement. They also use financial statements to keep a close watch on the lifeblood of the business: cash flows. Managers must know how to read their financial statements. Also, they should take advantage of proven accounting tools and techniques to assist them in making profit, controlling cash flow, and keeping the business in good financial condition.

Managers need a good accounting model for analysing profit; they can use budgeting to plan, make projections, and achieve the financial goals of the business, which is the essence of management control. Business managers and owners must decide which ownership structure to use, taking into account risk to personal wealth and the prospects for tax minimisation. Finally, managers should clearly understand how the costs of the business are determined, and they should get involved in choosing the basic accounting methods for measuring profit and for recording values of their assets and liabilities. This often involves making choices that can best be made when managers and accountants are speaking the same language, not always easily achieved as finance is awash with ambiguous terms. This part of the book, in short, explains how accounting helps managers achieve the financial goals of the business and to be better able to communicate effectively with their accountants and finance staff.

Chapter 9

Managing Profit Performance

As a manager you get paid to make profit happen. That's what separates you from the non-manager employees at your business. Of course, you have to be a motivator, innovator, consensus builder, lobbyist and maybe sometimes a babysitter too. But the real purpose of your job is to control and improve the profit of your business. No matter how much your staff love you (or do they love those doughnuts you bring in every Monday?), if you don't meet your profit goals, you're facing the unemployment line.

You have to be relentless in your search for better ways to do things. Competition in most industries is fierce, and you can never take profit performance for granted. Changes take place all the time – changes initiated by the business and changes pressured by outside forces. Maybe a new superstore down the street is causing your profit to fall off, and you decide that you'll have a huge sale, complete with splashy ads on TV, to draw customers into the shop.

Slow down, not so fast! First make sure that you can afford to cut prices and spend money on advertising and still turn a profit. Maybe price cuts and splashy ads will keep your cash register singing and the kiddies smiling, but you need to remember that making sales does not guarantee that you make a profit. As all you experienced business managers know, profit is a two headed beast – profit comes from making sales *and* controlling expenses.

So how do you determine what effect price cuts and advertising costs may have on your bottom line? By turning to your beloved accounting staff, of course, and asking for some *what-if* reports (like 'What if we offer a 15 per cent discount?').

This chapter shows you how to identify the key variables that determine what your profit would be if you changed certain factors (such as prices).

Redesigning the External Profit and Loss Account

To begin, Figure 9-1 presents the profit and loss account of a business (the same example as is used in Chapter 8). Figure 9-1 shows an *external profit and loss account* – the profit and loss account that's reported to the outside investors and creditors of the business. The expenses in Figure 9-1 are presented as they are usually disclosed in an external statement. (Chapter 5 explains sales revenue, expenses and the format of the external profit and loss account.)

(Amounts in thousands)	
External Profit and Loss Account For Year	
Sales Revenue	£ 52,000
Cost of Goods Sold Expense	31,200
Gross Margin	£ 20,800
Sales, Administration, and General Expenses	15,600
Depreciation Expense	1,650
Earnings Before Interest and Tax	£ 3,550
Interest Expense	750
Earnings Before Tax	£ 2,800
Tax Expense	900
Net Income	£ 1,900

Figure 9-1: Example of a business's external profit and loss account.

The managers of the business should understand this profit and loss account, of course. But, the external profit and loss account is not entirely adequate for management decision-making; this profit report falls short of providing all the information about expenses needed by managers. But, before moving on to the additional information managers need, take a quick look at the external profit and loss account (Figure 9-1).

For more information about the external profit and loss account and all its sundry parts, see Chapter 5. Let us just point out the following here about this particular financial statement:

✔ The business represented by this profit and loss account sells products and therefore has a *cost of goods sold expense.* In contrast, companies that sell services (airlines, cinemas, consultants and so on) don't have a cost of goods sold expense, as all their sales revenue goes toward meeting operating expenses and then providing profit.

✔ The external profit and loss account shown in Figure 9-1 is prepared according to authorised accounting methods and disclosure standards, but keep in mind that these financial reporting standards are designed for reporting information *outside* the business. Once a profit and loss account is released to people outside the business, a business has no control over the circulation of its statement. The accounting profession, in deciding on the information for disclosure in external profit and loss accounts, has attempted to strike a balance. On the one side are the needs of those who have invested capital in the business and have loaned money to the business; clearly they have the right to receive enough information to evaluate their investments in the business and their loans to the business. On the other side is the need of the business to keep certain information confidential and out of the hands of its competitors. What it comes down to is that certain information that outside investors and creditors might find interesting and helpful does not, in fact, legally have to be disclosed.

✔ The profit and loss account does not report the *financial effects* of the company's profit-making activities – that is, the increases and decreases in its assets and liabilities caused by revenue and expenses. Managers need to control these financial effects for which purpose they need the complete financial picture provided by the two other primary financial statements (the balance sheet and the cash flow statement) in addition to the profit and loss account. See Chapters 6 and 7 for more about these two other primary financial statements.

Basic Model for Management Profit and Loss Account

Figure 9-2 presents a model for a *management* profit and loss account using the same business as the example whose external profit and loss account is shown in Figure 9-1. Many lines of information are exactly the same – sales revenue and cost of goods sold expense for instance – and thus gross margins are the same. The last five lines in the two statements are the same, starting with operating profit (earnings before interest and corporation tax) down to the bottom line. In other respects, however, there are critical differences between the two profit reports.

Management Profit and Loss Account For Year		
(Amounts in thousands)	Totals for Period	Per Unit
Unit Sales Volume =	520,000	
Sales Revenue	£52,000	£100
Cost of Goods Sold Expense	31,200	60
Gross Margin	£20,800	£40
Revenue-driven Operating Expenses	4,160	8
Contribution Margin	£16,640	£32
Fixed Operating Expenses	13,090	
Operating Profit, or Earnings Before Interest and Tax Expenses (EBIT)	£ 3,550	
Interest Expense	750	
Earnings Before Tax	£ 2,800	
Tax Expense	900	
Net Income	£ 1,900	

Figure 9-2: Management profit and loss account model.

First, note that total *unit sales volume* and *per unit amounts* are included in the management profit and loss account (Figure 9-2). The business appears to sell only one product; the 520,000 units total sales volume is from sales of this product. In fact, most businesses sell a mix of many different products. The company's various managers need detailed sales revenue and cost information for each product, or product line, or segment of the business they are responsible for. To keep the illustration easy to follow we have collapsed the business's entire sales into one 'average' product. Instead of grappling with 100 or 1,000 different products, we condensed them all into one proxy product. The main purpose of Figure 9-2 is to show a basic template, or model, that can be used for the more detailed reports to different managers in the business organisation.

Variable versus fixed operating expenses

Another fundamental difference between the external profit report (Figure 9-1) and the internal profit report (Figure 9-2) is that the company's *operating expenses* (sales, administration and general expenses plus depreciation expense) are separated into two different categories in the management report:

- **Variable expenses:** The *revenue-driven expenses* that depend directly on the total sales revenue amount for the period. These expenses move in step with changes in total sales revenue. Commissions paid to salespersons based on a percentage of the amount of sales are a common example of variable operating expenses.

- **Fixed expenses:** The operating expenses that are relatively fixed in amount for the period, regardless of whether the company's total unit sales (sales volume) had been substantially more, or substantially less, than the 520,000 units that it actually sold during the year. An example of a fixed operating expense is the annual business rates on the company's property. Also, depreciation is a fixed expense; a certain amount of depreciation expense is recorded to the year regardless of actual sales volume.

The management profit and loss account does not, we repeat *not*, present different profit numbers for the year compared with the profit numbers reported in the company's external profit and loss account. Note that operating profit for the year (or earnings before interest and tax expenses) is the same as reported outside the business – in Figures 9–1 and 9–2 this number is the same. And in reading down the rest of the two profit and loss accounts, note that earnings before tax and bottom-line net income are the same in both the external and internal reports. The external profit and loss account of the business reports a broad, all-inclusive group of 'Sales, Administration and General Expenses', and a separate expense for depreciation. In contrast, the management profit and loss account reveals information about *how the operating expenses behave relative to the sales of the business*. The actual reporting of expenses in external profit and loss accounts varies from business to business – but you never see profit and loss accounts in which operating expenses are sorted between variable and fixed.

Virtually every business has *variable operating expenses*, which move up and down in tight proportion to changes in unit sales volume or sales revenue. Here are some examples of common variable operating expenses:

- ✔ Cost of goods sold expense – the cost of the products sold to customers.

- ✔ Commissions paid to salespeople based on their sales.

- ✔ Transportation costs of delivering products to customers.

- ✔ Fees that a business pays to a bank when a customer uses a credit card such as Visa, MasterCard or American Express.

The management profit and loss account (Figure 9-2) can be referred to as the *internal profit report*, since it is for management eyes only and does not circulate outside the business – although it may be the target of industrial intelligence gathering and perhaps even industrial espionage by competitors. Remember that in the external profit and loss account only one lump sum for the category of sales, administrative and general (SA&G) expenses is reported – a category for which some of the expenses are fixed but some are variable. What you need to do is have your accountant carefully examine these expenses to determine which are fixed and which are variable. (Some expenses may have both fixed and variable components, but we don't go into these technical details.)

Further complicating the matter somewhat is the fact that the accountant needs to divide variable expenses between those that vary with sales *volume* (total number of units sold) and those that vary with sales *revenue* (total pounds of sales revenue). The following examples outline this important distinction:

- ✔ An example of an expense driven by sales volume is the cost of shipping and packaging. This cost depends strictly on the *number* of units sold and generally is the same regardless of how much the item inside the box costs.

- ✔ An example of an expense driven by sales revenue are sales commissions paid to salespersons, which directly depend on the amounts of sales made to customers. Other examples are franchise fees based on total sales revenue of retailers, business premises rental contracts that include a clause that bases monthly rent on sales revenue, and royalties that are paid for the right to use a well-known name or a trademarked logo in selling the company's products and which are based on total sales revenue.

The business represented in Figure 9-2 has just one variable operating expense – an 8 per cent sales commission, resulting in an expense total of £4,160,000 (£52 million sales revenue × 8 per cent). Of course, a real business probably would have many different variable operating expenses, some driven by unit sales volume and some driven by total sales revenue pounds. But the basic idea is the same for all of them and one variable operating expense serves the purpose here. Also, cost of goods sold expense is itself a sales volume driven expense (see Chapter 13 regarding different accounting methods for measuring this expense). The example shown in Figure 9-2 is a bit oversimplified – the business sells only one product and has only one variable operating expense – but the main purpose is to present a general template that can be tailored to fit the particular circumstances of a business.

Fixed operating expenses are the many different costs that a business is obliged to pay and cannot decrease over the short run without major surgery on the human resources and physical facilities of the business. You must distinguish fixed expenses from your variable operating expenses.

As an example of fixed expenses, consider a typical self-service car wash business – you know, the kind where you drive in, put some coins in a box, and use the water spray to clean your car. Almost all the operating costs of this business are fixed: Rent on the land, depreciation of the structure and the equipment and the annual insurance premium cost don't depend on the number of cars passing through the car wash. The only variable expenses are probably the water, soap and electricity.

If you want to decrease fixed expenses significantly, you need to downsize the business (lay off workers, sell off property and so on). When looking at the various ways you have for improving your profit, significantly cutting down on fixed expenses is generally the last-resort option. Refer to 'Improving profit' later in this chapter for the better options.

Better than anyone else, managers know that sales for the year could have been lower or higher. A natural question is, 'What difference in the profit would there have been at the lower or higher level of sales?' If you'd sold 10 per cent fewer total units during the year, what would your net income (bottom-line profit) have been? You might guess that profit would have slipped 10 per cent but that would *not* have been the case. In fact, profit would have slipped by much more than 10 per cent. Are you surprised? Read on for the reasons.

Why wouldn't profit fall the same percentage as sales? The answer is because of the nature of fixed expenses – just because your sales are lower doesn't mean that your expenses are lower. *Fixed expenses* are the costs of doing business that, for all practical purposes, are stuck at a certain amount over the short term. Fixed expenses do not react to changes in the sales level. Here are some examples of fixed expenses:

- Interest on money that the business has borrowed
- Employees' salaries and benefits
- Business Rates
- Fire insurance

A business can downsize its assets and therefore reduce its fixed expenses to fit a lower sales level, but that can be a drastic reaction to what may be a temporary downturn. After deducting cost of goods sold, variable operating expenses and fixed operating expenses, the next line in the management profit and loss account is operating profit, which is also called *earnings before interest and tax* (or *EBIT*). This profit line in the report is a critical juncture that managers need to fully appreciate.

From operating profit (EBIT) to the bottom line

After deducting all operating expenses from sales revenue, you get to earnings before interest and tax (EBIT), which is £3,550,000 in the example. *Operating* is an umbrella term that includes cost of goods sold expense and all other expenses of making sales and operating your business – but not interest and tax. Sometimes EBIT is called *operating profit*, or *operating earnings*, to emphasise that profit comes from making sales and controlling operating expenses. This business earned £3,550,000 operating profit from its £52 million sales revenue – which seems satisfactory. But is its £3,550,000 EBIT really good enough? What's the reference for answering this question?

The main benchmark for judging EBIT is whether this amount of profit is adequate to cover the *cost of capital* of the business. Chapter 6 explains the various assets that a business needs to make sales and earn profit. A business must secure money to invest in its various assets – and this capital has a cost. A business has to pay interest on its debt capital, and it should earn enough after-tax net income (bottom-line profit) to satisfy its owners who have put their capital in the business. See the sidebar 'How much net income is needed to make owners happy?' in this chapter.

Nobody – not even the most die-hard humanitarian – is in business to make a zero EBIT. You simply can't do this, because profit is an absolutely necessary part of doing business – and recouping the cost of capital is why profit is needed.

Don't treat the word *profit* as something that's whispered in the hallways. Profit builds owners' value and provides the basic stability for a business. Earning a satisfactory EBIT is the cornerstone of business. Without earning an adequate operating profit, a business could not attract capital, and you can't have a business without capital.

How much net income is needed to make owners happy?

People who invest in a business usually aren't philanthropists who don't want to make any money on the deal. No, these investors want a business to protect their capital investment, earn a good bottom-line profit for them and enhance the value of their investment over time. They understand that a business may not earn a profit but suffer a loss – that's the risk they take as owners.

As described in Chapters 6 and 11, how much of a business's net income (bottom-line profit) is distributed to the owners depends on the business and the arrangement that it made with the owners. But regardless of how much money the owners actually receive, they still have certain expectations of how well the business will do – that is, what the business's earnings before interest and tax will be. After all, they've staked their money on the business's success.

One test of whether the owners will be satisfied with the net income (after interest and tax) is to compute the *return on equity* (ROE), which is the ratio of net income to total owners' equity (net income ÷ owners' equity). In this chapter's business example, the bottom-line profit is £1.9 million. Suppose that the total owners' equity in the business is £15.9 million (as shown in Figure 8–1 for the business example). Thus, the ROE is 12 per cent (£1.9 million ÷ £15.9 million). Is 12 per cent a good ROE? Well, that depends on how much the owners could earn from an alternative investment. We'd say that a 12 per cent ROE isn't bad. By the way, ROE is also known as ROSI: *return on shareholders' investment.*

Note: ROE does not imply that all the net income was distributed in cash to the owners. Usually, a business needs to retain a good part of its bottom-line net income to provide capital for growing the business. Suppose, in this example, that none of the net income is distributed in cash to its owners. The ROE is still 12 per cent; ROE does not depend on how much, if any, of the net income is distributed to the owners. (Of course, the owners may prefer that a good part of the net income be distributed to them.)

Travelling Two Trails to Profit

How is the additional information in the management profit and loss account useful? Well, with this information you can figure out how the business earned its profit for the year. We're not referring to how the company decided which products to sell, and the best ways to market and advertise its products, and how to set sales prices, and how to design an efficient and smooth running organisation, and how to motivate its employees, and all the other things every business has to do to achieve its financial goals. We're talking about an *accounting explanation of profit* that focuses on methods for calculating profit – going from the basic input factors of sales price, sales volume and costs to arrive at the amount of profit that results from the interaction of the factors. Business managers should be familiar with these accounting calculations. They are responsible for each factor and for profit, of course. With this in mind, therefore: How did the business earn its profit for the year?

First path to profit: Contribution margin minus fixed expenses

We can't read your mind. But, if we had to hazard a guess regarding how you would go about answering the profit question, we'd bet that, after you had the chance to study Figure 9-2, you would do something like the following, which is correct as a matter of fact:

Computing Profit Before Tax	
Contribution margin per unit	£32
× Unit sales volume	520,000
Equals: Total contribution margin	£16,640,000
Less: Total fixed operating expenses	£13,090,000
Equals: Operating profit (EBIT)	£3,550,000
Less: Interest Expense	£750,000
Equals: Earnings before tax	£2,800,000

Note that we stop at the *earnings before tax* line in this calculation. You're aware, of course, that business profit is subject to tax. Chapter 3 provides a general overview of the taxation of business profit. This chapter focuses on profit above the taxation expense line. Nevertheless, please keep in mind as a broad rule of thumb that taxable income of a regular business corporation is subject to around 30 per cent tax in addition to value added – except small businesses whose taxable income is taxed at a lower rate.

Contribution margin is what's left over after you subtract cost of goods sold expense and other variable expenses from sales revenue. On a *per unit* basis the business sells its product for £100, its variable product cost (cost of goods sold) is £60 and its variable operating cost per unit is £8 – which yields £32 contribution margin per unit. *Total* contribution margin for a period equals contribution margin per unit times the units sold during the period – in the business example, £32 × 520,000 units, which is £16,640,000 total contribution margin. Total contribution margin is a measure of profit *before fixed expenses are deducted*. To pay for its fixed operating expenses and its interest expense, a business needs to earn a sufficient amount of total contribution margin. In the example, the business earned more total contribution margin than its fixed expenses, so it earned a profit for the year.

> ## How variable expenses mow down your sales price
>
> Consider a retail hardware store that sells, say, a lawnmower to a customer. The purchase cost per unit that the retailer paid to the lawnmower manufacturer when the retailer bought its shipment is the *product cost* in the contribution margin equation. The retailer also provides one free servicing of the lawnmower after the customer has used it a few months (cleaning it and sharpening the blade) and also pays its salesperson a commission on the sale. These two additional expenses, for the service and the commission, are examples of variable expenses in the margin equation.

Here are some other concepts associated with the term *margin*, which you're likely to encounter:

- **Gross margin, also called gross profit:** Gross margin = sales revenue – cost of goods sold expense. Gross margin is profit from sales revenue *before* deducting the other variable expenses of making the sales. So gross margin is one step short of the final contribution margin earned on making sales. Businesses that sell products must report gross margin on their *external* profit and loss accounts. However, generally accounting standards do *not* require that you report other variable expenses of making sales on external profit and loss accounts. In their external financial reports, very few businesses divulge other variable expenses of making sales. In other words, managers do not want the outside world and competitors to know their contribution margins. Most businesses carefully guard information about contribution margins because the information is very sensitive.

- **Gross margin ratio:** Gross margin ratio = gross margin ÷ sales revenue. In the business we use as an example in this chapter, the gross margin on sales is 40 per cent. Gross margins of companies vary from industry to industry, from over 50 per cent to under 25 per cent – but very few businesses can make a bottom-line profit with less than a 20 per cent gross margin.

- **Markup:** Generally refers to the amount added to the product cost to determine the sales price. For example, suppose a product that cost £60 is marked up (based on cost) by 66⅔ per cent to determine its sales price of £100 – for a gross margin of £40 on the product. *Note:* The markup based on *cost* is 66⅔ per cent (£40 markup ÷ £60 product cost). But the gross margin ratio is only 40 per cent, which is based on *sales price* (£40 ÷ £100).

Second path to profit: Excess over break-even volume × contribution margin per unit

The second method of computing a company's profit starts with a particular sales volume as the point of reference. So, the first step is to compute this specific sales volume of the business (which is not its actual sales volume for the year) by dividing its total annual fixed expenses by its contribution margin per unit. Interest expense is treated as a fixed expense (because for all practical purposes it is more or less fixed in amount over the short-run). For the business in the example, the interest expense is £750,000 (see Figure 9–2), which, added to the £13,090,000 fixed operating expenses, gives total fixed expenses of £13,840,000. The company's *break-even point*, also called its *break-even sales volume*, is computed as follows:

> £13,840,000 total annual fixed expenses for year ÷ £32 contribution margin per unit = 432,500 units break-even point (or, break-even sales volume) for the year

In other words, if you multiply £32 contribution margin per unit by 432,500 units you get a total contribution margin of £13,840,000, which exactly equals the company's total fixed expenses for the year. The business actually sold more than this number of units during the year but, if it had sold only 432,500 units, the company's profit would have been exactly zero. Below this sales level the business suffers a loss, and above this sales level the business makes profit. The break-even sales volume is the crossover point from the loss column to the profit column. Of course, a business's goal is to do better than just reaching its break-even sales volume.

Calculating its break-even point calls attention to the amount of fixed expenses hanging over a business. As explained earlier, a business is committed to its fixed expenses over the short run and cannot do much to avoid these costs – short of breaking some of its contracts and taking actions to downsize the business that could have disastrous long-run effects. Sometimes the total fixed expenses for the year are referred to as the 'nut' of the business – which may be a hard nut to crack (by exceeding its break-even sales volume).

In the example (see Figure 9–2) the business actually sold 520,000 units during the year, which is 87,500 units more than its break-even sales volume (520,000 units sold minus its 432,500 break-even sales volume). Therefore, you can determine the company's earnings before tax as follows:

Second Way of Computing Profit

Contribution margin per unit	£32
× Units sold in excess of break-even point	87,500
Equals: Earnings before tax	£2,800,000

This second way of analysing profit calls attention to the need of the business to achieve and exceed its break-even point to make profit. The business makes no profit until it clears its break-even hurdle, but once over this level of sales it makes profit hand over fist because the units sold from here on are not burdened with any fixed costs, which have been covered by the first 432,500 units sold during the year. Be careful in thinking that only the last 87,500 units sold during the year generate all the profit for the year. The first 432,500 units sold are necessary to get the business into position in order for the next 87,500 units to make profit.

The key point is that once the business has reached its break-even sales volume (thereby covering its annual fixed expenses), each additional unit sold brings in pre-tax profit equal to the contribution margin per unit. Each additional unit sold brings in 'pure profit' of £32 per unit, which is the company's contribution margin per unit. A business has to get into this upper region of sales volume to make a profit for the year.

Calculating the margin of safety

The *margin of safety* is the excess of its actual sales volume over a company's break-even sales volume. This business sold 520,000 units, which is 87,500 units above its break-even sales volume – a rather large cushion against any downturn in sales. Only a major sales collapse would cause the business to fall all the way down to its break-even point, assuming that it can maintain its £32 contribution margin per unit and that its fixed costs don't change. You may wonder what a 'normal' margin of safety is for most businesses. Sorry, we can't give you a definitive answer on this. Due to the nature of the business or industry-wide problems, or due to conditions beyond its control, a business may have to operate with a smaller margin of safety than it would like.

Doing What-If Analysis

Managing profit is like driving a car – you need to be glancing in the rear-view mirror constantly as well as looking ahead through the windscreen. You have to know your profit history to see your profit future. Understanding the past is the best preparation for the future.

The model of a *management profit and loss account* shown in Figure 9-2 allows you to compare your actual profit with what it would've looked like if you'd done something differently – for example, raised prices and sold fewer units. With the profit model, you can test-drive adjustments before putting them into effect. It lets you plan and map out your profit strategy for the *coming* period. Also, you can analyse why profit went up or down from the *last* period, using the model to do hindsight analysis.

The management profit and loss account profit model focuses on the key factors and variables that drive profit. Here's what you should know about these factors:

- Even a small decrease in the contribution margin per unit can have a drastic impact on profit because fixed expenses don't go down over the short run (and may be hard to reduce even over the long run).

- Even a small increase in the contribution margin per unit can have a dramatic impact on profit because fixed expenses won't go up over the short run – although they may have to be increased in the long run.

- Compared with changes in contribution margin per unit, sales volume changes have secondary profit impact; sales volume changes are not trivial, but even relatively small margin changes can have a bigger effect on profit.

- You can, perhaps, reduce fixed expenses to improve profit, but you have to be very careful to cut fat and not muscle; reducing fixed expenses may very well diminish the capacity of your business to make sales and deliver a high-quality service to customers.

The following sections expand on these key points.

Lower profit from lower sales – but that much lower?

The management profit and loss account shown in Figure 9-2 is designed for managers to use in profit analysis – to expose the critical factors that drive profit. Remember what information has been added that isn't included in the external profit and loss account:

- **Unit sales volume** for the year
- **Per-unit values**
- **Fixed versus variable** operating expenses
- **Contribution margin** – total and per unit

Handle this information with care. The contribution margin per unit is confidential, for your eyes only. This information is limited to you and other managers in the business. Clearly, you don't want your competitors to find out your margins. Even within a business, the information may not circulate to all managers – just those who need to know.

The contribution margin per unit is one of the three most important determinants of profit performance, along with sales volume and fixed expenses – as shown in the upcoming sections.

With the information provided in the management profit and loss account, you're ready to paint a what-if scenario. We're making you the chief executive officer of the business in this example. What if you had sold 5 per cent fewer units during this period? In this example, that would mean you had sold only 494,000 units rather than 520,000 units, or 26,000 units less. The following computation shows you how much profit damage this seemingly modest drop in sales volume would've caused.

Impact of 5% Lower Sales Volume on Profit

Contribution margin per unit	£32
× 26,000 fewer units sold	26,000
Equals: Decrease in earnings before tax	£832,000

By selling 26,000 fewer units you missed out on the £832,000 profit that these units would have produced – this is fairly straightforward. What is not so obvious, however, is that this £832,000 decrease in profit would have been a 30 per cent drop in profit: £832,000 decrease ÷ £2,800,000 profit = 30 per cent decrease. Lose just 5 per cent of your sales and lose 30 per cent of your profit? How can such a thing happen? The next section expands on how a seemingly small decrease in sales volume can cause a stunning decrease in profit. Read on.

Violent profit swings due to operating leverage

First, the bare facts for the business in the example: The company's contribution margin per unit is £32 and, before making any changes, the company sold 520,000 units during the year, which is 87,500 units in excess of its break-even sales volume. The company earned a total contribution margin of £16,640,000 (see Figure 9-2), which is its contribution per unit times its total units sold during the year. If the company had sold 5 per cent less during the year (26,000 fewer units), you'd expect its total contribution margin to decrease 5 per cent, and you'd be absolutely correct – £832,000 decrease ÷ £16,640,000 = 5 per cent decrease. Compared with its £2,800,000 profit before tax, however, the £832,000 drop in total contribution margin equals a *30 per cent* fall-off in profit.

The main focus of business managers and investors is on profit, which in this example is profit before tax. Therefore, the 30 per cent drop in profit would get more attention than the 5 per cent drop in total contribution margin. The much larger percentage change in profit caused by a relatively small change in sales volume is the effect of *operating leverage*. Leverage means that there is a multiplier effect – that a relatively small percentage change in one factor can cause a much larger change in another factor. A small push can cause a large movement – this is the idea of leverage.

In the above scenario for the 5 per cent, 26,000 units decrease in sales volume, note that the 5 per cent is based on the total 520,000 units sales volume of the business. But, if the 26,000 units decrease in sales volume is divided by the 87,500 units in excess of the company's break-even point – which are the units that generate profit for the business – the sales volume decrease equals 30 per cent. In other words, the business lost 30 per cent of its profit layer of sales volume and, thus, the company's profit would have dropped 30 per cent. This dramatic drop is caused by the operating leverage effect.

Note: If the company had sold 5 per cent *more* units, with no increase in its fixed expenses, its pre-tax profit would have *increased* by 30 per cent, reflecting the operating leverage effect. The 26,000 additional units sold at a £32 contribution margin per unit would increase its total contribution margin by £832,000 and this increase would increase profit by 30 per cent. You can see why businesses are always trying to increase sales volume.

Cutting sales price, even a little, can gut profit

So, what effect would a 5 per cent decrease in the sales price have caused? Around a 30 per cent drop similar to the effect of a 5 per cent decrease in sales volume? Not quite. Check out the following computation for this 5 per cent sales price decrease scenario:

Impact of 5% Lower Sales Price on Profit	
Contribution margin per unit decrease	£4.60
× Units sold during year	520,000
Equals: Decrease in earnings before tax	£2,392,000

Hold on! Earnings before tax would drop from £2,800,000 at the £100 sales price (refer to Figure 9–2) to only £408,000 at the £95 sales price – a plunge of 85 per cent. What could cause such a drastic dive in profit?

The sales price drops £5 per unit – a 5 per cent decrease of the £100 sales price. But, contribution margin per unit does not drop by the entire £5 because the variable operating expense per unit (sales commissions in this example) would also drop 5 per cent, or £40 per unit – for a net decrease of £4.60 per unit in the contribution margin per unit. (This is one reason for identifying the expenses that depend on sales revenue – as shown in the management profit and loss account in Figure 9-2.) For this what-if scenario that examines the case of the company selling all units at a 5 per cent lower sales price than it did, the company's contribution margin would have been only £27.40 per unit. Such a serious reduction in its contribution margin per unit would have been intolerable.

At the lower sales price, the company's contribution margin would be £27.40 per unit (£32.00 in the original example minus the £4.60 decrease = £27.40). As a result, the break-even sales volume would be much higher, and the company's 520,000 sales volume for the year would have been only 14,891 units over its break-even point. So, the lower £27.40 contribution margin per unit would yield only £408,000 profit before tax.

The moral of the story is to protect contribution margin per unit above all else. Every pound of contribution margin per unit that's lost – due to decreased sales prices, increased product cost or increases in other variable costs – has a tremendously negative impact on profit. Conversely, if you can increase the contribution margin per unit without hurting sales volume, you reap very large profit benefits, as described next.

Improving profit

The preceding sections explore the downside of things – that is, what would've happened to profit if sales volume or sales prices had been lower. The upside – higher profit – is so much more pleasant to discuss and analyse, don't you think?

Profit improvement boils down to the three critical profit-making factors, listed in order from the most effective to the least effective:

- ✔ Increasing the contribution margin per unit
- ✔ Increasing sales volume
- ✔ Reducing fixed expenses

Say you want to improve your bottom-line profit from the £1,900,000 net income you earned the year just ended to £2,110,000 next year. How can you pump up your net income by £210,000? (By the way, this is the only place in the chapter we bring the tax factor into the analysis.)

First of all, realise that to increase your net income *after taxes* by £210,000, you need to increase your before-tax profit by much more – to provide for the amount that goes to tax. Your accountant calculates that you would need a £312,000 increase in earnings before tax next year because your tax increase would be about £102,000 on the £312,000 increase in pre-tax earnings. So, you have to find a way to increase earnings, before tax, by £312,000.

You should also take into account the possibility that fixed costs and interest expense may rise next year, but for this example we're assuming that they won't. We're also assuming that the business can't cut any of its fixed operating expenses without hurting its ability to maintain and support its present sales level (and a modest increase in the sales level). Of course, in real life, every business should carefully scrutinise its fixed expenses to see if some of them can be cut.

- ✔ Increase your contribution margin per unit by £0.60, which would raise the total contribution margin by £312,000, based on a 520,000 units sales volume (£0.60 × 520,000 = £312,000).

- ✔ Sell 9,750 additional units at the current contribution margin per unit of £32, which would raise the total contribution margin by £312,000 (9,750 × £32 = £312,000).

- ✔ Use a combination of these two approaches: Increase both the margin per unit and the sales volume.

The second approach is obvious – you just need to set a sales goal of increasing the number of products sold by 9,750 units. (How you motivate your already overworked sales staff to accomplish that sales volume goal is up to you.) But how do you go about the first approach, increasing the contribution margin per unit by £0.60?

The simplest way to increase contribution margin per unit by £0.60 would be to decrease your product cost per unit by £0.60. Or you could attempt to reduce sales commissions from £8 per £100 of sales to £7.40 per £100 – which may adversely affect the motivation of your sales force, of course. Or you could raise the sales price about £0.65 (remember that 8 per cent comes off the top for the sales commission, so only £0.60 would remain from that £0.65 to improve the unit contribution margin). Or you could combine two or more such changes so that your unit contribution next year would increase £0.60. However you do it, the improvement would increase your earnings before tax the desired amount:

Impact of $0.60 Higher Unit Contribution Margin on Profit

Contribution margin per unit increase	$0.60
× Units sold during year	520,000
Equals: Increase in earnings before tax	$312,000

Cutting prices to increase sales volume: A very tricky game to play!

A word of warning: Be sure to *run the numbers* (accountant speak for using a profit model) before deciding to drop sales prices in an effort to gain more sales volume. Suppose, for example, you're convinced that if you decrease sales prices by 5 per cent your sales volume will increase by 10 per cent. Seems like an attractive trade-off, one that would increase both profit performance and market share. But are you sure that those positive changes are the results you'll get?

The impact on profit may surprise you. Get a piece of notepaper and do the computation for this lower sales price and higher sales volume scenario:

Lower Sales Price and Higher Sales Volume Impact on Profit

New sales price (lower)	$95.00
Less: Product cost per unit (same)	$60.00
Less: Variable operating expenses (lower)	$7.60
Equals: New unit contribution margin (lower)	$27.40
× Sales volume (higher)	572,000
Equals: Total contribution margin	$15,672,800
Less: Previous total contribution margin	$16,640,000
Equals: Decrease in total contribution margin	$967,200

Your total contribution margin would not go up; instead, it would go down $967,200! In dropping the sales price by $5, you would give up too much of your contribution margin per unit. The increase in sales volume would not make up for the big dent in unit contribution margin. You may gain more market share, but would pay for it with a $967,200 drop in earnings before tax.

To keep profit the same, you would have to increase sales volume more than 10 per cent. By how much? Divide the total contribution margin for the 520,000 units situation by the contribution margin per unit for the new scenario:

£16,640,000 ÷ £27.40 = 607,300 units

In other words, just to keep your total contribution margin the same at the lower sales price, you would have to increase sales volume to 607,300 units – an increase of 87,300 units, or a whopping 17 per cent. That would be quite a challenge, to say the least.

Cash flow from improving profit margin versus improving sales volume

This chapter discusses increasing profit margin versus increasing sales volume to improve bottom-line profit. Improving your profit margin is the better way to go, compared with increasing sales volume. Both actions increase profit, but the profit margin tactic is much better in terms of cash flow. When sales volume increases, so does stock. On the other hand, when you improve profit margin (by raising the sales price or by lowering product cost), you don't have to increase stock – in fact, reducing product cost may actually cause stock to decrease a little. In short, increasing your profit margin yields a higher cash flow from profit than does increasing your sales volume.

The SCORE website offers a downloadable Excel spreadsheet that enables you to do as many 'what if' calculations as you like (go to www.score. org, register and click on Templates and Tools). You can push your selling price up and down, add in and strip out costs, and see what your break-even point will be. By adding in your target profit as a 'fixed cost' at the last line where you're asked for the 'Owner's Draw' (in other words, what money the shareholder(s) expects), you can work out break-even volumes to meet those profit goals. You can shortcut the route to this spreadsheet by going on Microsoft's template site (http://office.microsoft.com/en-us/templates/break-even-analysis-TC001017515.aspx).

A Final Word or Two

Recently, some friends pooled their capital and opened an up-market off-licence in a rapidly growing area. The business has a lot of promise. We can tell you one thing they should have done before going ahead with this new venture – in addition to location analysis and competition analysis, of course. They should have used the basic profit model (in other words, the management profit and loss account) discussed in this chapter to figure out their break-even sales volume – because we're sure they have rather large fixed expenses. And they should have determined how much more sales revenue over their break-even point that they will need to earn a satisfactory return on their investment in the business.

During their open house for the new shop we noticed the very large number of different beers, wines and spirits available for sale – to say nothing of the different sizes and types of containers many products come in. Quite literally, the business sells thousands of distinct products. The shop also sells many products like soft drinks, ice, corkscrews and so on. Therefore, the company does not have a single sales volume factor (meaning the number of units sold) to work with in the basic profit model. So, you have to adapt the profit model to get along without the sales volume factor.

The trick is to determine your *average contribution margin as a percentage of sales revenue*. We'd estimate that an off-licence's average gross margin (sales revenue less cost of goods sold) is about 25 per cent. The other variable operating expenses of the shop probably run about 5 per cent of sales. So, the average contribution margin would be 20 per cent of sales (25 per cent gross margin less 5 per cent variable operating expenses). Suppose the total fixed operating expenses of the shop are about £100,000 per month (for rent, salaries, electricity and so on), which is £1.2 million per year. So, the shop needs £6 million in sales per year just to break even:

> £1.2 million fixed expenses ÷ 20% average contribution margin = £6 million annual sales to break even

Selling £6 million of product a year means moving a lot of booze. The business needs to sell another £1 million to provide £200,000 of operating earnings (at the 20 per cent average contribution margin) – to pay interest expense, tax and to leave enough net income for the owners who invested capital in the business and who expect a good return on their investment.

By the way, some disreputable off-licence owners are known (especially to HM Revenue and Customs) to engage in *sales skimming*. This term refers to not recording all sales revenue; instead, some cash collected from customers is put in the pockets of the owners. They don't report the profit in their tax returns or in the profit and loss accounts of the business. Our friends who started the off-licence are honest business people, and we're sure they won't engage in sales skimming – but they do have to make sure that none of their store's employees skim off some sales revenue.

When sales skimming is being committed, not all of the actual sales revenue for the year is recorded, even though the total cost of all products sold during the year is recorded. Obviously, this distorts the profit and loss account and throws off normal ratios of gross profit and operating profit to sales revenue. If you have the opportunity to buy a business, please be alert to the possibility that some sales skimming may have been done by the present owner. Indeed, we've been involved in situations in which the person selling the business bragged about how much he was skimming off the top.

Chapter 10

Business Budgeting

A business can't open its doors each day without having some idea of what to expect. And it can't close its doors at the end of the day not knowing what happened. In the Boy Scouts, the motto is 'Be Prepared'. Likewise, a business should plan and be prepared for its future, and should control its actual performance to reach its financial goals. The only question is how.

Budgeting is one answer. Please be careful with this term. Budgeting does *not* refer to putting a financial straitjacket on a business. Instead, business budgeting refers to setting specific goals and having the detailed plans necessary to achieve the goals. Business budgeting is built on realistic forecasts for the coming period, and demands that managers develop a thorough understanding of the profit blueprint of the business as well as the financial effects of the business's profit-making activities. A business budget is an integrated plan of action – not simply a few trend lines on a financial chart. Business managers have two broad options – they can wait for results to be reported to them on a 'look back' basis, or they can look ahead and plan what profit and cash flow should be, and then compare actual results against the plan. Budgeting is the method used to enact this second option.

The financial statements included in the annual financial report of a business are prepared *after the fact*; that is, the statements are based on actual transactions that have already taken place. Budgeted financial statements, on the other hand, are prepared *before the fact*, and are based on future transactions that you expect to take place based on the business's profit and financial strategy and goals. These forward-looking financial statements are referred to as *pro forma*, which is Latin for 'provided in advance'. ***Note:*** Budgeted financial statements are not reported outside the business; they are strictly for internal management use.

You can see a business's budget most easily in its set of *budgeted financial statements* – its budgeted profit and loss account, balance sheet and cash flow statement. Preparing these three budgeted financial statements requires a lot of time and effort; managers do detailed analysis to determine how to improve the financial performance of the business. The vigilance required in budgeting helps to maintain and improve profit performance and to plan cash flow.

Budgeting is much more than slap-dashing together a few figures. A budget is an integrated financial plan put down on paper, or these days we should say entered in computer spreadsheets. Planning is the key characteristic of budgeting. The budgeted financial statements encapsulate the financial plan of the business for the coming year.

The Reasons for Budgeting

Managers don't just look out the window and come up with budget numbers. Budgeting is not pie-in-the-sky wishful thinking. Business budgeting – to have real value – must start with a critical analysis of the most recent actual performance and position of the business by the managers who are responsible for the results. Then the managers decide on specific and concrete goals for the coming year. Budgets can be done for more than one year, but the key stepping-stone into the future is the budget for the coming year – see the sidebar 'Taking it one game at a time'.

In short, budgeting demands a fair amount of management time and energy. Budgets have to be worth this time and effort. So why should a business go to the trouble of budgeting? Business managers do budgeting and prepare budgeted financial statements for three quite different reasons – distinguishing them from each other is useful.

The modelling reasons for budgeting

To construct budgeted financial statements, you need good models of the profit, cash flow and financial condition of your business. Models are blueprints, or schematics of how things work. A business budget is, at its core, a financial blueprint of the business.

Taking it one game at a time

A company generally prepares one-year budgets, although many businesses also develop budgets for two, three and five years. However, reaching out beyond a year becomes quite tentative and very iffy. Making forecasts and estimates for the next 12 months is tough enough. A one-year budget is much more definite and detailed in comparison to longer-term budgets.

As they say in the sports world, a business should take it one game (or year) at a time.

Looking down the road beyond one year is a good idea, to set long-term goals and to develop long-term strategy. But long-term planning is different than long-term budgeting.

Note: Don't be intimidated by the term model. It simply refers to an explicit, condensed description of how profit, cash flow, and assets and liabilities behave. For example, Chapter 9 presents a model of a management profit and loss account. A model is analytical, but not all models are mathematical. In fact, none of the financial models in this book is the least bit mathematical – but you do have to look at each factor of the model and how it interacts with one or more other factors. The simple accounting equation, assets = liabilities + owners' equity, is a model of the balance sheet, for example. And, as Chapter 9 explains, profit = contribution margin per unit × units sold in excess of the break-even point.

Budgeting relies on financial models, or blueprints, that serve as the foundation for each budgeted financial statement. These blueprints are briefly explained, as follows:

- **Budgeted management profit and loss account:** Chapter 9 presents a design for the internal profit and loss account that provides the basic information that managers need for making decisions and exercising control. This internal (for managers only) profit report contains information that is not divulged outside the business. The management profit and loss account shown in Figure 9-2 serves as a hands-on profit model – one that highlights the critical variables that drive profit. This management profit and loss account separates variable and fixed expenses and includes sales volume, contribution margin per unit, as well as other factors that determine profit performance. The management profit and loss account is like a schematic that shows the path to the bottom line. It reveals the factors that must be improved in order to improve profit performance in the coming period.

- **Budgeted balance sheet:** The key connections and ratios between sales revenue and expenses and their related assets and liabilities are the elements of the basic model for the budgeted balance sheet. These vital connections are explained throughout Chapters 5 and 6; Chapter 8 (specifically Figure 8–1) also presents an overview of these connections.

✔ **Budgeted cash flow statement:** The changes in assets and liabilities from their balances at the end of the year just concluded and the balances at the end of the coming year determine cash flow from profit for the coming year. These changes constitute the basic model of cash flow from profit, which Chapter 7 explains (see Figure 7-3 in particular). The other sources and uses of cash depend on managers' strategic decisions regarding capital expenditures that will be made during the coming year, and how much new capital will be raised by increased debt and from owners' additional investment of capital in the business.

In short, budgeting requires good working models of profit performance, financial condition (assets and liabilities), and cash flow from profit. Constructing good budgets is a strong incentive for businesses to develop financial models that not only help in the budgeting process but also help managers make day-to-day decisions.

Planning reasons for budgeting

One main purpose of budgeting is to develop a definite and detailed financial plan for the coming period. To do budgeting, managers have to establish explicit financial objectives for the coming year and identify exactly what has to be done to accomplish these financial objectives. Budgeted financial statements and their supporting schedules provide clear destination points – the financial flight plan for a business.

The process of putting together a budget directs attention to the specific things that you must do to achieve your profit objectives and to optimise your assets and capital requirements. Basically, budgets are a form of planning, and planning pushes managers to answer the question 'How are we going to get there from here?'

Budgeting also has other planning-related benefits:

✔ **Budgeting encourages a business to articulate its vision, strategy and goals.** A business needs a clearly-stated strategy guided by an overarching vision, and should have definite and explicit goals. It is not enough for business managers to have strategy and goals in their heads – and nowhere else. Developing budgeted financial statements forces managers to be explicit and definite about the objectives of the business, and to formulate realistic plans for achieving the business objectives.

✔ **Budgeting imposes discipline and deadlines on the planning process.** Many busy managers have trouble finding enough time for lunch, let alone planning for the upcoming financial period. Budgeting pushes managers to set aside time to prepare a detailed plan that serves as a road map for the business. Good planning results in a concrete course of action that details how a company plans to achieve its financial objectives.

Management control reasons for budgeting

Budgets can be and usually are used as a means of *management control*, which involves comparing budgets against actual performance and holding individual managers responsible for keeping the business on schedule in reaching its financial objectives. The board of directors of a corporation focus their attention on the master budget for the whole business: the budgeted management profit and loss account, the budgeted balance sheet and the budgeted cash flow statement for the coming year.

The chief executive officer and the chairman of the business focus on the master budget. They also look at how each manager in the organisation is doing on his or her part of the master budget. As you move down the organisation chart of a business, managers have narrower responsibilities – say, for the business's north-eastern territory or for one major product line – therefore, the master budget is broken down into parts that follow the business's organisational structure. In other words, the master budget is put together from many pieces, one for each separate organisational unit of the business. So, for example, the manager of one of the company's far-flung warehouses has a separate budget for expenses and stock levels for his or her area.

By using budget targets as benchmarks against which actual performance is compared, managers can closely monitor progress toward (or deviations from) the budget goals and timetable. You use a budget plan like a navigation chart to keep your business on course. Significant variations from budget raise red flags, in which case you can determine that performance is off course or that the budget needs to be revised because of unexpected developments.

For management control, the annual budgeted management profit and loss account is divided into months or quarters. The budgeted balance sheet and budgeted cash flow statement are also put on a monthly or quarterly basis. The business should not wait too long to compare budgeted sales revenue and expenses against actual performance (or to compare actual cash flows and asset levels against the budget timetable). You need to take prompt action when problems arise, such as a divergence between budgeted expenses and actual expenses. Profit is the main thing to pay attention to, but debtors and stock can get out of control (become too high relative to actual sales revenue and cost of goods sold expense), causing cash flow problems. (Chapter 7 explains how increases in debtors and stock are negative factors on cash flow from profit.) A business cannot afford to ignore its balance sheet and cash flow numbers until the end of the year.

Other benefits of budgeting

Budgeting has advantages and ramifications that go beyond the financial dimension and have more to do with business management in general. These points are briefly discussed as follows:

- **Budgeting forces managers to do better forecasting.** Managers should constantly scan the business environment to identify sea changes that can impact the business. Vague generalisations about what the future might hold for the business are not quite good enough for assembling a budget. Managers are forced to put their predictions into definite and concrete forecasts.

- **Budgeting motivates managers and employees by providing useful yardsticks for evaluating performance and for setting managers' compensation when goals are achieved.** The budgeting process can have a good motivational impact on employees and managers by involving managers in the budgeting process (especially in setting goals and objectives) and by providing incentives to managers to strive for and achieve the business's goals and objectives. Budgets can be used to reward good results. Budgets provide useful information for superiors to evaluate the performance of managers. Budgets supply baseline financial information for incentive compensation plans. The profit plan (budget) for the year can be used to award year-end bonuses according to whether designated goals are achieved.

- **Budgeting is essential in writing a business plan.** New and emerging businesses must present a convincing *business plan* when raising capital. Because these businesses may have little or no history, the managers and owners of a small business must demonstrate convincingly that the company has a clear strategy and a realistic plan to make money. A coherent, realistic budget forecast is an essential component of a business plan. Venture capital sources definitely want to see the budgeted financial statements of the business.

In larger businesses, budgets are typically used to hold managers accountable for their areas of responsibility in the organisation; actual results are compared against budgeted goals and timetables, and variances are highlighted. Managers don't mind taking credit for *favourable* variances, or when actual comes in better than budget. Beating the budget for the period, after all, calls attention to outstanding performance. But *unfavourable* variances are a different matter. If the manager's budgeted goals and targets are fair and reasonable, the manager should carefully analyse what went wrong and what needs to be improved. But if the manager perceives the budgeted goals and targets to be arbitrarily imposed by superiors and not realistic, serious motivational problems can arise.

In reviewing the performance of their subordinates, managers should handle unfavourable variances very carefully. Stern action may be called for, but managers should recognise that the budget benchmarks may not be entirely fair, and should make allowances for unexpected developments that occur after the budget goals and targets are established.

Budgeting and Management Accounting

What we say earlier in the chapter can be likened to an advertisement for budgeting – emphasising the reasons for and advantages of budgeting by a business. So every business does budgeting, right? Nope. Smaller businesses generally do little or no budgeting – even many larger businesses avoid budgeting. The reasons are many, and mostly practical in nature.

Some businesses are in relatively mature stages of their life cycle or operate in an industry that is mature and stable. These companies do not have to plan for any major changes or discontinuities. Next year will be a great deal like last year. The benefits of going through a formal budgeting process do not seem worth the time and cost to them. At the other extreme, a business may be in a very uncertain environment; attempting to predict the future seems pointless. A business may lack the expertise and experience to prepare budgeted financial statements, and it may not be willing to pay the cost for an accountant or outside consultant to help.

In applying for a loan, the lender may be impressed that your business plan includes a well-thought-out budget. I (John) served on a local bank's board of directors for several years, and I reviewed many loan requests. Our bank did not expect a business to include a set of budgeted financial statements in the loan request package. Of course, we did demand to see the latest financial statements of the business. Very few of our smaller business clients prepared budgets. Although many businesses do not prepare budgets, they do establish detailed goals and performance objectives that serve as good benchmarks for management control.

Every business – whether it does budgeting or not – should design internal accounting reports that provide the information managers need to control the business. Obviously, managers should keep close tabs on what's going on throughout the business. Some years ago, in one of my classes, I (Colin) asked students for a short definition of management control. One student answered that management control means 'watching everything'. That's not bad.

A business may not do any budgeting, and thus it does not prepare budgeted financial statements. But its managers should receive regular profit and loss accounts, balance sheets and cash flow statements – and these key internal financial statements should contain detailed management control information. Other specialised accounting reports may be needed as well.

Most business managers, in our experience, would tell you that the accounting reports they get are reasonably good for management control. Their accounting reports provide the detailed information they need for keeping a close watch on the thousand and one details about the business (or their particular sphere of responsibility in the business organisation). Their main criticisms are that too much information is reported to them and all the information is flat, as if all the information is equally relevant. Managers are very busy people, and have only so much time to read the accounting reports coming to them. Managers have a valid beef on this score, we think. Ideally, significant deviations and problems should be highlighted in the accounting reports they receive – but separating the important from the not-so-important is easier said than done.

If you were to ask a cross section of business managers how useful their accounting reports are for making decisions, you would get a different answer than how good the accounting reports are for management control. Business managers make many decisions affecting profit: setting sales prices, buying products, determining wages and salaries, hiring independent contractors and purchasing fixed assets are just a few that come to mind. Managers should carefully analyse how their actions would impact profit before reaching final decisions. Managers need internal profit and loss accounts that are good profit models – that make clear the critical variables that affect profit (see Figure 9-2 for an example). Well-designed management profit and loss accounts are absolutely essential for helping managers make good decisions.

Keep in mind that almost all business decisions involve non-financial and non-quantifiable factors that go beyond the information included in management accounting reports. For example, the accounting department of a business can calculate the cost savings of a wage cut, or the elimination of overtime hours by employees, or a change in the retirement plan for employees – and the manager would certainly look at this data. But such decisions must consider many other factors such as effects on employee morale and productivity, the possibility of the union going out on strike, legal issues and so on. In short, accounting reports provide only part of the information needed for business decisions, though an essential part for sure.

Needless to say, the internal accounting reports to managers should be clear and straightforward. The manner of presentation and means of communication should be attention getting. A manager should not have to call the accounting department for an explanation. Designing management accounting reports is a separate topic – one beyond the limits of this book.

In the absence of budgeting by a business, the internal accounting reports to its managers become the major – often the only – regular source of financial information to them. Without budgeting, the internal accounting reports have to serve a dual function – both for control and for planning. The managers use the accounting reports to critically review what's happened (control), and use the information in the reports to make decisions for the future (planning).

Before leaving the topic, we have one final observation to share with you. Many management accounting reports that we've seen could be improved. Accounting systems, unfortunately, give so much attention to the demands of preparing external financial statements and tax returns that the needs managers have for good internal reports are too often overlooked or ignored. The accounting reports in many businesses do not speak to the managers receiving them – the reports are too voluminous and technical, and are not focused on the most urgent and important problems facing the managers. Designing good internal accounting reports for managers is a demanding task, to be sure. Every business should take a hard look at its internal management accounting reports and identify what needs to be improved.

Budgeting in Action

Suppose you're the general manager of one of a large company's several divisions. You have broad authority to run this division, as well as the responsibility for meeting the financial expectations for your division. To be more specific, your profit responsibility is to produce a satisfactory annual operating profit, or earnings before interest and tax (EBIT). (Interest and tax expenses are handled at a higher level in the organisation.)

The CEO has made clear to you that she expects your division to increase EBIT during the coming year by about 10 per cent ($256,000, to be exact). In fact, she has asked you to prepare a budgeted management profit and loss account showing your plan for increasing your division's EBIT by this target amount. She also has asked you to prepare a budgeted cash flow from profit based on your profit plan for the coming year.

Figure 10-1 presents the management profit and loss account of your division for the year just ended. The format of this accounting report follows the profit model discussed in Chapter 9, which explains profit behaviour and how to increase profit. Note that fixed operating expenses are separated from the two variable operating expenses. To simplify the discussion, we've significantly condensed your management profit and loss account. (Your actual reports would include much more detailed information about sales and expenses.) Also, we assume that you sell only one product to keep the number crunching to a minimum.

	Totals for Period	Per Unit
Unit Sales Volume =	26,000	
Sales Revenue	£ 26,000,000	£1,000.00
Cost of Goods Sold Expense	14,300,000	550.00
Gross Margin	£ 11,700,000	£450.00
Revenue-driven Operating Expenses	2,080,000	80.00
Volume-driven Operating Expenses	1,300,000	50.00
Contribution Margin	£ 8,320,000	£320.00
Fixed Operating Expenses	5,720,000	
Operating Profit	£ 2,600,000	

Figure 10-1: Management profit and loss account for year just ended.

Most businesses, or the major divisions of a large business, sell a mix of several different products. General Motors, for example, sells many different makes and models of cars and commercial vehicles, to say nothing about its other products. The next time you visit your local hardware store, look at the number of products on the shelves. The assortment of products sold by a business and the quantities sold of each that make up its total sales revenue is referred to as its *sales mix*. As a general rule, certain products have higher profit margins than others. Some products may have extremely low profit margins, which are called *loss leaders*. The marketing strategy for loss leaders is to use them as magnets to get customers to buy your higher profit margin products along with their purchase of the loss leaders. Shifting the sales mix to a higher proportion of higher profit margin products has the effect of increasing the average profit margin on all products sold. (A shift to lower profit margin products would have the opposite effect, of course.) Budgeting sales revenue and expenses for the coming year must include any planned shifts in the company's sales mix.

Developing your profit strategy and budgeted profit and loss account

Suppose that you and your managers, with the assistance of your accounting staff, have analysed your fixed operating expenses line by line for the coming year. Some of these fixed expenses will actually be reduced or eliminated next year. But the large majority of these costs will continue next year, and most are subject to inflation. Based on careful studies and estimates, you and your staff forecast that your total fixed operating expenses for next year will be £6,006,000 (including £835,000 depreciation expense, compared with the £780,000 depreciation expense for last year).

Thus, you will need to earn £8,862,000 total contribution margin next year:

£2,856,000	EBIT goal (£2,600,000 last year plus £256,000 budgeted increase)
+ 6,006,000	Budgeted fixed operating expenses next year
£8,862,000	Total contribution margin goal next year

This is your main profit budget goal for next year, assuming that fixed operating expenses are kept in line. Fortunately, your volume-driven variable operating expenses should not increase next year. These are mainly transportation costs, and the shipping industry is in a very competitive 'hold-the-price-down' mode of operations that should last through the coming year. The cost per unit shipped should not increase, but if you sell and ship more units next year, the expense will increase in proportion.

You have decided to hold the revenue-driven operating expenses at 8 per cent of sales revenue during the coming year, the same as for the year just ended. These are sales commissions, and you have already announced to your sales staff that their sales commission percentage will remain the same during the coming year. On the other hand, your purchasing manager has told you to plan on a 4 per cent product cost increase next year – from £550 per unit to £572 per unit, or an increase of £22 per unit. Thus, your unit contribution margin would drop from £320 to £298 (if the other factors that determine margin remain the same).

One way to attempt to achieve your total contribution margin objective next year is to load all the needed increase on sales volume and keep sales price the same. (We're not suggesting that this strategy is a good one, but it's a good point of departure.) At the lower unit contribution margin, your sales volume next year would have to be 29,738 units:

£8,862,000 total contribution margin goal ÷ £298 contribution margin per unit = 29,738 units sales volume

Compared with last year's 26,000 units sales volume, you would have to increase your sales by over 14 per cent. This may not be feasible.

After discussing this scenario with your sales manager, you conclude that sales volume cannot be increased 14 per cent. You'll have to raise the sales price to provide part of the needed increase in total contribution margin and to offset the increase in product cost. After much discussion, you and your sales manager decide to increase the sales price by 3 per cent. Based on the 3 per cent sales price increase and the 4 per cent product cost increase, your unit contribution margin next year is determined as follows:

Unit Contribution Margin Next Year	
Sales price	£1,030.00
Less: Product cost	572.00
Less: Revenue-driven operating expenses	82.40
Less: Volume-driven variable operating expenses	50.00
Equals: Contribution margin per unit	£325.60

At this £325.60 budgeted contribution margin per unit, you determine the total sales volume needed next year to reach your profit goal as follows:

> £8,862,000 total contribution margin goal next year ÷ £325.60 contribution margin per unit = 27,217 units sales volume

This sales volume is about 5 per cent higher than last year (1,217 additional units over the 26,000 sales volume last year = about 5 per cent increase).

If you don't raise the sales price, your division has to increase sales volume by 14 per cent (as calculated above). If you increase the sales price by just 3 per cent, the sales volume increase you need to achieve your profit goal next year is only 5 per cent. Does this make sense? Well, this is just one of many alternative strategies for next year. Perhaps you could increase sales price by 4 per cent. But, you know that most of your customers are sensitive to a sales price increase, and your competitors may not follow with their own sales price increase.

After lengthy consultation with your sales manager, you finally decide to go with the 3 per cent sales price increase combined with the 5 per cent sales volume growth as your official budget strategy. Accordingly, you forward your budgeted management profit and loss account to the CEO. Figure 10-2 summarises this profit budget for the coming year. This summary-level budgeted management profit and loss account is supplemented with appropriate schedules to provide additional detail about sales by types of customers and other relevant information. Also, your annual profit plan is broken down into quarters (perhaps months) to provide benchmarks for comparing actual performance during the year against your budgeted targets and timetable.

	Totals for Period	Per Unit
Unit Sales Volume =	27,217	
Sales Revenue	£ 28,033,968	£1,030.00
Cost of Goods Sold Expense	15,568,378	572.00
Gross Margin	£ 12,465,590	£458.00
Revenue-driven Operating Expenses	2,242,717	82.40
Volume-driven Operating Expenses	1,360,872	50.00
Contribution Margin	£ 8,862,000	£325.60
Fixed Operating Expenses	6,006,000	
Operating Profit	£ 2,856,000	

Figure 10-2: Budgeted profit and loss account for coming year.

Budgeting cash flow from profit for the coming year

The budgeted profit plan (refer to Figure 10-2) is the main focus of attention, but the CEO also requests that all divisions present a *budgeted cash flow from profit* for the coming year. **Remember:** The profit you're responsible for as general manager of the division is earnings before interest and tax (EBIT) – not net income after interest and tax.

Chapter 7 explains that increases in debtors, stock and prepaid expenses *hurt* cash flow from profit and that increases in creditors and accrued liabilities *help* cash flow from profit. You should compare your budgeted management profit and loss account for the coming year (Figure 10–2) with your actual statement for last year (Figure 10–1). This side-by-side comparison (not shown here) reveals that sales revenue and all expenses are higher next year.

Therefore, your short-term operating assets, as well as the liabilities that are driven by operating expenses, will increase at the higher sales revenue and expense levels next year – unless you can implement changes to prevent the increases.

For example, sales revenue increases from £26,000,000 last year to the budgeted £28,033,968 for next year – an increase of £2,033,968. Your debtors balance was five weeks of annual sales last year. Do you plan to tighten up the credit terms offered to customers next year – a year in which you will raise the sales price and also plan to increase sales volume? We doubt it. More likely, you will keep your debtors balance at five weeks of annual sales. Assume that you decide to offer your customers the same credit terms next year. Thus, the increase in sales revenue will cause debtors to increase by £195,574 (5⁄52 × £2,033,968 sales revenue increase).

Last year, stock was 13 weeks of annual cost of goods sold expense. You may be in the process of implementing stock reduction techniques. If you really expect to reduce the average time stock will be held in stock before being sold, you should inform your accounting staff so that they can include this key change in the balance sheet and cash flow models. Otherwise, they will assume that the past ratios for these vital connections will continue next year.

Figure 10-3 presents a summary of your budgeted cash flow from profit (the EBIT for your division) based on the information given for this example and using the ratios explained in Chapter 7 for short-term operating assets and liabilities. For example, debtors increases by £195,574, as just explained. And, stock increases by £317,095 (13⁄52 × £1,268,378 cost of goods sold expense increase). *Note:* Increases in accrued interest payable and income tax payable are not included in your budgeted cash flow. Your profit responsibility ends at the operating profit line, or earnings before interest and income tax expenses.

You submit this budgeted cash flow from profit statement (Figure 10–3) to top management. Top management expects you to control the increases in your short-term assets and liabilities so that the actual cash flow generated by your division next year comes in on target. The cash flow from profit of your division (minus the small amount needed to increase the working cash balance held by your division for operating purposes) will be transferred to the central treasury of the business.

Figure 10-3: Budgeted cash flow from profit statement for coming year.

Budgeted Operating Profit (See Figure 10-2)	£2,856,000
Accounts Receivable Increase	(195,574)
Inventory Increase	(317,095)
Prepaid Expenses Increase	(26,226)
Depreciation Expense	835,000
Accounts Payable Increase	34,968
Accrued Expenses Payable Increase	52,453
Budgeted Cash Flow From Operating Profit	£3,239,526

Business budgeting versus government budgeting: Only the name is the same

Business and government budgeting are more different than alike. Government budgeting is preoccupied with allocating scarce resources among many competing demands. From national agencies down to local education authorities, government entities have only so much revenue available. They have to make very difficult choices regarding how to spend their limited tax revenue.

Formal budgeting is legally required for almost all government entities. First, a budget request is submitted. After money is appropriated, the budget document becomes legally binding on the government agency. Government budgets are legal straitjackets; the government entity has to stay within the amounts appropriated for each expenditure category. Any changes from the established budgets need formal approval and are difficult to get through the system.

A business is not legally required to use budgeting. A business can use its budget as it pleases and can even abandon its budget in midstream. Unlike the government, the revenue of a business is not constrained; a business can do many things to increase sales revenue. In short, a business has much more flexibility in its budgeting. Both business and government should apply the general principle of cost/benefits analysis to make sure that they are getting the best value for money. But a business can pass its costs to its customers in the sales prices it charges. In contrast, government has to raise taxes to spend more.

Capital Budgeting

This chapter focuses on profit budgeting for the coming year, and budgeting the cash flow from that profit. These two are hardcore components of business budgeting – but not the whole story. Another key element of the budgeting process is to prepare a *capital expenditures budget* for top management review and approval. A business has to take a hard look at its long-term operating assets – in particular, the capacity, condition and efficiency of these resources – and decide whether it needs to expand and modernise its fixed assets. In most cases, a business would have to invest substantial sums of money in purchasing new fixed assets or retrofitting and upgrading its old fixed assets. These long-term investments require major cash outlays. So, a business (or each division of the business) prepares a formal list of the fixed assets to be purchased or upgraded. The money for these major outlays comes from the central treasury of the business. Accordingly, the capital expenditures budget goes to the highest levels in the organisation for review and final approval. The chief financial officer, the CEO and the board of directors of the business go over a capital expenditure budget request with a fine-tooth comb.

At the company-wide level, the financial officers merge the profit and cash flow budgets of all divisions. The budgets submitted by one or more of the divisions may be returned for revision before final approval is given. One main concern is whether the collective total of cash flow from all the units provides enough money for the capital expenditures that have to be made during the coming year for new fixed assets – and to meet the other demands for cash, such as for cash distributions from profit. The business may have to raise more capital from debt or equity sources during the coming year to close the gap between cash flow from profit and its needs for cash. The financial officers need to be sure that any proposed capital expenditures make good business sense. We look at this in the next three sections. If the expenditure is worthwhile, they may need to raise more money to pay for it. We cover that subject in Chapter 18.

Deducing payback

The simplest way to evaluate an investment is to calculate *payback* – how long it takes you to get your money back. Figure 10-4 shows an investment that calls for £20,000 cash up front in the expectation of getting £25,000 cash back over the next five years. The investment is forecasted to return a total of £20,000 by the end of year 4, so we say that this investment has a four-year payback.

	£
Initial cost of investment	20,000
Annual net cash inflows	
Year 1	1,000
Year 2	4,000
Year 3	8,000
Year 4	7,000
Year 5	5,000
Total cash in	25,000

Figure 10-4: Calculating payback.

When calculating the return on long-term investments, we use cash rather than profit. This is because we need to compare like with like: Investments are paid for in cash or by committing cash, so we need to calculate the return using cash, too.

Let's suppose that we have two competing projects from which we have to choose only one. Figure 10-5 sets out the maths. Both projects have a four-year payback, in that the outlay is recovered in that period; so this technique tells us that both projects are equally acceptable, as long as we are content to recover our outlay by year 4.

However, this is only part of the story. We can see at a glance that Project 2 produces £9,000 more cash over five years than Project 1 does. We also get a lot more cash back in the first two years with Project 2, which must be better – as well as safer for the investor. Payback fails to send those signals, but is still a popular tool because of its simplicity.

Figure 10-5:
Comparing
investments
using
payback.

	£ Project 1	£ Project 2
Initial cost of investment	20,000	20,000
Annual net cash inflows		
Year 1	1,000	3,000
Year 2	4,000	5,000
Year 3	8,000	8,000
Year 4	7,000	8,000
Year 5	5,000	10,000
Total cash in	25,000	34,000

Discounting cash flow

A pound today is more valuable than a pound in one, two or more years' time. For us to make sound investment decisions, we need to ask how much we would pay now to get a pound back at some date in the future. If we know we can earn 10 per cent interest from a bank, then we would only pay out 90p now to get that pound in one year's time. The 90p represents the *Net Present Value* (NPV) of that pound – the amount we would pay now to get the cash at some future date.

In effect what we're doing is discounting the future cash flow using a percentage that equates to the minimum return that we want to earn. The further out that return, the less we would pay now in order to get it.

The formula we use to discount the cash flow is:

$$\text{Present Value } (PV) = \pounds P \times 1/(1+r)^n$$

where £P is the initial investment, r is the interest expressed as a decimal, and n is the year when the cash will flow in. (For example, in year 1 $n =1$, in year 2 it will be 2 and so on). So if we require a 15 per cent return, we should only be prepared to pay £0.87 now to get £1 in one year's time, £0.76 for a pound in two years' time and just £0.50 now for a pound coming in five years' time.

Take a look at Figure 10-6. If we use a discount rate of 15 per cent (which is a very average return on capital for a business) the picture doesn't look so rosy. Far from paying back in four years and producing £25,000 cash for an outlay of £20,000, Project 1 is actually paying out less money (£15,642) in real terms, allowing for the time value of money, than we have paid out.

Figure 10-6:
Comparing cash with the Net Present Value of that cash at 15 per cent discount rate.

	Year 1	Year 2	Year 3	Year 4	Year 5	Total
Cash in	1,000	4,000	8,000	7,000	5,000	25,000
NPV of cash	870	3,025	5,260	4,002	2,486	15,642

Calculating the internal rate of return

Net Present Value is a powerful concept, though a slightly esoteric one. All we know so far about our attempt to evaluate Project 1 is that if we aim for a return of 15 per cent, our returns will be disappointing. So, we move on to the next stage in our quest for a sound way to appraise capital investment proposals – calculating exactly what the return on investment will be.

To arrive at this figure we need to calculate the actual return the project made on the discounted cash flow – the *Internal Rate of Return* (IRR). To do this, we need to find the value for 'r' in the Net Present Value formula (see the section 'Discounting cash flow') that ensures the present value of the future cash flow equals the cost of the investment. In the case of Project 1, the IRR is just short of 7 per cent. You would fare little worse by leaving the money on deposit in a bank, in this case.

The IRR is a number you can use to compare one project with another to assess quickly which is superior from a financial point of view. For example, Project 2 has an IRR of 17 per cent, which is clearly better than that of Project 1, a fact not revealed by using the payback method.

The Solutions Matrix website (www.solutionmatrix.com) has a very neat tool for working out payback, discounted cash flow, Internal Rate of Return and a whole lot more calculations relating to capital budgeting. You have to register on the site first before downloading their free capital budgeting spreadsheet suite and tutorial. Just go to the home page and click on 'Download Center' and 'Download Financial Metrics Lite for Microsoft Excel'.

Arriving at the cost of capital

No new capital investment would make much sense if it didn't at least cover the cost of the capital used to finance it. This cost is known in the trade as the *hurdle rate*, as that is the level of return any project has to beat. Say you've worked out the cost of equity (steam ahead to Chapter 11 if you're less than familiar with this term) as being 15 per cent. That should cover the dividends and the fairly high costs associated with raising the dosh. Next comes the cost of borrowed capital (and that of any other long-term source of finance such as hire purchase or mortgages). That figure is usually fairly self-evident as the lender will state this up front; however you may have to make a judgment call here if your loans have a *variable rate of interest*; that is, one that can go up and down with the general bank rate. Then you have to make an educated guess as to what that might be over the life of the loan.

Next you need to combine the cost of equity and debt capital into one overall cost of capital figure; in essence, your hurdle rate.

An average cost is required because you don't usually identify each individual project with one particular source of finance. Generally businesses take the view that all projects have been financed from a common pool of money except for the relatively rare case when project specific finance is raised.

 Assume your company intends to keep the gearing ratio of borrowed capital to equity in the proportion of 20:80. (Push ahead to chapter 14 if gearing is not a term in your Scrabble vocabulary). The cost of new capital from these sources has been assessed, say, at 10 per cent and 15 per cent respectively and corporation tax is 30 per cent. The calculation of the overall weighted average cost is as follows:

Type of capital	Proportion(a)	After-tax cost (b)	Weighted cost (a x b)
10% loan capital	0.20	7.0%	1.4%
Equity	0.80	15.0%	12.0%
			13.4%

The resulting weighted average cost of 13.4 per cent is the minimum rate that this company should accept on proposed investments. Any investment that isn't expected to achieve this return isn't a viable proposition.

Reporting On Variances

Any performance needs to be carefully monitored and compared against the budget as the year proceeds, and corrective action must be taken where necessary to keep the two consistent. This has to be done on a monthly basis (or using shorter time intervals if required), showing both the company's performance during the month in question and throughout the year so far.

Looking at Figure 10-7 you can see at a glance that the business is behind on sales for this month, but ahead on the yearly target. The convention is to put all unfavourable variations in brackets. Hence, a higher-than-budgeted sales figure doesn't have brackets, while a higher materials cost does. You can also see that, while profit is running ahead of budget, the profit margin is slightly behind (–0.30 per cent). This is partly because other direct costs, such as labour and distribution in this example, are running well ahead of budgeting variances.

Figure 10-7:
Fixed Budget – note figures rounded up and down to nearest thousand may affect percentages.

Heading	Month			Year to date		
	Budget	Actual	Variance	Budget	Actual	Variance
Sales	805*	753	(52)	6,358	7,314	956
Materials	627	567	60	4,942	5,704	(762)
Materials margin	178	186	8	1,416	1,610	194
Direct costs	74	79	(5)	595	689	(94)
Gross profit	104	107	3	820	921	101
Percentage	**12.92**	**14.21**	**1.29**	**12.90**	**12.60**	**(0.30)**

Flexing your budget

A budget is based on a particular set of sales goals, few of which are likely to be met exactly in practice. Figure 10-7 shows that the business has used £762,000 more materials than budgeted. As more has been sold, this is hardly surprising. The way to manage this situation is to flex the budget to show what would be expected to happen to expenses, given the sales that actually occurred. This is done by applying the budget ratios to the actual data. For example, materials were planned to be 22.11 per cent of sales in the budget. By applying that to the actual month's sales, you arrive at a materials cost of £587,000.

Looking at the flexed budget in Figure 10-8 you can see that the business has spent £19,000 more than expected on the material given the level of sales actually achieved, rather than the £762,000 overspend shown in the fixed budget. The same principle holds for other direct costs, which appear to be running £94,000 over budget for the year. When you take into account the extra sales shown in the flexed budget, you can see that the company has actually spent £4,000 over budget on direct costs. While this is serious, it isn't as serious as the fixed budget suggests. The flexed budget allows you to concentrate your efforts on dealing with true variances in performance.

Figure 10-8:
Flexed
Budget –
note figures
rounded up
and down
to nearest
thousand
may affect
percent-
ages.

Heading	Month			Year to date		
	Budget	**Actual**	**Variance**	**Budget**	**Actual**	**Variance**
Sales	753*	753	–	7,314	7,314	–
Materials	587	567	20	5,685	5,704	(19)
Materials margin	166	186	20	1,629	1,610	(19)
Direct costs	69	79	(10)	685	689	(4)
Gross profit	97	107	10	944	921	(23)
Percentage	**12.92**	**14.21**	**1.29**	**12.90**	**12.60**	**(0.30)**

Staying Flexible with Budgets

One thing never to lose sight of is that budgeting is a *means to an end*. It's a tool for doing something better than you could without the tool. Preparing budgeted financial statements is not the ultimate objective; a budget is not an end in itself. The budgeting process should provide definite benefits, and businesses should use their budgeted financial statements to measure progress toward their financial objectives – and not just file them away someplace.

Budgets are not the only tool for management control. Control means accomplishing your financial objectives. Many businesses do not use budgeting and do not prepare budgeted financial statements. But they do lay down goals and objectives for each period and compare actual performance against these targets. Doing at least this much is essential for all businesses.

Keep in mind that budgets are not the only means for controlling expenses. Actually, we shy away from the term *controlling* because we've found that, in the minds of most people, *controlling* expenses means minimising them. The *cost/benefits* idea captures the better view of expenses. Spending more on advertising, for example, may have a good payoff in the additional sales volume it produces. In other words, it's easy to cut advertising to zero if you really want to minimise this expense – but the impact on sales volume may be disastrous.

Business managers should eliminate any *excessive* amount of an expense – the amount that really doesn't yield a benefit or add value to the business. For example, it's possible for a business to spend too much on quality inspection by doing unnecessary or duplicate steps, or by spending too much time testing products that have a long history of good quality. But this doesn't mean that the business should eliminate the expense entirely. Expense control means trimming the cost down to the right size. In this sense, expense control is one of the hardest jobs that business managers do, second only to managing people, in our opinion.

Chapter 11

Choosing the Right Ownership Structure

....

In This Chapter

▶ Seeing profit as a small piece of the sales revenue pie

▶ Taking stock of the company as an important ownership structure

▶ Watching out for negative factors affecting share value

▶ Discerning profit allocation and liability issues

▶ Looking out for Number One in a sole proprietorship

▶ Deciding on the best ownership structure for tax purposes

....

*T*he obvious reason for investing in a business as an owner rather than a safer kind of investment is the potential for greater rewards. As one of the partners or shareholders of a business, you're entitled to part of the business's profit – and you're also subject to the risk that the business will go down the tubes, taking your money down with it. This chapter shows you how ownership structure affects your share of the profit – especially how changes beyond your control can make your share less valuable. It also explains how the ownership structure has a dramatic impact on the taxes paid by the business and its owners.

From the Top Line to the Bottom Line

Chapter 5 explains the business profit-making process and the accounting profit report for a period, which is called the *profit and loss account*. The chapter focuses on the financial effects on the various operating assets and operating liabilities of a business of its sales revenue and expense activities. To make sense of a company's *balance sheet* (its statement of financial condition at the end of the profit period), which is explained in Chapter 6, you need to understand how its sales revenue and expenses propel the company's operating assets and operating liabilities. And to round out the financial picture of a business, you need to look at its sources and uses of cash flows for the period, which are presented in its *cash flow statement* – see Chapter 7.

Whew! These three business financial statements present a lot of information. But, if you're a manager or owner of a business you should have a good grip on these three *accounting reports* (as they're sometimes called). Accounting is often called the language of business, and learning the basic vocabulary of accounting is extraordinarily helpful, if not downright essential, for business managers and owners.

There is one aspect of the business profit-making process that it is easy to lose sight of when reading a profit and loss account. How does a business get from the top line in its profit and loss account (sales revenue) down to its bottom line (net income)?

In our free enterprise, largely unregulated and non-government-controlled economy, business managers have the responsibility of negotiating the prices paid for labour, subject only to minimum wages legislation, and most of the other services, supplies and other factors used in the profit-making process. This book isn't the place to delve into the fields of labour economics and political economy. But we would point out that business profit and loss accounts are one key source of information for scholars who do research in these areas. In particular, the financial statements prepared by accountants report how sales revenue is divided among the different parties in a business's profit-making process.

A business collects money from its customers and then redistributes that sales revenue to the many parties clamouring for their fair share. You may think that the second part of this process would be the easy part, but business managers sometimes have a tough time deciding what constitutes a fair share for each claimant. For example, in deciding how much to pay employees in regular wages and fringe benefits, business managers have to ask what value each employee adds to the business, whether to raise sales prices in order to pay higher wages and so on.

The distribution of total sales revenue among the various claimants on the revenue is a *zero-sum game*. This means that if one party gets a bigger piece of the revenue pie then some other party gets a smaller piece, keeping the size of the pie (total sales revenue) the same. (The alternative is for the business to increase the size of its sales revenue pie – by raising its sales prices or selling more units.) If a business increases compensation to its employees, for instance, without changing the prices paid for all other services and supplies, then the shares of total sales revenue going to the Chancellor in tax and to the owners as after-tax net income decrease. (Note that a business may increase wages expecting that labour productivity gains will offset the wage gains.) Business managers must constantly calculate how changes in the prices they charge customers and changes in the prices they pay for labour, materials, products, utilities and many other expenses affect bottom-line profit.

Net income, or net profit as it is often referred to, is the bottom-line profit that the business earned this period (or, to be more precise, the period just concluded, which often is called 'this period' to mean the most recent period). This figure is the starting point for determining how much cash – if any – to distribute to the owners. Businesses are not legally required to distribute any of their profit for the period, but if they do distribute some or all of their profit, the amounts distributed to each owner depend on the business's ownership structure, as described in the following section, 'What Owners Expect for Their Money'.

The owners of a business, in a real sense, stand at the end of the line for their piece of the sales revenue pie. How can you tell whether a business is doing well for its owners? What's a good net income figure? One test is to compare bottom-line profit with sales revenue. Dividing profit by sales revenue gives the *profit ratio*, which is expressed as a percentage. Many people don't really know what's a typical profit ratio for a business. They think it's high – 20 per cent, 30 per cent or even 50 per cent of sales revenue. In fact, the large majority of businesses earn profit ratios of less than 10 per cent.

Although profit ratio is a useful test of profit performance, it ignores the amount of capital the owners have tied up in the business. Every business needs owners' capital to invest in the assets needed for making profit. The ratio of profit over owners' equity is called *return on equity*. To calculate a business's return on equity (ROE) you divide net income by total owners' equity (you can find owners' equity listed on the business's balance sheet). Compare the ROE of a business with the ROEs of investment alternatives that have the same kinds of risks and advantages when you're deciding whether to invest in a business. Business managers keep a close watch on their ROE in order to judge their business's profit performance relative to the amount of its owners' capital being used to make that profit.

Equity is a term used to describe the capital put in by the owners either on start-up, left in from past profits generated, or by way of additional investment to help the venture grow. It is also referred to as owners' equity, because those who put up equity own the business. The term *risk capital* is also used, as the owners of a business put their capital at risk. If things go seriously wrong they can lose their shirts, and more besides. Lenders such as banks enjoy a measure of protection because their money is usually secured against an asset such as property, equipment, machinery or even a motor vehicle. All such assets are likely to have some value worth recovering, even though it might not be enough to cover the whole sum involved.

Usually, managers have an ownership interest in the business – although in large, public companies, managers usually own only a small percentage of the total owners' equity. For a small business, the two or three chief managers may be the only owners. But many small businesses have outside, non-manager investors who put money in the business and share in the profit that the business earns. Chapter 14 explains more about ROE and other ways outside investors interpret the information in a business's external financial report.

What Owners Expect for Their Money

Every business – regardless of how big it is and whether it's publicly or privately owned – has owners; no business can get all the financing it needs just by borrowing. An *owner* is someone who:

- ✔ Invested money in the business when it originally raised capital from its owners or who bought ownership shares from one of the existing owners of the business.

- ✔ Expects the business to earn profit on the owners' capital and expects to share in that profit by receiving cash distributions from profit and by benefiting from increases in the value of the ownership shares – with no guarantee of either.

- ✔ Directly participates in the management of the business or hires others to manage the business – in smaller businesses an owner may be one of the managers or may sit on the board of directors of the business, but in very large businesses you are just one of thousands of owners who elect a representative board of directors to oversee the managers of the business and to protect the interests of the owners.

- ✔ Receives a proportionate share of the proceeds if the business is sold or if the business sells off its assets.

- ✔ Takes risks and may lose the amount of their shareholding.

When owners invest money in a business, the accountant records the amount of money received as an increase in the company's *cash* account (note the account is not called 'money'). And, to keep things in balance, the amount invested in the business is recorded as an increase in an *owners' equity* account. (This is one example of *double entry accounting*, which is explained in Chapter 2.) Owners' equity also increases when a business makes profit. Because of the two different reasons for increases, the owners' equity of a business is divided into two separate accounts:

- ✔ **Share capital (also referred to as invested capital):** Represents the amounts of money that owners have invested in the business, which could have been many years ago. Owners may invest additional capital from time to time, but generally speaking they cannot be forced to put additional money in a business.

- ✔ **Retained earnings (also referred to as reserves):** Represents the profit earned by a business over the years that has not been distributed to its owners. If all profit has been distributed every year, retained earnings will have a zero balance. (If a business has never made a profit, its accumulated loss will cause retained earnings to have a negative balance, called a *deficit*.) If none of the annual profits of a business have been distributed to its owners, the balance in retained earnings will be the cumulative profit earned by the business since it opened its doors.

The account title *retained earnings* for the profit that a business earns and does not distribute to its owners is appropriate for any type of business entity. Business companies – one of the most common types of business entities – use this title. The other types of business entities discussed in this chapter may use this title, but they may collapse both sources of owners' equity into just one account for each owner. Companies are legally required to distinguish between the two sources of owners' equity: invested capital versus retained earnings. The other types of business entities may not be.

Whether to retain some or all of annual net income is one of the most important decisions that a business makes; distributions from profit have to be decided at the highest level of a business. A growing business needs additional capital for expanding its assets, and increasing the debt load of the business usually cannot supply all the additional capital. So, the business *ploughs back* some of its profit for the year – it keeps some (perhaps all) of the profit, rather than giving it out to the owners. In the long run this may be the best course of action, a step back before a leap forward.

Banks are one major source of loans to businesses. Of course, banks charge interest on the loans; a business and its bank negotiate an interest rate acceptable to both. Also, many other conditions are negotiated, such as the term (time period) of the loan, whether collateral is required to secure the loan and so on. The loan contract between a business and its lender may prohibit the business from distributing profit to owners during the period of the loan. Or, the loan agreement may require that the business maintain a minimum cash balance – which could mean that money the business would like to distribute to owners from profit has to stay in its cash account instead.

The chairman or other appropriate officer of the business signs the lending agreement with the bank. In addition, the bank may ask the major investors in the business to sign the agreement *as individuals*, in their personal capacities – and perhaps ask their spouses to sign the agreement as well. You should definitely understand your personal obligations if you are considering signing a lending agreement for a business. You take the risk that you may have to pay some part – or perhaps all – of the loan out of your personal assets.

Now, who are the owners and how do they organise themselves? A business may have just one owner, or two or more owners. A one-owner business may choose to operate as a *sole trader* or *proprietorship*; a multi-owner business must choose to be a *partnership*, a *limited partnership* or a *limited liability company*. The most ordinary type of business is a sole trader – there are 1.5 million of them in the UK. Around a million limited companies are in operation at present, too.

No ownership structure is inherently better than another; which one is right for a particular business is something that the business's managers and owners need to decide (or should consult a tax adviser about, as discussed later in this chapter). The following discussion focuses on how ownership structure affects profit distribution to owners. Later, this chapter explains how the ownership structure determines the tax paid by the business and its owners – which is always an important consideration.

Companies

The law views a *company* as a person. Like an adult, a company is treated as a distinct and independent individual who has rights and responsibilities. A company's 'birth certificate' is the legal form that is filed if the company is domiciled in the UK. A company must have a legal name, of course, like an individual. Just as a child is separate from his or her parents, a company is separate from its owners. The company is responsible for its own debts, just like a person is. The bank can't come after you if your neighbour defaults on his or her loan, and the bank can't come after you if the company you have invested money in goes belly up. If a company doesn't pay its debts, its creditors can seize only the company's assets, not the assets of the company's owners.

You can find out everything you need to know about registering a company from Companies House at www.companieshouse.gov.uk/infoAndGuide/companyRegistration.shtml.

This important legal distinction between the obligations of the business entity and its individual owners is known as *limited liability* – that is, the limited liability of the owners. Even if the owners are excessively wealthy they have no legal liability for the unpaid debts of the company (unless they've used the corporate shell to defraud creditors, or are trading in some fraudulent or illegal manner). So, when you invest money in a company as an owner, you know that the most you can lose is the same amount you put in. You may lose every pound you put in, but that's the most you can lose. The company's creditors cannot reach through the corporate entity to grab your assets to pay off the liabilities of the business.

Stock shares

A company issues ownership shares to persons who invest money in the business. These ownership shares are documented by *stock certificates*, which state the name of the owner and how many shares are owned. The company has to keep a *register* (list) of how many shares everyone owns, of course. (An owner can be another company, or any other legal entity.) The owners of a company are called its *shareholders* because they own *shares* issued by the company. The shares are fully *negotiable*, which means the owner can sell them at any time to anyone willing to buy them without having to get the approval of the company or the other shareholders to sell the shares. *Publicly owned companies* are those whose shares are traded in public markets, most notably the London Stock Exchange, the New York Stock Exchange and NASDAQ (National Association of Securities Dealers Automated Quotation).

One share is one unit of ownership; how much one share is worth with respect to the value of the whole business depends on the total number of shares that the business issues. If a business has issued 400,000 shares and you own 40,000 of them, you own ⅒ of the business. But suppose that the business issues an additional 40,000 shares; you now have 40,000 of 440,000, giving you a ⅟₁₁ interest in the business. The more shares a business issues, the smaller the percentage of total owners' equity each share represents. Issuing additional shares may dilute, or decrease the value of each share of stock. A good example is when a publicly owned company doubles the number of its shares by issuing a two-for-one stock split. Each shareholder gets one new share for each share presently owned, without investing any additional money in the business. As you would expect, the market value of the stock drops in half – which is exactly the purpose of the split, because the lower stock price is better for stock market trading (according to conventional wisdom).

If new shares are issued at a price equal to the going value of the shares, the value of the existing shares should not be adversely affected. But if new shares are issued at a discount from the going value, the value of each share after the additional shares are issued may decline. For example, assume you own shares in a business and the shares are selling for £100 per share. Suppose the company issues some shares for £50 per share. Each new share adds only £50 value to the business, which drags down the average value of all shares of the company. We quickly admit here that the valuation of company shares is not nearly so simple – but our purpose is to emphasise that shareholders should pay attention to the issue of additional shares for less than the going market price of a company's shares. Management stock options are the prime example of issuing shares at below market prices.

Many publicly owned companies give their managers share options in addition to their salaries and other benefits. A *share option* gives a manager the legal right to buy a certain number of shares at a fixed price starting at some time in the future – assuming conditions of continued employment and other requirements are satisfied. Usually the *exercise price* (also called the *strike price*) of a management share option is set equal to or higher than the present market value of the shares. So, granting the manager the share option does not produce any immediate gain to the manager – and these options can't be exercised for some time anyway. If the market price of the shares rises above the exercise price of the share option sometime in the future, the share options become valuable – indeed, many managers have become multi-millionaires from their share options.

Suppose that the market value of a company's shares has risen to, say, £100 and that the exercise price of the share options awarded to several managers a few years ago was set at £50 per share. And, assume that all the other conditions of the share options are satisfied. The managers' share options will certainly be exercised to realise their gains. It would seem, therefore, that the management share options would have a negative impact on the market price of the company's shares – because the total value of the business has to be divided over a larger number of shares and this results in a smaller value per share. On the other hand, it can be argued that the total value of the business is higher than it would have been without the management share options, because better qualified managers were attracted to the business or the managers performed better because of their options. Even with the decrease in the value per share, it is argued, the shareholders are better off than they would have been if no share options had been awarded to the managers. The shares' market value may have been only £90 or £80 without the management share options – so the story goes.

Classes of shares

Before you invest in shares, you should ascertain whether the company has issued just one *class* of share. A class is one group, or type, of share all having identical rights; every share is the same as every other share. A company can issue two or more different classes of shares. For example, a business may offer Class A and Class B shares, where Class A shareholders are given the vote in elections for the board of directors but Class B shareholders do not get a vote. Of course, if you want to vote in the annual election of directors you should buy Class A shares. Laws generally are very liberal regarding the different classes of shares that can be issued by companies. For a whimsical example, one class could get the best seats at the annual meetings of the shareholders. To be serious, differences between classes of shares are very significant and affect the investment value of the shares of each class of share.

Two classes of corporate shares are fundamentally different: *ordinary shares* (called *common shares* in the US) and *preference shares*. Preference shareholders are promised a certain amount of cash dividends each year (note we said 'promised', not 'guaranteed') – but the company makes no such promises to its ordinary shareholders. If the business ends up liquidating its assets and after paying off its liabilities returns money to its owners, the preference shareholders have to be paid before any money goes to the ordinary shareholders. The ordinary shareholders are at the top of the risk chain: A business that ends up in deep financial trouble is obligated to pay off its liabilities first, and then its preferred shareholders, and by the time the ordinary shareholders get their turn the business may have no money left to pay them. So, preference shareholders have the promise of annual dividends and stand ahead of ordinary shareholders in the liquidation of the business. What's the attraction of ordinary shares, therefore? The main advantage of ordinary shares is that they have unlimited upside potential. After obligations to its preference shareholders are satisfied, the rest of the profit earned by the company accrues to the benefit of its ordinary shareholders.

The main difference between preference shares and ordinary shares concerns *cash dividends* – what the business pays its owners from its profit. Here are the key points:

- A business must pay dividends to its preference shareholders because it has a contractual obligation to do so, whereas each year the board of directors must decide how much, if any, cash dividends to distribute to its ordinary shareholders. You can find details of the average dividend paid by companies at any one time in the *Financial Times*. At the time of writing, this average stands at 3.1 per cent.

- Preference shareholders usually are promised a fixed (limited) dividend per year and typically don't have a claim to any profit beyond the stated amount of dividends. (Some companies issue *participating preference shares* or convertible preference shares, which give the preference shareholders a contingent right to more than just their basic amount of dividends, something which gets too technical for this book.)

- Preference shareholders don't have voting rights – unless they don't receive dividends for one period or more. In other words, preference shareholders usually do not have voting rights in electing the company's board of directors or on other critical issues facing the company. Needless to say, these matters can become complex, and they vary from company to company – no wonder there are so many corporate lawyers! If you need more information we recommend *Investing For Dummies* by Tony Levene (Wiley).

Here are some other general things to know about ordinary shares:

- Each share is equal to every other share in its class. This way, ownership rights are standardised, and the main difference between two shareholders is how many shares each owns.

- The only way a business has to return shareholders' capital (composed of invested capital and retained earnings) is if the majority of shareholders vote to liquidate the business in part or in total. Other than that, the business's managers don't have to worry about losing the shareholders' capital. Of course, shareholders are free to sell their shares at any time, as noted next.

- A shareholder can sell his or her shares at any time, without the approval of the other shareholders. However, shareholders of a privately owned business may have agreed to certain restrictions on this right when they invested in the business. Additionally, the stock market takes a dim view of shareholders who also work in a business suddenly dumping a whole lot of shares without having a compelling reason to do so. You can find details of directors' dealings in their own shares by going to `www.investegate.co.uk` and clicking on 'Company Announcements' followed by 'News'.

✔ Shareholders can either put themselves in key management positions or delegate the task of selecting top managers and officers to a *board of directors*, which is a small group of persons selected by the shareholders to set the business's policies and represent shareholders' interests. If you put up more than half the money in a business, you can put yourself on the board and elect yourself president of the business. The shareholders who own 50 per cent plus one share constitute the controlling group that decides who goes on the board of directors.

If you want to sell your shares, how much can you get for them? Shares in privately owned businesses aren't publicly traded, so how can you determine the value of your shares in such a business? To be frank, you can't really. Until you actually sell your shares for a certain price per share, you simply don't know their market value for sure. On the other hand, you can use certain benchmarks, or valuation methods, to estimate market value. For example, you could look to the *book value per share*, which is based on values reported on the business's latest balance sheet:

Total shareholders' equity ÷ total number of shares = book value per share

Book values are historical – based on the past transactions of the business – whereas market pricing looks to how the business is likely to do in the future. The past is important, but the future prospects of the business are more important in setting a value on the business. Market value depends on forecast profit performance (future earnings), which in many cases is much more important than book value per share. One way of estimating the value of your shares in a private business company is the *earnings multiple* method, in which you calculate the theoretical value of a share by using a certain multiple of the business's earnings (net income) per share.

Suppose a privately owned business company earned £3.20 net income per share last year. You calculate the book value per share at the end of the year, which, let's assume, is £20. You may be able to sell your shares at ten times earnings per share, or £32 per share, which is considerably more than the book value per share. If someone paid £32 per share for the shares and the business earned £3.20 per share next year, the new shareholder might be satisfied to earn 10 per cent on his or her £32 investment – calculated by dividing the £3.20 earnings per share by the £32 cost of the share. (Not all of the £3.20 may be paid out as a cash dividend, so part of the 10 per cent earnings on the investment consists of the increase in retained earnings of the business.)

Keep in mind that the £32 market value is only an estimate and just a theoretical price. However, you don't know the market price until you sell the shares. As potential investors in the business, we may be willing to offer you £35 or £40 per share – or we may offer less than the book value per share.

Shareholders and managers

Shareholders (including managers who own shares in the business) are concerned, first and foremost, with the profit performance of their business.

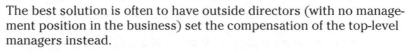

The dividends they receive, and the value of their shares, depend on profit. Managers, too, are concerned with profit – their jobs depend on living up to the business's profit goals. But even though shareholders and managers strive toward the common goal of making the business profitable, they have an inherent conflict of interest that revolves around money and power:

✔ The more money that managers make in wages and benefits, the less shareholders see in the bottom-line net income. Shareholders obviously want the best managers for the job, but they don't want to pay any more than they have to. In many companies, top-level managers, for all practical purposes, set their own salaries and compensation packages.

The best solution is often to have outside directors (with no management position in the business) set the compensation of the top-level managers instead.

✔ Who should control the business: the managers, who were hired for their competence and are intimately familiar with the business, or the shareholders, who probably have no experience relevant to running this particular business but who put up the money that the business is running on? In ideal situations, the two sides respect each other's importance to the business and use this tension constructively. Of course, the real world is far from ideal, and you have situations in which managers are controlling the board of directors rather than the other way around. But this book isn't the proper place to get into all that.

In particular, watch out for actions that cause a *dilution effect* on the value of your shares – that is, cause each share to drop in value. Now, the dilution effect may be the result of a good business decision, so even though your share of the business has decreased in the short term, the long-term profit performance of the business (and, therefore, your investment) may benefit. But you need to watch these decisions closely. The following situations cause a dilution effect:

✔ A business issues additional shares at the going market value, but doesn't really need the additional capital – the business is in no better profit-making position than it was before issuing the new shares. For example, a business may issue new shares in order to let a newly hired chief executive officer buy them. The immediate effect may be a dilution in the market value per share. Over the long term, however, the new CEO may turn the business around and lead it to higher levels of profit performance that increase the share's value.

✔ A business issues new shares at a discount below its shares' current value. For example, the business may issue a new batch of shares at a price lower than the current market value to employees who take advantage of an employee share-purchase plan. Selling shares at a discount, by itself, has a dilution effect on the market value of the shares. But in the grand scheme of things, the share-purchase plan may motivate its employees to achieve higher productivity levels, which leads to superior profit performance of the business.

Where profit goes in a company

Suppose that your business earned £1.32 million in net income for the year just ended and has issued a total of 400,000 shares of capital stock. Divide net income by the number of shares, and you come up with earnings per share of £3.30.

The cash flow statement reports that the business paid £400,000 total cash dividends during the year, or £1 per share. (Cash dividends are usually paid half-yearly or sometimes quarterly, so the business most likely paid £0.25 dividends per share each of the four quarters.) The rest of the net income – £920,000 – remains in the retained earnings account. (**Remember:** Net income is first entered as an increase in the retained earnings account, and distributions are taken out of this account.) The retained earnings account thus increased by £2.30 per share (the difference between the net income, or earnings per share, and the dividends per share).

Although shareholders don't have the cash to show for it, their investment is better off by £2.30 per share – which shows up in the balance sheet as an increase in the retained earnings account in owners' equity. They can just hope that the business will use the cash flow provided from profit this year to make more

profit in the future, which should lead to higher cash dividends.

If the business is a publicly owned company whose shares are actively traded, its shareholders look to the change in the *market price* of the stock shares during the year. Did the market value go up or down during the year? You may think that the market value should increase £2.30 per share, because the business earned this much per share that it kept in the business and did not distribute to its shareholders. Your thinking is quite logical: Profit is an increase in the net assets of a business (assets less liabilities). The business is £2.30 per share richer at the end of the year than it was at the start of the year, due to profit earned and retained.

Yet it's entirely possible that the market price of the stock shares actually *decreased* during the year. Market prices are governed by psychological, political and economic factors that go beyond the information in the financial reports of a business. Financial statements are one – but only one – of the information sources that stock investors use in making their buy-and-sell decisions. Chapter 14 explains how stock investors use the information in financial reports.

Partnerships and limited partnerships

Suppose you're starting a new business with one or more other owners, but you do not want it to be a company. You can choose to form a *partnership* or a *limited partnership*, which are the main alternatives to the corporate form of a business. *Note:* A partnership is sometimes also called a *firm*. (You don't see this term used to refer to a company nearly as often as you do to a partnership.) The term firm connotes an association of a group of individuals working together in a business or professional practice, as in a *firm of lawyers*.

Compared with the relatively rigid structure of companies, partnership and limited partnership ownership structures allow the division of management authority, profit sharing, and ownership rights among the owners to be very flexible. Here are the key features of these two ownership structures:

✔ **Partnerships:** Partnerships avoid the double-taxation feature that companies are subject to (see 'Choosing the Right Legal Structure for Tax Purposes', later in this chapter, for details). Partnerships also differ from companies with respect to liability. A partnership's owners fall into two categories:

- **General partners** are subject to *unlimited liability*. If a business can't pay its debts, its creditors can reach into general partners' personal assets. General partners have the authority and responsibility to manage the business. They are roughly equivalent to the managing director and other high-level managers of a business company. The general partners usually divide authority and responsibility among themselves, and often they elect one member of their group as the senior general partner or elect a small executive committee to make major decisions.

- **Limited partners** escape the unlimited liability that the general partners have hanging around their necks. You can reduce the more painful consequences of entering a partnership by having your involvement registered as a limited partnership. A limited partnership is very different from a 'general' partnership. It is a legal animal that, in certain circumstances, combines the best attributes of a partnership and a corporation.

A limited partnership works like this. There must be one or more general partners with the same basic rights and responsibilities (including unlimited liability) as in any general partnership and one or more limited partners who are usually passive investors. The big difference between a general partner and a limited partner is that the limited partner isn't personally liable for debts of the partnership. The most a limited partner can lose is the amount that he or she paid or agreed to pay into the partnership as a capital contribution; or received from the partnership after it became insolvent.

To keep this limited liability, a limited partner may not participate in the management of the business, with very few exceptions. A limited partner who does get actively involved in the management of the business risks losing immunity from personal liability and having the same legal exposure as a general partner.

Caution: We would advise you as a member of a partnership, either as a general or limited partner, to get up to speed on the special accounting practices of the business regarding how salaries and other payments for services to owners and partners are accounted for in the entity's financial statements and how they are treated in determining annual taxable income. Don't take anything for granted; investigate first. Call a tax professional if you have questions or need advice in this area.

Partnerships are effectively collections of sole traders or proprietors. It is a common structure used by people who started out on their own, but want to expand. There are very few restrictions to setting up in business with another person (or persons) in partnership, and several definite advantages. By pooling resources you may have more capital; you will be bringing, hopefully, several sets of skills to the business; and if you are ill, the business can still carry on.

The legal regulations governing partnerships in essence assume that competent businesspeople should know what they are doing. The law merely provides a framework of agreement, which applies 'in the absence of agreement to the contrary'. It follows from this that many partnerships are entered into without legal formalities and sometimes without the parties themselves being aware that they have entered a partnership! Just giving the impression that you are partners may be enough to create an 'implied partnership'.

In the absence of an agreement to the contrary, these rules apply to partnerships:

- ✔ All partners contribute capital equally.

- ✔ All partners share profits and losses equally.

- ✔ No partner shall have interest paid on their capital.

- ✔ No partner shall be paid a salary.

- ✔ All partners have an equal say in the management of the business.

It is unlikely that all these provisions will suit you, so you would be well advised to get a partnership agreement drawn up in writing before trading.

Partnerships have three serious financial drawbacks that merit particular attention.

1. **If your partner makes a business mistake, perhaps by signing a disastrous contract without your knowledge or consent, every member of the partnership must shoulder the consequences.** Under these circumstances, your personal assets could be taken to pay the creditors, even though the mistake was no fault of your own.

2. **If your partner goes bankrupt in their personal capacity, for whatever reason, his or her creditors can seize their share of the partnership.** As a private individual you are not liable for your partner's private debts, but having to buy them out of the partnership at short notice could put you and the business in financial jeopardy.

3. **If your partnership breaks up for any reason, those continuing with it will want to recover control of the business; those who remain shareholders will want to buy back shares; the leaver wants a realistic price.** The agreement you have on setting up the business should specify the procedures, and how to value the leaver's share, otherwise resolving the situation will be costly. The traditional route to value the leaver's share is to ask an independent accountant. This is rarely cost-effective. The valuation costs money and worst of all it is not definite and consequently there is room for argument. Another way is to establish a formula, an agreed eight times the last audited pre-tax profits, for example. This approach is simple but difficult to get right. A fast-growing business is undervalued by a formula using historic data unless the multiple is high; a high multiple may overvalue 'hope' or goodwill, thus unreasonably profiting the leaver. Under a third option, one partner offers to buy out the others at a price he specifies. If they do not accept his offer, the continuing partners must buy the leaver out at that price. In theory, such a price should be acceptable to all.

Even death may not release you from partnership obligations and in some circumstances your estate can remain liable. Unless you take public leave of your partnership by notifying your business contacts, and legally bringing your partnership to an end, you will remain liable indefinitely.

The partnership agreement specifies how to divide profit among the owners. Whereas owners of a company receive a portion of profit that's directly proportional to the number of shares they own and, therefore, how much they invested, a partnership does not have to divide profit according to how much each owner invested. Invested capital is only one of three factors that generally play into profit allocation in partnerships:

✔ **Treasure:** Owners may be rewarded according to how much of the 'treasure' – invested capital – they contributed; they get back a certain percentage (return) on their investment. So if Joe invested twice as much as Jane did, his cut of the profit may be set at twice as much as Jane's.

✔ **Time:** Owners who invest more time in the business may receive more of the profit. In some businesses, a partner may not contribute much more than capital and his or her name, whereas other partners work long hours. This way of allocating profit works like a salary.

✔ **Talent:** Regardless of capital or time, some partners bring more to the business than others. Whatever it is that they do for the business, they contribute much more to the business's success than their capital or time suggests.

Note: A partnership needs to maintain a separate capital (or *ownership*) account for each partner. The total profit of the entity is allocated into these capital accounts, as spelled out in the partnership agreement. The agreement also specifies how much money each partner can withdraw from his capital account – for example, partners may be limited to withdrawing no more than 80 per cent of their anticipated share of profit for the coming year, or they may be allowed to withdraw only a certain amount until they've built up their capital accounts.

Sole proprietorships

A *sole proprietorship* or, as it is frequently known, *sole tradership*, is basically the business arm of an individual who has decided *not* to carry on his or her business activity as a separate legal entity (as a partnership, or limited liability company) – it's the default option. An individual may do house repair work for homeowners on a part-time basis, or be a full-time barber who operates on his own. Both are sole proprietorships. Anytime you regularly provide services for a fee, or sell things at a flea market, or engage in any business activity whose primary purpose is to make profit, you are a sole proprietor. If you carry on business activity to make profit or income, HM Revenue and Customs requires that you file a separate schedule summarising your profit or loss from trading with your annual individual income tax return. If your business activities are substantial, the Revenue may ask for both a profit and loss account and a balance sheet, but for most small businesses a few lines of figures showing income, main cost categories, and the resultant profit will be sufficient. As the sole owner (proprietor), you have *unlimited liability*, meaning that if your business can't pay all its liabilities, the creditors to whom your business owes money can come after your personal assets. Many part-time entrepreneurs may not know this or may put it out of their minds, but this is a big risk to take.

One other piece of advice for sole proprietors: Although you don't have to separate invested capital from retained earnings like companies do, you should still keep these two separate accounts for owners' equity – not only for the purpose of tracking the business but for the benefit of any future buyers of the business as well.

Spreading the joy of profit to your employees and customers: Business co-operatives

A *co-operative* pays its customers *patronage dividends* based on its profit for the year – each customer receives a year-end refund based on his or her purchases from the business over the year. Imagine that.

A co-operative is also an enterprise owned and controlled by the people working in it. Once in danger of becoming extinct, the workers' cooperative is enjoying something of a comeback with thousands being set up each year around Europe.

If this is to be your chosen legal form, you can pay from £90 to register with the Chief Registrar of Friendly Societies. You must have at least seven members at the outset, though they do not all have to be full-time workers at first. Like a limited company, a registered co-operative has limited liability (see 'Limited Liability Companies') for its members and must file annual accounts, but there is no charge for this. Not all co-operatives bother to register, as it is not mandatory, in which case they are treated in law as a partnership with unlimited liability.

Limited companies (Ltd) and public limited companies (plc)

As the name suggests, in this form of business your liability is limited to the amount you contribute by way of share capital.

 A *limited company* has a legal identity of its own, separate from the people who own or run it. This means that, in the event of failure, creditors' claims are restricted to the assets of the company. The shareholders of the business are not liable as individuals for the business debts beyond the paid-up value of their shares. This applies even if the shareholders are working directors, unless of course the company has been trading fraudulently. In practice, the ability to limit liability is restricted these days as most lenders, including the banks, often insist on personal guarantees from the directors. Other advantages include the freedom to raise capital by selling shares.

Disadvantages include the legal requirement for the company's accounts to be audited and filed for public inspection.

A limited company can be formed by two shareholders, one of whom must be a director. A company secretary must also be appointed, who can be a shareholder, director or an outside person such as an accountant or lawyer.

The company can be bought 'off the shelf' from a registration agent, then adapted to suit your own purposes. This will involve changing the name, shareholders and articles of association and takes a couple of weeks to arrange. Alternatively, you can form your own company. But before you can form a company, you need to decide which of the two main structures of company to use.

A limited company (Ltd) is the most common type. This is a private company limited by shares. A limited company can be started with, say, an authorised share capital of £1,000. This is then divided into 1,000 × £1 shares. You can then issue as few or as many of the shares as you want. As long as the shares you have issued are paid for in full, if the company liquidates, the shareholders have no further liabilities. If the shares have not been paid for, the shareholders are liable for the value, that is, if they have 100 £1 shares, they only are liable for £100.

A *plc company* is a public limited company and may be listed on the Stock Exchange. Before a plc can start to trade it must have at least £50,000 of shares issued and at least 25 per cent of the value must have been paid for. A plc company has a better status due to its larger capital.

Choosing the Right Legal Structure for Tax Purposes

In deciding which type of ownership structure is best for securing capital and managing their business, owners should also consider the tax factor.

Taxable-entity companies pay tax on their annual taxable profit amounts. Their shareholders pay income tax on cash dividends that the business distributes to them from profit, making the company and its owners subject to double taxation. The owners (shareholders) of a company include in their individual income tax returns the cash distributions from profit paid to them by the business.

In the following examples, we assume that the business uses the same accounting methods in preparing its profit and loss account that it uses for determining its taxable income – a realistic assumption.

Companies

Whether trading as a limited company or public limited company, the tax rules are much the same. True, a small company, defined as one making less than a certain amount of profit, currently around £300,000 a year, may end up paying less tax than its bigger brothers, but the basic deal is the same.

Suppose you have a company with the following abbreviated profit and loss account (see Chapter 5 for details on profit and loss accounts):

Sales revenue	£26,000,000
Expenses, except corporation tax	(23,800,000)
Earnings before tax	£2,200,000
Corporation Tax	(748,000)
Net income	£1,452,000

The £748,000 corporation tax is determined by the fact that this business's £2.2 million taxable income puts it in the 34 per cent tax bracket (corporate taxable income rates have moved around the 30 per cent rate in recent years, but have been much higher and may yet be again. The actual rate makes no difference to the argument developed in this example):

£2,200,000 taxable income × 34% tax rate = £748,000 tax

That's a big chunk of the business's hard-earned profit. You must also consider the so-called *double taxation* of corporate profit – a most unpleasant topic if you're a shareholder in a company. Not only does the company have to pay £748,000 corporation tax on its profit (as we just calculated), but when the business distributes some of its after-tax profit to its shareholders as their just rewards for investing capital in the business, the shareholders include these cash dividends as income in their individual income tax returns and pay a second tax.

For a rather dramatic example, suppose that this business distributed its entire after-tax net income as cash dividends to its shareholders. (Even though most businesses don't pay 100 per cent cash dividends from their net incomes.) Its shareholders must include the cash dividends in their individual income tax returns. How much each individual pays in taxes depends on his or her total taxable income for the year, but let us make an arbitrary (but reasonable) assumption that the shareholders are, on average, in the marginal 31 per cent tax bracket. In this example, the shareholders would combine to pay £450,120 total individual income tax on their dividend incomes:

£1,452,000 dividends × 31% income tax rate = £450,120 total individual income tax paid by shareholders

You can calculate the total tax paid by both the company and its shareholders as follows:

£748,000	paid by the company on its £2,200,000 taxable income
£450,120	paid by its shareholders on £1,452,000 in cash dividends
£1,198,120	total tax paid by both the company and its shareholders

Compare this to the company's £2,200,000 of taxable income. Out of the £2,200,000 pre-tax profit that the business earned, £1,198,120 is quite a bit of total tax to pay – more than half. On the other hand, if the company had retained all of its after-tax profit and paid no cash dividends, then at least for now the individual shareholders would not have to pay the second tax. Distributing no cash dividends may not go down well with all the shareholders, however. Most companies – but by no means all – pay part of their after-tax net income as cash dividends to their shareholders.

The distribution of profit to the shareholders in the dividend payment gives the appearance of taxing the same profit twice, but through a process of *tax credits* this double taxation doesn't generally occur. When a shareholder gets a dividend from a company, it comes with a tax credit attached. This means that any shareholder on the basic rate of tax won't have to pay any further tax. Higher rate taxpayers, however, have a further amount of tax to pay. So every shareholder takes a tax cash hit when dividends are distributed, but only higher rate taxpayers actually end up losing out.

Partnerships, limited liability partnerships and sole proprietorships

Sole traders (self-employed) have all their income from every source brought together and taxed as one entity. Partnerships are treated as a collection of sole traders for tax purposes, and each partner's share of that collective liability has to be worked out. Under the self-assessment tax system in the UK, the basis of a period of a year of assessment is the accounting year ending within that tax year. There are special rules that apply for the first year and the last year of trading that should ensure tax is charged fairly.

If your turnover is low, currently in the UK less than circa £15,000 per year, you can put in a three-line account on your standard tax return: sales, expenses and profit. No need for expensive accountancy advice here. If it is over whatever the current low figure is, then you have to summarise your accounts to show turnover, gross profit and expenses by main heading.

You will have a personal allowance: the current threshold below which you don't pay tax. That amount is deducted from the profit figure. All these rates and amounts are constantly changing, but the broad principles remain.

Partners don't actually get paid salaries, although partners may take monthly draws (withdrawals from the partnership) that may look like salaries. These may be listed as *drawings*. Partners are not employees but rather owners whose compensation consists of sharing in the profit of the partnership. A partner's share of profit may be disproportionately large, as a substitute for a salary, if that partner puts in more hours at the business or otherwise makes a disproportionate contribution. But the amount paid out is a withdrawal of profit by the partner and not a true salary.

Deciding which legal structure is best

The most important rule is never to let the 'tax tail wag the business dog'. Tax is just one aspect of business life. If you want to keep your business's finances private, then the public filing of accounts required of companies will not be for you. On the other hand, if you feel that you want to protect your private assets from creditors if things go wrong, then being a sole trader or partner is probably not the best route to take.

Company profits and losses are locked into the company, so if you have several lines of business using different trading entities, you cannot easily settle losses in one area against profits in another. But as sole traders are treated as one entity for all their sources of income, there is more scope for netting off gains and losses. Some points to bear in mind here are:

✔ If your profits are likely to be small, say below £60,000, for some time, then from a purely tax point of view you may pay less tax as a sole trader. This is because as an individual you get a tax-free allowance. Your first few thousand pounds of income are not taxable. This amount varies with personal circumstances, if you are married or single, for example, and can be changed in the budget each year.

✔ If you expect to be making higher rates of profit (above £60,000) and want to reinvest a large portion of those profits back into your business, then you could be better off forming a company. That is because companies don't start paying higher rates of tax until their profits are above £300,000. Even then they don't pay tax at 40 per cent. A sole trader would be taxed at the 40 per cent rate by the time their profits had reached about £35,000, taking allowances into account. So a company making £300,000 taxable profits could have around £50,000–£60,000 more to reinvest in financing future growth than would a sole trader in the same line of work.

✔ Non-salary benefits are more favourably treated for the sole trader. You can generally get tax relief on the business element of costs that are only partly business related, such as running a vehicle. A director of a company will be taxed on the value of the vehicle's list price and will not be allowed travel to and from work as a business expense.

Bear in mind that these calculations change with every change of tax rates in each budget.

Don't let the tax tail wag the business dog! Your business needs to be structured to let you operate without taking undue financial risks. Tax is just one of a number of factors to weigh up when deciding how to legally structure your business. Although important, don't let tax be the deciding factor.

Chapter 12

Cost Conundrums

. . . .

In This Chapter

▶ Determining costs: The second most important thing accountants do

▶ Comprehending the different needs for cost information

▶ Contrasting costs to understand them better

▶ Determining product cost for manufacturers

▶ Padding profit by manufacturing too many products

. . . .

Measuring costs is the second most important thing accountants do, right after measuring profit. But really, can measuring a cost be very complicated? You just take numbers off a purchase invoice and call it a day, right? Not if your business manufactures the products you sell – that's for sure! Businesses must carefully record all their costs correctly so that profit can be determined each period, and so that managers have the information they need to make decisions and to control profit performance.

Previewing What's Coming Down the Road

One main function of accounting for a manufacturing business is measuring *product cost*. Examples are the cost of a new car just rolling off the assembly line or the cost of this book, *Understanding Business Accounting For Dummies*. Most production (manufacturing) processes are fairly complex, so measuring product cost is also fairly complex in most cases. Every step in the production process has to be tracked very carefully from start to finish. One major problem is that many manufacturing costs cannot be directly matched with particular products; these are called *indirect costs*. To arrive at the *full cost* of each separate product manufactured, accountants devise methods for allocating the indirect production costs to specific products. Different accountants use different allocation methods. In other respects, as well, product cost accounting is characterised by a diversity of methods. Generally accepted accounting principles provide very little guidance for measuring product cost. Manufacturing businesses have a lot of leeway in how their product costs are determined; even businesses in the same industry use different product cost accounting methods.

In addition to measuring product costs of manufacturers, accountants in all businesses determine many other costs: the costs of the departments and other organisational units of the business; the cost of pensions for the company's employees; the cost of marketing initiatives and advertising campaigns; and, on occasion, the cost of restructuring the business or the cost of a major recall of products sold by the business. A common refrain among accountants is 'different costs for different purposes'. True enough, but at its core, cost accounting serves two broad purposes – measuring profit and providing relevant information to managers.

This chapter covers cost concepts and cost measurement methods that are used by both retail and manufacturing businesses, along with additional stuff for manufacturers to worry about. We also discuss how having a good handle on cost issues can help you recognise when a business is monkeying around with product cost to deliberately manipulate its profit figure. Service businesses – which sell a service such as transportation or entertainment – have a break here. They do not encounter the cost-accounting problems of manufacturers, but they have plenty of cost allocation issues to deal with in assessing the profitability of each of their separate sales revenue sources.

What Makes Cost So Important?

Without good cost information, a business operates in the dark. Cost data is needed for different purposes in business, including the following:

- **Setting sales prices:** The common method for setting sales prices (known as *cost-plus* or *mark-up on cost*) starts with cost and then adds a certain percentage.

- **Measuring gross margin:** Investors and managers judge business performance by the bottom-line profit figure. This profit figure depends on the *gross margin* figure that you get when you subtract your cost of goods sold expense from your sales revenue. Gross margin (also called *gross profit*) is the first profit line in the profit and loss account (see Figures 9–1 and 12–2 for examples).

- **Valuing assets:** The balance sheet reports cost values for many assets, and these values are, of course, included in the overall financial position of your business.

✔ **Making optimal choices:** You often must choose one alternative over others in making business decisions. The best alternative depends heavily on cost factors, and you have to be careful to distinguish *relevant* costs from *irrelevant* costs, as described in the section 'Relevant versus irrelevant (sunk) costs', later in this chapter.

In most situations, the book value of a fixed asset is an *irrelevant* cost. Say the book value is £35,000 for a machine used in the manufacturing operations of the business. This is the amount of original cost that has not yet been charged to depreciation expense since it was acquired, and it may seem quite relevant. However, in deciding between keeping the old machine or replacing it with a newer, more efficient machine, the *disposable value* of the old machine is the relevant amount, not the non-depreciated cost balance of the asset. Suppose the old machine has only a £20,000 salvage value at this time. This is the relevant cost for the alternative of keeping it for use in the future – not the £35,000 that hasn't been depreciated yet. In order to keep using it, the business forgoes the £20,000 it could get by selling the asset, and this £20,000 is the relevant cost in the decision situation. Making decisions involves looking at the future cash flows of each alternative – not looking back at historical-based cost values.

Sharpening Your Sensitivity to Costs

The following sections explain important distinctions between costs that managers should understand in making decisions and exercising control. Also, these cost distinctions help managers better appreciate the cost figures that accountants attach to products that are manufactured or purchased by the business. In a later section we focus on the special accounting methods and problems of computing product costs of *manufacturers*. Retailers purchase products in a condition ready for sale to their customers – although the products have to be removed from shipping containers and a retailer does a little work making the products presentable for sale and putting the products on display.

Manufacturers don't have it so easy; their product costs have to be 'manufactured' in the sense that the accountants have to compile production costs and compute the cost per unit for every product manufactured. We cannot exaggerate the importance of correct product costs (for businesses that sell products, of course). The total cost of goods (products) sold is the first, and usually the largest, expense deducted from sales revenue in measuring profit. The bottom-line profit amount reported in the profit and loss account of a business for the period depends heavily on whether its product costs have been measured properly. Also, keep in mind that product cost is the value for the stock asset reported in the balance sheet of a business.

Direct versus indirect costs

What's the difference between these costs? Well:

- **Direct costs:** Can be clearly attributed to one product or product line, or one source of sales revenue, or one organisational unit of the business, or one specific operation in a process. An example of a direct cost in the book publishing industry is the cost of the paper that a book is printed on; this cost can be squarely attached to one particular phase of the book production process.

- **Indirect costs:** Are far removed from and cannot be obviously attributed to specific products, organisational units or activities. A book publisher's phone bill is a cost of doing business but can't be tied down to just one step in the book's editorial and production process. The salary of the purchasing officer who selects the paper for all the books is another example of a cost that is indirect to the production of particular books.

Indirect costs are allocated according to some methods to different products, sources of sales revenue, organisational units and so on. Most allocation methods are far from perfect, and in the last analysis end up being rather arbitrary. Business managers should always keep an eye on the allocation methods used for indirect costs, and take the cost figures produced by these methods with a grain of salt.

The cost of filling the fuel tank in driving your car from London to Bristol and back is a direct cost of making the trip. The annual road tax that the government charges you is an indirect cost of the trip, although it is a direct cost of having the car available during the year.

Fixed versus variable costs

Two other costs you need to know about are:

- **Fixed costs** remain the same over a relatively broad range of sales volume or production output. For example, the cost of renting office space doesn't change regardless of how much a business's sales volume increases or decreases. Fixed costs are like a dead weight on the business. Its total fixed costs form the hurdle that the business must overcome by selling enough units at high enough profit margins per unit in order to avoid a loss and move into the profit zone. (Chapter 9 explains the break-even point, which is the level of sales needed to cover fixed costs for the period.)

- **Variable costs** increase and decrease in proportion to changes in sales or production level. If you increase the number of books that your business produces, the cost of the paper and ink also goes up.

Breaking even

The saying goes that every picture is worth a thousand words. Well, 'finance' and 'pictures' are words that don't come together too often, but they certainly do when you look at costings.

Take a look at Figure 12-1. The bottom horizontal axis represents volume, starting at 0 and rising as the company produces more product. The vertical axis represents value, starting at 0 and rising, as you'd expect, with any increase in volume. The horizontal line in the middle of the chart represents *fixed costs* – those costs that remain broadly unchanged with increases in volume, rents and so on. The line angling upwards from the fixed cost line represents the *variable cost* – the more we produce, the higher the cost. We arrive at the total costs by adding the fixed and variable costs together.

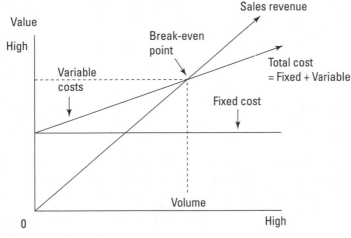

Figure 12-1:
A break-
even chart.

On the hopeful assumption that our sales team has been hard at work, we should then see sales revenue kicking in. The line representing those sales starts at 0 (no sales means no money is coming in) then rises as sales grow. The crucial information this chart shows is the *break–even point*, when total costs have been covered by the value of sales revenue and the business has started to make profit. The picture makes it easier to appreciate why lowering cost, either fixed or variable, or increasing selling prices, helps a business to break even at lower volumes and hence start making profit sooner and be able to make even more profit from any given amount of assets.

Conversely, a business that only reaches break even when sales are so high that there is virtually no spare capacity is shown as being vulnerable, because that business has a small *margin of safety* if events don't turn out as planned.

Relevant versus irrelevant (sunk) costs

Is there such a thing as an irrelevant cost in business accounting? Sure:

- ✔ **Relevant costs:** Costs that should be considered when deciding on a future course of action. Relevant costs are *future* costs – costs that you would incur, or bring upon yourself, depending on which course of action you take. For example, say that you want to increase the number of books that your business produces next year in order to increase your sales revenue, but the cost of paper has just shot up. Should you take the cost of paper into consideration? Absolutely: That cost will affect your bottom-line profit and may negate any increases in sales volume that you experience (unless you increase the sales price). The cost of paper is a relevant cost.

- ✔ **Irrelevant (or sunk) costs:** Costs that should be disregarded when deciding on a future course of action: If brought into the analysis, these costs could cause you to make the wrong decision. An irrelevant cost is a vestige of the past; that money is gone, so get over it. For example, suppose that your supervisor tells you to expect a load of new recruits next week. All your staff members use computers now, but you have loads of typewriters gathering dust in the cupboard. Should you consider the cost paid for those typewriters in your decision to buy computers for all the new staff? Absolutely not: That cost should have been written off and is no match for the cost you'd pay in productivity (and morale) for new employees who are forced to use typewriters.

Generally speaking, fixed costs are irrelevant when deciding on a future course of action, assuming that they're truly fixed and can't be increased or decreased over the short term. Most variable costs are relevant because they depend on which alternative is decided on.

Fixed costs are usually irrelevant in decision-making because these costs will be the same no matter which course of action you decide upon. Looking behind these costs, you usually find that the costs provide *capacity* of one sort or another – so much building space, so many machine-hours available for use, so many hours of labour that will be worked and so on. Managers have to figure out the best overall way to utilise these capacities.

Separating between actual, budgeted and standard costs

Other costs to know about are:

- ✔ **Actual costs:** Historical costs, based on actual transactions and operations for the period just ended, or going back to earlier periods.

Financial statement accounting is based on a business's actual transactions and operations; the basic approach to determining annual profit is to record the financial effects of actual transactions and allocate historical costs to the periods benefited by the costs.

✔ **Budgeted costs:** Future costs, for transactions and operations expected to take place over the coming period, based on forecasts and established goals. Note that fixed costs are budgeted differently than variable costs – for example, if sales volume is forecast to increase by 10 per cent, variable costs will definitely increase accordingly, but fixed costs may or may not need to be increased to accommodate the volume increase (see 'Fixed versus variable costs', earlier in this chapter). Chapter 10 explains the budgeting process and budgeted financial statements.

✔ **Standard costs:** Costs, primarily in manufacturing, that are carefully engineered based on detailed analysis of operations and forecast costs for each component or step in an operation. Developing standard costs for variable production costs is relatively straightforward because many of these are direct costs, whereas most fixed costs are indirect, and standard costs for fixed costs are necessarily based on more arbitrary methods (see 'Direct versus indirect costs' earlier in this chapter). *Note:* Some variable costs are indirect and have to be allocated to specific products in order to come up with a full (total) standard cost of the product.

Product versus period costs

Product costs differ from period costs:

✔ **Product costs:** Costs attached to particular products. The cost is recorded in the stock asset account until the product is sold, at which time the cost goes into the cost of goods sold expense account. (See Chapters 5 and 6 for more about these accounts; also, see Chapter 13 for alternative methods for selecting which product costs are first charged to the cost of goods sold expense.) One key point to keep in mind is that product cost is deferred and not recorded to expense until the product is sold.

The cost of a new car sitting on a dealer's showroom floor is a product cost. The dealer keeps the cost in the stock asset account until you buy the car, at which point the dealer charges the cost to the cost of goods sold expense.

✓ **Period costs:** Costs that are *not* attached to particular products. These costs do not spend time in the 'waiting room' of stock. Period costs are recorded as expenses immediately; unlike product costs, period costs don't pass through the stock account first. Advertising costs, for example, are accounted for as period costs and recorded immediately in an expense account. Also, research and development costs are treated as a period cost.

Separating between product costs and period costs is particularly important for manufacturing businesses, as you find out in the following section.

Putting Together the Pieces of Product Cost for Manufacturers

Businesses that manufacture products have several additional cost problems to deal with. We use the term *manufacture* in the broadest sense: Car makers assemble cars, beer companies brew beer, oil companies refine oil, ICI makes products through chemical synthesis and so on. *Retailers*, on the other hand, buy products in a condition ready for resale to the end consumer. For example, Levi Strauss manufactures clothing, and Selfridges is a retailer that buys from Levi Strauss and sells the clothes to the public.

The following sections describe costs that are unique to manufacturers and address the issue of determining the cost of products that are manufactured.

Minding manufacturing costs

Manufacturing costs consist of four basic types:

✓ **Raw materials:** What a manufacturer buys from other companies to use in the production of its own products. For example, The Ford Motor Company buys tyres from Goodyear (and other tyre manufacturers) that then become part of Ford's cars.

✓ **Direct labour:** The employees who work on the production line.

✓ **Variable overhead:** Indirect production costs that increase or decrease as the quantity produced increases or decreases. An example is the cost of electricity that runs the production equipment: You pay for the electricity for the whole plant, not machine by machine, so you can't attach this cost to one particular part of the process. But if you increase or decrease the use of those machines, the electricity cost increases or decreases accordingly.

✔ **Fixed overhead:** Indirect production costs that do *not* increase or decrease as the quantity produced increases or decreases. These fixed costs remain the same over a fairly broad range of production output levels (see 'Fixed versus variable costs' earlier in this chapter). Three significant fixed manufacturing costs are:

- Salaries for certain production employees who don't work directly on the production line, such as department managers, safety inspectors, security guards, accountants, and shipping and receiving workers.

- Depreciation of production buildings, equipment and other manufacturing fixed assets.

- Occupancy costs, such as building insurance, property rental, and heating and lighting charges.

Figure 12-2 shows a sample management profit and loss account for a manufacturer, including supplementary information about its manufacturing costs. Notice that the cost of goods sold expense depends directly on the product cost from the manufacturing cost summary that appears below the management profit and loss account. A business may manufacture 100 or 1,000 different products, or even more. To keep the example easy to follow, Figure 12-2 presents a scenario for a one-product manufacturer. The example is realistic yet avoids the clutter of too much detail. The multi-product manufacturer has some additional accounting problems, but these are too technical for a book like this. The fundamental accounting problems and methods of all manufacturers are illustrated in the example.

The information in the manufacturing cost summary schedule below the profit and loss account (see Figure 12-2) is highly confidential and for management eyes only. Competitors would love to know this information. A company may enjoy a significant cost advantage over its competitors and definitely would not want its cost data to get into the hands of its competitors.

Unlike a retailer, a manufacturer does not *purchase* products but begins by buying the raw materials needed in the production process. Then the manufacturer pays workers to operate the machines and equipment and to move the products into warehouses after they've been produced. All this is done in a sprawling plant that has many indirect overhead costs. All these different production costs have to be funnelled into the product cost so that the product cost can be entered in the stock account, and then to the cost of goods sold expense when products are sold.

Management Profit and Loss Account for Year

	Per Unit	Totals
Sales Volume	110,000 Units	
	Per Unit	**Totals**
Sales Revenue	£1,400	£154,000,000
Cost of Goods Sold Expense	(760)	(83,600,000)
Gross Margin	£640	£70,400,000
Variable Operating Expenses	(300)	(33,000,000)
Contribution Margin	£340	£37,400,000
Fixed Operating Expenses	(195)	(21,450,000)
Earnings Before Interest and Tax (EBIT)	£145	£15,950,000
Interest Expense		(2,750,000)
Earnings Before Tax		£13,200,000
Corporation Tax Expense		(4,488,000)
Net Income		£8,712,000

Manufacturing Cost Summary for Year

	Per Unit	Totals
Annual Production Capacity	150,000 Units	
Actual Output	120,000 Units	
Production Cost Components	**Per Unit**	**Totals**
Raw Materials	£215	£25,800,000
Direct Labour	125	15,000,000
Variable Overhead	70	8,400,000
Total Variable Manufacturing Costs	£410	£49,200,000
Fixed Overhead	350	42,000,000
Total Manufacturing Costs	£760	£91,200,000
To 10,000 Units Stock Increase		(7,600,000)
To 110,000 Units Sold		£83,600,000

Figure 12-2: Example for determining product cost of a manufacturer.

Allocating costs properly: Not easy!

Two vexing issues rear their ugly heads in determining product cost for a manufacturer:

  ✔ **Drawing a defining line between manufacturing costs and non-manufacturing operating costs:** The key difference here is that manufacturing costs are categorised as product costs, whereas non-manufacturing operating costs are categorised as period costs (refer to 'Product versus period costs' earlier in this chapter). In calculating product cost, you factor in only manufacturing costs and not other costs. Period costs are recorded right away as an expense – either in variable operating expenses or fixed operating expenses for the example shown in Figure 12-2.

Wages paid to production line workers are a clear-cut example of a manufacturing cost. Salaries paid to salespeople are a marketing cost and are not part of product cost; marketing costs are treated as period costs, which means these costs are recorded immediately to the expenses of the period. Depreciation on production equipment is a manufacturing cost, but depreciation on the warehouse in which products are stored after being manufactured is a period cost. Moving the raw materials and works-in-progress through the production process is a manufacturing cost, but transporting the finished products from the warehouse to customers is a period cost. In short, product cost stops at the end of the production line – but every cost up to that point should be included as a manufacturing cost. The accumulation of direct and variable production costs starts at the beginning of the manufacturing process and stops at the end of the production line. All fixed and indirect manufacturing costs during the year are allocated to the actual production output during the year.

If you mis-classify some manufacturing costs as operating costs, your product cost calculation will be too low (refer to 'Calculating product cost' later in this chapter).

✔ **Whether to allocate indirect costs among different products, organisational units or assets:** Indirect *manufacturing* costs must be allocated among the products produced during the period. The full product cost includes both direct and indirect manufacturing costs. Coming up with a completely satisfactory allocation method is difficult and ends up being somewhat arbitrary – but must be done to determine product cost. For non-manufacturing operating costs, the basic test of whether to allocate indirect costs is whether allocation helps managers make better decisions and exercise better control. Maybe, maybe not. In any case, managers should understand how manufacturing indirect costs are allocated to products and how indirect non-manufacturing costs are allocated, keeping in mind that every allocation method is arbitrary and that a different allocation method may be just as convincing. (See the sidebar 'Allocating indirect costs is as simple as ABC – not!')

Allocating indirect costs is as simple as ABC – not!

Accountants for manufacturers have developed loads of different methods and schemes for allocating indirect overhead costs, many based on some common denominator of production activity such as direct labour hours. The latest method to get a lot of press is called *activity-based costing* (ABC).

With the ABC method, you identify each necessary, supporting activity in the production process and collect costs into a separate pool for each identified activity. Then you develop a *measure* for each activity – for example, the measure for the engineering department may be hours, and the measure for the maintenance department may be square feet. You use the activity measures as *cost drivers* to allocate cost to products. So if Product A needs 200 hours of the engineering department's time and Product B is a simple product that needs only 20 hours of engineering, you allocate ten times as much of the engineering cost to Product A.

The idea is that the engineering department doesn't come cheap – including the cost of their computers and equipment as well as their salaries and benefits, the total cost per hour for those engineers could be £100 to £200. The logic of the ABC cost-allocation method is that the engineering cost per hour should be allocated on the basis of the number of hours (the driver) required by each product. In similar fashion, suppose the cost of the maintenance department is £10 per square foot per year. If Product C uses twice as much floor space as Product D, it will be charged with twice as much maintenance cost.

The ABC method has received much praise for being better than traditional allocation methods, especially for management decision making, but keep in mind that it still requires rather arbitrary definitions of cost drivers – and having too many different cost drivers, each with its own pool of costs, is not too practical. Cost allocation always involves arbitrary methods. Managers should be aware of which methods are being used and should challenge a method if they think that it's misleading and should be replaced with a better (though still somewhat arbitrary) method. We don't mean to put too fine a point on this, but to a large extent, cost allocation boils down to a 'my arbitrary method is better than your arbitrary method' argument.

Note: Cost allocation methods should be transparent to managers who use the cost data provided to them by accountants. Managers should never have to guess about what methods are being used, or have to call upon the accountants to explain the allocation methods.

Calculating product cost

The basic equation for calculating product cost is as follows (using the example of the manufacturer from Figure 12–2):

£91.2 million total manufacturing costs ÷ 120,000 units production output = £760 product cost per unit

Looks pretty straightforward, doesn't it? Well, the equation itself may be simple, but the accuracy of the results depends directly on the accuracy of your manufacturing cost numbers. And because manufacturing processes are fairly complex, with hundreds or thousands of steps and operations, your accounting systems must be very complex and detailed to keep accurate track of all the manufacturing costs.

As we explain earlier, when introducing the example, this business manufactures just one product. Also, its product cost per unit is determined for the entire year. In actual practice, manufacturers calculate their product costs monthly or quarterly. The computation process is the same, but the frequency of doing the computation varies from business to business.

In this example the business manufactured 120,000 units and sold 110,000 units during the year. As just computed, its product cost per unit is £760. The 110,000 total units sold during the year is multiplied by the £760 product cost to compute the £83,600,000 cost of goods sold expense, which is deducted against the company's revenue from selling 110,000 units during the year. The company's total manufacturing costs for the year were £91,200,000, which is £7,600,000 more than the cost of goods sold expense. This remainder of the total annual manufacturing costs is recorded as an increase in the company's stock asset account, to recognise the 10,000 units increase of units awaiting sale in the future. In Figure 12-2, note that the £760 product cost per unit is applied both to the 110,000 units sold and to the 10,000 units added to stock.

Note: As just mentioned, most manufacturers determine their product costs monthly or quarterly rather than once a year (as in the example). Product costs likely will vary each successive period the costs are determined. Because the product costs vary from period to period, the business must choose which cost of goods sold and stock cost method to use – unless product cost remains absolutely flat and constant period to period, in which case the different methods yield the same results. Chapter 13 explains the alternative accounting methods for determining cost of goods sold expense and stock cost value.

Fixed manufacturing costs and production capacity

Product cost consists of two very distinct components: *variable manufacturing costs* and *fixed manufacturing costs*. In Figure 12-2 note that the company's variable manufacturing costs are £410 per unit and that its fixed manufacturing costs are £350 per unit. Now, what if the business had manufactured just one more unit? Its total variable manufacturing costs would have been £410 higher; these costs are driven by the actual number of units produced, so even one more unit would have caused the variable costs to increase. But, the company's total fixed costs would have been the same if it had produced one more unit, or 10,000 more units for that matter. Variable manufacturing costs are bought on a per unit basis, as it were, whereas fixed manufacturing costs are bought in bulk for the whole period.

Fixed manufacturing costs are needed to provide *production capacity* – the people and physical resources needed to manufacture products – for the period. Once the business has the production plant and people in place for the year, its fixed manufacturing costs cannot be easily scaled down. The business is stuck with these costs over the short run. It has to make the best use it can from its production capacity.

Production capacity is a critical concept for business managers to grasp. You need to plan your production capacity well ahead of time because you need plenty of lead time to assemble the right people, equipment, land and buildings. When you have the necessary production capacity in place, you want to make sure that you're making optimal use of that capacity. The fixed costs of production capacity remain the same even as production output increases or decreases, so you may as well make optimal use of the capacity provided by those fixed costs.

The fixed cost component of product cost is called the *burden rate*. In our manufacturing example the burden rate is computed as follows (see Figure 12-2 for data):

£42.0 million total fixed manufacturing costs for period ÷ 120,000 units production output for period = £350 burden rate

Note that the burden rate depends on the number divided into total fixed manufacturing costs for the period; that is, the production output for the period. Now, here's a very important twist on our example: Suppose the company had manufactured only 110,000 units during the period – equal exactly to the quantity sold during the year. Its variable manufacturing cost per unit would have been the same, or £410 per unit. But, its burden rate would have been £381.82 per unit (computed by dividing the £42 million total fixed manufacturing costs by the 110,000 units production output). Each unit sold, therefore, would have cost £31.82 more simply because the company produced fewer units (£381.82 burden rate at the 110,000 output level compared with the £350 burden rate at the 120,000 output level).

In this alternative scenario (in which only 110,000 units were produced), the company's product cost would have been £791.82 (£410 variable costs plus the £381.82 burden rate). The company's cost of goods sold, therefore, would have been £3,500,000 higher for the year (£31.82 higher product cost × 110,000 units sold). This rather significant increase in its cost of goods sold expense is caused by the company producing fewer units, although it did produce all the units that it needed for sales during the year. The same total amount of fixed manufacturing costs would be spread over fewer units of production output.

Shifting the focus back to the example shown in Figure 12-2, the company's cost of goods sold benefited from the fact that it produced 10,000 more units than it sold during the year – these 10,000 units absorbed £3.5 million of its total fixed manufacturing costs for the year, and until the units are sold, this £3.5 million stays in the stock asset account. It's entirely possible that the higher production level was justified – to have more stock on hand for sales growth next year. But production output can get out of hand – see the following section, 'Excessive production output for puffing up profit'.

For the example illustrated in Figure 12-2, the business's production capacity for the year is 150,000 units. However, this business produced only 120,000 units during the year, which is 30,000 units fewer than it could have produced. In other words, it operated at 80 per cent of production capacity, which is 20 per cent *idle capacity* (which isn't unusual):

> 120,000 units output ÷ 150,000 units capacity = 80% utilisation

Running at 80 per cent of production capacity, this business's burden rate for the year is £350 per unit (£42 million total fixed manufacturing costs ÷ 120,000 units output). The burden rate would have been higher if the company had produced, say, only 110,000 units during the year. The burden rate, in other words, is sensitive to the number of units produced. This can lead to all kinds of mischief, as explained next.

Excessive production output for puffing up profit

Whenever production output is higher than sales volume, be on guard. Excessive production can puff up the profit figure. How? Until a product is sold, the product cost goes in the stock asset account rather than the cost of goods sold expense account, meaning that the product cost is counted as a *positive* number (an asset) rather than a *negative* number (an expense). The burden rate is included in product cost, which means that this cost component goes into stock and is held there until the products are sold later. In short, when you overproduce, more of your fixed manufacturing costs for the period are moved to the stock asset account and less are moved into cost of goods sold expense, which is based on the number of units sold.

The actual costs/actual output method and when not to use it

To determine its product cost, the business in the Figure 12-2 example uses the *actual cost/actual output method,* in which you take your actual costs – which may have been higher or lower than the budgeted costs for the year – and divide by the actual output for the year.

The actual costs/actual output method is appropriate in most situations. However, this method is not appropriate and would have to be modified in two extreme situations:

✔ **Manufacturing costs are grossly excessive or wasteful due to inefficient production operations:** For example, suppose that the business represented in Figure 12–2 had to throw away £1.2 million of raw materials during the year. The £1.2 million is included in the total raw materials cost, but should be removed from the calculation of the raw material cost per unit. Instead, you treat it as a period cost – meaning that you take it directly into expense. Then the cost of

goods sold expense would be based on £750 per unit instead of £760, which lowers this expense by £1.1 million (based on the 110,000 units sold). But you still have to record the £1.2 million expense for wasted raw materials, so EBIT would be £100,000 lower.

✔ **Production output is significantly less than normal capacity utilisation:** Suppose that the Figure 12-2 business produced only 75,000 units during the year but still sold 110,000 units because it was working off a large stock carryover from the year before. Then its production capacity would be 50 per cent instead of 80 per cent. In a sense, the business wasted half of its production capacity, and you can argue that half of its fixed manufacturing costs should be charged directly to expense on the profit and loss account and not included in the calculation of product cost.

You need to judge whether a stock increase is justified. Be aware that an unjustified increase may be evidence of profit manipulation or just good old-fashioned management bungling. Either way, the day of reckoning will come when the products are sold and the cost of stock becomes cost of goods sold expense – at which point the cost subtracts from the bottom line.

Recapping the example shown in Figure 12-2: The business manufactured 10,000 more units than it sold during the year. With variable manufacturing costs at $410 per unit, the business took on $4.1 million more in manufacturing costs than it would have if it had produced only the 110,000 units needed for its sales volume. In other words, if the business had produced 10,000 fewer units, its variable manufacturing costs would have been $4.1 million less. That's the nature of variable costs. In contrast, if the company had manufactured 10,000 fewer units, its *fixed* manufacturing costs would not have been any less – that's the nature of fixed costs.

Of its £42 million total fixed manufacturing costs for the year, only £38.5 million ended up in the cost of goods sold expense for the year (£350 burden rate × 110,000 units sold). The other £3.5 million ended up in the stock asset account (£350 burden rate × 10,000 units stock increase). Let us be very clear here: We're not suggesting any hanky-panky. But the business did help its pre-tax profit to the amount of £3.5 million by producing 10,000 more units than it sold. If the business had produced only 110,000 units, equal to its sales volume for the year, then all the fixed manufacturing costs would have gone into cost of goods sold expense. As explained above, the expense would have been £3.5 million higher, and EBIT would have been that much lower.

Now suppose that the business manufactured 150,000 units during the year and increased its stock by 40,000 units. This may be a legitimate move if the business is anticipating a big jump in sales next year. But on the other hand, a stock increase of 40,000 units in a year in which only 110,000 units were sold may be the result of a serious overproduction mistake, and the larger stock may not be needed next year. In any case, Figure 12-3 shows what happens to production costs and – more importantly – what happens to profit at the higher production output level.

The additional 30,000 units (over and above the 120,000 units manufactured by the business in the original example) cost £410 per unit. (The precise cost may be a little higher than £410 per unit because, as you start crowding your production capacity, some variable costs may increase a little.) The business would need about £12.3 million more for the additional 30,000 units of production output:

> £410 variable manufacturing cost per unit × 30,000 additional units produced = £12,300,000 additional variable manufacturing costs invested in stock

But check out the business's EBIT in Figure 12-3: £23.65 million, compared with £15.95 million in Figure 12-2 – a £7.70 million increase, even though sales volume, sales prices and operating costs all remain the same. Whoa! What's going on here? The simple answer is that the cost of goods sold expense is £7.70 million less than before. But how can cost of goods sold expense be less? The business sells 110,000 units in both scenarios and variable manufacturing costs are £410 per unit in both cases.

The burden rate component of product cost in the first case is £350 (see Figure 12-2). In the second case the burden rate is only £280 (see Figure 12-3). Recall that the burden rate is computed by dividing total fixed manufacturing costs for the period by the production output during the period. Dividing by 150,000 units compared with 120,000 units reduces the burden rate from £350 to £280. The £70 lower burden rate multiplied by the 110,000 units sold results in a £7.7 million smaller cost of goods sold expense for the period, and a higher pre-tax profit of the same amount.

Management Profit and Loss Account for Year

Sales Volume	110,000 Units	
	Per Unit	**Totals**
Sales Revenue	£1,400	£154,000,000
→ Cost of Goods Sold Expense	(690)	(75,900,000)
Gross Margin	£710	£78,100,000
Variable Operating Expenses	(300)	(33,000,000)
Contribution Margin	£410	£45,100,000
Fixed Operating Expenses	(195)	(21,450,000)
Earnings Before Interest and Tax (EBIT)	£215	£23,650,000
Interest Expense		(2,750,000)
Earnings Before Tax		£20,900,000
Corporation Tax Expense		(7,106,000)
Net Income		£13,794,000

Manufacturing Cost Summary for Year

Annual Production Capacity	150,000 Units	
Actual Output	150,000 Units	
Production Cost Components	**Per Unit**	**Totals**
Raw Materials	£215	£32,250,000
Direct Labour	125	18,750,000
Variable Overhead	70	10,500,000
Total Variable Manufacturing Costs	£410	£61,500,000
Fixed Overhead	280	42,000,000
Total Manufacturing Costs	£690	£103,500,000
To 40,000 Units Stock Increase		(27,600,000)
To 110,000 Units Sold		£75,900,000

Figure 12-3: Example in which production output greatly exceeds sales volume, thereby boosting profit for the period.

In the first case the business puts £3.5 million of its total annual fixed manufacturing costs into the increase in stock (10,000 units increase × £350 burden rate). In the second case, in which the production output is at capacity, the business puts £11.2 million of its total fixed manufacturing costs into the increase in stock (40,000 units increase × £280 burden rate). Thus, £7.7 million more of its fixed manufacturing costs go into stock rather than cost of goods sold expense. But don't forget that stock increased 40,000 units, which is quite a large increase compared with the annual sales of 110,000 during the year just ended.

Who was responsible for the decision to go full blast and produce up to production capacity? Do the managers really expect sales to jump up enough next period to justify the much larger stock level? If they prove to be right, they'll look brilliant. But if the output level was a mistake and sales do not go up next year, they'll have you-know-what to pay next year, even though profit looks good this year. An experienced business manager knows to be on guard when stock takes such a big jump.

A View from the Top Regarding Costs

The CEO of a business gets paid to take the big-picture point of view. Using the business example in the chapter (refer to Figure 12-2 again), a typical CEO would study the management profit and loss account and say something like the following:

> *Not a bad year. Total costs were just about 90 per cent of sales revenue. EBIT per unit was a little more than 10 per cent of sales price (£145 per unit ÷ £1,400 sales price). I was able to spread my fixed operating expenses over 110,000 units of sales for an average of £195 per unit. Compared with the £340 contribution margin per unit, this yielded £145 EBIT per unit. I can live with this.*

> *I'd like to improve our margins, of course, but even if we don't, we should be able to increase sales volume next year. In fact, I notice that we produced 10,000 units more than we sold this year. So, I'll put pressure on the sales manager to give me her plan for increasing sales volume next year.*

> *I realise that cost numbers can be pushed around by my sharp-pencil accountants. They keep reminding me about cost classification problems between manufacturing and non-manufacturing costs – but, what the heck, it all comes out in the wash sooner or later. I watch the three major cost lines in my profit and loss account – cost of goods sold, variable operating expenses and fixed operating expenses.*

> *I realise that some costs can be classified in one or another of these groupings. So, I expect my accountants to be consistent period to period, and I have instructed them not to make any changes without my approval. Without consistency of accounting methods, I can't reliably compare my expense numbers from period to period. In my view, it's better to be arbitrary in the same way, period after period, rather than changing cost methods to keep up with the latest cost allocation fads.*

Chapter 13

Choosing Accounting Methods

. . . .

In This Chapter

▶ Having a choice of accounting methods

▶ Understanding the alternatives for calculating cost of goods sold expense and stock cost

▶ Dealing with depreciation

▶ Writing down stock and debtors

▶ Keeping two sets of books

. . . .

Some people put a great deal of faith in numbers: 2 + 2 = 4, and that's the end of the story. They see a number reported to the last digit on an accounting report, and they get the impression of exactitude. But accounting isn't just a matter of adding up numbers. It's not an exact science.

Accountants *do* have plenty of rules that they must follow. The official rule book of generally accepted accounting principles laid down by the Accounting Standards Board (and its predecessors) is more than 1,200 pages long and growing fast. In addition there are the rules and regulations issued by the various government regulatory agencies that govern financial reporting and accounting methods and those issued by publicly owned companies such as the London Stock Exchange. Also, the Institute of Chartered Accountants and the other professional accountancy institutes also play a role in setting accounting standards.

Although we're still in the early stages, standards are going *international* – the goal being to establish worldwide accounting standards. With the advent of the European Union and the ever-increasing amount of international trade and investing, business and political leaders in many nations recognise the need to iron out differences in accounting methods and disclosure standards from country to country.

Perhaps the most surprising thing – considering that formal rule-making activity has been going on since the 1930s – is that a business still has options for choosing among alternative accounting methods. Different methods lead to inconsistent profit measures from company to company. The often-repeated goal for standardising accounting methods is to make like things look alike and different things look different – but the accounting profession hasn't reached this stage of nirvana yet. In addition, accounting methods change over the years, as the business world changes. Accounting rules too are, to one degree or another, in a state of flux.

Because the choice of accounting methods directly affects the profit figure for the year and the values reported in the ending balance sheet, business managers (and investors) need to know the difference between accounting methods. You don't need to probe into these accounting methods in excruciating, technical detail, but you should at least know whether one method versus another yields higher or lower profit measures and higher or lower asset values in financial statements. This chapter explains accounting choices for measuring cost of goods sold, depreciation and other expenses. Get involved in making these important accounting decisions – it's your business, after all.

Decision-Making Behind the Scenes in Profit and Loss Accounts

Chapter 5 introduces the conventional format for presenting profit and loss accounts in *external* financial reports. (Also see Figure 9-1 for another example.) Figure 13-1 presents another profit and loss account for a business – with certain modifications that you won't see in actual external profit and loss accounts. For explaining the choices between alternative accounting methods, certain specific expenses are broken down under the company's sales, administrative and general expenses (SA&G) category in Figure 13-1. Of these particular expenses, only depreciation is disclosed in external profit and loss accounts. Don't expect to find in external profit and loss accounts the other expenses shown under the SA&G category in Figure 13-1. Businesses are very reluctant to divulge such information to the outside world.

Profit and Loss Account for Year

Sales Revenue		£26,000,000
Cost of Goods Sold Expense		14,300,000
Gross Margin		£11,700,000
Sales, Administrative, and General Expenses:		
Stock Shrinkage and Write-downs	£378,750	
Bad Debts	385,000	
Asset Impairment Write-downs	287,000	
Depreciation	780,000	
Warranty and Guarantee Expenses	967,250	
All Other SA&G Expenses	6,302,000	
Total		9,100,000
Earnings Before Interest and Tax		£2,600,000
Interest Expense		400,000
Earnings Before Tax		£2,200,000
Corporation Tax Expense		880,000
Net Income		£1,320,000

Figure 13-1:
A profit and loss account including certain expenses that are not reported outside the business.

Here's a quick overview of the accounting matters and choices relating to each line in the profit and loss account shown in Figure 13-1, from the top line to the bottom line:

- ✔ **Sales revenue:** Timing the recording of sales is something to be aware of. Generally speaking, sales revenue timing is not a serious accounting problem, but businesses should be consistent from one year to the next. However, for some businesses– such as software and other high-tech companies, and companies in their early start-up phases – the timing of recording sales revenue is a major problem. A footnote to the company's financial statements should explain its revenue recognition method if there is anything unusual about it.

  Note: If products are returnable and the deal between the seller and buyer does not satisfy normal conditions for a completed sale, then recognition of sales revenue should be postponed until the return privilege no longer exists. For example, some products are sold *on approval*, which means the customer takes the product and tries it out for a few days or longer to see if they really want it. This area is increasingly significant with the continuing rapid growth of the Internet as a medium for selling. In response, the UK introduced the Distance Selling Regulations in October 2001. These regulations give consumers additional rights to obtain full refunds on goods bought over the Internet and through mail order without having to give a reason for doing so.

✔ **Cost of goods sold expense:** Whether to use the first-in, first-out (FIFO) method, or the last-in, first-out (LIFO) method, or the average cost method (each of which is explained in the section 'Calculating Cost of Goods Sold and Cost of Stock' later in this chapter), cost of goods sold is a big expense for companies that sell products and naturally the choice of method can have a real impact.

✔ **Gross margin:** Can be dramatically affected by the method used for calculating cost of goods sold expense (and the method of revenue recognition, if this is a problem).

✔ **Stock write-downs:** Whether to count and inspect stock very carefully to determine loss due to theft, damage and deterioration, and whether to apply the net realisable value (NRV) method strictly or loosely are the two main questions that need to be answered. See 'Identifying Stock Losses: Net Realisable Value (NRV)' later in this chapter. Stock is a high-risk asset that's subject to theft, damage and obsolescence.

✔ **Bad debts expense:** When to conclude that the debts owed to you by customers who bought on credit (debtors) are not going to be paid – the question is really when to *write down* these debts (that is, remove the amounts from your asset column). You can wait until after you've made a substantial effort at collecting the debts, or you can make your decision before that time. See 'Collecting or Writing Off Bad Debts' later in this chapter.

✔ **Asset impairment write-downs:** Whether (and when) to *write down* or *write off* an asset – that is, remove it from the asset column. Stock shrinkage, bad debts and depreciation by their very nature are asset write-downs. Other asset write-downs are required when any asset becomes *impaired*, which means that it has lost some or all of its economic utility to the business and has little or no disposable value. An asset write-down reduces the book (recorded) value of an asset (and at the same time records an expense or loss of the same amount). A *write-off* reduces the asset's book value to zero and removes it from the accounts, and the entire amount becomes an expense or loss.

For example, your delivery truck driver had an accident. The repair of the truck was covered by insurance, so no write-down is necessary. But the products being delivered had to be thrown away and were not insured while in transit. You write off the cost of the stock lost in the accident.

✔ **Depreciation expense:** Whether to use a short-life method and load most of the expense over the first few years, or a longer-life method and spread the expense evenly over the years. Refer to 'Appreciating Depreciation Methods' later in this chapter. Depreciation is a big expense for some businesses, making the choice of method even more important.

✔ **Warranty and guarantee (post-sales) expenses:** Whether to record an expense for products sold with warranties and guarantees in the same period that the goods are sold (along with the cost of goods sold expense, of course) or later, when customers actually return products for repair or replacement. Businesses can usually forecast the percentage of products sold that will be returned for repair or replacement under the guarantees and warranties offered to customers – although a new product with no track record can be a problem in this regard.

✔ **All other SA&G expenses:** Whether to disclose separately one or more of the specific expenses included in this conglomerate total. For example, the SEC requires that *advertising* and *repairs and maintenance* expenses be disclosed in the documents businesses file with the SEC, but you hardly ever see these two expenses reported in external profit and loss accounts. Nor do you find individual top management compensation revealed in external profit and loss accounts, other than that for directors. GAAP does not require such disclosures – much less revealing things like bribes or other legally questionable payments by a business.

✔ **Earnings before interest and tax (EBIT):** This profit measure equals sales revenue less all the expenses above this line; therefore, EBIT depends on the particular choices made for recording sales revenue and expenses. Having a choice of accounting methods means that an amount of wriggle is inherent in recording sales revenue and many expenses. How much wriggle effect do all these accounting choices have on the EBIT profit figure? This is a very difficult question to answer. The business itself may not know. We would guess (and it's no more than a conjecture on our part) that the EBIT for a period reported by most businesses could easily be 10–20 per cent lower or higher if different accounting choices had been made.

✔ **Interest expense:** Usually a cut-and-dried calculation, with no accounting problems. (Well, we can think of some really hairy interest accounting problems, but we won't go into them here.)

✔ **Corporation tax expense:** You can use different accounting methods for some of the expenses reported in your profit and loss account than you use for calculating taxable income. Oh, crikey! The hypothetical amount of taxable income, if the accounting methods used in the profit and loss account were used in the tax return, is calculated; then the corporation tax based on this hypothetical taxable income is figured. This is the corporation tax expense reported in the profit and loss account. This amount is reconciled with the actual amount of corporation tax owed based on the accounting methods used for tax purposes. A reconciliation of the two different tax amounts is provided in a rather technical footnote to the financial statements. See 'Reconciling Corporation Tax' later in this chapter.

✔ **Net income:** Like EBIT, can vary considerably depending on which accounting methods you use for measuring expenses. (See also Chapter 8 on *profit smoothing*, which crosses the line from choosing acceptable accounting methods into the grey area of 'earnings management' through means of accounting manipulation.)

Whereas bad debts, post-sales expenses and asset write-downs vary in importance from business to business, cost of goods sold and depreciation methods are so important that a business must disclose which methods it uses for these two expenses in the footnotes to its financial statements. (Chapter 8 explains footnotes to financial statements.) HM Revenue and Customs requires that a company actually record in its cost of goods sold expense and stock asset accounts the amounts determined by the accounting method they use to determine taxable income – a rare requirement in company tax law.

Considering how important the bottom-line profit number is, and that different accounting methods can cause a major difference on this all-important number, you'd think that accountants would have developed clear-cut and definite rules so that only one accounting method would be correct for a given set of facts. No such luck. The final choice boils down to an arbitrary decision, made by top-level accountants in consultation with, and with consent of, managers. If you own a business or are a manager in a business, we strongly encourage you to get involved in choosing which accounting methods to use for measuring your profit and for presenting your balance sheet. Chapter 17 explains that a manager has to answer questions about his or her financial reports on many occasions, and so should know which accounting methods are used to prepare the financial statements.

Accounting methods vary from business to business more than you'd probably suspect, even though all of them stay within the boundaries of acceptable practice. The rest of this chapter expands on the methods available for measuring certain expenses. Sales revenue accounting can be a challenge as well, but profit accounting problems lie mostly on the expense side of the ledger.

Calculating Cost of Goods Sold and Cost of Stock

One main accounting problem of companies that sell products is how to measure their *cost of goods sold expense*, which is the sum of the costs of the products sold to customers during the period. You deduct cost of goods sold from sales revenue to determine *gross margin* – the first profit line on the profit and loss account (see Chapter 5 for more about profit and loss accounts, and Figure 9-1 for a typical profit and loss account). Cost of goods sold is therefore a very important figure, because if gross margin is wrong, bottom-line profit (net income) is wrong.

First a business acquires products, either by buying them (retailers) or by producing them (manufacturers). Chapter 12 explains how manufacturers determine product cost; for retailers product cost is simply the purchase cost. (Well, it's not entirely this simple, but you get the point.) Product cost is entered in the stock asset account and is held there until the products are sold. Then, but not before, product cost is taken out of stock and recorded in the cost of goods sold expense account. You must be absolutely clear on this point. Suppose that you clear £700 from your salary for the week and deposit this amount in your bank account. The money stays in there and is an asset until you spend it. You don't have an expense until you write a cheque.

Likewise, not until the business sells products does it have a cost of goods sold expense. When you write a cheque, you know how much it's for – you have no doubt about the amount of the expense. But when a business withdraws products from its stock and records cost of goods sold expense, the expense amount is in some doubt. The amount of expense depends on which accounting method the business selects.

The essence of this accounting issue is that you have to divide the total cost of your stock between the units sold (cost of goods sold expense, in the profit and loss account) and the unsold units that remain on hand waiting to be sold next period (stock asset, in the balance sheet).

For example, say you own a shop that sells antiques. Every time an item sells, you need to transfer the amount you paid for the item from the stock asset account into the cost of goods sold expense account. At the start of a fiscal period, your cost of goods sold expense is zero, and if you own a medium-sized shop selling medium-quality antiques, your stock asset account may be £20,000. Over the course of the fiscal period, your cost of goods sold expense should increase (hopefully rapidly, as you make many sales).

You probably want your stock asset account to remain fairly static, however. If you paid £200 for a wardrobe that sells during the period, the £200 leaves the stock asset account and finds a new home in the cost of goods sold expense account. However, you probably want to turn around and replace the item you sold, ultimately keeping your stock asset account at around the same level – although more complicated businesses have more complicated strategies for dealing with stock and more perplexing accounting problems.

You have three methods to choose from when you measure cost of goods sold and stock costs: You can follow a first-in, first-out (FIFO) cost sequence, follow a last-in, first-out cost sequence (LIFO), or compromise between the two methods and take the average costs for the period. Other methods are acceptable, but these three are the primary options. ***Caution:*** Product costs are entered in the stock asset account in the order acquired, but they are not necessarily taken out of the stock asset account in this order. The different methods refer to the order in which product costs are *taken out* of the stock asset account. You may think that only one method is appropriate – that the sequence in should be the sequence out. However, generally accepted accounting principles permit other methods.

In reality, the choice boils down to FIFO versus LIFO; the average cost method runs a distant third in popularity. If you want our opinion, FIFO is better than LIFO for reasons that we explain in the next two sections. You may not agree, and that's your right. For your business, you make the call.

The FIFO method

With the FIFO method, you charge out product costs to cost of goods sold expense in the chronological order in which you acquired the goods. The procedure is that simple. It's like the first people in line to see a film get in the cinema first. The usher collects the tickets in the order in which they were bought.

We think that FIFO is the best method for both the expense and the asset amounts. We hope that you like this method, but also look at the LIFO method before making up your mind. You should make up your mind, you know. Don't just sit on the sidelines. Take a stand.

Suppose that you acquire four units of a product during a period, one unit at a time, with unit costs as follows (in the order in which you acquire the items): £100, £102, £104 and £106. By the end of the period, you have sold three of those units. Using FIFO, you calculate the cost of goods sold expense as follows:

$$£100 + £102 + £104 = £306$$

In short, you use the first three units to calculate cost of goods sold expense. (You can see the benefit of having such a standard method if you sell hundreds or thousands of different products.)

The ending stock asset, then, is £106, which is the cost of the most recent acquisition. The £412 total cost of the four units is divided between the £306 cost of goods sold expense for the three units sold and the £106 cost of the one unit in ending stock. The total cost has been taken care of; nothing fell between the cracks.

FIFO works well for two reasons:

- ✔ In most businesses, products actually move into and out of stock in a first-in, first-out sequence: The earlier acquired products are delivered to customers before the later acquired products are delivered, so the most recently purchased products are the ones still in ending stock to be delivered in the future. Using FIFO, the stock asset reported on the balance sheet at the end of the period reflects the most recent purchase cost and therefore is close to the current *replacement cost* of the product.

- ✔ When product costs are steadily increasing, many (but not all) businesses follow a first-in, first-out sales price strategy and hold off on raising sales prices as long as possible. They delay raising sales prices until they have sold all lower-cost products. Only when they start selling from the next batch of products, acquired at a higher cost, do they raise sales prices. We strongly favour using the FIFO cost of goods sold expense method when the business follows this basic sales pricing policy because both the expense and the sales revenue are better matched for determining gross margin.

The LIFO method

Remember the cinema usher we mentioned earlier? Think about that usher going to the *back* of the line of people waiting to get into the next showing and letting them in from the rear of the line first. In other words, the later you bought your ticket, the sooner you get into the cinema. This is the LIFO method, which stands for *last-in, first-out*. The people in the front of the queue wouldn't stand for it, of course, but the LIFO method is quite acceptable for determining the cost of goods sold expense for products sold during the period. The main feature of the LIFO method is that it selects the *last* item you purchased first and then works backward until you have the total cost for the total number of units sold during the period. What about the ending stock, the products you haven't sold by the end of the year? Using the LIFO method, you never get back to the cost of the first products acquired (unless you sold out your entire stock); the earliest cost remains in the stock asset account.

Using the same example from the preceding section, assume that the business uses the LIFO method instead of FIFO. The four units, in order of acquisition, had costs of £100, £102, £104, and £106. If you sell three units during the period, LIFO gives you the following cost of goods sold expense:

£106 + £104 + £102 = £312

The ending stock cost of the one unit not sold is £100, which is the oldest cost. The £412 total cost of the four units acquired less the £312 cost of goods sold expense leaves £100 in the stock asset account. Determining which units you actually delivered to customers is irrelevant; when you use the LIFO method, you always count backward from the last unit you acquired.

If you really want to argue in favour of using LIFO – and we have to tell you that we won't back you up on this one – here's what you can say:

✔ Assigning the most recent costs of products purchased to the cost of goods sold expense makes sense because you have to replace your products to stay in business and the most recent costs are closest to the amount you will have to pay to replace your products. Ideally, you should base your sales prices not on original cost but on the cost of replacing the units sold.

✔ During times of rising costs, the most recent purchase cost maximises the cost of goods sold expense deduction for determining taxable income, and thus minimises the taxable income. In fact, LIFO was invented for income tax purposes. True, the cost of stock on the ending balance sheet is lower than recent acquisition costs, but the profit and loss account effect is more important than the balance sheet effect.

The more product cost you take out of the stock asset to charge to cost of goods sold expense, the less product cost you have in the ending stock. In maximising cost of goods sold expense, you minimise the stock cost value.

But here are the reasons why LIFO, in our view, is usually the wrong choice (the following sections of this chapter go into more details about these issues):

✔ Unless you base your sales prices on the most recent purchase costs or you raise sales prices as soon as replacement costs increase – and most businesses don't follow either of these pricing policies – using LIFO depresses your gross margin and, therefore, your bottom-line net income.

✔ The LIFO method can result in an ending stock cost value that's seriously out-of-date, especially if the business sells products that have very long lives.

✔ Unscrupulous managers can use the LIFO method to manipulate their profit figures if business isn't going well. Refer to 'Manipulating LIFO stock levels to give profit a boost' later in the chapter.

Note: In periods of rising product costs, it's true that FIFO results in higher taxable income than LIFO does – something you probably want to avoid, we're sure. Nevertheless, even though LIFO may be preferable in some circumstances, we still say that FIFO is the better choice in the majority of situations, for the reasons discussed earlier, and you may come over to our way of thinking after reading the following sections. By the way, if the products are intermingled such that they cannot be identified with particular purchases, then the business has to use FIFO for its income tax returns.

The greying of LIFO stock cost

If you sell products that have long lives and for which your product costs rise steadily over the years, using the LIFO method has a serious impact on the ending stock cost value reported on the balance sheet and can cause the balance sheet to look misleading. Over time, the cost of replacing products becomes further and further removed from the LIFO-based stock costs. Your 2012 balance sheet may very well report stock based on 1985, 1975 or 1965 product costs. As a matter of fact, the product costs used to value stock can go back even further.

Suppose that a major manufacturing business has been using LIFO for more than 45 years. The products that this business manufactures and sells have very long lives – in fact, the business has been making and selling many of the same products for many years. Believe it or not, the difference between its LIFO and FIFO cost values for its ending stock is about £2 billion because some of the products are based on costs going back to the 1950s, when the company first started using the LIFO method. The FIFO cost value of its ending stock is disclosed in a footnote to its financial statements; this disclosure is how you can tell the difference between a business's LIFO and FIFO cost values. The gross margin (before income tax) over the business's 45 years would have been £2 billion higher if the business had used the FIFO method – and its total taxable income over the 45 years would have been this much higher as well.

Of course, the business's income taxes over the years would have been correspondingly higher as well. That's the trade-off.

Note: A business must disclose the difference between its stock cost value according to LIFO and its stock cost value according to FIFO in a footnote on its financial statements – but, of course, not too many people outside of stock analysts and professional investment managers read footnotes. Business managers get involved in reviewing footnotes in the final steps of getting annual financial reports ready for release (refer to Chapter 8). If your business uses FIFO, your ending stock is stated at recent acquisition costs, and you do not have to determine what the LIFO value may have been. Annual financial reports do not disclose the estimated LIFO cost value for a FIFO-based stock.

Many products and raw materials have very short lives; they're regularly replaced by new models (you know, with those 'New and Improved!' labels) because of the latest technology or marketing wisdom. These products aren't around long enough to develop a wide gap between LIFO and FIFO, so the accounting choice between the two methods doesn't make as much difference as with long-lived products.

Manipulating LIFO stock levels to give profit a boost

The LIFO method opens the door to manipulation of profit – not that you would think of doing this, of course. Certainly, most of the businesses that choose LIFO do so to minimise current taxable income and delay paying taxes on it as long as possible – a legitimate (though perhaps misguided in some cases) goal. However, some unscrupulous managers know that they can use the LIFO method to 'create' some profit when business isn't going well.

So if a business that uses LIFO sells more products than it purchased (or manufactured) during the period, it has to reach back into its stock account and pull out older costs to transfer to the cost of goods sold expense. These costs are much lower than current costs, leading to an artificially low cost of goods sold expense, which in turn leads to an artificially high gross margin figure. This dipping into old cost layers of LIFO-based stock is called a *LIFO liquidation gain*.

This unethical manipulation of profit is possible for businesses that have been using LIFO for many years and have stock cost values far lower than the current purchase or manufacturing costs of products. By not replacing all the quantities sold, they let stock fall below normal levels.

Suppose that a retailer sold 100,000 units during the year and normally would have replaced all units sold. Instead, it purchased only 90,000 replacement units. Therefore, the other 10,000 units were taken out of stock, and the accountant had to reach back into the old cost layers of stock to record some of the cost of goods sold expense. To see the impact of LIFO liquidation gain on the gross margin, check out what the gross margin would look like if this business had replaced all 100,000 units versus the gross margin for replacing only 90,000. In this example, the old units in stock carry a LIFO-based cost of only £30, whereas the current purchase cost is £65. Assume that the units have a £100 price tag for the customer.

Gross margin if the business replaced all 100,000 of the units sold		
Sales revenue (100,000 units at £100 per unit)		£10,000,000
Cost of goods sold expense (100,000 units at £65 per unit)		6,500,000
Gross margin		£3,500,000

Gross margin if the business replaced only 90,000 of the units sold		
Sales revenue (100,000 units at £100 per unit)		£10,000,000
Cost of goods sold expense:		
Units replaced (90,000 units at £65 per unit)		£5,850,000
Units from stock (10,000 units at £30 per unit)	300,000	6,150,000
Gross margin		£3,850,000

The LIFO liquidation gain (the difference between the two gross margins) in this example is £350,000 – the £35 difference between the old and the current unit costs multiplied by 10,000 units. Just by ordering fewer replacement products, this business padded its gross margin – but in a very questionable way.

Of course, this business may have a good, legitimate reason for trimming stock by 10,000 units – to reduce the capital invested in that asset, for example, or to anticipate lower sales demand in the year ahead. LIFO liquidation gains may also occur when a business stops selling a product and that stock drops to zero. Still, we have to warn investors that when you see a financial statement reporting a dramatic decrease in stock and the business uses the LIFO method, you should be aware of the possible profit manipulation reasons behind the decrease.

Note: A business must disclose in the footnotes to its financial statements any substantial LIFO liquidation gains that occurred during the year. The outside auditor should make sure that the company includes this disclosure. (Chapter 15 discusses audits of financial statements by auditors.)

The average cost method

Although not nearly as popular as the FIFO and LIFO methods, the average cost method seems to offer the best of both worlds. The costs of many things in the business world fluctuate; business managers focus on the average product cost over a time period. Also, the averaging of product costs over a period of time has a desirable smoothing effect that prevents cost of goods sold from being overly dependent on wild swings of one or two purchases.

To many businesses, the compromise aspect of the method is its *worst* feature. Businesses may want to go one way or the other and avoid the middle ground. If they want to minimise taxable income, LIFO gives the best effect during times of rising prices. Why go only halfway with the average cost method? Or if the business wants its ending stock to be as near to current replacement costs as possible, FIFO is better than the average cost method. Even using computers to keep track of averages, which change every time product costs change, is a nuisance. No wonder the average cost method is not popular! But it *is* an acceptable method.

Identifying Stock Losses: Net Realisable Value (NRV)

Regardless of which method you use to determine stock cost, you should make sure that your accountants apply the *net realisable value (NRV)* test to stock. (Just to confuse you, this test is sometimes called the *lower of cost or market (LCM)* test.) A business should go through the NRV routine at least once a year, usually near or at year-end. The process consists of comparing the cost of every product in stock – meaning the cost that's recorded for each product in the stock asset account according to the FIFO or LIFO method (or whichever method the company uses) – with two benchmark values:

- ✔ The product's *current replacement cost* (how much the business would pay to obtain the same product right now).

- ✔ The product's *net realisable value* (how much the business can sell the product for).

If a product's cost on the books is higher than either of these two benchmark values, your accountant should decrease product cost to the lower of the two. In other words, stock losses are recognised *now* rather than *later*, when the products are sold. The drop in the replacement cost or sales value of the product should be recorded now, on the theory that it's better to take your medicine now than to put it off. Also, the stock cost value on the balance sheet is more conservative because stock is reported at a lower cost value.

Buying and holding stock involves certain unavoidable risks. Asset write-downs, explained in the 'Decision-Making behind the Scenes in Profit and Loss Accounts' section of this chapter, are recorded to recognise the consequences of two of those risks – stock shrinkage and losses to natural disasters not fully covered by insurance. NRV records the losses from two other risks of holding stock:

✔ **Replacement cost risk:** After you purchase or manufacture a product, its replacement cost may drop permanently below the amount you paid (which usually also affects the amount you can charge customers for the products, because competitors will drop their prices).

✔ **Sales demand risk:** Demand for a product may drop off permanently, forcing you to sell the products below cost just to get rid of them.

Determining current replacement cost values for every product in your stock isn't easy! Applying the NRV test leaves much room for interpretation.

Keeping accurate track of your stock costs is important to your bottom line both now and in the future, so don't fall into the trap of doing a quick NRV scan and making a snap judgment that you don't need a stock write-down.

Some shady characters abuse NRV to cheat on their company tax returns. They *write down* their ending stock cost value – decrease ending stock cost more than can be justified by the NRV test – to increase the deductible expenses on their tax returns and thus decrease taxable income. A product may have a proper cost value of £100, for example, but a shady character may invent some reason to lower it to £75 and thus record a £25 stock write-down expense in this period for each unit – which is not justified by the facts. But, even though the person can deduct more this year, he or she will have a lower stock cost to deduct in the future. Also, if the person is selected for an HM Revenue and Customs audit and the tax inspectors discover an unjustified stock write-down, the person may end up being charged with tax evasion.

Most accounting software packages either support or have plug-in modules that allow you to run all these costing methods and compare their effect on your apparent financial performance. For example, the Sage Pro Inventory Control module (check out their website at `www.sageproerp.com/products/accounting/ic`) supports LIFO, FIFO, average weighted and standard cost inventory valuation methods.

Managing Your Stock Position

Businesses have to carry a certain minimum amount of stock to ensure the production pipeline works efficiently and likely demand is met. So the costs associated with ordering large quantities infrequently and so reducing the order cost but increasing the cost of holding stock has to be balanced with placing frequent orders, which pushes the cost of orders up, but reduces stock holding costs. Economic Order Quantity (EOQ) is basically an accounting formula that calculates the most cost-effective quantity to order; the point at which the combination of order costs and inventory carrying costs are at the minimum.

The formula for EOQ is:

$$\text{Economic Order Quantity} = \sqrt{\frac{(2 \times R \times O)}{C}}$$

Where: R = Annual demand in units; O = Cost of placing an order; C = Cost of carrying a unit of inventory for the year.

Appreciating Depreciation Methods

In theory, depreciation expense accounting is straightforward enough: You divide the cost of a fixed asset among the number of years that the business expects to use the asset. In other words, instead of having a huge lump-sum expense in the year that you make the purchase, you charge a fraction of the cost to expense for each year of the asset's lifetime. Using this method is much easier on your bottom line in the year of purchase, of course.

But theories are rarely as simple in real life as they are on paper, and this one is no exception. Do you divide the cost *evenly* across the asset's lifetime, or do you charge more to certain years than others? Furthermore, when it eventually comes time to dispose of fixed assets, the assets may have some disposable, or *salvage*, value. Only cost minus the salvage value should be depreciated, right? Or, should salvage value estimates be ignored and the total cost of a fixed asset be depreciated? And how do you estimate how long an asset will last in the first place? Do you consult an accountant psychic hot line?

As it turns out, HM Revenue and Customs runs its own little psychic business on the side, with a crystal ball known as the HM Revenue and Customs Code. The HM Revenue and Customs Code doesn't give you predictions of how long your fixed assets will *last*; it only tells you what kind of timeline to use for income tax purposes, as well as how to divide the cost along that timeline. HM Revenue and Customs have a little help in their psychic predictions. They have a direct line to their boss, the Chancellor of the Exchequer, who varies these rules every year or so to stimulate capital spending by businesses. This is done by varying the *writing down allowance*, which is tax speak for the amount of depreciation expense you can get tax relief for. So if the Chancellor wants to encourage businesses to buy computers, he can set a 100 per cent writing down allowance for the first year, whereas the asset may well have an economic life of three years or more. Confused? Well at least you know what you are getting for your money when you hire a tax accountant.

Hundreds of books have been written on depreciation, but the only book that counts is the HM Revenue and Customs Code. Most businesses adopt the useful lives allowed by the income tax law for their financial statement accounting; they don't go to the trouble of keeping a second depreciation schedule for financial reporting. Why complicate things if you don't have to? Why keep one depreciation schedule for income tax and a second for preparing your financial statements? However, they do tell you what their policy is.

Tesco's annual report contains this explanation of their depreciation policy:

Depreciation is provided on a straight-line basis over the anticipated useful economic lives of the assets. The following rates applied for the Group and are consistent with the prior year:

- ✔ Land premiums paid in excess of the alternative use value – at 2.5 per cent of cost.

- ✔ Freehold and leasehold buildings with greater than 40 years unexpired – at 2.5 per cent of cost.

- ✔ Leasehold properties with less than 40 years unexpired are amortised by equal annual instalments over the unexpired period of the lease.

- ✔ Plant, equipment, fixtures and fittings, and motor vehicles – at rates varying from 10 per cent to 33 per cent.

By the way, keeping two depreciation schedules is an example of *keeping two sets of books*. In some situations a person using this term is referring to the illegal tactic of keeping one set of accounts for the actual amounts of sales revenue and expenses and keeping a second set of fictional accounts for income tax purposes. (We've never seen two sets of books in actual practice – although, we have seen cases of skimming sales revenue and inflating expenses on the books to minimise the taxable income of a business.)

Note: Taxation laws can change at any time and can get extremely technical. Please use the following information for a basic understanding of the procedures and *not* as tax advice. There are a number of annual income tax guides, such as *Tolley's Tax Guides*, published by Butterworths.

HM Revenue and Customs' rules give guidance on which of two depreciation methods to use for particular types of assets:

✔ **Straight-line depreciation method:** With this method, you divide the cost evenly among the years of the asset's estimated lifetime. So if a new building owned and used by a business costs £390,000 and its useful life is 39 years, the depreciation expense is £10,000 (⅟₃₉ of the cost) for each of the 39 years. (See the example of Tesco above.) You must use straight-line depreciation for buildings and may choose to use it for other types of assets; once you start using this method for a particular asset, you can't change your mind and switch to another method later.

✔ **Accelerated depreciation method:** Actually, this term is a generic catch-all for several different kinds of methods. What they all have in common is that they're *front-loading* methods, meaning that you charge a larger amount of depreciation expense in the early years and a smaller amount in the later years. *Accelerated depreciation method* also refers to adopting useful lives that are shorter than realistic estimates (very few cars are useless after five years, for example, but they can be fully depreciated over five years).

One popular accelerated method is the *double-declining balance* (DDB) depreciation method. With this method, you calculate the straight-line depreciation rate and then you double that percentage. You apply that doubled percentage to the declining balance over the course of the asset's depreciation time line. After a certain number of years, you switch back to the straight-line method for the remainder of the asset's depreciation years to ensure that you depreciate the full cost by the end of the predetermined number of years. See the sidebar 'The double-declining balance depreciation method' for an example.

By the way, the salvage value of fixed assets (the estimated disposal values when the assets are taken to the junkyard or sold off at the end of their useful lives) is ignored in the calculation of depreciation for income tax. Put another way, if a fixed asset is held to the end of its entire depreciation life, then its original cost will be fully depreciated, and the fixed asset from that time forward will have a zero book value. (Recall that book value is equal to the cost minus the balance in the accumulated depreciation account.) Fully depreciated fixed assets are grouped with all other fixed assets in external balance sheets. All these long-term resources of a business are reported in one asset account called *property, plant and equipment* (instead of fixed assets). If all its fixed assets were fully depreciated, the balance sheet of a company would look rather peculiar – the cost of its fixed assets would be completely offset by its accumulated depreciation. We've never seen this, but it would be possible for a business that hasn't replaced any of its fixed assets for a long time.

The straight-line method has strong advantages: It's easy to understand and it stabilises the depreciation expense from year to year. But many business managers and accountants favour the accelerated depreciation method. Keep in mind, however, that the depreciation expense in the annual profit and loss account is higher in the early years when you use an accelerated depreciation method, and so bottom-line profit is lower until later years. Nevertheless, many accountants and businesses like accelerated depreciation because it paints a more conservative (a lower, or a more moderate) picture of profit performance in the early years. Who knows? Fixed assets may lose their economic usefulness to a business sooner than expected. If this happens, using the accelerated depreciation method would look good in hindsight.

Minimising taxable income and corporation tax in the early years to hang on to as much cash as possible is very important to many businesses, and they pay the price of reporting lower net income in order to defer paying corporation tax as long as possible. Or they may use the straight-line method in their financial statements even though they use an accelerated method in their annual tax returns, which complicates matters. (Refer to the section 'Reconciling Corporation Tax' for more information.)

The double-declining balance depreciation method

Suppose that a business pays £100,000 for a fixed asset that has a five-year useful life and for which the double-declining balance depreciation method is used. The annual depreciation expense by the straight-line method is $\frac{1}{5}$, or 20 per cent, of cost per year – which in this example would be £20,000 per year. With the DDB method, you double that percentage to 40 per cent, which gives £40,000 depreciation for the first year. After the first year, however, the 40 per cent rate of depreciation is applied to the declining balance of the fixed asset. For example, in the second year, depreciation equals the £60,000 non-depreciated balance of the fixed asset (£100,000 cost less the £40,000 first year depreciation) multiplied by the 40 per cent rate – which gives £24,000 depreciation for the second year. The third year's depreciation is 40 per cent of £36,000 (£100,000 cost minus the £64,000 accumulated depreciation balance).

You then switch to the straight-line method on the remaining amount of non-depreciated cost for the last two years in this example (the exact number of years depends on the number of years in the asset's depreciation timeline) – meaning that you divide the remaining balance by the number of remaining years. In this example, you need to use the straight-line method after the third year because if you applied the 40 per cent rate to the non-depreciated balance of the fixed asset at the start of the fourth year and again in the following year on the declining balance, the fixed asset's cost would not be completely depreciated by the end of five years.

Got all that? Good, because things get even more technical and complicated in company tax law. For example, businesses that buy fixed assets in the later part of a year must follow the *half-year* convention, which requires that the business use a midpoint date in the year that an asset is acquired and placed in service. We don't want to get into all the details here; suffice it to say that you need a good tax-law accountant to get the most out of your depreciation expense deduction.

Except for brand-new enterprises, a business typically has a mix of fixed assets – some in their early years of depreciation, some in their middle years and some in their later years. So, the overall depreciation expense for the year may not be that different than if the business had been using straight-line depreciation for all its fixed assets. A business does *not* have to disclose in its external financial report what its depreciation expense would have been if it had been using an alternative method. Readers of the financial statements cannot tell how much difference the choice of depreciation method made in that year.

Collecting or Writing Off Bad Debts

A business that allows its customers to pay on credit granted by the business is always subject to *bad debts* – debts that some customers never pay off. You are allowed, provided that you demonstrate serious efforts to recover the money owed, to write the loss in value off against your tax bill. You may also recover any VAT paid in respect of the invoice concerned. Don't forget in your role as an unpaid tax collector you will have charged your defaulting customer Value-Added Tax, paid that over to HM Revenue and Customs as required, but failed to recover the loot from the said customer, along with the rest of the boodle owed.

Reconciling Corporation Tax

Corporation tax is a heavy influence on a business's choice of accounting methods. Many a business decides to minimise its current taxable income by recording the maximum amount of deductible expenses. Thus, taxable income is lower, corporation tax paid to the Treasury is lower and the business's cash balance is higher. Using these expense maximisation methods to prepare the profit and loss account of the business has the obvious effect of minimising the profit that's reported to the owners of the business. So, you may ask whether you can use one accounting method for corporation tax but an alternative method for preparing your financial statements. Can a business eat its cake (minimise corporation tax) and have it too (report more profit in its profit and loss account)?

The answer is yes, you can. You may decide, however, that using two different accounting methods is not worth the time and effort. In other areas of accounting for profit, businesses use one method for income tax and an alternative method in the financial statements (but we don't want to go into the details here).

When recording an expense, either an asset is decreased or a liability is increased. In this example, a special type of liability is increased to record the full amount of corporation tax expense: *deferred tax payable*. This unique liability account recognises the special contingency hanging over the head of the business to anticipate the time in the future when the business exhausts the higher depreciation amounts deducted in the early years by accelerated depreciation, and moves into the later years when annual depreciation amounts are less than amounts by the straight-line depreciation method. This liability account does not bear interest. Be warned that the accounting for this liability can get very complicated. The business provides information about this liability in a footnote to its financial statements, as well as reconciling the amount of corporation tax expense reported in its profit and loss account with the tax owed the government based on its tax return for the year. These footnotes are a joy to read – just kidding.

Dealing With Foreign Exchange

Foreign exchange poses a tricky problem when it comes to accounting reports. Currencies just aren't stable and they certainly don't respect year-end. A business can have all sorts of currency swishing around, pounds, dollars, euros, yen . . . You need to include a note in your accounts to explain the extent of your use of foreign exchange and the way in which you've handled the conversion of currencies. In this section I explain three areas to pay particular attention to.

Transaction exposure

Transaction exposure occurs when a business incurs costs or generates revenues in any currency other than the one shown in its filed accounts. Two types of event can lead to this:

- ✔ A mismatch between cost of sales (manufacturing and so on) incurred in one currency and the actual sales income generated in another.

- ✔ A time lag between setting the selling price in one currency and the date the customer actually pays up.

As exchange rates frequently change, you need to explain how you handled the conversions.

Translation exposure

Translation exposure refers to the effects of movements in the exchange rate on the balance sheet and profit and loss account that occur between reporting dates on assets and liabilities denominated in foreign currencies. In practice, any company that has assets or liabilities denominated in a currency other than the currency shown on their reported accounts has to 'translate' those back into the company's reporting currency when the consolidated accounts have to be produced. This can be up to four times a year for major trading businesses. Any changes in the foreign exchange rate between the countries involved cause movements in the accounts.

Comparing performance

Exchange rate movements can make it difficult to compare one year with another; an essential accounting task if management is to keep track of how a business is performing. For example, if a UK company sold 1,000 of its products into a eurozone country, its selling price expressed in pounds sterling could be as much as ten percent higher or lower (a euro was anything from 80.68p to 90.43p in the most recent 52-week period while we prepared this edition).

Accountants usually handle this movement by stating that current year revenue is compared to the prior financial year, translated on consistent exchange rates to eliminate distortions due to fluctuations in exchange rates. In any event, you need to include a note in the accounts showing how you've handled currency movements.

Two Final Issues to Consider

We think that you have been assuming all along that *all* expenses should be recorded by a business. Of course, you're correct on this score. Many accountants argue that two expenses, in fact, are not recorded by businesses, but should be. A good deal of controversy surrounds both items. Many think one or both expenses should be recognised in measuring profit and in presenting the financial statements of a business:

   ✔ **Share options:** As part of their compensation packages, many public companies award their high-level executives share options, which give them the right to buy a certain number of shares at fixed prices after certain conditions are satisfied (years of service and the like). If the market price of the company's shares in the future rises above the exercise (purchase) prices of the share options – assuming the other conditions of these contracts are satisfied – the executives use their share options to buy shares below the going market price of the shares.

Should the difference between the going market price of the shares and the exercise prices paid for the shares by the executives be recognised as an expense? Generally accepted accounting principles (GAAP) do not require that such an expense be recorded (unless the exercise price was below the market price at the time of granting the share option). However, the business must present a footnote disclosing the number of shares and exercise prices of its stock options, the theoretical cost of the share options to the business, and the dilution effect on earnings per share that exercising the share options will have. But this is a far cry from recording an expense in the profit and loss account. Many persons, including Warren Buffett, who is Chair of Berkshire Hathaway, Inc, are strongly opposed to share options – thinking that the better alternative is to pay the executives in cash and avoid diluting earnings per share, which depresses the market value of the shares.

In brief, the cost to shareholders of share options is off the books. The dilution in the market value of the shares of the corporation caused by its share options is suffered by the shareholders, but does not flow through the profit and loss account of the business.

✔ **Purchasing power of pound loss caused by inflation:** Due to inflation, the purchasing power of one pound today is less than it was one year ago, two years ago and so on back in time. Yet accountants treat all pounds the same, regardless of when the pound amounts were recorded on the books. The cost balance in a fixed asset account (a building, for instance) may have been recorded 10 or 20 years ago; in contrast, the cost balance in a current asset account (stock, for instance) may have been recorded only one or two months ago (assuming the business uses the FIFO method). So, depreciation expense is based on very old pounds that had more purchasing power back then, and cost of goods sold expense is based on current pounds that have less purchasing power than in earlier years.

Stay tuned for what might develop in the future regarding these two expenses. If we had to hazard a prediction, we would say that the pressure for recording the expense of share options will continue and might conceivably succeed – although we would add that powerful interests oppose recording share options expense. On the other hand, the loss of purchasing power of the pound caused by inflation has become less important in an era signified by low inflation rates around the world. However, an enormous increase in the rate of inflation would resurrect this argument, and with rates of 5 per cent and more prevailing in some parts of 'new' Europe, 7 per cent in India, 10 per cent in Russia and 11 per cent in Turkey, the beast is not quite as dead as economists would like us to believe.

Part IV
Financial Reports in the Outside World

'Oh no! Not another bad company
financial report.'

In this part . . .

This part looks at accounting and financial reporting from the outside investor's, or non-manager's point of view. Outside investors in a business – the owners who are not on the inside managing the business – depend on the financial reports from the business as their main source of information about the business. Investors should know how to read and interpret the financial statements and what to look for in the footnotes to the statements. Their main concerns are the business's profit and cash flow performance and its financial health. Lenders to the business have similar interests in how the business is doing. Key ratios are calculated to test the success of the business in making profit and keeping its financial affairs in order. You can use the same ratios on the accounts of your competitors, customers, suppliers or potential acquisition targets to see how they're performing.

Investors should also read the independent auditor's report, which provides some, though far from conclusive, assurance that the financial statements have been prepared properly. The auditor's report may reveal serious shortcomings in the statements (if they find any), and warns investors in the event that the business is standing on thin financial ice and may not be able to continue as a going concern. Investors should also look and see from a financial perspective how comparable businesses are performing.

Chapter 14

How Investors Read a Financial Report

In This Chapter

▶ Looking after your investments

▶ Keeping financial reports private versus making them public

▶ Using ratios to understand profit performance

▶ Using ratios to interpret financial condition and cash flow

▶ Scanning footnotes and identifying the important ones

▶ Paying attention to what the auditor has to say

*1*n reading financial reports, directors, managers, business owners and investors need to know how to navigate through the financial statements to find the vital signs of progress and problems. The financial statement ratios explained in this chapter point the way – these ratios are signposts on the financial information highway. You can also keep abreast of business affairs by reading financial newspapers and investment magazines, and investment newsletters are very popular. These sources of financial information refer to the ratios discussed in this chapter on the premise that you know what the ratios mean. Most managers or individual investors in public companies don't have the time or expertise to study a financial report thoroughly enough to make decisions based on the report, so they rely on stockbrokers, investment advisers and publishers of credit ratings (like Standard & Poor's) for interpretations of financial reports. The fact is that the folks who prepare financial reports have this kind of expert audience in mind; they don't include explanations or mark passages with icons to help *you* understand the report.

Sure you may have your own accountant or investment adviser on tap so why should you bother reading this chapter if you rely on others to interpret financial reports anyway? Well, the more you understand the factors that go into interpreting a financial report, the better prepared you are to evaluate the commentary and advice of stock analysts and other investment experts. If you can at least nod intelligently while your stockbroker talks about a business's P/E and EPS, you'll look like a savvy investor – and may get more favourable treatment. (P/E and EPS, by the way, are two of the key ratios explained later in the chapter.)

This chapter gives you the basics for comparing companies' financial reports, including the points of difference between private and public companies, the important ratios that you should know about and the warning signs to look out for on audit reports. Part II of this book explains the three primary financial statements that are the core of every financial report: the profit and loss account, the balance sheet and the cash flow statement. In this chapter, we also suggest how to sort through the footnotes that are an integral part of every financial report to identify those that have the most importance to you. Believe us, the pros read the footnotes with a keen eye.

Financial Reporting by Private versus Public Businesses

The main impetus behind the continued development of generally accepted accounting principles (GAAP) has been the widespread public ownership and trading in the securities (stocks and bonds) issued by thousands of companies. The 1929 stock market crash and its aftermath plainly exposed the lack of accounting standards, as well as many financial reporting abuses and frauds. Landmark federal securities laws were passed in the US in 1933 and 1934, and a federal regulatory agency with broad powers – the Securities and Exchange Commission (SEC) – was created and given jurisdiction over trading in corporate securities. In the UK, the Government has enacted a series of Companies Acts, culminating in one consolidated act in 2006, that have strengthened the protection for shareholders. Financial reports and other information must be filed with The London Stock Exchange or the relevant authorities elsewhere, such as the SEC in the US, and made available to the investing public.

Accounting standards are not limited to public companies whose securities are traded on public exchanges, such as the London and New York Stock Exchanges and NASDAQ. These financial accounting and reporting standards apply with equal force and authority to private businesses whose ownership shares are not traded in any open market. When the shareholders of a private business receive its periodic financial reports, they are entitled to assume that the company's financial statements and footnotes are prepared in accordance with the accounting rules in force at the time. Even following the rules leaves a fair amount of wriggle room – look back to Chapter 13 if you need a refresher on this subject. So it always pays to check over the figures yourself to be sure of what is really going on. The bare-bones content of a private business's annual financial report includes the three primary financial statements (balance sheet, profit and loss account, and cash flow statement) plus several footnotes. We've seen many private company financial reports that don't even have a letter from the chairman – just the three financial statements plus a few footnotes and nothing more. In fact, we've seen financial reports of private businesses (mostly small companies) that don't even include a cash flow statement; only the balance sheet and profit and loss account are presented. Omitting a cash flow statement violates the rules – but the company's shareholders and its lenders may not demand to see the cash flow statement, so the company can get away with it.

Publicly owned businesses must comply with an additional layer of rules and requirements that don't apply to privately owned businesses. These rules are issued by the Stock Exchange, the agency that regulates financial reporting and trading in stocks and bonds of publicly owned businesses. The Stock Exchange has no jurisdiction over private businesses; those businesses need only worry about GAAP, which don't have many hard-and-fast rules about financial report formats. Public businesses have to file financial reports and other forms with the Stock Exchange that are made available to the public. These filings are available to the public on the London Stock Exchange's website www.londonstockexchange.com/ or for US companies on the Securities Exchange Commission's (SEC's) EDGAR database at the SEC's website – www.sec.gov/edgar/quickedgar.htm.

The best known of these forms is the annual 10-K, which includes the business's annual financial statements in prescribed formats with all the supporting schedules and detailed disclosures that the SEC requires.

Here are some (but not all) of the main financial reporting requirements that publicly owned businesses must adhere to. (Private businesses may include these items as well if they want, but they generally don't.)

- ✔ **Management discussion and analysis (MD&A) section:** Presents the top managers' interpretation and analysis of a business's profit performance and other important financial developments over the year.

- ✔ **Earnings per share (EPS):** The only ratio that a public business is *required* to report, although most public businesses do report a few other ratios as well. See 'Earnings per share, basic and diluted' later in this chapter. Note that private businesses' reports generally don't include any ratios (but you can, of course, compute the ratios yourself).

- ✔ **Three-year comparative profit and loss account:** See Chapter 5 for more information about profit and loss accounts.

Note: A publicly-owned business can make the required filings with the Stock Exchange or SEC and then prepare a different annual financial report for its shareholders, thus preparing two sets of financial reports. This is common practice. However, the financial information in the two documents can't differ in any material way. A typical annual financial report to shareholders is a glossy booklet with excellent art and graphic design including high-quality photographs. The company's products are promoted and its people are featured in glowing terms that describe teamwork, creativity and innovation – we're sure you get the picture. In contrast, the reports to the London Stock Exchange or SEC look like legal briefs – nothing fancy in these filings. The core of financial statements and footnotes (plus certain other information) is the same in both the Stock Exchange filings and the annual reports to shareholders. The Stock Exchange filings contain more information about certain expenses and require much more disclosure about the history of the business, its main markets and competitors, its principal officers, any major changes on the horizon and so on. Professional investors and investment managers read the Stock Exchange filings.

Most public companies solicit their shareholders' votes in the annual election of persons to the board of directors (whom the business has nominated) and on other matters that must be put to a vote at the annual shareholders' meeting. The method of communication for doing so is called a *proxy statement* – the reason being that the shareholders give their votes to a *proxy*, or designated person, who actually casts the votes at the annual meeting. The Stock Exchange requires many disclosures in proxy statements that are not found in annual financial reports issued to shareholders or in the business's annual accounts filed at Companies House. For example, compensation paid to the top-level officers of the business must be disclosed, as well as their shareholdings. If you own shares in a public company, take the time to read through all the financial statements you receive through the post and any others you can get your hands on.

Analysing Financial Reports with Ratios

Financial reports have lots of numbers in them. (Duh!) The significance of many of these numbers is not clear unless they are compared with other numbers in the financial statements to determine the relative size of one number to another number. One very useful way of interpreting financial reports is to compute *ratios* – that is, to divide a particular number in the financial report by another. Financial report ratios are also useful because they enable you to compare a business's current performance with its past performance or with another business's performance, regardless of whether sales revenue or net income was bigger or smaller for the other years or the other business. In other words, using ratios cancels out size differences.

The following sections explain the ten financial statement ratios that you're most likely to run into. Here's a general overview of why these ratios are important:

- ✔ **Gross margin ratio and profit ratio:** You use these ratios to measure a business's profit performance with respect to its sales revenue. Sales revenue is the starting point for making profit; these ratios measure the percentage of total sales revenue that is left over as profit.

- ✔ **Earnings per share (EPS), price/earnings (P/E) ratio and dividend yield:** These three ratios revolve around the market price of shares, and anyone who invests in publicly owned businesses should be intimately familiar with them. As an investor, your main concern is the return you receive on your invested capital. Return on capital consists of two elements:

  - Periodic **cash dividends** distributed by the business.

  - Increase (or decrease) in the **market price** of the shares.

  Dividends and market prices depend on earnings – and there you have the relationship among these three ratios and why they're so important to you, the investor. Major newspapers report P/E ratios and dividend yields in their stock market activity tables; stockbrokers' investment reports focus mainly on forecasts of EPS and dividend yield.

- ✔ **Book value per share and return on equity (ROE):** Shares for private businesses have no ready market price, so investors in these businesses use the ROE ratio, which is based on the value of their ownership equity reported in the balance sheet, to measure investment performance. Without a market price for the shares of a private business, the P/E ratio cannot be determined. EPS can easily be determined for a private business but does not have to be reported in its profit and loss account.

- ✔ **Current ratio and acid-test ratio:** These ratios indicate whether a business should have enough cash to pay its liabilities.

- ✔ **Return on assets (ROA):** This ratio is the first step in determining how well a business is using its capital and whether it's earning more than the interest rate on its debt, which causes financial leverage gain (or loss).

The profit and loss account and balance sheet of the business example that we first use in Chapter 8 are repeated here so that you have a financial statement for reference – see Figures 14-1 (profit and loss account) and 14-2 (balance sheet). Notice that a cash flow statement is not presented here – mainly because no ratios are calculated from data in the cash flow statement. (Refer to the sidebar 'The temptation to compute cash flow per share: Don't give in!') The footnotes to the company's financial statements are not presented here, but the use of footnotes is discussed in the following sections.

(Amounts in thousands, except per share amounts)	
Profit and Loss Account for Year	
Sales Revenue	£ 52,000
Cost of Goods Sold Expense	31,200
Gross Margin	£ 20,800
Sales, Administration, and General Expenses	15,600
Depreciation Expense	1,650
Earnings Before Interest and Tax	£ 3,550
Interest Expense	750
Earnings Before Tax	£ 2,800
Corporation Tax Expense	900
Net Income	£ 1,900
Earnings Per Share	£ 2.39

Figure 14-1: A sample profit and loss account.

(Amounts in thousands)		
Balance Sheet at End of Year		
Assets		
Cash	£ 3,500	
Debtors	5,000	
Stock	7,800	
Prepaid Expenses	900	
Current Assets		£ 17,200
Fixed Assets	£ 19,500	
Accumulated Depreciation	(6,825)	12,675
Total Assets		£ 29,875
Liabilities		
Creditors	£ 1,500	
Accrued Expenses Payable	2,400	
Tax Payable	75	
Overdraft	4,000	
Current Liabilities		£ 7,975
Long-term Loans		6,000
Owners' Equity		
Share Capital (795,000 shares)	£ 4,000	
Retained Earnings	11,900	15,900
Total Liabilities and Owners' Equity		£ 29,875

Figure 14-2: A sample balance sheet.

Gross margin ratio

Making bottom-line profit begins with making sales and earning enough gross margin from those sales, as explained in Chapters 5 and 9. In other words, a business must set its sales prices high enough over product costs to yield satisfactory gross margins on its products, because the business has to worry about many more expenses of making sales and running the business, plus interest expense and income tax expense. You calculate the _gross margin ratio_ as follows:

$$\text{Gross margin} \div \text{sales revenue} = \text{gross margin ratio}$$

So a business with a £20.8 million gross margin and £52 million in sales revenue (refer to Figure 14-1) ends up with a 40 per cent gross margin ratio. Now, if the business had only been able to earn a 41 per cent gross margin, that one additional point (one point is 1 per cent) would have caused a jump in its gross margin of £520,000 (1 per cent × £52 million sales revenue) – which would have trickled down to earnings before income tax. Earnings before income tax would have been 19 per cent higher (a £520,000 bump in gross margin ÷ £2.8 million income before income tax). Never underestimate the impact of even a small improvement in the gross margin ratio!

Outside investors know only the information disclosed in the external financial report that the business releases. They can't do much more than compare the gross margin for the two- or three-yearly profit and loss accounts included in the annual financial report. Although publicly owned businesses are required to include a management discussion and analysis (MD&A) section that should comment on any significant change in the gross margin ratio, corporate managers have wide latitude in deciding what exactly to discuss and how much detail to go into. You definitely should read the MD&A section, but it may not provide all the answers you're looking for. You have to search further in stockbroker releases, in articles in the financial press, or at the next professional business meeting you attend.

As explained in Chapter 9, managers focus on _contribution margin per unit_ and _total contribution margin_ to control and improve profit performance business. Contribution margin equals sales revenue minus product cost and other variable operating expenses of the business. Contribution margin is profit before the company's total fixed costs for the period are deducted. Changes in the contribution margins per unit of the products sold by a business and changes in its total fixed costs are extremely important information in managing profit.

However, businesses do not disclose contribution margin information in their _external_ financial reports – they wouldn't even think of doing so. This information is considered to be proprietary in nature; it should be kept confidential and out of the hands of its competitors. In short, investors do not have access to information about the business's contribution margin. Neither accounting standards nor the Stock Exchange requires that such information be disclosed. The external profit and loss account discloses gross margin and operating profit, or earnings before interest and income tax expenses. However, the expenses between these two profit lines in the profit and loss account are not separated between variable and fixed (refer to Figure 14-1).

Profit ratio

Business is motivated by profit, so the *profit ratio* is very important to say the least. The profit ratio indicates how much net income was earned on each £100 of sales revenue:

Net income ÷ sales revenue = profit ratio

For example, the business in Figure 14-1 earned £1.9 million net income from its £52 million sales revenue, so its profit ratio is 3.65 per cent, meaning that the business earned £3.65 net income for each £100 of sales revenue.

A seemingly small change in the profit ratio can have a big impact on the bottom line. Suppose that this business had earned a profit ratio of 5 per cent instead of 3.65 per cent. That increase in the profit ratio translates into a £700,000 increase in bottom-line profit (net income) on the same sales revenue.

Profit ratios vary widely from industry to industry. A 5–10 per cent profit ratio is common in most industries, although some high-volume retailers, such as supermarkets, are satisfied with profit ratios around 1 per cent or 2 per cent.

You can turn any ratio upside down and come up with a new way of looking at the same information. If you flip the profit ratio over to be sales revenue divided by net income, the result is the amount of sales revenue needed to make £1 profit. Using the same example, £52 million sales revenue ÷ £1.9 million net income = 27.37 to 1 upside-down profit ratio, which means that this business needs £27.37 in sales to make £1 profit. So you can say that net income is 3.65 per cent of sales revenue, or you can say that sales revenue is 27.37 times net income – but the standard profit ratio is expressed as net income divided by sales revenue.

Earnings per share, basic and diluted

Publicly owned businesses, according to generally accepted accounting principles (GAAP), must report *earnings per share (EPS)* below the net income line in their profit and loss accounts – giving EPS a certain distinction among the ratios. Why is EPS considered so important? Because it gives investors a means of determining the amount the business earned on their share investments: EPS tells you how much net income the business earned for each share you own. The essential equation for EPS is as follows:

Net income ÷ total number of capital stock shares = EPS

For the example in Figures 14-1 and 14-2, the company's $1.9 million net income is divided by the 795,000 shares of stock the business has issued to compute its $2.39 EPS.

Note: Private businesses do not have to report EPS if they don't want to. Considering the wide range of issues covered by GAAP, you find surprisingly few distinctions between private and public businesses – these authoritative accounting rules apply to all businesses. But EPS is one area where GAAP makes an exception for privately owned businesses. EPS is extraordinarily important to the shareholders of businesses whose shares are publicly traded. These shareholders focus on market price *per share*. They want the total net income of the business to be communicated to them on a per share basis so that they can easily compare it with the market price of their shares. The shares of privately owned companies are not actively traded, so there is no readily available market value for their shares. The thinking behind the rule that privately owned businesses should not have to report EPS is that their shareholders do not focus on per share values and are more interested in the business's total net income performance.

The business in the example is too small to be publicly owned. So we turn here to a larger public company example. This publicly owned company reports that it earned $1.32 billion net income for the year just ended. At the end of the year, this company has 400 million shares *outstanding*, which refers to the number of shares that have been issued and are owned by its shareholders. Thus, its EPS is $3.30 ($1.32 billion net income ÷ 400 million stock shares). But here's a complication: The business is committed to issuing additional capital shares in the future for share options that the company has granted to its managers, and it has borrowed money on the basis of debt instruments that give the lenders the right to convert the debt into its capital stock. Under terms of its management share options and its convertible debt, the business could have to issue 40 million additional capital shares in the future. Dividing net income by the number of shares outstanding plus the number of shares that could be issued in the future gives the following computation of EPS:

$1.32 billion net income ÷ 440 million capital stock shares = $3.00 EPS

This second computation, based on the higher number of shares, is called the *diluted* earnings per share. (*Diluted* means thinned out or spread over a larger number of shares.) The first computation, based on the number of shares actually outstanding, is called *basic* earnings per share. Publicly owned businesses have to report two EPS figures – unless they have a *simple capital structure* that does not require the business to issue additional shares in the future. Generally, publicly owned companies have *complex capital structures* and have to report two EPS figures. Both are reported at the bottom of the profit and loss account. So the company in this example reports £3.30 basic EPS and £3.00 diluted EPS. Sometimes it's not clear which of the two EPS figures is being used in press releases and in articles giving investment advice. Fortunately, *The Financial Times* and most other major financial publications leave a clear trail of both EPS figures.

Calculating basic and diluted EPS isn't always as simple as our examples may suggest. An accountant would have to adjust the EPS equation for the following complicating things that a business may do:

- ✔ Issue additional shares during the year and buy back some of its shares (shares of its stock owned by the business itself that are not formally cancelled are called *treasury stock*).

- ✔ Issue more than one class of share, causing net income to be divided into two or more pools – one pool for each class of share.

- ✔ Go through a merger (business combination) in which a large number of shares are issued to acquire the other business.

The shareholders should draw comfort from the fact that the top management of many businesses in which they invest are probably just as anxiously reviewing EPS performance as they are. This extract from Tesco's annual accounts reveals much:

Annual bonuses based on achieving stretching EPS growth targets and specific corporate objectives.

- ✔ Annual bonuses are paid in shares. On award, the Executive can elect to defer receipt of the shares for a further two years, which is encouraged, with additional matching share awards.

- ✔ Longer-term bonus based on a combination of relative total shareholder return, and the achievement of stretching EPS growth targets and specific corporate objectives. Longer-term bonuses are paid in shares, which must be held for a further four years. Executive Directors are encouraged to hold shares for longer than four years with additional matching share awards. Further details are provided below.

- ✔ Share options are granted to Executive Directors at market value and can only be exercised if EPS growth exceeds Retail Price Index (RPI) plus 9 per cent over any three years from grant.

- ✔ Executive Directors are required to build and hold a shareholding with a value at least equal to their basic salary; full participation in the Executive Incentive scheme is conditional upon meeting this target.

Price/earnings (P/E) ratio

The *price/earnings (P/E) ratio* is another ratio that's of particular interest to investors in public businesses. The P/E ratio gives you an idea of how much you're paying in the current price for the shares for each pound of earnings, or net income, being earned by the business. Remember that earnings prop up the market value of shares, not the book value of the shares that's reported in the balance sheet. (Read on for the book value per share discussion.)

The P/E ratio is, in one sense, a reality check on just how high the current market price is in relation to the underlying profit that the business is earning. Extraordinarily high P/E ratios are justified only when investors think that the company's EPS has a lot of upside potential in the future.

The P/E ratio is calculated as follows:

> Current market price of stock ÷ most recent trailing 12 months diluted EPS = P/E ratio

If the business has a simple capital structure and does not report a diluted EPS, its basic EPS is used for calculating its P/E ratio. (See the earlier section 'Earnings per share, basic and diluted'.)

Assume that the stock shares of a public business with a £3.65 diluted EPS are selling at £54.75 in the stock market. ***Note:*** From here forward, we will use the briefer term EPS in reference to P/E ratios; we assume you understand that it refers to diluted EPS for businesses with complex capital structures and to basic EPS for businesses with simple capital structures.

The actual share price bounces around day to day and is subject to change on short notice. To illustrate the P/E ratio, we use this price, which is the closing price on the latest trading day in the stock market. This market price means that investors trading in the stock think that the shares are worth 15 times diluted EPS (£54.75 market price ÷ £3.65 diluted EPS = 15). This value may be below the broad market average that values shares at, say, 20 times EPS. The outlook for future growth in its EPS is probably not too good.

Dividend yield

The *dividend yield* tells investors how much *cash flow income* they're receiving on their investment. (The dividend is the cash flow income part of investment return; the other part is the gain or loss in the market value of the investment over the year.)

Market cap – not a cap on market value

One investment number you see a lot in the financial press is the *market cap.* No, this does not refer to a cap, or limit, on the market value of a company's capital shares. The term is shorthand for *market capitalisation,* which refers to the total market value of the business that is determined by multiplying the stock's current market price by the total number of shares issued by the company. Suppose a company's stock is selling at £50 per share in the stock market and it has 200 million shares outstanding. Its market cap is £10 billion. Another business may be willing to pay higher than £50 per share for the company. Indeed, many acquisitions and mergers involve the acquiring company paying a hefty premium over the going market price of the shares of the company being acquired.

Suppose that a stock of a public company that is selling for £60 paid £1.20 cash dividends per share over the last year. You calculate dividend yield as follows:

£1.20 annual cash dividend per share ÷ £60 current market price of stock = 2% dividend yield

You use dividend yield to compare how your stock investment is doing to how it would be doing if you'd put that money in corporate or Treasury bonds, gilt edged stock (UK government borrowings) or other debt securities that pay interest. The average interest rate of high-grade debt securities has recently been three to four times the dividend yields on most public companies; in theory, market price appreciation of the shares over time makes up for that gap. Of course, shareholders take the risk that the market value will not increase enough to make their total return on investment rate higher than a benchmark interest rate. (At the time of writing, this yield gap has shrunk to nothing and is causing an agonizing reappraisal of the value of equities, in relation to debt, as an investment medium.)

Assume that long-term government gilt edged stock are currently paying 6 per cent annual interest, which is 4 per cent higher than the business's 2 per cent dividend yield in the example just discussed. If this business's shares don't increase in value by at least 4 per cent over the year, its investors would have been better off investing in the debt securities instead. (Of course, they wouldn't have had all the perks of a share investment, like those heartfelt letters from the chairman and those glossy financial reports.) The market price of publicly traded debt securities can fall or rise, so things get a little tricky in this sort of investment analysis.

Book value per share

Book value per share is one measure, but it's certainly not the only amount, used for determining the value of a privately owned business's shares. As discussed in Chapter 6, book value is not the same thing as market value. The asset values that a business records in its books (also known as its *accounts*) are *not* the amounts that a business could get if it put its assets up for sale. Book values of some assets are generally lower than what the cost would be for replacing the assets if a disaster (such as a flood or a fire) wiped out the business's stock or equipment. Recording current market values in the books is really not a practical option. Until a seller and a buyer meet and haggle over price, trying to determine the market price for a privately owned business's shares is awfully hard.

You can calculate book value per share for publicly owned businesses too. However, market value is readily available, so shareholders (and investment advisers and managers) do not put much weight on book value per share. EPS is the main factor that affects the market prices of stock shares of public companies – not the book value per share. We should add that some investing strategies, known as *value investing*, search out companies that have a high book value per share compared to their going market prices. But by and large, book value per share plays a secondary role in the market values of stock shares issued by public companies.

Although book value per share is generally not a good indicator of the market value of a private business's shares, you do run into this ratio, at least as a starting point for haggling over a selling price. Here's how to calculate book value per share:

Total owners' equity ÷ total number of stock shares = book value per share

The business shown in Figure 14-2 has issued 795,000 shares: Its £15.9 million total owners' equity divided by its 795,000 shares gives a book value per share of £20. If the business sold off its assets exactly for their book values and paid all its liabilities, it would end up with £15.9 million left for the shareholders, and it could therefore distribute £20 per share. But the company will not go out of business and liquidate its assets and pay off its liabilities. So book value per share is a theoretical value. It's not totally irrelevant, but it's not all that definitive, either.

Return on equity (ROE) ratio

The *return on equity (ROE) ratio* tells you how much profit a business earned in comparison to the book value of shareholders' equity. This ratio is useful for privately owned businesses, which have no way of determining the current value of owners' equity (at least not until the business is actually sold). ROE is also calculated for public companies, but, just like book value per share, it plays a secondary role and is not the dominant factor driving market prices. (Earnings are.) Here's how you calculate this key ratio:

Net income ÷ owners' equity = ROE

The owners' equity figure is at book value, which is reported in the company's balance sheet. Chapter 6 explains owners' equity and the difference between share capital and retained earnings, which are the two components of owners' equity.

The business whose profit and loss account and balance sheet are shown in Figures 14-1 and 14-2 earned £1.9 million net income for the year just ended and has £15.9 million owners' equity. Therefore, its ROE is 11.95 per cent (£1.9 million net income ÷ £15.9 million owners' equity = 11.95 per cent). ROE is net income expressed as a percentage of the amount of total owners' equity of the business, which is one of the two sources of capital to the business, the other being borrowed money, or interest-bearing debt. (A business also has non-interest-bearing operating liabilities, such as creditors.) The cost of debt capital (interest) is deducted as an expense to determine net income. So net income 'belongs' to the owners; it increases their equity in the business, so it makes sense to express net income as the percentage of improvement in the owners' equity.

Gearing or leverage

Your company's liquidity keeps you solvent from day to day and month to month and we come to that next when we look at the current ratio and acid test. But what about your ability to pay back long-term debt year after year? Two financial ratios indicate what kind of shape you're in over the long term.

If you've read this chapter from the beginning, you may be getting really bored with financial ratios by now, but your lenders – bankers and bondholders, if you have them – find these long-term ratios to be incredibly fascinating, for obvious reasons.

The first ratio gauges how easy it is for your company to continue making interest payments on the debt:

> Times interest earned = earnings before interest and taxes ÷ interest expense

Don't get confused – earnings before any interest expense and taxes are paid (EBIT) is really just the profit that you have available to make those interest payments in the first place. Figure 14-1, for example, shows an EBIT of £3,550 (thousand) and an interest expense of £750 (thousand) this year for a times-interest-earned ratio of 4.73. In other words, this business can meet its interest expense 4.73 times over.

You may also hear the same number called an *interest coverage*. Lenders get mighty nervous if this ratio ever gets anywhere close to 1.0, because at that point, every last penny of profits goes for interest payments on the long-term debt.

The second ratio tries to determine whether the principal amount of your debt is in any danger:

Debt-to-equity ratio = long-term liabilities ÷ owners' equity

The debt-to-equity ratio says a great deal about the general financial structure of your company. After all, you can raise money to support your company in only two ways: borrow it and promise to pay it back with interest, or sell pieces of the company and promise to share all the rewards of ownership. The first method is debt; the second, equity.

Figure 14-2, for example, shows a debt-to-equity ratio of £6,000 ÷ £15,900, or .38. This ratio means that the company has around three times more equity financing than it does long-term debt.

Lenders love to see lots of equity supporting a company's debt because then they know that the money they loan out is safer. If something goes wrong with the company, they can go after the owners' money. Equity investors, on the other hand, actually want to take on some risk. They like to see relatively high debt-to-equity ratios because that situation increases their leverage and (as the following section points out) can substantially boost their profits. So the debt-to-equity ratio that's just right for your company depends not only on your industry and how stable it is, but also on who you ask.

Current ratio

The *current ratio* is a test of a business's *short-term solvency* – its capability to pay off its liabilities that come due in the near future (up to one year). The ratio is a rough indicator of whether cash-on-hand plus the cash flow from collecting debtors and selling stock will be enough to pay off the liabilities that will come due in the next period.

As you can imagine, lenders are particularly keen on punching in the numbers to calculate the current ratio. Here's how they do it:

Current assets ÷ current liabilities = current ratio

Note: Unlike with most of the other ratios, you don't multiply the result of this equation by 100 and represent it as a percentage.

Businesses are expected by their creditors to maintain a minimum current ratio (2.0, meaning a 2-to-1 ratio, is the general rule) and may be legally required to stay above a minimum current ratio as stipulated in their contracts with lenders. The business in Figure 14-2 has £17.2 million in current assets and £7,975,000 in current liabilities, so its current ratio is 2.16 and it shouldn't have to worry about lenders coming by in the middle of the night to break its legs. Chapter 6 discusses current assets and current liabilities and how they are reported in the balance sheet.

How much working capital, ready or nearly ready money do you need to ensure survival? Having the liquid assets available when you absolutely need them to meet short-term obligations is called *liquidity*. You don't have to have cash in the till to be liquid. Debtors (that is, people who owe you money and can be reasonably expected to cough up soon) and stock ready to be sold are both part of your liquid assets. You can use several financial ratios to test a business's liquidity, including the current ratio and the acid test. You can monitor these ratios year by year and measure them against your competitors' ratios and the industry averages.

Acid-test ratio

Most serious investors and lenders don't stop with the current ratio for an indication of the business's short-term solvency – its capability to pay the liabilities that will come due in the short term. Investors also calculate the *acid-test ratio* (also known as the *quick ratio* or the *pounce ratio*), which is a more severe test of a business's solvency than the current ratio. The acid-test ratio excludes stock and prepaid expenses, which the current ratio includes, and limits assets to cash and items that the business can quickly convert to cash. This limited category of assets is known as *quick* or *liquid* assets.

You calculate the acid-test ratio as follows:

Liquid assets ÷ total current liabilities = acid-test ratio

Note: Unlike most other financial ratios, you don't multiply the result of this equation by 100 and represent it as a percentage.

For the business example shown in Figure 14-2, the acid-test ratio is as follows:

Cash	£3,500,000
Marketable securities	none
Debtors	5,000,000
Total liquid assets	£8,500,000
Total current liabilities	£7,975,000
Acid-test ratio	1.07

A 1.07 acid-test ratio means that the business would be able to pay off its short-term liabilities and still have a little bit of liquid assets left over. The general rule is that the acid-test ratio should be at least 1.0, which means that liquid assets equal current liabilities. Of course, falling below 1.0 doesn't mean that the business is on the verge of bankruptcy, but if the ratio falls as low as 0.5, that may be cause for alarm.

This ratio is also known as the *pounce ratio* to emphasise that you're calculating for a worst-case scenario, where a pack of wolves (more politely known as *creditors*) has pounced on the business and is demanding quick payment of the business's liabilities. But don't panic. Short-term creditors do not have the right to demand immediate payment, except under unusual circumstances. This is a very conservative way to look at a business's capability to pay its short-term liabilities – too conservative in most cases.

Keeping track of stock and debtor levels

Two other areas that effect liquidity need to be monitored carefully: how fast your stock is selling out (if your business requires holding goods for sale), and how fast your customers are paying up.

Here's the ratio for stock levels:

> Stock turnover = cost of goods sold ÷ stock

Stock turnover tells you something about how liquid your stocks really are. This ratio divides the cost of goods sold, as shown in your yearly profit and loss account, by the average value of your stock. If you don't know the average, you can estimate it by using the stock figure listed in the balance sheet at the end of the year.

For the business represented in Figures 14-1 and 14-2, the stock turnover is £31,200 ÷ £7,800, or 4.0. This ratio means that this business turns over its stocks four times each year. Expressed in days, the business carries a 91.25-day (365 ÷ 4.0) supply of stock.

Is a 90-day plus inventory good or bad? It depends on the industry and even on the time of year. A car dealer who has a 90-day supply of cars at the height of the season may be in a strong stock position, but the same stock position at the end of the season could be a real weakness. As Just In Time (JIT) supply chains and improved information systems make business operations more efficient across all industries, stock turnover is on the rise, and the average number of days that stock of any kind hangs around continues to shrink.

What about debtor levels?

> Debtor turnover = sales on credit ÷ debtors

Debtor turnover tells you something about liquidity by dividing the sales that you make on credit by the average debtors. If an average isn't available, you can use the debtors from a balance sheet.

If the business represented in Figures 14-1 and 14-2 makes 80 per cent of its sales on credit, its debtor turnover is (£52,000 × 0.8) ÷ £5,000, or 8.3. In other words, the company turns over its debtors 8.3 times per year, or once every 44 days, on average. That's not too bad: payment terms are 30 days. But remember, unlike fine wine, debtors don't improve with age.

Return on assets (ROA) ratio

As discussed in Chapter 6 (refer to the sidebar 'Trading on the equity: Taking a chance on debt'), one factor affecting the bottom-line profit of a business is whether it used debt to its advantage. For the year, a business may have realised a *financial leverage gain* – it earned more profit on the money it borrowed than the interest paid for the use of that borrowed money. So a good part of its net income for the year may be due to financial leverage. The first step in determining financial leverage gain is to calculate a business's *return on assets (ROA) ratio*, which is the ratio of EBIT (earnings before interest and tax) to the total capital invested in operating assets.

Here's how to calculate ROA:

EBIT ÷ net operating assets = ROA

Note: This equation calls for *net operating assets*, which equals total assets less the non-interest-bearing operating liabilities of the business. Actually, many stock analysts and investors use the total assets figure because deducting all the non-interest-bearing operating liabilities from total assets to determine net operating assets is, quite frankly, a nuisance. But we strongly recommend using net operating assets because that's the total amount of capital raised from debt and equity.

Compare ROA with the interest rate: If a business's ROA is 14 per cent and the interest rate on its debt is 8 per cent, for example, the business's net gain on its debt capital is 6 per cent more than what it's paying in interest. There's a favourable spread of 6 points (one point = 1 per cent), which can be multiplied by the total debt of the business to determine how much its total earnings before income tax is traceable to financial leverage gain.

 In Figure 14-2, notice that the company has £10 million total interest-bearing debt (£4 million short-term plus £6 million long-term). Its total owners' equity is £15.9 million. So its net operating assets total is £25.9 million (which excludes the three short-term non-interest-bearing operating liabilities). The company's ROA, therefore, is

£3.55 million earnings before interest and tax ÷ £25.9 million net operating assets = 13.71% ROA

The business earned £1,371,000 (rounded) on its total debt – 13.71 per cent ROA times £10 million total debt. The business paid only £750,000 interest on its debt. So the business had £621,000 financial leverage gain before income tax (£1,371,000 less £750,000). Put another way, the business paid 7.5 per cent interest on its debt but earned 13.71 per cent on this money for a favourable spread of 6.21 points – which, when multiplied by the £10 million debt, yields the £621,000 pre-tax financial gain for the year.

ROA is a useful earnings ratio, aside from determining financial leverage gain (or loss) for the period. ROA is a *capital utilisation* test – how much profit before interest and tax was earned on the total capital employed by the business. The basic idea is that it takes money (assets) to make money (profit); the final test is how much profit was made on the assets. If, for example, a business earns £1 million EBIT on £20 million assets, its ROA is only 5 per cent. Such a low ROA signals that the business is making poor use of its assets and will have to improve its ROA or face serious problems in the future.

Using combined ratios

You wouldn't use a single ratio to decide whether one vehicle was a better or worse buy than another. MPG, MPH, annual depreciation percentage and residual value proportion are just a handful of the ratios that you'd want to review. So it is with a business. You can use a combination of ratios to form an opinion on the financial state of affairs at any one time.

The best known of these combination ratios is the Altman Z-Score (`www.creditguru.com/CalcAltZ.shtml`) that uses a combined set of five financial ratios derived from eight variables from a company's financial statements linked to some statistical techniques to predict a company's probability of failure. Entering the figures into the onscreen template at this website produces a score and an explanatory narrative giving a view on the businesses financial strengths and weaknesses.

Appreciating the limits of ratios

A danger with ratios is to believe that because you have a precise number, you have a right figure to aim for. For example, a natural feeling with financial ratios is to think that high figures are good ones, and an upward trend represents the right direction. This theory is, to some extent, encouraged by the personal feeling of wealth that having a lot of cash engenders.

Unfortunately, no general rule exists on which way is right for financial ratios. In some cases a high figure is good; in others, a low figure is best. Indeed, in some circumstances, ratios of the same value aren't as good as each other. Look at the two working capital statements in Table 14-1.

Table 14-1	Difficult Comparisons			
	1			2
Current Assets				
Stock	10,000			22,990
Debtors	13,000			100
Cash	100	23,100	10	23,100
Less Current Liabilities				
Overdraft	5,000		90	
Creditors	1,690	6,690	6,690	6,690
Working Capital		16,410		16,410
Current Ratio		3.4:1		3.4:1

The amount of working capital in examples 1 and 2 is the same, £16,410, as are the current assets and current liabilities, at £23,100 and £6,690 respectively. It follows that any ratio using these factors would also be the same. For example, the current ratios in these two examples are both identical, 3.4:1, but in the first case there's a reasonable chance that some cash will come in from debtors, certainly enough to meet the modest creditor position. In the second example there's no possibility of useful amounts of cash coming in from trading, with debtors at only £100, while creditors at the relatively substantial figure of £6,600 will pose a real threat to financial stability.

So in this case the current ratios are identical, but the situations being compared are not. In fact, as a general rule, a higher working capital ratio is regarded as a move in the wrong direction. The more money a business has tied up in working capital, the more difficult it is to make a satisfactory return on capital employed, simply because the larger the denominator, the lower the return on capital employed.

In some cases the right direction is more obvious. A high return on capital employed is usually better than a low one, but even this situation can be a danger signal, warning that higher risks are being taken. And not all high profit ratios are good: sometimes a higher profit margin can lead to reduced sales volume and so lead to a lower Return on Capital Employed (ROCE).

In general, business performance as measured by ratios is best thought of as lying within a range; liquidity (current ratio), for example, staying between 1.2:1 and 1.8:1. A change in either direction may represent a cause for concern.

The temptation to compute cash flow per share: Don't give in!

Businesses are prohibited from reporting a *cash flow per share* number on their financial reports. The accounting rule book specifically prohibits very few things, and cash flow per share is on this small list of contraband. Why? Because – and this is somewhat speculative on our part – the powers that be were worried that the cash flow number would usurp net income as the main measure for profit performance. Indeed, many writers in the financial press were talking up the importance of cash flow from profit, so we see the concern on this matter. Knowing how important EPS is for

market value of stocks, the authorities declared a similar per share amount for cash flow out of bounds and prohibited it from being included in a financial report. Of course, you could compute it quite easily – the rule doesn't apply to how financial statements are interpreted, only to how they are reported.

Should we dare give you an example of cash flow per share? Here goes: A business with £42 million cash flow from profit and 4.2 million total capital stock shares would end up with £10 cash flow per share. Shhh.

The Biz/ed (www.bized.co.uk/compfact/ratios/index.htm) and Harvard Business School (http://harvardbusinessonline.hbsp. harvard.edu/b02/en/academic/edu_tk_acct_fin_ratio.jhtml) websites contain free tools that calculate financial ratios from company accounts. They also provide useful introductions to ratio analysis and definitions of each ratio and the formula used to calculate it. To download their spreadsheet, you first need to register with the Harvard website.

By registering (for free) with the Proshare website (go to www.proshare clubs.co.uk and click on 'Research Centre' and 'Performance Tables'), you have access to a number of tools that crunch public company ratios for you. Select the companies you want to look at, and then the ratios you're most interested in (EPS, P/E, ROI, Dividend Yield and so on). All is revealed within a couple of seconds. You can then rank the companies by performance in more or less any way you want. You can find more comprehensive tools on the Internet, on the websites of share traders for example, but Proshare is a great site to cut your teeth on – and the price is right!

Frolicking through the Footnotes

Reading the footnotes in annual financial reports is no picnic. The investment pros have to read them because in providing consultation to their clients, they are required to comply with due diligence standards or because of their legal duties and responsibilities of managing other peoples' money.

We suggest you do a quick read-through of the footnotes and identify the ones that seem to have the most significance. Generally, the most important footnotes are those dealing with the following matters:

- **Share options awarded by the business to its executives:** The additional shares issued under share options dilute (thin out) the earnings per share of the business, which in turn puts downside pressure on the market value of its shares, everything else being the same.

- **Pending legal actions, litigation and investigations by government agencies:** These intrusions into the normal affairs of the business can have enormous consequences.

- **Segment information for the business:** Most public businesses have to report information for the major segments of the organisation – sales and operating profit by territories or product lines. This gives a better glimpse of the different parts making up the whole business. (However, segment information may be reported elsewhere in an annual financial report than in the footnotes.)

These are just three of the many important pieces of information you should look for in footnotes. But you have to stay alert for other critical matters that a business may disclose in its footnotes – scan each and every footnote for potentially important information. Finding a footnote that discusses a major lawsuit against the business, for example, may make the shares too risky for your portfolio.

Checking for Ominous Skies on the Audit Report

The value of analysing a financial report depends directly and entirely on the accuracy of the report's numbers. Top management wants to present the best possible picture of the business in its financial report (which is understandable, of course). The managers have a vested interest in the profit performance and financial condition of the business.

Independent auditors are like umpires in the financial reporting process. The auditor comes in, does an audit of the business's accounting system and procedures, and gives a report that is attached to the company's financial statements. You should check the audit report included with the financial report. Publicly owned businesses are required to have their annual financial reports audited by an independent accountancy firm, and many privately owned businesses have audits done, too, because they know that an audit report adds credibility to the financial report.

What if a private business's financial report doesn't include an audit report? Well, you have to trust that the business prepared accurate financial statements that follow generally accepted accounting principles and that the footnotes to the financial statements provide adequate disclosure.

Unfortunately, the audit report gets short shrift in financial statement analysis, maybe because it's so full of technical terminology and accountant doublespeak. But even though audit reports are a tough read, anyone who reads and analyses financial reports should definitely read the audit report. Chapter 15 provides a lot more information on audits and the auditor's report.

The auditor judges whether the business used accounting methods and procedures in accordance with accepted accounting principles. In most cases, the auditor's report confirms that everything is hunky-dory, and you can rely on the financial report. However, sometimes an auditor waves a yellow flag – and in extreme cases, a red flag. Here are the two most important warnings to watch out for in an audit report:

✔ The business's capability to continue normal operations is in doubt because of what are known as *financial exigencies*, which may mean a low cash balance, unpaid overdue liabilities or major lawsuits that the business doesn't have the cash to cover.

✔ One or more of the methods used in the report is not in line with the prevailing accounting body rules, leading the auditor to conclude that the numbers reported are misleading or that disclosure is inadequate.

Although auditor warnings don't necessarily mean that a business is going down the tubes, they should turn on that light bulb in your head and make you more cautious and sceptical about the financial report. The auditor is questioning the very information on which the business's value is based, and you can't take that kind of thing lightly.

In very small businesses it is likely that the accounts will not be independently audited and their accounts come with a rather alarming caveat, running something like this: *These accounts have been prepared on the basis of information provided by the owners and have not been independently verified.* A full audit is an expensive process and few businesses that don't have to will go to the expense and trouble just to be told what they probably already know anyway.

Just because a business has a clean audit report doesn't mean that the financial report is completely accurate and above board. As discussed in Chapter 15, auditors don't necessarily catch everything. Keep in mind that the accounting rules are pretty flexible, leaving a company's accountants with room for interpretation and creativity that's just short of *cooking the books* (deliberately defrauding and misleading readers of the financial report).

Window dressing and profit smoothing – two common examples of massaging the numbers – are explained in Chapter 8.

Finding Financial Facts

Understanding how to calculate financial ratios and how to interpret that data is all fine and dandy, but before you can do anything useful you need to get a copy of the accounts in the first place. Seeing the accounts for your own business shouldn't be too much of a problem. If you're the boss, the accounts should be on your desk right now; if you're not the boss, try snuggling up to the accounts department. If they're too coy to let you have today's figures, the latest audited accounts are in the public domain anyway filed away at Companies House (www.companieshouse.gov.uk), as required by law.

Public company accounts

Most companies make their glossy annual financial reports available to download from their websites, which you can find by typing the company name into an Internet search engine. You need to have Adobe Acrobat Reader on your computer to open the files. No problem, though: Adobe Acrobat Reader is free and you can easily download the program from Adobe's website (http://adobe-reader.download-start.net/download). The software enables you to search for key words in the annual report – a handy feature indeed for tracking down the sections of the report that you're most interested in.

Yahoo has direct online links to several thousand public company reports and accounts and performance ratios at http://uk.finance.yahoo.com (enter the name of the company you're looking for in the box on the left of the screen under Investing. It appears after you've entered about three letters, click and follow the threads). Paying this site a visit saves you the time and trouble of hunting down company websites.

Private company accounts

Finding financial information on private companies is often a time-consuming and frustrating job. Not for nothing do these companies call themselves 'private'. Businesses, and particularly smaller businesses, can be very secretive about their finances and have plenty of tricks to hide information from prying eyes. Many smaller businesses can elect to file abbreviated accounts with Companies House that provide only the barest details. You can find out just what these shortened accounts must contain at the Business Link website (go to www.businesslink.gov.uk and click on 'Taxes, returns, & payroll', 'Introduction to business taxes' and 'Accounting and audit exceptions for small companies'). The accounts of very small companies don't need to be audited, so the objective reliability of the scant data given may be questionable. Having said that, tens of thousands of private companies file full and generally reliable accounts.

Two fruitful sources of private company accounts exist:

- ✔ **Companies House** (www.companieshouse.gov.uk) is the official repository of all company information in the UK. Their WebCHeck service offers a free Company Names and Address Index that covers 2 million companies, searchable either by company name or by company registration numbers. You can use WebCHeck to purchase (at a cost of £1 per company) a company's latest accounts that give details of sales, profits, margins, directors, shareholders and bank borrowings.

- ✔ **Keynote** (www.keynote.co.uk) offers business ratios and trends for 140 industry sectors and provides information to assess accurately the financial health of each industry sector. This service enables you to find out how profitable a business sector is and how successful the main companies operating in each sector are. Executive summaries are free, but expect to pay between £250 and £500 for most reports.

Scoring credit

If all you want is a quick handle on whether a company is likely to be around long enough to pay its bills, including a dividend to shareholders, then a whole heap of information exists about credit status for both individual sole traders and companies of varying complexity. Expect to pay anywhere from £5 for basic information up to £200 for a very comprehensive picture of a company's credit status. So you can avoid trading unknowingly with individuals or businesses that pose a credit risk.

Experian (www.ukexperian.com), Dun & Bradstreet (www.dnb.com), Creditgate.com (www.creditgate.com) and Credit Reporting (www.creditreporting.co.uk/b2b) are the major agencies compiling and selling credit histories and small-business information. Between them they offer a comprehensive range of credit reports instantly available online that include advice about credit limits.

Using FAME (Financial Analysis Made Easy)

FAME (Financial Analysis Made Easy) is a powerful database that contains information on 7 million companies in the UK and Ireland. Typically, the following information is included: contact information including phone, email and web addresses plus main and other trading addresses; activity details; 29 profit and loss account and 63 balance sheet items; cash flow and ratios; credit score and rating; security and price information (listed companies only); names of bankers, auditors, previous auditors and advisors; details of holdings and subsidiaries (including foreign holdings and subsidiaries); names of current and previous directors with home addresses and shareholder indicator; heads of department; and shareholders. You can compare each company with detailed financials with its peer group based on its activity codes and the software lets you search for companies that comply with your own criteria, combining as many conditions as you like. FAME is available in business libraries and on CD from the publishers, who also offer a free trial (www.bvdinfo.com/Products/Company-Information/National/FAME.aspx).

Looking beyond financial statements

Investors can't rely solely on the financial report when making investment decisions. Analysing a business's financial statements is just one part of the process. You may need to consider these additional factors, depending on the business you're thinking about investing in:

✔ Industry trends and problems.

✔ National economic and political developments.

✔ Possible mergers, friendly acquisitions and hostile takeovers.

✔ Turnover of key executives.

✔ International markets and currency exchange ratios.

✔ Supply shortages.

✔ Product surpluses.

Whew! This kind of stuff goes way beyond accounting, obviously, and is just as significant as financial statement analysis when you're picking stocks and managing investment portfolios. A good book for new investors to read is *Investing For Dummies* by Tony Levene.

Chapter 15

Professional Auditors and Advisers

- -

In This Chapter

▶ Cutting the deck for a fair deal: Why audits are needed

▶ Interpreting the auditor's report

▶ Knowing what auditors catch and don't catch

▶ Growing beyond audits: Professional accountancy practices as advisers and consultants

▶ Questioning the independence of auditors

- -

*I*f we'd written this chapter 50 years ago, we would have talked almost exclusively about the role of the professional chartered or certified accountant as the *auditor* of the financial statements and footnotes presented in a business's annual financial report to its owners and lenders. Back then, in the 'good old days', audits were a professional accountancy firm's bread-and-butter service – audit fees were a large share of these firms' annual revenue. Audits were the core function that accountants performed then. In addition to audits, accountants provided accounting and tax advice to their clients – and that was pretty much all they did.

Today, accountants do a lot more than auditing. In fact, the profession has shifted away from the expression *auditing* in favour of broader terms like *assurance* and *attestation*. More importantly, accountants have moved into consulting and advising clients on matters other than accounting and tax matters. The movement into the consulting business while continuing to do audits – often for the same clients – has caused all sorts of problems, which this chapter looks at after discussing audits by accountants.

Why Audits?

When I (John) graduated from college, I went to work for a big national accountancy firm. The transition from textbook accounting theory to real-world accounting practice came as a shock. Some of our clients dabbled in window dressing (refer to Chapter 8), and more than a few used earnings management tactics (see profit smoothing in Chapter 8). A few of our clients were engaged in accounting fraud, but just a very few. I was surprised how many businesses cut corners to get things done. Sometimes they were close to acting illegally, and some went over the edge. I soon realised that I had been rather naive, and I came to tolerate most of the questionable practices in the rough and tumble world of business.

I mention my early experience in public accounting to remind you that the world of business is not like Sunday school. Not everything is pure and straight. Nevertheless, legal and ethical lines of conduct separate what is tolerated and what isn't. If you cross the lines, you are subject to legal sanctions and can be held liable to others. For instance, a business can deliberately deceive its investors and lenders with false or misleading numbers in its financial report. Instead of 'What You See Is What You Get' in its financial statements, you get a filtered and twisted version of the business's financial affairs – more of a 'What I Want You to See Is What You Get' version. That's where audits come in.

Audits are the best practical means for keeping fraudulent and misleading financial reporting to a minimum. A business having an independent accounting professional who comes in once a year to check up on its accounting system is like a person getting a physical exam once a year – the audit exam may uncover problems that the business was not aware of, and knowing that the auditors come in once a year to take a close look at things keeps the business on its toes.

The basic purpose of an annual financial statement audit is to make sure that a business has followed the accounting methods and disclosure requirements required by law – in other words, to make sure that the business has stayed in the ballpark of accounting rules. After completing an audit examination, the accountant prepares a short auditor's report stating that the business has prepared its financial statements according to the rules – or has not, as the case may be. In this way, audits are an effective means of enforcing accounting standards.

An audit by an independent accountant provides assurance (but not an iron-clad guarantee) that the business's financial statements follow accepted accounting methods and provide adequate disclosure. This is the main reason why accountancy firms are paid to do annual audits of financial reports. The auditor must be *independent* of the business being audited. The auditor can have no financial stake in the business or any other relationship with the client that may compromise his or her objectivity. However, the independence of auditors has come under scrutiny of late. See the section 'From Audits to Advising' later in the chapter.

The core of a business's financial report is its three primary financial statements – the profit and loss account, the cash flow statement and the balance sheet – and the necessary footnotes to these statements. A financial report may consist of just these statements and footnotes and nothing more. Usually, however, there's more – in some cases, a lot more. Chapter 8 explains the additional content of financial reports of public business corporations, such as the transmittal letter to the owners from the chief executive of the business, historical summaries, supporting schedules and listings of directors and top-level managers – items not often included in the financial reports of private businesses.

The auditor's opinion covers the financial statements and the accompanying footnotes. The auditor, therefore, does not express an opinion of whether the chairman's letter to the shareholders is a good letter – although if the chairman's claims contradicted the financial statements, the auditor would comment on the inconsistency. In short, auditors audit the financial statements and their footnotes but do not ignore the additional information included in annual financial reports.

Although the large majority of audited financial statements are reliable, a few slip through the audit net. Auditor approval is not a 100 per cent guarantee that the financial statements contain no erroneous or fraudulent numbers, or that the statements and their footnotes provide all required disclosures, as the all too frequent Enron-like events attest.

Who's Who in the World of Audits

Chapter 1 explains that to be a qualified accountant, a person usually has to hold a degree, has to pass a rigorous national exam, have audit experience and satisfy continuing education requirements. Many accountants operate as sole practitioners, but many form partnerships (also called firms). An accountancy firm has to be large enough to assign enough staff auditors to the client so that all audit work can be completed in a relatively short period – financial reports are generally released about four to six weeks after the close of the fiscal year. Large businesses need large accountancy firms, and very large global business organisations need very large international accountancy firms. The public accounting profession consists of four very large international firms, several good-sized second-tier national firms, often with international network arrangements, many regional firms, small local firms, and sole practitioners.

All businesses whose ownership units (shares) are traded in public markets in the UK, the US and most other countries with major stock markets are required to have annual audits by independent auditors. Every stock you see listed on the LSE (London Stock Exchange), the NYSE (New York Stock Exchange), NASDAQ (National Association of Securities Dealers Automated Quotations) and other stock-trading markets must be audited by an outside accountancy firm. The Big Four international accountancy firms are household names in the business world. (Big Five until Arthur Andersen sank in the wake of the Enron debacle.)

The Big Four are:

- ✔ **Ernst & Young**
- ✔ **PricewaterhouseCoopers**
- ✔ **Deloitte & Touche**
- ✔ **KPMG**

The next ten accountancy firms, in terms of size are:

- ✔ Grant Thornton UK
- ✔ BDO Stoy Hayward
- ✔ RSM Tenon Group
- ✔ Baker Tilly
- ✔ Smith & Williamson
- ✔ PKF (UK)
- ✔ Moore Stephens UK
- ✔ Mazars
- ✔ Vantis
- ✔ Begbies Traynor

These guys bob up and down and, on occasion, even dip out of the top spots in this list. Accountancy Age (www.accountancyage.com and select 'Top 50+50' from top menu bar) keeps tabs on their movements each year.

Though these ten are pretty big bears, their combined fee income is less than that of Ernst & Young, the smallest of the Big Four.

The firms are legally organised as limited liability partnerships, so you see *LLP* after their names. The big four international accountancy firms and a handful of those in the second tier audit almost all of the large public corporations in the UK and the US. For these corporations the annual audit is a cost of doing business; it's the price they pay for going into public markets for their capital and for having their shares traded in a public marketplace – which provides liquidity for their shares.

Banks and other lenders to closely held businesses whose ownership shares are not traded in any public marketplace may insist on audited financial statements. We would say that the amount of a bank loan, generally speaking, has to be more than $5 million or $10 million before a lender will insist that the business pay for the cost of an audit. If outside non-manager investors – for example venture capital providers or business angels – have much invested in a business, they will almost certainly insist on an annual audit to be carried out by a substantial firm such as those listed earlier.

Instead of an audit, which they couldn't realistically afford, many smaller businesses have an outside accountant come in regularly to look over their accounting methods and give advice on their financial reporting. Unless an accountant has done an audit, he or she has to be very careful not to express an opinion of the external financial statements. Without a careful examination of the evidence supporting the account balances, the accountant is in no position to give an opinion on the financial statements prepared from the accounts of the business.

In the grand scheme of things, most audits are a necessary evil that does not uncover anything seriously wrong with a business's accounting system and the accounting methods it uses to prepare its financial statements. Overall, the financial statements end up looking virtually the same as they would have looked without an audit. Still, an audit has certain side benefits. In the course of doing an audit, an accountant watches for business practices that could stand some improvement and is alert to potential problems. And fraudsters beware: Accountants may face legal action if they fail to report any dodgy dealings they discover.

The auditor usually recommends ways in which the client's _internal controls_ can be strengthened. For example, an auditor may discover that accounting employees are not required to take holidays and let someone else do their jobs while they're gone. The auditor would recommend that the internal control requiring holidays away from the office be strictly enforced. Chapter 2 explains that good internal controls are extremely important in an accounting system. Also, in many audits that we've worked on, we caught several technical errors that were corrected and we suggested minor improvements that were made – the end result being that the financial statements were marginally better than they would have been without the audit.

What an Auditor Does before Giving an Opinion

An auditor does two basic things: *examines evidence* and *gives an opinion* about the financial statements. The lion's share of audit time is spent on examining evidence supporting the transactions and accounts of the business. A very small part of the total audit time is spent on writing the auditor's report, in which the auditor expresses an opinion of the financial statements and footnotes.

This list gives you an idea of what the auditor does 'in the field' – that is, on the premises of the business being audited:

- ✔ Evaluates the design and operating dependability of the business's accounting system and procedures.

- ✔ Evaluates and tests the business's internal accounting controls that are established to deter and detect errors and fraud.

- ✔ Identifies and critically examines the business's accounting methods – especially whether the methods conform to generally accepted accounting rules), which are the touchstones for all businesses.

- ✔ Inspects documentary and physical evidence for the business's revenues, expenses, assets, liabilities and owners' equities – for example, the auditor counts products held in stock, observes the condition of those products and confirms checking account balances directly with the banks.

The purpose of all the audit work (examining evidence) is to provide a convincing basis for expressing an opinion of the business's financial statements, attesting that the company's financial statements and footnotes (as well as any directly supporting tables and schedules) can be relied on – or not, in some cases. The auditor puts that opinion in the auditor's report.

The auditor's report is the only visible part of the audit process to financial statement readers – the tip of the iceberg. All the readers see is the auditor's one-page report (which is based on the evidence examined during the audit process, of course). For example, PricewaterhouseCoopers LLP spend thousands of hours auditing Sainsbury's, but the only thing that the shareholders see is the final one-page audit report.

What's in an Auditor's Report

The audit report, which is included in the financial report near the financial statements, serves two useful purposes:

- ✔ It reassures investors and creditors that the financial report can be relied upon or calls attention to any serious departures from established financial reporting standards and principles.

- ✔ It prevents (in the large majority of cases, anyway) businesses from issuing sloppy or fraudulent financial reports. Knowing that your report will be subject to an independent audit really keeps you on your toes!

The large majority of audit reports on financial statements give the business a clean bill of health, or a *clean opinion*. At the other end of the spectrum, the auditor might state that the financial statements are misleading and should not be relied upon. This negative audit report is called an *adverse opinion*. That's the big stick that auditors carry: They have the power to give a company's financial statements an adverse opinion, and no business wants that. Notice that we say here that the audit firms 'have the power' to give an adverse opinion. In fact, the threat of an adverse opinion almost always motivates a business to give way to the auditor and change its accounting or disclosure in order to avoid getting the kiss of death of an adverse opinion. An adverse audit opinion, if it were actually given, states that the financial statements of the business are misleading, and by implication fraudulent. The LSE and the SEC do not tolerate adverse opinions; they would stop trading in the company's shares if the company received an adverse opinion from its auditor.

Between the two extremes of a clean opinion and an adverse opinion, an auditor's report may point out a flaw in the company's financial statements – but not a fatal flaw that would require an adverse opinion. These are called *qualified opinions*. The following section looks at the most common type of audit report: the clean opinion, in which the auditor certifies that the business's financial statements conform to the rules and are presented fairly.

True and fair, a clean opinion

If the auditor finds no serious problems, the audit firm states that the accounts give a true and fair view of the state of affairs of the company. In the US, the auditor gives the financial report an *unqualified opinion*, which is the correct technical name, but most people call it a *clean opinion*. This expression has started to make its way in UK accounting parlance as the auditing business becomes more international. The clean-opinion audit report runs to about 100 words and three paragraphs, with enough defensive legal language to make even a seasoned accountant blush. This is a clean, or unqualified, opinion in the standard three-paragraph format:

In our opinion:

> *The financial statements give a true and fair view of the state of affairs of the company and the Group at 22 February 2012 and of the profit and cash flows of the Group for the year then ended;*

> *The financial statements have been properly prepared in accordance with the Companies Act 1985; and*

> *Those parts of the Directors' remuneration report required by Part 3 of Schedule 7A to the Companies Act 1985 have been properly prepared in accordance with the Companies Act 1985.*

1st paragraph	We did the audit, but the financial statements are the responsibility of management; we just express an opinion of them.
2nd paragraph	We carried out audit procedures that provide us a reasonable basis for expressing our opinion, but we don't necessarily catch everything.
3rd paragraph	The company's financial statements conform to GAAP and are not misleading.

Figure 15-1 presents a clean opinion but in a *one*-paragraph format – given by PricewaterhouseCoopers on one of Caterpillar's financial statements. For many years, Price Waterhouse (as it was known before its merger with Coopers) was well known for its maverick one-paragraph audit report.

Figure 15-1: A one-paragraph audit report.

REPORT OF INDEPENDENT ACCOUNTANTS

PRICEWATERHOUSE(COOPERS

To the Board of Directors and Stockholders of Caterpillar Inc.: We have audited, in accordance with auditing standards generally accepted in the United States, the consolidated financial position of Caterpillar Inc. and its subsidiaries as of December 31, 1999, 1998 and 1997, and the related consolidated results of their operations and their consolidated cash flow for each of the three years in the period ended December 31, 1999, (not presented herein); and in our report dated January 21, 2000, we expressed an unqualified opinion on those consolidated financial statements.

In our opinion, the information set forth in the accompanying condensed consolidated financial statements is fairly stated, in all material respects, in relation to the consolidated financial statements from which it has been derived.

PricewaterhouseCoopers LLP

Peoria, Illinois
January 21, 2000

Other kinds of audit opinions

An audit report that does *not* give a clean opinion may look very similar to a clean-opinion audit report to the untrained eye. Some investors see the name of an audit firm next to the financial statements and assume that everything is okay – after all, if the auditor had seen a problem, the cops would have pounced on the business and put everyone in jail, right? Well, not exactly.

How do you know when an auditor's report may be something other than a straightforward, no-reservations clean opinion? *Look for a fourth paragraph*; that's the key. Many audits require the audit firm to add additional, explanatory language to the standard, unqualified (clean) opinion.

One modification to an auditor's report is very serious – when the audit firm expresses the view that it has substantial doubts about the capability of the business to continue as a going concern. A *going concern* is a business that has sufficient financial wherewithal and momentum to continue its normal operations into the foreseeable future and would be able to absorb a bad turn of events without having to default on its liabilities. A going concern does not face an imminent financial crisis or any pressing financial emergency. A business could be under some financial distress, but overall still be judged a going concern. Unless there is evidence to the contrary, the auditor assumes that the business is a going concern.

But in some cases, the auditor may see unmistakable signs that a business is in deep financial waters and may not be able to convince its creditors and lenders to give it time to work itself out of its present financial difficulties. The creditors and lenders may force the business into involuntary bankruptcy, or the business may make a pre-emptive move and take itself into voluntary bankruptcy. The equity owners (shareholders of a company) may end up holding an empty bag after the bankruptcy proceedings have concluded. (This is one of the risks that shareholders take.) If an auditor has serious concerns about whether the business is a going concern, these doubts are spelled out in the auditor's report.

Auditors also point out any accounting methods that are inconsistent from one year to the next, whether their opinion is based in part on work done by another audit firm, on limitations on the scope of their audit work, on departures from the rules (if they're not serious enough to warrant an adverse opinion) or on one of several other more technical matters. Generally, businesses – and auditors, too – want to end up with a clean bill of health; anything less is bound to catch the attention of the people who read the financial statements. Every business wants to avoid that sort of attention if possible.

Do Audits Always Catch Fraud?

Business managers and investors should understand one thing: Having an audit of a business's financial statements does not guarantee that all fraud, embezzlement, theft and dishonesty will be detected. Audits have to be cost-effective; auditors can't examine every transaction that occurred during the year. Instead, auditors carefully evaluate businesses' internal controls and rely on sampling – they examine only a relatively small portion of transactions closely and in depth. The sample may not include the transactions that would tip off the auditor that something is wrong, however. Perpetrators of fraud and embezzlement are usually clever in concealing their wrongdoing and often prepare fake evidence to cover their tracks.

Looking for errors and fraud

Auditors look in the high-risk areas where fraud and embezzlement are most likely to occur and in areas where the company's internal controls are weak. But again, auditors can't catch everything. High-level management fraud is extraordinarily difficult to detect because auditors rely a great deal on management explanations and assurances about the business. Top-level executives may lie to auditors, deliberately mislead them and conceal things that they don't want auditors to find out about. Auditors have a particularly difficult time detecting management fraud.

Under tougher auditing standards adopted recently, auditors have to develop a detailed and definite plan to search for indicators of fraud, and they have to document the search procedures and findings in their audit working papers. Searching is one thing, but actually finding fraud is quite another. There had been many cases in which high-level management fraud went on for some time before it was discovered, usually not by auditors. The new auditing standard was expected to lead to more effective audit procedures that would reduce undetected fraud.

Unfortunately, it does not appear that things have improved. Articles in the financial press since then have exposed many cases of accounting and management fraud that were not detected or, if known about, were not objected to by the auditors. This is most disturbing. It's difficult to understand how these audit failures and breakdowns happened. The trail of facts is hard to follow in each case, especially by just reading what's reported in the press. Nevertheless, we would say that two basic reasons explain why audits fail to find fraud.

First, business managers are aware that an audit relies on a very limited sampling from the large number of transactions. They know that there is only a needle-in-the-haystack chance of fraudulent transactions being selected for an in-depth examination by the auditor. Second, managers are in a position to cover their tracks – to conceal evidence and to fabricate false evidence. In short, well-designed and well-executed management fraud is extraordinarily difficult to uncover by ordinary audit procedures. Call this *audit evidence failure*; the auditor didn't know about the fraud.

In other situations, the auditor did know what was going on but didn't act on it – call this an *audit judgment failure.* In these cases, the auditor was overly tolerant of wrong accounting methods used by the client. The auditor may have had serious objections to the accounting methods, but the client persuaded the auditor to go along with the methods.

What happens when auditors spot fraud

In the course of doing an audit, the audit firm may make the following discoveries:

- **Errors in recording transactions:** These honest mistakes happen from time to time because of inexperienced bookkeepers, or poorly trained accountants, or simple failure to pay attention to details. No one is stealing money or other assets or defrauding the business. Management wants the errors corrected and wants to prevent them from happening again.

- **Theft, embezzlement and fraud against the business:** This kind of dishonesty takes advantage of weak internal controls or involves the abuse of positions of authority in the organisation that top management did not know about and was not involved in. Management may take action against the guilty parties.

- **Accounting fraud** (also called **financial fraud** or **financial reporting fraud**): This refers to top-level managers who know about and approve the use of misleading and invalid accounting methods for the purpose of disguising the business's financial problems or artificially inflating profit. Often, managers benefit from these improper accounting methods – by propping up the market price of the company's shares to make their stock options more valuable, for example.

- **Management fraud:** In the broadest sense, this includes accounting fraud, but in a more focused sense, it refers to high-level business managers engaging in illegal schemes to line their pockets at the business's expense or knowingly violating laws and regulations that put the business at risk of large criminal or civil penalties. A manager may conspire with competitors to fix prices or divide the market, for example. Accepting kickbacks or bribes from customers is an example of management fraud – although most management fraud is more sophisticated than taking under-the-table payments.

When the first two types of problems are discovered, the auditor's follow-up is straightforward. Errors are corrected, and the loss from the crime against the business is recorded. (Such a loss may be a problem if it is so large that the auditor thinks it should be disclosed separately in the financial report but the business disagrees and does not want to call attention to the loss.) In contrast, the auditor is between a rock and a hard place when accounting or management fraud is uncovered.

When an auditor discovers accounting or management fraud, the business has to clean up the fraud mess as best it can – which often involves recording a loss. Of course, the business should make changes to prevent the fraud from occurring again. And it may request the resignations of those responsible or even take legal action against those employees. Assuming that the fraud loss is recorded and reported correctly in the financial statements, the auditor then issues a clean opinion on the financial statements. But auditors can withhold a clean opinion and threaten to issue a qualified or adverse opinion if the client does not deal with the matter in a satisfactory manner in its financial statements. That's the auditor's real clout.

The most serious type of accounting fraud occurs when profit is substantially overstated, with the result that the market value of the corporation's shares was based on inflated profit numbers. Another type of accounting fraud occurs when a business is in deep financial trouble but its balance sheet disguises the trouble and makes things look more sound than they really are. The business may be on the verge of financial failure, but the balance sheet gives no clue. When the fraud comes out into the open, the market value takes a plunge, and the investors call their lawyers and sue the business and the auditor.

Investing money in a business or shares issued by a public business involves many risks. The risk of misleading financial statements is just one of many dangers that investors face. A business may have accurate and truthful financial statements but end up in the tank because of bad management, bad products, poor marketing or just bad luck.

All in all, audited financial statements that carry a clean opinion (the best possible auditor's report) are reliable indicators for investors to use – especially because auditors are held accountable for their reports and can be sued for careless audit procedures. (In fact, accountancy firms have had to pay many millions of pounds in malpractice lawsuit damages over the past 30 years, and Arthur Andersen was actually driven out of business.) Auditors usually handle clients for years, if not decades – PricewaterhouseCoopers LLP have been Sainsbury's auditors since 1995 – so if anyone knows where the bodies are it's the auditor. So don't overlook the audit report as a tool for judging the reliability of a business's financial statements. When you read the auditor's report on the annual financial statements from your pension fund manager, hopefully you'll be very reassured! That's your retirement money they're talking about, after all.

Auditors and the Rules

In the course of doing an audit, the accountant often catches certain accounting methods used by the client that violate the prevailing approved and authoritative methods and standards laid down by law that businesses must follow in preparing and reporting financial statements. All businesses are subject to these ground rules. An auditor calls to the attention of the business any departures from the rules, and he or she helps the business make adjustments to put its financial statements back on the right track. Sometimes, a business may not want to make the changes that the auditor suggests because its profit numbers would be deflated. Professional standards demand that the auditor secure a change (assuming that the amount involved is material). If the client refuses to make a change to an acceptable accounting method, the accountant warns the financial report reader in the auditor's report.

Auditors don't allow their good names to be associated with financial reports that they know are misleading if they can possibly help it. Every now and then, we read in the financial press about an audit firm walking away from a client ('withdraws from the engagement' is the official terminology). As mentioned earlier in this chapter, everything the auditor learns in the course of an audit is confidential and cannot be divulged beyond top management and the board of directors of the business. A *confidential relationship* exists between the auditor and the client – although it is not equal to the privileged communication between lawyers and their clients.

If an auditor discovers a problem, he or she has the responsibility to move up the chain of command in the business organisation to make sure that one level higher than the source of the problem is informed of the problem. But the board of directors is the end of the line. The auditor does not inform the LSE, the SEC or another regulatory agency of any confidential information learned during the audit.

However, most outside observers will work on the 'no smoke without fire' principle. No firm, yet alone an accountancy partnership with their partnership profit share on the line, willingly gives up a lucrative client.

Auditors, on the other hand, are frequently being replaced, often for cost reasons – auditing is a negotiable deal too – but also because the firm being audited may have simply outgrown the auditor. This happens fairly frequently when a business is going for a public listing of its shares. The guy round the corner, who was cheap and competent, cuts no ice with the big wheels at the LSE and the placing houses that have to sell the shares. They want a big name auditor to help the PR push.

We can't exaggerate the importance of reliable financial statements that are prepared according to uniform standards and methods for measuring profit and putting values on assets, liabilities and owners' equity. Not to put too fine a point on it, the flow of capital into businesses and the market prices of shares traded in the public markets (the London Stock Exchange, the New York Stock Exchange and over the NASDAQ network) depend on the information reported in financial statements.

The US Sarbanes-Oxley Act (known less commonly but better understood as the Public Company Accounting Reforms and Investor Protection Act – 2002) and the UK 'Companies (Audit, Investigations and Community Enterprise) Act – 2004' were brought in to ensure truthfulness in financial accounting (refer to Chapter 1 for more details about Sarbanes-Oxley). Despite the pain involved for businesses, the end result of complying with the acts will hopefully be a set of audited accounts that outsiders place more reliance on than ever before.

Also, smaller, privately owned businesses would have a difficult time raising capital from owners and borrowing money from banks if no one could trust their financial statements. Generally accepted accounting principles, in short, are the gold standard for financial reporting. Once financial reporting standards have been put into place, how are the standards enforced? To a large extent, the role of auditors is to do just that – to enforce the rules. The main purpose of having annual audits, in other words, is to keep businesses on the straight-and-narrow path and to prevent businesses from issuing misleading financial statements. Auditors are the guardians of the financial reporting rules. We think most business managers and investors agree that financial reporting would be in a sorry state of affairs if auditors weren't around.

From Audits to Advising

If Accountant Rip van Winkle woke up today after his 20-year sleep, he would be shocked to find that accountancy firms make most of their money not from doing audits but from advising clients. A recent advertisement by one of the Big Four international accountancy firms listed the following services: 'assurance, business consulting, corporate finance, eBusiness, human capital, legal services, outsourcing, risk consulting, and tax services'. (Now, if the firm could only help you with your back problems!) Do you see audits in this list? No? Well, it's under the first category – assurance. Why have accountancy firms moved so far beyond audits into many different fields of consulting?

We suspect that many businesses do not view audits as adding much value to their financial reports. True, having a clean opinion by an auditor on financial statements adds credibility to a financial report. At the same time, managers tend to view the audit as an intrusion, and an override on their prerogatives regarding how to account for profit and how to present the financial report of the business. Most audits, to be frank about it, involve a certain amount of tension between managers and the audit firm. After all, the essence of an audit is to second-guess the business's accounting methods and financial reporting decisions. So it's quite understandable that accountancy firms have looked to other types of services they can provide to clients that are more value-added and less adversarial – and that are more lucrative.

Nevertheless, many people have argued that accountancy firms should get out of the consulting and advising business – at least to the same clients they audit. For the first years of this millennium, things seemed to be moving in this direction, and new legislation gave them a none-too-gentle prod. Arthur Andersen only just split their consultancy business off before they went under themselves. Luckily, they changed the name of the consulting business from Andersen to Accenture, ditching a fair amount of the bad odour that attached itself to the accountancy practice's name. Now the pendulum is swinging back and big accountancy firms are pushing an integrated approach, arguing that clients don't want to have to explain largely the same business facts to different teams of 'visiting firemen'. Although the Big Four are back in the consulting game, figures from the Management Consultancies Association suggest that accountancy firms only have 16 per cent of the market for consultancy services, right now at least.

Sometimes we take the pessimistic view that in the long run accountants will abandon audits and do only taxes and consulting. Who will do audits then? Well, a team of governmental auditors could take over the task – but we don't think this would be too popular.

Part V
The Part of Tens

'Before we get down to business, I couldn't help noticing what an unusually large shredder you have.'

In this part . . .

The Part of Tens contains four shorter chapters. The first chapter presents ten tools and techniques that are useful in running a business and getting the most from your accounting system. These top ten topics are summarised and condensed, and constitute a compact accounting tool kit for managers. The second chapter looks at the range of options available to finance a business and covers the field from international stock markets to government grants. The third chapter provides investors with a checklist of the top ten things they should look for when reading a financial report in order to gain the maximum amount of information in the minimum amount of time. The final chapter provides insights on getting to grips with the future; a veritable financial crystal ball.

Chapter 16

Ten Ways Savvy Business Managers Use Accounting

. . . .

In This Chapter

▶ Making better profit decisions

▶ Leveraging – both the operating kind and the financial kind

▶ Putting your finger on the pulse of cash flow

▶ Better budgeting for planning and control

▶ Developing financial controls

▶ Taking charge of the accounting function

▶ Explaining your financial statements to others

. . . .

So how can accounting help make you a better business manager? This is the bottom-line question. Speaking of the bottom line, that's exactly the place to start. Accounting provides the financial information and analysis tools you need for making insightful profit decisions – and stops you from plunging ahead with gut decisions that may feel right but that don't hold water after diligent analysis.

Make Better Profit Decisions

Making profit starts with earning margin on each unit sold and then selling enough units to overcome your total fixed expenses for the period (the basic concept that we explain more fully in Chapter 9). We condense the accounting model of profit into the following equation:

(Margin per unit × sales volume) – fixed expenses = profit

Note: Profit here is *before* corporation tax. Regular corporations pay tax based on the amount of their taxable income; different rates apply to different brackets of taxable income. The bottom-line net income in the profit and loss account of a business is after-tax income. A business may distribute all, part or none of its profit for the year to its owners.

Insist that your accountant determines the margin per unit for all products you sell. The margin is also called the *contribution margin* to emphasise that it contributes toward the business's fixed expenses. Here's an example for determining the *margin per unit* for a product:

Margin Factors	Amount
Sales price	£100.00
Less product cost	60.00
Equals gross margin	£40.00
Less sales revenue-driven expenses	8.00
Less sales volume-driven expenses	5.00
Equals margin per unit	£27.00

We'd bet that your accountant provides the gross margin (also called *gross profit*) on your products. So far, so good. But don't stop at the gross margin line. Push your accountant to determine the two variable expenses for each product. In this example, you don't make £40 per unit sold; you make only £27 from selling the product. Two products may have the same £40 gross profit, but one could provide a £27 margin and the other a £32 margin because the second one's variable expenses are lower.

Have your accountant differentiate between *revenue*-driven and *volume*-driven variable expenses for each product. Suppose you raise the sales price to £110.00, a 10 per cent increase. The sales revenue-driven expense increases by 10 per cent as well, to £8.80, because these expenses (such as sales commission) are a certain *percentage* of the sales price. Your margin increases not £10.00, but only £9.20 (the £10.00 sales price increase minus the £0.80 expense increase). In contrast, the higher sales price by itself does not increase the sales volume-driven expenses (such as shipping costs); these expenses remain at £5.00 per unit unless other factors cause them to increase.

You earn profit (or to be precise, profit before tax) by selling enough products that your total margin is higher than your total fixed expenses for the period. The excess of total margin over fixed expenses is profit before tax. Setting sales prices to generate an adequate total contribution margin is one of the most important functions of managers.

When thinking about changing sales price, focus on what happens to the *margin per unit*. Suppose, for example, that you're considering dropping the sales price 10 per cent from £100.00 to £90.00. You predict that your product cost and variable expenses will remain unchanged. Here's what would happen to your margin:

Margin Factors	After	Before
Sales price	£90.00	£100.00
Less product cost	<u>60.00</u>	<u>60.00</u>
Equals gross margin	£30.00	£40.00
Less sales revenue-driven expenses	7.20	8.00
Less sales volume-driven expenses	<u>5.00</u>	<u>5.00</u>
Equals margin per unit	£17.80	£27.00

Your margin would plunge £9.20 per unit – more than one-third!

Suppose you sold 100,000 units of this product during the year just ended. These sales generated £2.7 million total margin. If you drop the sales price, you give up £920,000 total margin. Where will the replacement come from for this £920,000 contribution margin? Higher sales volume? Sales volume would have to increase more than 50 per cent to offset the drastic drop in the contribution margin per unit. You'd better have a good answer. The profit model directs attention to this critical question and gives you the amount of margin sacrificed by dropping the sales price.

Understand That a Small Sales Volume Change Has a Big Effect on Profit

Is that big push before year-end for just 5 per cent more sales volume really that important? You understand that more sales mean more profit, of course. But what's the big deal? A 5 per cent increase in sales volume means just 5 per cent more profit, doesn't it? Oh no. If you think so, you need to read Chapter 9. Because fixed expenses are just that – fixed and unchanging over the short run. Seemingly small changes in sales volume cause large swings in profit. This effect is called *operating leverage*.

The following example illustrates operating leverage. Suppose your £12.5 million annual fixed expenses provide the personnel and physical resources to sell 625,000 units over the year. However, you didn't hit capacity; your company's actual sales volume was 500,000 units for the year, or 80 per cent of sales capacity – which isn't bad. Your average margin across all products is £30 per unit. Using the basic profit equation, you determine profit before income tax as follows:

$$[£30 \text{ margin per unit} \times 500{,}000 \text{ units}] = \begin{array}{ll} £15{,}000{,}000 & \text{contribution margin} \\ \underline{-\ 12{,}500{,}000} & \text{fixed expenses} \\ = £2{,}500{,}000 & \text{pre-tax profit} \end{array}$$

Now, what if you had sold 25,000 more units, which is just 5 per cent more sales volume? Your fixed expenses would have been the same because sales volume would still be well below the sales capacity provided by your fixed expenses. Therefore, the profit increase would have been the £30 margin per unit times the 25,000 additional units sold, or £750,000. This is a 5 per cent gain in contribution margin. But compared to the £2,500,000 pre-tax profit, the additional £750,000 is a 30 per cent gain – from only a 5 per cent sales volume gain, which is a 6-to-1 payoff!

Operating leverage refers to the wider swing in profit rather than the smaller swing in sales volume. In this example, a 5 per cent increase in sales volume would cause a 30 per cent increase in profit. Unfortunately, operating leverage cuts both ways. If your sales volume had been 5 per cent less, your profit would have been £750,000 less, which would have resulted in 30 per cent less profit.

Here's a quick explanation of operating leverage. In this example, total contribution margin is 6 times profit: £15 million contribution margin ÷ £2.5 million profit = 6. So a 5 per cent swing in contribution margin has a 6-times effect, or a 30 per cent impact on profit. Suppose a business had no fixed expenses (highly unlikely). In this odd situation, there is no operating leverage. The percentage gain or loss in profit would equal the percentage gain or loss in sales volume.

The fundamental lesson of operating leverage is to make the best use you can of your fixed expenses – that is, take advantage of the capacity provided by the resources purchased with your fixed expenses. If your sales volume is less than your sales capacity, the unsold quantity would have provided a lot more profit. Most businesses are satisfied if their actual sales volume is 80–90 per cent of their sales capacity. But keep in mind one thing: That last 10 or 20 per cent of sales volume would make a dramatic difference in profit!

Fathom Profit and Cash Flow from Profit

Profit equals sales revenue minus expenses – you don't need to know much about accounting to understand this definition. However, business managers should dig a little deeper. First, you should be aware of the accounting problems in measuring sales revenue and expenses. Because of these problems, profit is not a clear-cut and precise number. Second, you should know the real stuff of profit and know where to find profit in your financial statements.

Profit is not a politically correct term. Instead, business financial reports call profit *net income* or *net earnings*. So don't look for the term *profit* in external financial statements. Remember, net income (or net earnings) = bottom-line profit after tax.

Profit accounting methods are like hemlines

Profit is not a hard-and-fast number but is rather soft and flexible on the edges. For example, profit depends on which accounting method is selected to measure the cost-of-goods-sold expense, which is usually the largest expense for businesses that sell products. The rules of the game, called *generally accepted accounting principles* (or GAAP for short), permit two or three alternative methods for measuring cost of goods sold and for other expenses as well. (Chapter 13 discusses accounting methods.)

When evaluating the profit performance of your own business or when sizing up the net income record of a business you're considering buying, look carefully at whether profit measurement is based on stingy (conservative) or generous (liberal) accounting methods. You can assume that profit is in the GAAP ballpark, but you have to determine whether profit is in the right field or the left field (or perhaps in centre field). Businesses are not required to disclose how different the profit number would have been for the period if different accounting methods had been used, but they do have to reveal their major accounting methods in the footnotes to their annual financial statements.

The real stuff of profit

Most people know that, in the general sense of the word, *profit* is a gain, or an increase in wealth, or how much better off you are. But managers and investors hit the wall when asked to identify the real stuff of profit earned by a business. To make our point, suppose that your business's latest annual profit and loss account reports £10 million sales revenue and £9.4 million expenses, which yields £600,000 bottom-line net income. Your profit ratio is 6 per cent of sales revenue, which is about typical for many businesses. But we digress.

Our question is this: *Where is that £600,000 of profit?* Can you find and locate the profit earned by your business? Is it in cash? If not, where is it? If you can't answer this question, aren't you a little embarrassed? Quick – go and read Chapter 5!

Profit accounting is more complicated than simple cash-in, cash-out book-keeping. Sales for cash increase cash, of course, but sales on credit initially increase an asset called debtors. So *two* assets are used in recording sales revenue. Usually, a minimum of four assets and two liabilities are used in recording a business's expenses. To locate profit, you have to look at all the assets and liabilities that are changed by revenue and expenses. The *measure* of profit is found in the profit and loss account. But the *substance* of profit is found in assets and liabilities, which are reported in the *balance sheet*.

Your accountant will have determined that your £600,000 net income consists of the following three components:

£600,000 profit = £420,000 cash + £290,000 net increase in other assets – £110,000 increase in liabilities

This is a typical scenario for the makeup of profit – we don't mean the pound amounts but rather the three components of profit. The pound amounts of the increases or decreases in assets and liabilities vary from business to business, of course, and from year to year. But rarely would the profit equation be

£600,000 profit = £600,000 cash

Cash is only one piece of the profit pie. Business managers need accounting to sort out how profit is divided among the three components – in particular, you need to know the cash flow generated from profit.

Govern Cash Flow Better

A business wants to make profit, of course, but equally important, a business must convert its profit into *usable cash flow*. Profit that is never turned into cash or is not turned into cash for a long time is not very helpful. A business needs cash flow from profit to provide money for three critical uses:

✔ To distribute some of its profit to its equity (owner) sources of capital – to provide a cash income to them as compensation for their capital investment in the business.

✔ To grow the business – to invest in new fixed (long-term) operating assets and to increase its stock and other short-term operating assets.

✔ To meet its debt payment obligations and to maintain the general liquidity and solvency of the business.

One expense, depreciation, is not a cash outlay in the period it's recorded as an expense. Rather, depreciation expense for a period is an allocated amount of the original cost of the business's fixed assets that were bought and paid for in previous years. More importantly, the sales revenue collected by the business includes money for its depreciation expense. Thus the business converts back into cash some of the money that it put in its fixed assets years ago. Understanding how depreciation works in cash flow analysis is very important.

In one sense, you can say that depreciation generates cash flow. But please be careful here. This does *not* mean that if you had recorded more depreciation expense, you would have had more cash flow. What it means is that through making sales at prices that include recovery of some of the cost of fixed assets, your sales revenue (to the extent that it is collected by year-end) includes cash flow to offset the depreciation expense.

To illustrate this critical point, suppose a business did not make a profit for the year but did manage to break even. In this zero-profit situation, there is cash flow from profit because of depreciation. The company would realise cash flow equal to its depreciation for the year – assuming that it collected its sales revenue. Depreciation is a process of recycling fixed assets back into cash during the year, whether or not the business makes a profit.

In the example in the preceding section, the business earned $600,000 net income (profit). But its cash increased only $420,000. Why? The *cash flow statement* provides the details. In addition to reporting the depreciation for the year, the first section of the cash flow statement reports the short-term operating asset and liability changes caused by the business's sales and expenses. These changes either help or hurt cash flow from profit (from operating activities, to use the correct technical accounting term).

An increase in debtors hurts cash flow from profit because the business did not collect all its sales on credit for the year. An increase in stock hurts cash flow from profit because the business replaces the products sold and spends more money to increase its stock of products. On the other hand, an increase in creditors or accrued expenses payable helps cash flow from profit. These two liabilities are, basically, unpaid expenses. When these liabilities increase, the business did not pay all its expenses for the year – and its cash outflows for expenses were less than its expenses.

Generally speaking, growth hurts cash flow from profit. To grow its sales and profit, a business usually has to increase its debtors and stock. Some of this total increase is offset by increases in the business's short-term operating liabilities. Usually, the increase in assets is more than the increase in liabilities, particularly when growth is faster than usual, and therefore cash flow from profit suffers. When a business suffers a decline in sales revenue, its bottom-line profit usually goes down – but its cash flow from profit may not drop as much as net profit, or perhaps not at all. A business should decrease its debtors and stock at the lower sales level; these decreases help cash flow from profit. Even if a business reported a loss for the year, its cash flow from profit could be positive because of the depreciation factor and because the business may have reduced its debtors and stock.

Call the Shots on Your Management Accounting Methods

Business managers too often defer to their accountants in choosing accounting methods for measuring sales revenue and expenses. You should get involved in making these decisions. The best accounting method is the one that best fits the operating methods and strategies of your business. As a business manager, you know these operating methods and strategies better than your accountant. Chapter 13 gives you the details on various accounting methods.

For example, consider sales prices. How do you set your sales prices? Many factors affect your sales prices, of course. What we're asking here concerns your general sales pricing policy relative to product cost changes. For example, if your product cost goes up, do you allow your 'old' stock of these products to sell out before you raise the sales price? In other words, do you generally wait until you start selling the more recently acquired, higher-cost products before you raise your sales price? If so, you're using the first-in, first-out (FIFO) method. You might prefer to keep your cost-of-goods-sold expense method consistent with your sales pricing method. But the accountant may choose the last-in, first-out (LIFO) expense method, which would mismatch the higher-cost products with the lower-sales-price products.

The point is this: Business managers formulate a basic strategy regarding expense recovery. Sales revenue has to recoup your expenses to make a profit. How do you pass along your expenses to your customers in the sales prices you charge them? Do you attempt to recover the cost of your fixed assets as quickly as possible and set your sales prices on this basis? Then you should use a fast, or *accelerated*, depreciation method. On the other hand, if you take longer to recover the cost of your fixed assets through sales revenue, then you should probably use the longer-life *straight-line* depreciation method.

In short, we encourage you to take charge and choose the accounting methods that best fit your strategic profit plan. You need to speak some of the accounting language and know which accounting methods are available. In short, business managers should take charge of the accounting function just like they take charge of marketing and other key functions of the business.

This applies only to management accounting. Your accountants and auditors will call the shots when preparing accounts for the outside world.

Build Better Budgets

Budgeting (explained in Chapter 10) provides important advantages – first, for understanding the profit dynamics and financial structure of your business, and second, for planning for changes in the coming period. Budgeting forces you to focus on the factors that have to improve in order to increase profit and helps you prepare for the future. The basic profit model provides the framework for the profit budget. A good profit model is the essential starting point for budgeting. To develop your profit plan for the coming year, focus on the following:

- ✔ Margins
- ✔ Sales volume
- ✔ Fixed expenses

The profit budget, in turn, lays the foundation for changes in your operating assets and liabilities that are driven by sales revenue and expenses. Suppose you project a 10 per cent rise in sales revenue. How much will your debtors asset increase? Suppose your sales volume target for next year is 15 per cent higher than this year. How much will your stock increase? The budgeted changes in sales revenue and expenses for next year lead directly to the budgeted changes in operating assets and operating liabilities. These changes, in turn, direct attention to two other key issues.

First, if things go according to plan, how much cash flow from profit will be generated? Second, will you need more capital, and where will you get this money? You need the budgeted cash flow from profit (operating activities) for the coming year for three basic financial planning decisions:

- ✔ **Cash distributions from profit to owners** (cash dividends to shareholders of companies and cash distributions to partners).
- ✔ **Capital expenditures** (purchases of new fixed assets to replace and upgrade old fixed assets and to expand the business's capacity).
- ✔ **Raising capital** from borrowing on debt and, possibly, raising new equity capital from owners.

The higher your budgeted cash flow from profit, the more flexibility you have in having money available for cash distributions from profit and for capital expenditures and the less pressure to go out and raise new capital from debt and equity sources of capital.

To sum up, your profit budget is dovetailed with the assets and liabilities budget and the cash flow budget. Your accountant takes your profit budget (your strategic plan for improving profit) and builds the budgeted balance sheet and the budgeted cash flow statement. This information is essential for good planning – focusing in particular on how much cash flow from profit will be realised and how much capital expenditures will be required, which in turn lead to how much additional capital you have to raise and how much cash distribution from profit you will be able to make.

Optimise Capital Structure and Financial Leverage

Our friend Ron, a florist, made this point one night: 'To make profit, you must make sales.' We quickly added that you also must invest in operating assets, which means that you must raise capital. Where do you get this money? Debt and equity are the two basic sources. *Equity* refers to the money that owners invest in a business with the hopes that the business will turn a profit. Profit builds the value of owners' equity; profit fundamentally is an increase in assets that accrues to the benefit of the owners. Chapter 11 discusses owner-ship structures; Chapter 6 covers debt and equity.

The return on the owners' equity interest in the business consists of two quite distinct parts:

- ✔ Cash distributions from profit to the owners.
- ✔ Increases in the value of their ownership interest in the business.

In contrast, lenders are paid a *fixed* rate of interest on the amount borrowed. This fixed nature of interest expense causes a *financial leverage* or *gearing* effect that either benefits or hurts the amount of profit remaining for the equity investors in the business.

Financial leverage refers in general to using debt in addition to equity capital. A financial leverage gain (or loss) refers to the difference between the earn-ings before interest and tax (EBIT) that a business can make on its debt capi-tal versus the interest paid on the debt. The following example illustrates a case of financial leverage gain.

Your business earned £2.1 million EBIT for the year just ended. Your net operating assets are £12 million – recall that net operating assets equal total assets less non-interest-bearing operating liabilities (mainly creditors and accrued expenses payable). Thus your total capital sources equal £12 million. Suppose you have £4 million debt. The other £8 million is owners' equity. You paid 8 per cent annual interest on your debt, or £320,000 total interest. Debt furnishes one-third of your capital, so one-third of EBIT is attributed to this capital source. One-third of EBIT is £700,000. But you paid only £320,000 interest for this capital. You earned £380,000 more than the interest. This is the amount of your pre-tax *financial leverage gain*.

Three factors determine financial leverage gain (or loss):

✔ Proportion of total capital provided from debt.

✔ Interest rate.

✔ Return on assets (ROA), or the rate of EBIT the business can earn on its total capital invested in its net operating assets.

In the example, your business earned 17.5 per cent on its net operating assets (£2.1 million EBIT ÷ £12 million total net operating assets). You used £4 million debt capital for the investment in your net operating assets, and you paid 8 per cent annual interest on the debt, which gives a favourable 9.5 per cent spread (17.5 per cent – 8 per cent). The 9.5 per cent favourable spread times £4 million debt equals the £380,000 leverage gain for the year (before tax).

Business managers should watch how much financial leverage gain contributes to the earnings for owners each year. In this example, the after-interest earnings for owners is £1,780,000 (equal to EBIT less interest expense). The £380,000 financial leverage gain provided a good part of this amount. Next year, one or more of the three factors driving the financial leverage gain may change. Savvy business managers sort out each year how much financial leverage impacts the earnings available for owners. Check out Chapter 14 for more on leverage, or *gearing* as it is also known.

A financial leverage gain enhances the earnings on owners' equity capital. The conventional wisdom is that a business should take advantage of debt that charges a lower interest rate than it can earn on the debt capital. Looking at the bigger picture, however, the long-run success of a business depends mainly on maintaining and improving the factors that determine its profit from operations (EBIT) – rather than going overboard and depending too much on financial leverage.

Develop Better Financial Controls

Experienced business managers can tell you that they spend a good deal of time dealing with problems. Things don't always go according to plan. Murphy's Law (if something can go wrong, it will, and usually at the worst possible time) is all too true. To solve a problem, you first have to know that you have one. You can't solve a problem if you don't know about it. Managers are problem solvers; they need to get on top of problems as soon as possible. In short, business managers need to develop good *financial controls*.

Financial controls act like trip wires that sound alarms and wave red flags for a manager's attention. Many financial controls are accounting-based. For example, actual costs are compared with budgeted costs or against last period's costs; serious variances are highlighted for immediate management attention. Actual sales revenue for product lines and territories are compared with budgeted goals or last period's numbers. Cash flow from profit period by period is compared with the budgeted amount of cash flow for the period from this source. These many different financial controls don't just happen. You should identify the handful of critical factors that you need to keep a close eye on and insist that your internal accounting reports highlight these operating ratios and numbers.

You must closely watch the margins on your products. Any deviation from the norm – even a relatively small deviation – needs your attention immediately. Remember that the margin per unit is multiplied by sales volume. If you sell 100,000 units of a product, a slippage of just 50 pence causes your total margin to fall £50,000. Of course, sales volume must be closely watched, too; that goes without saying. Fixed expenses should be watched in the early months of the year to see whether these costs are developing according to plan – and through the entire year.

Debtors' collections should be monitored closely. Average days before collection is a good control ratio to keep your eye on, and you should definitely get a listing of past-due customers' accounts. Stock is always a problem area. Watch closely the average days in stock before products are sold, and get a listing of slow-moving products. Experience is the best teacher. Over time you learn which financial controls are the most important to highlight in your internal accounting reports. The trick is to make sure that your accountants provide this information.

Minimise Tax

The first decision regarding tax concerns which type of legal ownership structure to use for carrying on the activities of the business, which is discussed in Chapter 11. When two or more owners provide capital for the business, you have two basic choices:

- A *partnership* – a specific contractual agreement among the owners regarding division of management authority, responsibilities and profit.

- A *limited liability company*, which has many characteristics of a partnership but is a separate legal entity, like a corporation.

Partnerships are *pass-through* tax entities. A pass-through business entity pays no tax on its taxable income but passes the obligation to its owners, who pick up their shares of the total taxable income in their individual income tax returns. In contrast, the individual shareholders of companies pay tax only on the amount of actual cash dividends from profit distributed by the company. Keep in mind here that the company pays corporation tax based on its taxable income. Factors other than tax affect the choice of ownership structure. You need the advice of tax professionals and financial consultants.

Regardless of the ownership structure, you should understand how accounting methods determine taxable income. Basically, the choice of accounting methods enables you to shift the timing of expenses – such as depreciation and cost of goods sold – between early years and later years. Do you want more expense deductions this year? Then choose the last-in, first-out (LIFO) method for cost-of-goods-sold expense and an accelerated method for depreciation. But keep in mind that what you gain today, you lose tomorrow. Higher expense deductions in early years cause lower deductions in later years. Also, these income-tax-driven accounting choices make the stock and fixed assets in your balance sheet look anaemic. Remember that expenses are asset decreases. You want more expense? Then lower asset values as reported in your balance sheet.

Think twice before jumping on the tax minimisation bandwagon. Knowing about accounting methods and their effects in both the profit and loss account and the balance sheet helps you make these important decisions.

Explain Your Financial Statements to Others

On many occasions, as a business manager you have to explain your financial statements to others:

- When applying for a loan.

- When talking with people or other businesses who may be interested in buying your business.

- When dealing with the press.

- ✔ When dealing with unions or other employee groups in setting new wages and benefit packages.

- ✔ When explaining the profit-sharing plan to your employees.

- ✔ When reporting financial statement data to national trade associations that collect this information from their members.

- ✔ When presenting the annual financial report before the annual meeting of owners.

Knowledge of financial statement reporting and accounting methods is also extremely useful when you sit on a bank's board of directors, or a hospital board, or any of several other types of oversight boards. In the preceding list, you're the explainer, the one who has to do the explaining. As a board member, you're the explainee, the person who has to make sense of the financial statements and accounting methods being presented. A good accounting foundation is invaluable.

Part II of this book shows you how to understand financial reports. In brief, you need a good grip on the purpose, nature and limitations of each of the three primary financial statements reported by a business:

- ✔ **The profit and loss account:** Many people think that bottom-line profit is cash in the bank, but you know better.

- ✔ **The cash flow statement:** Many people just add back depreciation to net income to determine cash flow from profit, but you know better.

- ✔ **The balance sheet:** Many people think that this financial statement reports the current values for assets, but you know better.

We'll tell you one disadvantage of knowing some accounting: The other members of the board will be very impressed with your accounting knowledge and may want to elect you chairperson.

A short word on massaging the numbers: Don't!

I (John) taught accounting to future business managers and accountants. I didn't encourage profit smoothing, window dressing and other techniques for manipulating accounting numbers to make a company's financial statements look better — no more than my marketing professor colleagues encouraged their students to engage in deceptive advertising tactics. Yet these things go on, and I felt obligated to expose my students to these practices as a warning that accountants face difficult moral decisions. In a similar vein, I caution you, a business manager, that you will surely face pressures from time to time to massage the accounting numbers — to make profit look smoother from year to year, or to make the short-term solvency of the business look better (by window dressing). Don't!

Chapter 17

Ten Places a Business Gets Money From

*A*ll business ventures need some cash to get going and need more money as they become more successful. They have to invest in staff, equipment and websites, and need to remain competitive and visible by keeping products and services up to date.

Many sources of funds are available to businesses, both big and small. However, not all of them are equally appropriate to all businesses at all times. Different sources of finance carry very different obligations, responsibilities and opportunities for profitable business. Having some appreciation of these differences enables business people to make informed choices.

Stock Markets

A stock market is quite simply a marketplace for trading company stock. A company listing on the London Stock Exchange, The New York Stock Exchange or FWB Frankfurt Stock Exchange is the way serious players raise money. The new breed of 'super exchanges' such as NYSE Euronext are also becoming popular. If you want a few hundred million, or a billion or so, stock markets are the places to come to.

All the stock markets have different rules and different outcomes. For example, the value placed on new companies on US stock markets is between 1.5 and 3 times that of UK and European markets.

To get listed on a major stock exchange, a company needs a track record of making substantial profits, with decent seven-figure sums being made in the year you plan to *float*, as this process is known. A large proportion (usually at least 25 per cent) of the company's shares must be put up for sale at the outset. Also, companies are expected to have 100 shareholders now and to demonstrate that 100 more will come on board as a result of the listing.

You can check out all the world stock markets from Amsterdam to Zagreb on the Stock Exchanges Worldwide Links website at `www.tdd.lt/slnews/Stock_Exchanges/Stock.Exchanges.htm` and at `www.worldwide-tax.com/stockexchanges/worldstockexchanges.asp`. Almost all stock exchange websites have pages in English. Look out for a term such as 'Listing Center', 'Listing' or 'Rules' and you'll find the latest criteria for floating a company on that exchange.

Junior stock markets such as London's Alternative Investment Market (AIM) were formed in the mid to late 1990's specifically to provide risk capital for new rather than established ventures. These markets have an altogether more relaxed atmosphere than the major exchanges.

These junior markets are an attractive proposition for entrepreneurs seeking equity capital. AIM is particularly attractive to any dynamic company of any size, age or business sector that has rapid growth in mind. The smallest firm on AIM entered to raise less than £1 million and the largest raised over £500 million.

As with the major stock markets, these junior versions expect something in return. The formalities for floating are minimal but the costs of entry are high, and you must have a nominated adviser such as a major accountancy firm, stockbroker or banker. The cost of floating on the junior market is around 6.5 per cent of all funds raised, and companies valued at less than £2 million can expect to shell out a quarter of funds raised in costs alone. The market is regulated by the London Stock Exchange. You can find out more by going to their website (`www.londonstockexchange.com`) and clicking on 'AIM'.

One rung down from AIM is PLUS-Quoted Market whose roots lie in the market formerly known as Ofex. It began life in November 2004 and was granted Recognised Investment Exchange (RIE) status by the Financial Services Authority (FSA) in 2007. Aimed at smaller companies wanting to raise up to £10 million, it draws on a pool of capital primarily from private investors. The market is regulated, but requirements aren't as stringent as those of AIM or the main market and the costs of flotation and ongoing costs are lower. Keycom used this market to raise £4.4 million in September 2008 to buy out a competitor to give them a combined contract to provide broadband access to 40,000 student rooms in UK universities. There are 174 companies quoted on PLUS with a combined market capitalisation of £2.3 billion. Even in 2009, a particularly bad year for stock market activity, 30 companies applied for entry to PLUS and 18 were admitted. You can find out more about PLUS at www.plusmarketsgroup.com.

Private Equity

Organisations known as *venture capitalists* provide private equity by investing other people's money, often from pension funds. They are likely to be interested in investing large sums of money, often more than can be raised on AIM. Some 7,000 or so companies worldwide get private equity backing each year, around half of which are in the US where the average deal is $7.8 million.

Venture capitalists generally expect their investment to pay off within seven years, but they are hardened realists. Two in every ten investments they make are total write-offs, and six perform averagely well at best. So, the one star in every ten investments they make has to cover a lot of duds. Venture capitalists have a target rate of return of over 30 per cent, to cover this poor hit rate.

Raising venture capital is an expensive option and deals are slow to arrange. Six months is not unusual, and over a year has been known. Every venture capitalist has a deal done in six weeks in its portfolio, but that truly is the exception rather than the rule.

PricewaterhouseCoopers produce the Money Tree Report (www.pwcmoney tree.com), which is a quarterly study of venture capital investment activity in the United States, and individual country associations do something similar for their own markets. The PSEPS Venture Capital and Private Equity Directory (www.pseps.com/associations.php) lists the venture capital associations of various countries.

The British Venture Capital Association (www.bvca.co.uk), the European Venture Capital Association (www.evca.com) and the National Venture Capital Association (www.nvca.org) in the US have online directories giving details of hundreds of venture capital providers both inside and outside of their respective countries and continents.

You can see how those negotiating with or receiving venture capital rate the firm in question at the Funded website (www.thefunded.com) in terms of the deal offered, the firm's apparent competence and how good they are at managing the relationship.

Business Angels

One possible first source of equity or risk capital is a private individual with his or her own funds and perhaps some knowledge of your type of business. In return for a share in the business, such investors will invest money at their own risk. About 40 per cent of these individuals suffer a partial or complete loss of their investment, which suggests that many are prepared to take big risks. They've been christened 'business angels', a term first coined to describe private wealthy individuals who backed a play on Broadway or in London's West End.

Most business angels have worked in a small firm or have owned their own businesses before, so know the business world well. They are more likely to invest in early-stage investments where relatively small amounts of money are needed. 10 per cent of business angel investment is for less than £10,000 and 45 per cent is for over £50,000. They are up to five times more likely to invest in start-ups and early-stage investments than venture capital providers in general. Most business angels invest close to home, and syndicated deals make up more than a quarter of all deals, proving that angels flock together!

In return for their investment, most angels want some involvement beyond merely signing a cheque and may hope to play a part in your business in some way. They are looking for big rewards. One angel who backed the fledgling software company Sage (who supply accounting, payroll and business management software for small and medium sized companies) with £10,000 in its first round of £250,000 financing saw his stake rise to £40 million. Various industry estimates suggest that upwards of £6.5 billion of angels' money is looking for investment homes, although the sum actually invested each year is probably much smaller than that.

To find a business angel, check out the online directory of the British Business Angels Association (www.bbaa.org.uk). The European Business Angels Network website has directories of national business angel associations both inside and outside of Europe. Go to www.eban.org and click on 'Members' to find individual business angels.

Corporate Venture Funds

Venture capital firms often get their hands dirty taking a hand in the management of the businesses they invest in. Another type of business is also in the risk capital business, without it necessarily being their main line of business. These firms, known as *corporate venturers*, usually want an inside track to new developments in and around the edges of their own fields of interest.

Sinclair Beecham and Julian Metcalfe founded takeaway food chain Pret a Manger with a £17,000 loan and a name borrowed from a boarded-up shop. They had global ambitions and they joined forces with the corporate venturing arm of a big firm. It was only by cutting in McDonald's, the burger giant, that they could see any realistic way to dominate the world. They sold a 33% stake for £25 million in 2001 to McDonald's Ventures, LLC, a wholly-owned subsidiary of McDonald's Corporation, the arm of McDonalds that looks after its corporate venturing activities. They could also have considered Cisco, Apple Computers, IBM and Microsoft who also all have corporate venturing arms.

For an entrepreneur, corporate venture funds can provide a 'friendly customer' and help to open doors. For the 'parent' it provides a privileged ringside seat as a business grows and so be able to decide if the area is worth plunging into more deeply, or at least gain valuable insights into new technologies or business processes.

Global Corporate Venturing (`www.globalcorporateventuring.com`) is a new website devoted to publishing information on who's who and who's doing what in the sector.

Banks

Banks are the principal, and frequently the only, source of finance for businesses that are not listed on a stock market or that don't have private equity backers.

For long-term lending, banks can provide term loans for a number of years, with either a variable interest rate payable or an interest rate fixed for a number of years ahead. The proportion of fixed-rate loans has increased from a third of all term loans to around one in two. In some cases, moving between a fixed interest rate and a variable one at certain intervals may be possible. Unlike in the case of an overdraft, the bank cannot pull the rug from under you if circumstances (or the local manager) change.

Bankers look for asset security to back their loan and to provide a near-certainty of getting their money back. They also charge an interest rate that reflects current market conditions and their view of the risk level of the proposal.

Bankers like to speak of the 'five Cs' of credit analysis – factors they look at when they evaluate a loan request.

> ✔ **Character.** Bankers lend money to borrowers who appear honest and who have a good credit history. Before you apply for a loan, obtain a copy of your credit report and clean up any problems.

You can check out your own business credit rating at CheckSure (www.checksure.biz). By using the comparative ratios for your business sector you can see how to improve your own rating. The service costs around £6 to £10 depending on the level of detail you require.

✔ **Capacity.** This is a prediction of the borrower's ability to repay the loan. For a new business, bankers look at the business plan. For an existing business, bankers consider financial statements and industry trends.

✔ **Collateral.** Bankers generally want a borrower to pledge an asset that can be sold to pay off the loan if the borrower lacks funds.

✔ **Capital.** Bankers scrutinise a borrower's net worth, the amount by which assets exceed debts.

✔ **Conditions.** Whether bankers give a loan can be influenced by the current economic climate as well as by the amount.

You can see an A to Z listing of business bank accounts at www.find.co.uk/commercial/commercial_banking_centre/business-banking where the top six or so are rated and reviewed.

Governments around the world have schemes to make raising money from banks easier for small and new businesses. These *Small Firm Loan Guarantee Schemes* are operated by banks at the instigation of governments. They are aimed at small and new businesses with viable business proposals that have tried and failed to obtain a conventional loan because of a lack of security. Loans are available for periods of between two and ten years on sums from £5,000 to £250,000. The government guarantees 70–90 per cent of the loan. In return for the guarantee, the borrower pays a premium of 1–2 per cent per year on the outstanding amount of the loan. The commercial aspects of the loan are matters between the borrower and the lender.

You can find out more about the UK Small Firms Loan Guarantee Scheme on the Business Link website (go to www.businesslink.gov.uk and click on 'Finance and grants', 'Finance options, 'Borrowing', and 'Government lending schemes').

As a means of short-term borrowing, banks can offer *overdrafts* – a facility to cover you when you want to withdraw more money from a bank account than it has funds available. The overdraft was originally designed to cover the timing differences of, say, having to acquire raw materials to manufacture finished goods that are later sold. However, overdrafts have become part of the core funding of most businesses, with a little over a quarter of all bank finance provided in this way.

Almost every type and size of business uses overdrafts. They are very easy to arrange and take little time to set up. That is also their inherent weakness. The key words in the arrangement document are *repayable on demand*, which leaves the bank free to make and change the rules as it sees fit. (This term is under constant review, and some banks may remove it from the arrangement.) With other forms of borrowing, as long as you stick to the terms and conditions, the loan is yours for the duration, but not with overdrafts. Small businesses can expect to pay interest at three to four per cent above base – the rate at which banks can borrow. Larger and more creditworthy firms may pay much less.

Bonds, Debentures and Mortgages

Bonds, debentures and mortgages are all kinds of borrowing with different rights and obligations for the parties concerned. A mortgage is much the same for a business as for an individual. The loan is for buying a particular property asset such as a factory, office or warehouse. Interest is payable and the loan itself is secured against the property, so if the business fails, the mortgage can substantially be redeemed.

Companies wanting to raise funds for general business purposes, rather than a mortgage where a particular property is being bought, issue debentures or bonds. These run for a number of years, typically three years and upwards, with the bond or debenture holder receiving interest over the life of the loan with the capital returned at the end of the period.

The key difference between debentures and bonds lies in their security and ranking. Debentures are unsecured, so in the event of the company being unable to pay interest or repay the sum, the loaner may well get little or nothing back. Bonds are secured against specific assets and so rank ahead of debentures for any pay out.

Unlike bank loans that are usually held by the issuing bank, bonds and debentures are sold to the public in much the same way as shares. The interest demanded is a factor of the prevailing market conditions and the financial strength of the borrower.

You can find out more about raising these forms of finance on the Business Link website (www.businesslink.gov.uk).

Leasing and Hire-Purchase

You can usually finance physical assets such as cars, vans, computers and office equipment by leasing them or buying them on hire purchase. This leaves other funds free to cover the less tangible elements in your cash flow.

In this way, a business gets the use of assets without paying the full cost all at once.

Companies take out *operating leases* where you use the equipment for less than its full economic life, as you might with a motor vehicle, for example. The lessor takes the risk of the equipment becoming obsolete, and assumes responsibility for repairs, maintenance and insurance. As you, the lessee, pay for this, the service is more expensive than a *finance lease*, where you lease the equipment for most of its economic life, taking care of the maintenance and insurance yourself. Leases can normally be extended, often for fairly nominal sums, in the latter years.

Businesses that need lots of fixed assets such as computers, machinery or vehicles are the big customers for leasing. The obvious attraction of leasing is that you need no deposit, which leaves your working capital free for more profitable use elsewhere. Also, you know the cost from the start, making forward planning simpler. Tax advantages over other forms of finance may even exist.

Hire purchase differs from leasing in that you have the option to eventually become the owner of the asset, after you make a series of payments.

You can find a leasing or hire purchase company through the Finance and Leasing Association. Their website (go to www.fla.org.uk and click on 'For Businesses' and 'Business Finance Directory') gives details of all UK-based businesses that offer this type of finance. The website also has general information on terms of trade and code of conduct. Euromoney produce an annual World Leasing Yearbook that contains details about 4,250 leasing companies worldwide (go to their website at www.euromoney.com and click on 'Leasing & Asset Finance' and 'Books' for ordering information). You can, however, see a listing of most countries' leasing associations for free in the 'Contributors' listing on this site.

Factoring and Invoice Discounting

Customers take on average around 60 to 90 days to pay their suppliers. In effect, this means that companies are granting a loan to customers for that time. In periods of rapid growth, this can put a strain on cash flow. One way to alleviate that strain is to *factor* creditworthy customers' bills to a financial institution and receive some of the funds as goods leave the door, and this speeds up the cash flow.

Factoring is an arrangement that allows a business to receive up to 80 per cent of the cash due from customers more quickly than normal. The factoring company in effect buys the trade debts, provides a 100 per cent protection against bad debts and can also provide a debtor accounting and administration service.

Factoring costs a little more than normal overdraft rates. The factoring service costs between 0.5 and 3.5 per cent of the turnover, depending on volume of work, the number of debtors, average invoice amount and other related factors.

Factoring is generally only available to a business that invoices other business customers for services provided. These customers can be either in the business's home market or overseas. Companies that sell directly to the public, sell complex and expensive capital equipment, or expect progress payments on long-term projects may find factoring their debtor book to be difficult, if not impossible.

Invoice discounting is a variation on the same theme. Factors collect in money owed by their clients' customers, take a fee and pass the balance on, whereas invoice discounters leave their clients to collect the money themselves. This could be an advantage for firms that fear the factoring method might reduce their contact with clients. Invoice discounting is, in any case, typically available only to businesses with a turnover in excess of £1 million.

You can find an invoice discounter or factoring business through the Asset Based Finance Association's directory at www.thefda.org.uk/public/membersList.asp.

Grants, Incentives and Competitions

Surprisingly, there really is such a thing as a free lunch in the money world. These free lunches come from benevolent governments whose agenda is either to get businesses to locate in an area bereft of business but jammed full of people looking for work, or to pioneer new, unproven and risky technologies. Absolutely no evidence exists that governments get any value out of this generosity, but that's the thing with governments – they feel they have to *govern*, and people are more prepared to listen to others that have open wallets.

Grants are constantly being introduced (and withdrawn), but no system exists to let you know automatically. You have to keep yourself informed. The Business Link website (go to www.businesslink.gov.uk and click on 'Finance and grants' and 'Grants and government support') has advice on how to apply for a grant as well as a directory of grants on offer. The Microsoft Small Business Centre (www.microsoft.com/uk/businesscentral/euga/home.aspx) has a European Union Grant Advisor with a search facility to help you find which of the 6,000 grants on offer might suit your business needs. www.grants.gov is a guide to how to apply for over 1,000 federal government grants in the US.

Governments aren't the only guys with open wallets. More than a thousand annual awards around the world aimed at businesses exist. They are awarded for such achievements as being the greenest, cleanest, fastest (growing, that is), best company to work for and a thousand other plausible superlatives to make you feel good. The guys giving these awards are in it for the publicity, and heck, if you can get your hands on some free money, swallow your pride and head on down. Business plans are central to most of these competitions, which are sponsored by banks, the major accountancy bodies, chambers of commerce, local or national newspapers, business magazines and the trade press. Government departments may also have their own competitions as a means of promoting their initiatives for exporting, innovation, job creation and so forth. You can find directories of business plan competitions at www.smallbusinessnotes.com/planning/competitions.html and www.awardsintelligence.co.uk.

Using the Pension Fund

This financing strategy is mostly available to private companies with a relatively limited number of participants – usually directors, partners, top managers and shareholders. In these cases, the company can pay money out of business profits, thus escaping tax, into either a Small Self-Administered Scheme (SSAS) or a Self-Invested Personal Pension Plan (SIPP). That scheme can then invest in a narrow range of asset classes such as the company's own shares, purchase of commercial property and loans to the company, subject to certain conditions and with the approval of the pension trustees. The trustees are themselves regulated by the Pensions Regulator (www.thepensionsregulator.gov.uk). The aim of any pension investment must be to enhance the value of the pension fund for the ultimate benefit of all the pensioners equally.

The fun doesn't stop at being able to use pensioners' money to invest in the business they work in. Both SSAS and SIPP schemes can (since April 2006) borrow up to 50 per cent of their net assets to purchase property. So, if an SSAS/SIPP has total assets of £100,000, it can borrow a further £50,000, thus providing up to £150,000 to invest in qualifying business assets.

You can get the lowdown on SSAS and SIPP pension schemes from companies such as Westerby Trustee Service (www.sipp-ssas-pensions.co.uk) and SIPPS Guide (www.sippsguide.com).

Chapter 18

Ten (Plus One) Questions Investors Should Ask When Reading a Financial Report

. . . .

In This Chapter

▶ Analysing sales and profit performance

▶ Investigating changes in assets and liabilities

▶ Looking for signs of financial distress

▶ Examining asset utilisation and return on capital investment

. . . .

*Y*ou have only so much time to search for the most important signals in a business's financial report. For a quick read through a financial report – one that allows you to decode the critical signals in the financial statements – you need a checklist of key questions to ask.

Before you read a business's annual financial report, get up to speed on which products and services the business sells and learn about the history of the business and any current problems it's facing. One place to find much of this information is the company's annual accounts filed at Companies House, which is a public document available to everyone. (You can also usually find this information on the company's website, in the investor affairs section.) Company profiles are prepared by securities brokers and investment advisers, and they're very useful. *The Economist*, *Investors Chronicle* and other national newspapers, such as *The Financial Times*, are good sources of information about public companies.

Did Sales Grow?

A business makes profit by making sales (although you do have to take controlling expenses into account). Sales growth is the key to long-run sustained profit growth. Even if profit is up, investors get worried when sales revenue is flat.

Start reading a financial report by comparing this year's sales revenue with last year's, and with all prior years included in the financial report. A company's sales trend is the most important factor affecting its profit trend. We dare you to find a business that has had a steady downward sales trend line but a steady upward profit line – you'd be looking for a long time.

Did the Profit Ratios Hold?

Higher sales from one year to the next don't necessarily mean higher profit. You also need to look at whether the business was able to maintain its profit ratio at the higher sales level. Recall that the *profit ratio* is net income divided by sales revenue. If the business earned, say, a 6 per cent profit ratio last year, did it maintain or perhaps improve this ratio on its higher sales revenue this year?

Also compare the company's *gross margin ratios* from year to year. Cost-of-goods-sold expense is reported by companies that sell products. Recall that gross margin equals sales revenue less cost of goods sold. Any significant slippage in a company's gross margin ratio (gross margin divided by sales revenue) is a very serious matter. Suppose that a company gives up two or three points (one point = 1 per cent) of its gross margin ratio. How can it make up for this loss? Decreasing its other operating expenses isn't easy or very practical – unless the business has allowed its operating expenses to become bloated.

In most external financial reports, profit ratios are *not* discussed openly, especially when things have not gone well for the business. You usually have to go digging for these important ratios and use your calculator. Articles in the financial press on the most recent earnings of public corporations focus on gross margin and profit ratios – for good reason. We always keep an eye on profit as a percentage of sales revenue, even though we have to calculate this key ratio for most businesses. We wish that all businesses would provide this ratio.

Were There Any Unusual or Extraordinary Gains or Losses?

Every now and then, a business records an *unusual* or *extraordinary* gain or loss. The first section of the profit and loss account reports sales revenue and the expenses of making the sales and operating the business. Also, interest and income tax expenses are deducted. Be careful: The profit down to this point may *not* be the final bottom line. The profit down to this point is from the business's ongoing, normal operations before any unusual, one-time gains or losses are recorded. The next layer of the profit and loss account reports these extraordinary, non-recurring gains or losses that the business recorded during the period.

These gains or losses are called extraordinary because they do not recur – or at least should not recur, although some companies report these gains and losses on a regular basis. These gains and losses are caused by a *discontinuity* in the business – such as a major organisational restructuring involving a reduction in the workforce and paying substantial severance packages to laid-off employees, selling off major assets and product lines of the business, retiring a huge amount of debt at a big gain or loss, or settling a huge lawsuit against the business. Generally, the gain or loss is reported on one line net of the corporation tax effect for each extraordinary item, and a brief explanation can be found in the footnotes to the financial statements.

Investors have to watch the pattern of these items over the years. An extraordinary gain or loss now and then is a normal part of doing business and is nothing to be alarmed about. However, a business that reports one or two of these gains or losses every year or every other year is suspect. These gains or losses may be evidence of past turmoil and future turbulence. We classify these businesses as high-risk investments – because you don't know what to expect in the future.

In any case, we advise you to consider whether an unusual loss is the cumulative result of inadequate accounting for expenses in previous years. A large legal settlement, for example, may be due to the business refusing to admit that it is selling unsafe products year after year; its liability finally catches up with it.

Did Earnings Per Share Keep Up with Profit?

Chapter 14 explains that a publicly owned business with a simple capital structure – meaning that the business is not required to issue additional shares in the future – reports just one earnings per share (EPS) for the period, which is called *basic* EPS. You calculate basic EPS by using the actual number of shares owned by shareholders. However, many publicly owned businesses have complex capital structures that require them to issue additional shares in the future. These businesses report *two* EPS numbers – basic EPS and *diluted* EPS. The diluted EPS figure is based on a larger number of shares that includes the additional number of shares that will be issued under terms of management share options, convertible debt and other contractual obligations that require the business to issue shares in the future.

In analysing earnings per share, therefore, you may have to put on your bifocals, as it were. For many businesses, you have to look at both basic EPS and diluted EPS. We suppose you could invest only in companies that report only basic EPS, but this investment strategy would eliminate a large number of businesses from your stock investment portfolio. Odds are, your stock investments include companies that report both basic and diluted EPS. The two EPS figures may not be too far apart, but then again, diluted EPS may be substantially less than basic EPS for some businesses.

Suppose you own stock in a public corporation that reports bottom-line net income that is 10 per cent higher than last year's. So far, so good. But you know that the market price of your shares depends on earnings per share (EPS). Ask what happened to basic and diluted EPS. Did both EPS figures go up 10 per cent? Not necessarily – the answer is often 'no', in fact. You have to check.

Public companies whose shares are traded on one of the national stock exchanges (London Stock Exchange, New York Stock Exchange, NASDAQ and so on) are required to report EPS in their profit and loss accounts, so you don't have to do any computations. (Private businesses whose shares are not traded do not have to report EPS.)

EPS increases exactly the same percentage that net income increases only if the total number of shares remains constant. Usually, this is not the case. Many public corporations have a fair amount of activity in their shares during the year. So they include a schedule of changes in shareholders' equity during the year. (Chapter 8 discusses this financial summary of changes in shareholders' equity.) Look at this schedule to find out how many shares were issued during the year. Also, companies may purchase some of their own shares during the year, which is reported in this schedule.

Suppose net income increased, say, 10 per cent, but basic EPS increased only 6.8 per cent because the number of shares issued by the business increased 3 per cent during the year. (You can check the computation if you like.) You should definitely look into why additional shares were issued. And if diluted EPS does not keep pace with the company's earnings increase, you should pinpoint why the number of shares included in the calculation of diluted EPS increased during the period. (Maybe more management share options were awarded during the year.) The number of shares may increase again next year and the year after. Businesses do not comment on why the percentage change in their EPS is not the same as the percentage change in their net income. We wish that companies were required to leave a clear explanation of any difference in the percentage of change in EPS compared with the percentage of change in net income. However, this is just wishful thinking on our part. You have to ferret out this information yourself, which we advise you to do.

An increase in EPS may not be due entirely to an increase in net income, but rather to a *decrease* in the number of shares. Cash-rich companies often buy their shares to reduce the total number of shares that is divided into net income, thereby increasing basic and diluted EPS. You should pay close attention to increases in EPS that result from decreases in the number of shares. The long-run basis of EPS growth is profit growth, although a decrease in the number of shares helps EPS and, hopefully, the market price of the shares.

Did the Profit Increase Generate a Cash Flow Increase?

Increasing profit is all well and good, but you also should ask: Did *cash flow from profit* increase? Cash flow from profit is found in the first section of the cash flow statement, which is one of the three primary financial statements included in a financial report. The cash flow statement begins with an explanation of cash flow from profit.

Accountants use the term *cash flow from operating activities* – which, in our opinion, is not nearly as descriptive as *cash flow from profit*. The term *profit* is avoided like the plague in external financial reports; it's not a politically correct word. So you may think that accountants would use the phrase *cash flow from net income*. But no, the official pronouncement on the cash flow statement mandated the term *cash flow from operating activities*. *Operating activities* refers simply to sales revenue and expenses, which are the profit-making operations of a business. We'll stick with *cash flow from profit* – please don't report us to the accounting authorities.

Almost all expenses are bad for cash flow, except one: depreciation. Depreciation expense is actually good for cash flow. Each year, a business converts part of the cost of its fixed assets back into cash through the cash collections from sales made during the year. Over time, fixed assets are gradually used up, so each year is charged with part of the fixed assets' cost by recording depreciation expense. And each year, a business retrieves cash for part of the cost of its fixed assets. Thus depreciation expense decreases profit but increases cash flow. But net income plus depreciation does not equal cash flow from profit – except in the imaginary scenario in which all the company's other operating assets (mainly debtors and stock) and all its operating liabilities (mainly creditors and accrued expenses payable) don't increase or decrease during the year.

Here's the key question: Should cash flow from profit change about the same amount as net income changed, or is it normal for the change in cash flow to be higher or lower than the change in net income?

As a general rule, sales growth penalises cash flow from profit in the short run. A business has to build up its debtors and stock, and these increases hurt cash flow – although, during growth periods, a business also increases its creditors and accrued expenses payable, which helps cash flow. The asset increases, in most cases, dominate the liability increases, and cash flow from profit suffers.

We strongly advise you to compare cash flow from operating activities (see, we use the officially correct term here) with net income for each of the past two or three years. Is cash flow from profit about the same percentage of net income each year? What does the trend look like? For example, last year, cash flow from profit may have been 90 per cent of net income, but this year it may have dropped to 50 per cent. Don't hit the panic button just yet.

A dip in cash flow from profit in one year actually may be good from the long-run point of view – the business may be laying a good foundation for supporting a higher level of sales. But then again, the slowdown in cash flow from profit could present a short-term cash problem that the business has to deal with.

A company's cash flow from profit may be a trickle instead of a stream. In fact, cash flow from profit could be *negative*; in making a profit, the company could be draining its cash reserves. Cash flow from profit is low, in most cases, because debtors from sales haven't been collected and because the business has made large increases in its inventories. These large increases raise questions about whether all the receivables will be collected and whether all the stock will be sold at regular prices. Only time can tell. But generally speaking, you should be cautious and take the net income number that the business reports with a grain of salt.

Analysing cash flow from *loss* (instead of from profit) is very important. When a company reports a loss for the year – instead of a profit – an immediate question is whether the company's cash reserve will buy it enough time to move out of the loss column into the profit column. When a business is in a loss situation (the early years of a start-up business, for example) and its cash flow from operating activities is negative, focus on the company's cash balance and how long the business can keep going until it turns the corner and becomes profitable. Stock analysts use the term *burn rate* to refer to how much cash outflow the business is using up each period. They compare this measure of how much cash the business is haemorrhaging each period to its present cash balance. The key question is this: Does the business have enough cash on hand to tide it over until it starts to generate positive cash flow from profit, and if not, where will it get more money to burn until it can record a profit?

Are Increases in Assets and Liabilities Consistent with the Business's Growth?

Publicly owned businesses present their financial statements in a three-year comparative format (or sometimes a two-year comparative format). Strictly speaking, you don't have to provide comparative financial statements – although all businesses, private and public, are encouraged to present comparative financial statements. Furthermore, business investors and lenders demand comparative financial statements. Thus, three columns of numbers are reported in profit and loss accounts, balance sheets and cash flow statements – for the current and two preceding years. To keep financial statement illustrations in this book as brief as possible, we present only one year; we do not include two additional columns for the two previous years. Please keep this point in mind.

Presenting financial statements in a three-year comparative format, as may be obvious, helps the reader make year-to-year comparisons. Of course, you have to deal with three times as many numbers in a three-year comparative financial statement compared with a one-year financial statement. And we should point out that the _amounts of changes_ are not presented; you either eyeball the changes or use a calculator to compute the amounts of changes during the year. For example, the ending balances of a business's property, plant and equipment asset account may be reported as follows (in millions of pounds): £4,097, £4,187 and £3,614 for the last three fiscal years. Only these ending balances are presented in the company's comparative balance sheet – the increase or decrease during the year is not presented.

A three-year comparative format enables you to see the general trend of sales revenue and expenses from year to year and the general drift in the amounts of the company's assets, liabilities and owners' equity accounts. You can easily spot any major differences in each line of the cash flow statement across the years. Whether you just cast a glance at adjacent amounts or actually calculate changes, ask yourself whether the increases of a company's assets and liabilities reported in its balance sheet are consistent with the sales growth of the business from year to year.

Unusually large increases in assets that are greatly out of line with the company's sales revenue growth put pressure on cash flow and could cast serious doubts on the company's solvency – which we explain in the next section.

Can the Business Pay Its Liabilities?

A business can build up a good sales volume and have very good profit margins, but if the company can't pay its bills on time, its profit opportunities could go down the drain. *Solvency* refers to the prospects of a business being able to meet its debt and other liability payment obligations on time. Solvency analysis asks whether a business will be able to pay its liabilities, looking for signs of financial distress that could cause serious disruptions in the business's profit-making operations. In short, even if a business has a couple of billion quid in the bank, you should ask: How does its solvency look?

To be solvent doesn't mean that a business must have cash in the bank equal to its total liabilities. Suppose, for example, that a business has £2 million in non-interest-bearing operating liabilities (mainly creditors and accrued expenses payable), £1.5 million in overdraft (due in less than one year) and £3.5 million in long-term debt (due over the next five years). Thus, its total liabilities are £7 million. To be solvent, the business does not need £7 million in its bank account. In fact, this would be foolish.

There's no point in having liabilities if all the money were kept in the bank. The purpose of having liabilities is to put the money to good use in assets other than cash. A business uses the money from its liabilities to invest in *non-cash* assets that it needs to carry on its profit-making operations. For example, a business buys products on credit and holds these goods in stock until it sells them. It borrows money to invest in its fixed assets.

Solvency analysis asks whether assets can be converted quickly back into cash so that liabilities can be paid on time. Will the assets generate enough cash flow to meet the business's liability payment obligations as they come due?

Short-term solvency analysis looks a few months into the future of the business. It focuses on the *current* assets of the business in relation to its *current* liabilities; these two amounts are reported in the balance sheet. A rough measure of a company's short-term liability payment ability is its *current ratio* – current assets (cash, debtors, stock and prepaid expenses) are divided by current liabilities (creditors and accrued expenses payable, plus interest-bearing debt coming due in the short term). A 2-to-1 current ratio usually is a reasonable benchmark for a business – but don't swallow this ratio hook, line and sinker.

A 2-to-1 current ratio is fairly conservative. Many businesses can get by on a lower current ratio without alarming their sources of short-term credit.

Business investors and creditors also look at a second solvency ratio called the *quick ratio*. This ratio includes only a company's *quick assets* – cash, debtors and short-term marketable investments in other company shares (if the company has any). Quick assets are divided by current liabilities to determine the quick ratio. It's also called the *acid-test ratio* because it's a very demanding test to put on a business. More informally, it's called the *pounce ratio*, as if all the short-term creditors pounced on the business and demanded payment in short order.

Many people consider a safe acid-test ratio to be 1-to-1 – £1 of quick assets for every £1 of current liabilities. However, be careful with this benchmark. It may not be appropriate for businesses that rely on heavy short-term debt to finance their inventories. For these companies, it's better to compare their quick assets with their quick liabilities and exclude their short-term notes payable that don't have to be paid until stock is sold.

The current and acid-test ratios are relevant. But the solvency of a business depends mainly on the ability of its managers to convince creditors to continue extending credit to the business and renewing its loans. The credibility of management is the main factor, not ratios. Creditors understand that a business can get into a temporary bind and fall behind on paying its liabilities. As a general rule, creditors are slow to pull the plug on a business. Shutting off new credit may be the worst thing lenders and other creditors could do. This may put the business in a tailspin, and its creditors may end up collecting very little. Usually, it's not in their interest to force a business into bankruptcy, except as a last resort.

Also check out the gearing. If borrowings are growing faster than retained profits or new shareholder investments, then gearing is going up, as are the financing risks. Have a look at Chapter 14 to see what gearing/leverage is all about.

Are There Any Unusual Assets and Liabilities?

Most businesses report a miscellaneous, catch-all account called *other assets*. Who knows what might be included in here? If the balance in this account is not very large, trust that the auditor did not let the business bury anything important in this account.

Marketable securities is the asset account used for investments in shares and bonds (as well as other kinds of investments). Companies that have more cash than they need for their immediate operating purposes put the excess funds to work earning investment income rather than let the money lie dormant in a bank checking account. The accounting rules for marketable securities are fairly tight; you needn't be concerned about this asset.

If you encounter an asset or liability you're not familiar with, look in the footnotes to the financial statements, which present a brief explanation of what the accounts are and whether they affect profit accounting. (We know, you don't like reading footnotes; neither do we.) For example, many businesses have large liabilities for unfunded pension plan obligations for work done in the past by their employees. The liability reveals that the business has recorded this component of labour expense in determining its profit over the years. The liability could be a heavy demand on the future cash flow of the business.

How Well Are Assets Being Utilised?

The overall test of how well assets are being used is the *asset turnover ratio*, which equals annual sales revenue divided by total assets. (You have to calculate this ratio; most businesses do not report this ratio in their financial statements, although a minority do.) This ratio tests the efficiency of using assets to make sales. Some businesses have low asset turnover ratios, less than 2-to-1. Some have very high ratios, such as 5-to-1. Each industry and retail sector in the economy has a standard asset turnover ratio, but these differ quite a bit from industry to industry and from sector to sector. There is no standard asset turnover ratio for all businesses. A supermarket chain couldn't make it if its annual sales revenues were only twice its assets. Capital-intensive heavy manufacturers, on the other hand, would be delighted with a 2-to-1 asset turnover ratio.

Financial report readers are wise to track a company's asset turnover ratio from year to year. If this ratio slips, the company is getting less sales revenue for each pound of assets. If the company's profit ratio remains the same, it gets less profit out of each pound of assets, which is not good news for equity investors in the business.

What Is the Return on Capital Investment?

We need a practical example to illustrate the *return on capital investment* questions you should ask. Suppose a business has £12 million total assets, and its creditors and accrued liabilities for unpaid expenses are £2 million. Thus, its *net operating assets* – total assets less its non-interest-bearing operating liabilities – are £10 million. We won't tell you the company's sales revenue for the year just ended. But we will tell you that its earnings before interest and tax (EBIT) were £1.32 million for the year. The basic question you should ask is this: How is the business doing in relation to the total capital used to make this profit?

EBIT is divided by assets (net operating assets, in our way of thinking) to get the *return on assets (ROA)* ratio. In this case, the company earned 13.2 per cent ROA for the year just ended:

£1,320,000 EBIT ÷ £10,000,000 net operating assets = 13.2% ROA

Was this rate high enough to cover the interest rate on its debt? Sure; it's doubtful that the business had to pay a 13.2 per cent interest rate. Now for the bottom-line question: How did the business do for its *owners*, who have a lot of capital invested in the business?

The business uses £4 million total debt, on which it pays 8 per cent annual interest. Thus, its total owners' equity is £6 million. The business is organised as a company that pays, for example, 30 per cent tax on its taxable income.

Given the company's capitalisation structure, its EBIT (or profit from operations) for the year just ended was divided three ways:

- **£320,000 interest on debt:** £4,000,000 debt × 8 per cent interest rate = £320,000

- **£300,000 income tax:** £1,320,000 EBIT – £320,000 interest = £1,000,000 taxable income; £1,000,000 taxable income × 30 per cent tax rate = £300,000 income tax

- **£700,000 net income:** £1,320,000 operating earnings – £320,000 interest – £300,000 income tax = £700,000 net income

Net income is divided by owners' equity to calculate the *return on equity (ROE)* ratio, which in this example is

£700,000 net income ÷ £6,000,000 owners' equity = 12% ROE

Some businesses report their ROE ratios, but many don't – generally accepted accounting principles don't require the disclosure of ROE. In any case, as an investor in the business, would you be satisfied with a 12 per cent return on your money?

You made only 4 per cent more than the debt holders, which may not seem much of a premium for the additional risks you take on as an equity investor in the business. But you may predict that the business has a bright future and over time your investment will increase two or three times in value. In any case, ROE is a good point of reference – although this one ratio doesn't give you a final answer regarding what to do with your capital. Reading Tony Levene's *Investing For Dummies* (Wiley) can help you make a wise decision.

What Does the Auditor Say?

A business pays a lot of money for its audit, and you should read what the auditor has to say. We'll be frank: The wording of the auditor's report is tough going. Talk about jargon! In any case, focus on the sentence that states the auditor's *opinion* on the financial statements. In rough terms, the auditor gives the financial statements a green light, a yellow light or a red light – green meaning that everything's okay (as far as can be ascertained by the process of the audit), yellow meaning that you should be aware of something that prevents the auditor from giving a green light and red meaning that the financial statements are seriously deficient.

Look for the key words *true and fair*. These code words mean that the audit firm has no serious disagreement with how the business prepared its financial statements. This unqualified opinion is called a *clean opinion*. Only in the most desperate situations does the auditor give an adverse opinion, which in essence says that the financial statements are misleading. If the audit firm can't give a clean opinion on the financial statements or thinks that something about the financial statements should be emphasised, a fourth paragraph is added to the standard three-paragraph format of the audit report (or additional language is added to the one-paragraph audit report used by the big accountancy firm PricewaterhouseCoopers). The additional language is the tip-off; look for a fourth paragraph (or additional language), and be sure to read it. The auditor may express doubt about the business being able to continue as a going concern. The solvency ratios discussed earlier should have tipped you off. When the auditor mentions it, things are pretty serious.

Chapter 19

Ten Ways to Get a Better Handle on the Financial Future

Managers are accustomed to using accounting to unravel the past. Accounts are usually a record of the effect of last year's, month's or week's decisions. Did your strategies for collecting money from customers more quickly or reducing stock levels actually happen, and if so, did they deliver better profits? (We cover this area in Chapter 6.)

But the past, as the saying goes, is another country. The future is where reputations are made and promotion achieved. Managers get maximum value from their grasp of accounting and finance from being able to blend that knowledge with some related skills to get a better handle on the ground ahead.

Sales Forecasts versus Sales Objectives

Sales drive much of a business's activities; they determine cash flow, stock levels, production capacity and ultimately how profitable or otherwise a business is. So, unsurprisingly, much effort goes into attempting to predict future sales. A sales forecast isn't the same as a sales objective. An *objective* is what you want to achieve and will shape a strategy to do so. A *forecast* is the most likely future outcome given what has happened in the past and the momentum that provides for the business.

A forecast is made up of three components and to get an accurate forecast you need to use the historic data to better understand the impact of each on the end result:

- ✔ **Underlying trend:** This is the general direction – up, flat or down – over the longer term, showing the rate of change.

- ✔ **Cyclical factors:** These are the short-term influences that regularly super-impose themselves on the trend. For example, in the summer months you expect sales of swimwear, ice cream and suntan lotion, to be higher than in the winter. Ski equipment would follow a reverse pattern.

- ✔ **Random movements:** These are irregular, random spikes up or down caused by unusual and unexplained factors.

Dealing with Demand Curves

The price you charge for your goods and services is perhaps the single most important number in the financial firmament. Predictions about what price to set influences everything from the amount of materials you have to buy to achieve a given level of profit (the higher the price, the less you have to purchase), to the amount of money you have to invest in fixed assets (a low price may involve selling a lot more to make a given level of profit, requiring a higher level of productive resources).

The main economic concept that underpins almost the whole subject of pricing is that of the *price elasticity of demand.* The concept itself is simple enough. The higher the price of an item or service, the less of it you're likely to sell. Obviously it's not quite that simple in practice; you also need to consider the number of buyers, their expectations, preference and ability to pay, and the availability of substitute products. Figure 19-1 shows a theoretical demand curve.

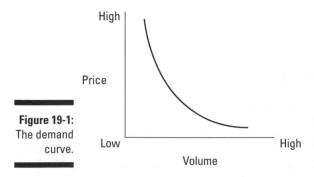

Figure 19-1:
The demand curve.

Figure 19-1 shows how the volume of sales of a particular good or service alters with changes in price. You calculate the elasticity of demand by dividing the percentage change in demand by the percentage change in price. If a price is reduced by 50% (say, from £100 to £50) and the quantity demanded increased by 100% (from 1,000 to 2,000), the elasticity of demand co-efficient is 2 (100/50). Here the quantity demanded changes by a bigger percentage than the price change, so demand is considered to be *elastic*. Were the demand in this case to rise by only 25%, then the elasticity of demand coefficient would be 0.5 (25/100). Here the demand is *inelastic*, as the percentage demand change is smaller than that of the price change.

Having a feel for elasticity is important in developing a business's financial strategy, but there's no perfect scientific way to work out what the demand coefficient is; it has to be assessed by 'feel'. Unfortunately the price elasticity changes at different price levels. For example, reducing the price of vodka from £10 to £5 might double sales, but halving it again may not have such a dramatic effect. In fact it could encourage a certain group of buyers, those giving it as a gift for example, to feel that giving something so cheap is rather insulting.

Maths Matters

The simplest way to predict the future is to assume that it will be more or less the same as the recent past. Despite Henry Ford's attributed quote that history is bunk, very often the past is a very good guide to what's likely to happen in the fairly immediate future – far enough ahead for budgeting purposes, if not for shaping long-term strategy.

The three most common mathematical techniques that use this approach are as follows:

- ✔ **Moving average** takes a series of data from the past, say, the last six months' sales, adds them up, divides by the number of months and uses that figure as the most likely forecast of what will happen in month seven. This method works well in a static, mature market place where change happens slowly, if at all.

- ✔ **Weighted moving average** gives more recent data more significance than earlier data because it gives a better representation of current business conditions. So before adding up the series of data, each figure is weighted by multiplying it by an increasingly higher factor as you get closer to the most recent data.

- ✔ **Exponential smoothing** is a more sophisticated averaging technique that gives exponentially decreasing weights as the data gets older. More recent data is given relatively more weight in making the forecasting. You can use double and triple exponential smoothing to help with different types of trend.

Fortunately all you need to know is that these and other statistical forecasting methods exist. The choice of which is the best forecasting technique to use is usually down to trial and error.

Various software programs calculate the best-fitting forecast by applying each of these techniques to the historic data you enter. See what actually happens and use the forecast technique that's closest to the actual outcome. Professor Hossein Arsham of the University of Baltimore provides a useful tool that enables you to enter data and see how different forecasting techniques perform. (`http://home.ubalt.edu/ntsbarsh/Business-stat/other applets/ForecaSmo.htm#rmenu`)

Duke University's Fuqua School of Business provides a helpful link to all their lecture material on forecasting (`www.duke.edu/~rnau/411home.htm`).

Averaging Out Averages

A common way forecasts are predicted is around a single figure that purports to be representative of a whole mass of often conflicting data. This single figure is usually known as an *average*, with the process of averaging seen as a way of smoothing over any conflicts. When some customers pay one price and others quite a different one, an average is used as the basis for forecasting. That would be all fine and dandy were it not for the fact that you have three different ways of measuring an average (the mean, median and mode). In fact, averages are the most frequently confused and misrepresented set of numbers in the whole field of forecasting.

To analyse anything for forecasting purposes you first need a data set such as that in Table 19-1.

Table 19-1	The Selling Prices of Company's Products to Different Customers
Customer	*Selling Price (£s)*
1	30
2	40
3	10
4	15
5	10

You then have three ways of working with the numbers:

✔ **The mean (or average):** This is the most common tendency measure and is used as a rough and ready check for many types of data. In Table 19-1 you add up the prices (£105) and divide by the number of customers (5), to arrive at a *mean*, or average selling price of £21.

✔ **The median:** The *median* is the value occurring at the centre of a data set. Recasting the figures in Table 19-1 in order puts Customer 4's purchase price of £15 in central position, with two higher and two lower prices. The median comes into its own in situations where the outlying values in a data set are extreme, as they are in the example, where, in fact, most of the customers buy for well below £21. In this case the median is a better measure of the average.

Always use the median when the distribution is skewed. You can use either the mean or the median when the population is symmetrical because they'll give very similar results.

✔ **The mode:** The mode is the observation in a data set that appears the most; in this example it is £10. So if you were surveying a sample of customers you'd expect more of them to say they were paying £10 for the products, even though you know the average price is £21.

Looking for Causes

Often when looking at historic data (the basis of all projections), a relationship between certain factors becomes apparent. Look at Figure 19-2, which is a chart showing the monthly sales of barbeques and the average temperature in the preceding month for the past eight months.

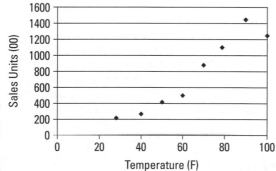

Figure 19-2:
Scatter
diagram.

You can clearly see a relationship between temperature (the *independent variable*) and sales (the *dependant variable*). By drawing the line that most accurately represents the slope, called the *line of best fit* (see Figure 19-3), you have a useful tool for estimating what sales might be next month, given the temperature that occurred this month.

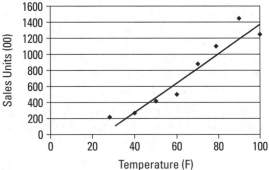

Figure 19-3: Scatter diagram with the line of best fit.

This example is a simple one. Real life data is usually more complicated, so it's harder to see a relationship between the independent and dependant variables with real life data than it is here. Fortunately, an algebraic formula known as *linear regression* can calculate the line of best fit for you.

A couple of calculations can test if a causal relationship is *strong* (even if strongly negative, the test is still useful for predictive purposes) and *significant* – the statisticians way of telling you if you can rely on the data as an aid to predicting the future. The tests are known as *R-Squared* and the *Students t test*, and all you need to know is that they exist and that you can probably find the software to calculate them on your computer.

Try Web-Enabled Scientific Services & Applications' (`www.wessa.net/slr.wasp`) free software, which covers almost every type of statistic calculation. For help in understanding statistical techniques, read Gerard E. Dallal's book *The Little Handbook of Statistical Practice* available free online (`www.tufts.edu/~gdallal/LHSP.HTM`). At Princeton University's website you can find a tutorial and lecture notes on the subject as taught to their Master of International Business students (`http://dss.princeton.edu/online_help/analysis/interpreting_regression.htm`).

Straddling Cycles

Economies tend to follow a cyclical pattern that moves from *boom*, when demand is strong, to *slump*, economists' shorthand for a downturn. Politicians believe they have become better managers of demand and proclaim the death of the cycle, but the 'this time it's different' school of thinking has been proved wrong time and time again. The cycle itself is caused by the collective behaviour of billions of people – the unfathomable 'animal spirits' of businesses and households. Maynard Keynes, the British economist whose strategy of encouraging governments to step up investment in bad times did much to alleviate the slump in the 1930s, explained animal spirits in the following way: 'Most, probably, of our decisions to do something positive, the full consequences of which will be drawn out over many days to come, can only be taken as the result of animal spirits – a spontaneous urge to action rather than inaction, and not as the outcome of a weighted average of quantitative benefits multiplied by quantitative probabilities'.

Added to the urge to act is the equally inevitable herd-like behaviour that leads to excessive optimism and pessimism. From the tulip mania in 17th-century Holland and the South Sea Bubble (1711–1720), to the Internet Bubble in 1999 and the collapse in US real estate in 2008, the story behind each bubble has been uncomfortably familiar. Strong market demand for some commodity (such as gold, copper or oil), currency, property or type of share leads the general public to believe the trend cannot end. Over-optimism leads the public at large to overextend itself in acquiring the object of the mania, while lenders fall over each other to fan the flames. Finally, either the money runs out or groups of investors become cautious. Fear turns to panic selling, so creating a vicious downward spiral that can take years to recover from.

Economics is a science of the indistinctly knowable rather than the exactly predictable. Although all cycles are difficult to understand or predict with much accuracy, they do have discernable patterns and some distinctive characteristics. Give some consideration to where you think you are in the cycle and build that into your projections.

Figure 19-4 shows an elegant curve, which depicts the theoretical textbook cycle.

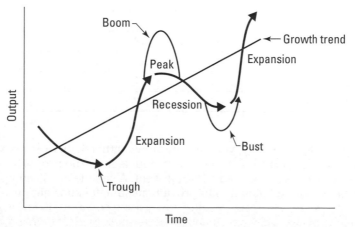

Figure 19-4:
The
textbook
economic
cycle.

The National Bureau of Economic Research provides a history of all US business cycle expansions and contractions since 1854 (www.nber.org/cycles.htm). The Foundation for the Study of Cycles, an international research and educational institution, provides a detailed explanation of different cycles (http://foundationforthestudyofcycles.org). The Centre for Growth and Business Cycle Research based in Manchester University's School of Social Sciences provides details of current research, recent publications and downloadable discussion papers on all aspects of business cycles (www.socialsciences.manchester.ac.uk/cgbcr).

Surveying Future Trends

Surveys are the most common research method used in organisations to get a handle on almost every aspect of future demand. If you ask your customers how much they plan to spend on their next holiday, car, haircut or laptop, you have a figure to base your projections on. Leaving aside the practical aspects of preparing and executing surveys (read *Statistics For Dummies* by Deborah J. Rumsey (Wiley) to find out about that), to be sure of the degree to which surveys are likely to be meaningful, you need a modest grasp of maths.

The size of the survey you undertake is vital to its accuracy. You frequently hear of political opinion polls taken on samples of 1,500–2,000 voters. This is because the accuracy of your survey clearly increases with the size of sample, as Table 19-2 shows:

Table 19-2	Survey Accuracy
Size of Sample	*95% of Surveys are Right within this many Percentage Points*
250	6.2
500	4.4
750	3.6
1,000	3.1
2,000	2.2
6,000	1.2

If on a sample size of 500, your survey showed that 40 per cent of your customers plan to spend £1,000 on your products, the true proportion would probably lie between 35.6 and 44.4 per cent. A sample of 250 completed replies is about the minimum to provide meaningful information.

Andrews University in the United States has a free set of lecture notes explaining the subject of sample size comprehensively (`www.andrews.edu/~calkins/ math/webtexts/prod12.htm`). At `www.auditnet.org/docs/statsamp. xls` you can find some great spreadsheets that do the boring maths of calculating sample size and accuracy for you.

Talking To The Troops

Financial forecasts are usually in the domain of top management and senior staff such as CFOs. However all the decisions that have a direct bearing on these forecasts rely on information provided by people on the front line. They know where the bodies are, so it makes good sense to talk to them early in the planning process. Also, you need their commitment because chances are they'll have a big influence on whether your projections bear fruit.

This process is known as *bottom up* projection. It involves, for example, building up a sales forecast customer by customer for every product or service they buy or may buy. Bottom up projection also requires an estimate of how many customers will be lost and won. Clearly only someone with detailed knowledge can prepare this. You can check this against your top down projection, based on, say, using a sales forecasting technique such as those covered earlier in this chapter. If you find a wide divergence between your theoretical projections and those made by the front line troops, discuss them and come up with a consensus that everyone can buy into.

Setting Out Assumptions

All future projections are based on assumptions – the stage of the economic cycle, government strategies on tax and expenditure, market size and growth rates, the level and type of competition . . . oh yes, and the weather comes into future projections too. The people running Heathrow hadn't expected the last week of 2010 to deliver so much snow it shut the airport just as peak Christmas demand was about to get underway.

Even the environment gets a look in here. Eyjafjallajökull, the Icelandic volcano that erupted in April 2010, caused air traffic around Europe and across the Atlantic to grind to a halt for six days. Airlines lost up to half their annual profits, business passengers were stranded for days and supply chains shortened by just-in-time purchasing strategies dried up. Now, arguably, business could do little directly or immediately to mitigate these problems, but the experience served to demonstrate the interconnection of seemingly remote environmental factors and made more obvious the reasons businesses have to take issues such as climate change seriously. Even if you are in no danger – unlike Lohachara, the first inhabited island to be wiped off the face of the Earth by global warming in 2006 – you'll eventually be affected by environmental issues. So build them into your thinking when making future financial projections, if only to state, for example, 'these plans are based on the assumption that the weather will be no more extreme than in the past fifty years'.

Pay particular attention to any outside factors that can have a significant effect on sales revenue – demand or price pressures; cost or availability of materials and key services; labour costs, rents, taxes and exchange rates.

Making Regular Revisions

Luca Paccioli, who wrote the world's first accounting book over 500 years ago, claimed that 'frequent accounting makes for long friendships'. No doubt he was hoping to sell more copies of his book (what author isn't?), but he could have said much the same about financial projections. The business world is dynamic, recently to an alarming degree. Frequently revisit your projections to see if they still hold good. Unforeseen and unforeseeable events such as the loss of a major customer or the entry of a new player into the market can throw plans off course. Sure, you may be able to get back on track, but that may mean making more changes in the short term to get to your long-term destination.

Some managers think revising projections to be a sign of weakness. Maynard Keynes, one of the greatest economic gurus of all time and a man who made a fortune out of the stock market over the period of the great depression, summed up the subject neatly: 'When the facts change, I change my mind.'

Revisions are one thing; constant sail trimming is something quite different. The army maxim – order, counter order, disorder – is one that holds good here. Rolling quarterly projections work best, giving the remaining planning period the once-over while adding a new quarter. That way you always have at least one full year's horizon to your projection.

Part VI
Appendixes

'I hate the end of the financial year.'

In this part...

We're not finished yet! We couldn't say goodbye without adding in a couple of helpful appendixes filled to the brim with extra information.

The world of accounting is a jargon-filled place, so we've included a glossary in Appendix A that enables you to understand the terms you're most likely to come across and to be clued-up when talking the talk.

Appendix B is another handy list, giving you the lowdown on different accounting software packages so that you can get deep down into the mine of invaluable information lying below the surface of the figures. Also included are some ideas on getting someone else to do that graft for you.

Appendix A

Glossary: Slashing through the Accounting Jargon Jungle

*Y*ou can keep up with the latest financial jargon on the Free Dictionary Web site at `http://financial-dictionary.thefreedictionary.com`.

accounting: The methods and procedures for analysing, recording, accumulating and storing financial information about the activities of an entity, and preparing summary reports of these activities internally for managers and externally for those entitled to receive financial reports about the entity.

accounting equation: Assets = Liabilities + Owners' Equity. This basic equation is the foundation for *double-entry accounting* and reflects the balance between a business's assets and the sources of capital that is invested in its assets.

Accounting Standards Board (ASB): The highest authoritative private-sector standard-setting body of the accounting profession in the United Kingdom. The ASB issues pronouncements that establish *generally accepted accounting principles (GAAP)*.

accrual-basis accounting: From the profit accounting point of view this refers to recording revenue at the time sales are made (rather than when cash is actually received from customers), and recording expenses to match with sales revenue or in the period benefited (rather than when the costs are paid). From the financial condition point of view this refers to recording several assets, such as receivables from customers, cost of stock (products not yet sold) and cost of long-term assets (fixed assets); and recording several liabilities in addition to debt (borrowed money), such as payables to vendors and payables for unpaid expenses.

accrued expenses payable: One main type of short-term liabilities of a business that arise from the gradual build-up of unpaid expenses, such as holiday pay earned by employees or profit-based bonus plans that aren't paid until the following period. *Caution:* The specific titles of this liability vary from business to business; you may see accrued liabilities, accrued expenses or some other similar account name.

accumulated depreciation: The total cumulative amount of depreciation expense that has been recorded since the fixed assets being depreciated were acquired. In the *balance sheet* the amount in this account is deducted from the cost of fixed assets. (Thus it is sometimes referred to as a contra account.) The purpose is to report how much of the total cost has been depreciated over the years. The balance of cost less accumulated depreciation is included in the total assets of a business – which is known as the *book value* of the assets.

acid-test ratio: See *quick ratio.*

activity based costing (ABC): The ABC approach classifies overhead costs into separate categories of support activities that are needed in manufacturing operations and in other areas of the business organisation (such as a sales territory). Cost drivers are developed for each support activity to measure the extent of usage of that support. The annual cost of each support activity is allocated to manufacturing and other areas according to how many cost driver units are used.

Alternative Investment Market (AIM): A stock market in London for shares in small and relatively unproven businesses.

annualised rate of interest and rate of return: The result of taking a rate of interest or a rate of return on investment for a period shorter than one year and converting it into an equivalent rate for the entire year. Suppose you earn 2 per cent interest rate every quarter (three months). Your annualised rate of interest (as if you received interest once a year at the end of the year) equals 8.24 per cent rounded – which is not simply 4 times the 2 per cent quarterly rate. (The annualised rate equals [1+0.02] raised to the fourth power minus one.) See also *compound interest.*

asset turnover ratio: A measure of how effectively assets were used during a period, usually one year. To find the asset turnover ratio, divide annual sales revenue either by total assets or by *net operating assets*, which equals total assets less short-term, non-interest-bearing liabilities.

Association of Chartered Accountants (ACA): The ACA designation is a widely recognised and respected badge of a professional accountant. A person must meet educational and experience requirements and pass a national uniform exam to qualify.

audit report: A one-page statement issued by an accountancy firm, after having examined a company's accounting system, records, and supporting evidence, that gives an opinion whether the company's financial statements and footnotes are presented fairly in conformity with *generally accepted accounting principles*. Annual audits are required by limited companies of publicly owned corporations; many privately held businesses also have audits. The auditor must be independent of the business. An auditor expresses doubts about the financial viability of a business if it is in dire financial straits.

bad debts: The particular expense that arises from a customer's failure to pay the amount owed to the business from a prior credit sale. When the credit sale was recorded, the accounts receivable asset account was increased. When it becomes clear that this debt owed to the business will not be collected, the asset account is written-off and the amount is charged to bad debts expense.

balance sheet: The *financial statement* that summarises the assets, liabilities and owners' equity of a business at an instant moment in time. Prepared at the end of every profit period, and whenever needed, the balance sheet shows a company's overall financial situation and condition.

basic earnings per share (EPS): Equals *net income* for the year (the most recent twelve months reported, called the trailing twelve months) divided by the number of shares of a business corporation that have been issued and are owned by shareholders (called the number of shares outstanding). See also *diluted earnings per share*. Basic EPS and diluted EPS are the most important factors that drive the market value of shares issued by publicly owned corporations.

book value of assets: Refers to the recorded amounts of assets which are reported in a *balance sheet* – usually the term is used to emphasise that the amounts recorded in the accounts of the business may be less than the current replacement costs of some assets, such as fixed assets bought many years ago that have been depreciated.

book value of owners' equity, in total or per share: Refers to the *balance sheet* value of owners' equity, either in total or on a per-share basis for corporations. Book value of owners' equity is not necessarily the price someone would pay for the business as a whole or per share, but it is a useful reference, or starting point for setting market price.

break-even point (sales volume): The annual sales volume (total number of units sold) at which total *contribution margin* equals total annual *fixed expenses* – that is, the exact sales volume at which the business covers its fixed expenses and makes a zero profit, or a zero loss depending on your point of view. Sales in excess of the break-even point contribute to profit, instead of having to go towards covering fixed expenses. The break-even sales volume is a useful point of reference for analysing profit performance and the effects of *operating leverage*.

budgeting: The process of developing and adopting a profit and financial plan with definite goals for the coming period – including forecasting expenses and revenues, assets, liabilities and cash flows based on the plan.

burden rate: An amount per unit that is added to the direct costs of manufacturing a product according to some method for the allocation of the total indirect fixed manufacturing costs for the period, which can be a certain percentage of direct costs or a fixed pound amount per unit of the common denominator on which the indirect costs are allocated across different products. Thus, the indirect costs are a 'burden' on the direct costs.

business angel: Private individuals who invest in entrepreneurial businesses with a view to making a substantial capital gain and perhaps helping with the management.

capital expenditures: Outlays for *fixed assets* – to overhaul or replace old fixed assets, or to expand and modernise the long-lived operating resources of a business. Fixed assets have useful lives from 3 to 39 (or more) years, depending on the nature of the asset and how it's used in the operations of the business. The term 'capital' here implies that substantial amounts of money are being invested that are major commitments for many years.

capital stock: The certificates of ownership issued by a corporation for capital invested in the business by owners; total capital is divided into units, called shares of capital stock. Holders of shares participate in cash dividends paid from profit, vote in board member elections, and receive asset liquidation proceeds; and have several other rights as well. A business corporation must issue at least one class of share called ordinary shares, which in the US are known as *common stock*. It may also issue other classes of stock, such as *preference shares*.

cash flow(s): In the most general and broadest sense this term refers to any kind of cash inflows and outflows during a period – monies coming in, and monies paid out.

cash flow from operating activities: See *cash flow from profit*.

cash flow from profit: In the *cash flow statement* this is called *cash flow from operating activities*, which equals net income for the period, adjusted for changes in certain assets and liabilities, and for depreciation expense. Some people call this *free cash flow* to emphasise that this source of cash is free from the need to borrow money, issue capital stock shares or sell assets. *Be careful:* The term free cash flow is also used to denote cash flow from profit minus capital expenditures. (Some writers deduct cash dividends also; usage has not completely settled down.)

cash flow statement: This financial statement of a business summarises its cash inflows and outflows during a period according to a threefold classification: *cash flow from profit* (or, *operating activities*), *investing activities* and *financing activities*.

chart of accounts: The official, designated set of accounts used by a business that constitute its *general ledger*, in which the transactions of the business are recorded.

Companies Acts: A series of UK laws governing the establishment and conduct of incorporated businesses, consolidated into the Companies Act 2006.

compound interest: 'Compound' is a code word for reinvested. Interest income *compounds* when you don't remove it from your investment, but instead leave it in and add it to your investment or savings account. Thus, you have a bigger balance on which to earn interest the following period.

comprehensive income: Includes net income which is reported in the *profit and loss account* plus certain technical gains and losses in assets and liabilities that are recorded but don't necessarily have to be included in the profit and loss account. Most companies report their comprehensive gains and losses (if they have any) in their *statement of changes in owners' equity*.

conservatism: If there is choice as to the amount of certain figures, when preparing accounts the lower figure for assets and the higher for liabilities should be used.

contribution margin: Equals sales revenue minus cost of goods sold expense and minus all *variable expenses* (in other words, contribution margin is profit before *fixed expenses* are deducted). On a per unit basis, contribution margin equals sales price less *product cost* per unit and less variable expenses per unit.

cooking the books: Refers to any one of several fraudulent (deliberately deceitful with intent to mislead) accounting schemes used to overstate profit and to make the financial condition look better than it really is. Cooking the books is different from *profit smoothing* and *window dressing*, which are tolerated – though not encouraged – in financial statement accounting. Cooking the books for income tax is just the reverse: It means overstating, or exaggerating, deductible expenses or understating revenue to minimize taxable income.

corporate venturing: Refers to large companies taking a share of small entrepreneurial ventures in order to have access to a new technology. If this approach works, they often buy out the whole business.

corporation tax: Tax paid by UK companies (with some exceptions) on 'chargeable profits'. Rates are fixed each year by the government. Reduced rates apply for small businesses.

cost-benefit analysis: Analysis of the costs and benefits of a particular investment or action, conducted to establish if that action is worthwhile from a purely accounting perspective.

cost of capital: For a business, this refers to joint total of the interest paid on debt capital and the minimum net income it should earn to justify the owner's equity capital. Interest is a contractually set amount of interest; no legally set amount of net income is promised to owners. A business's *return on assets (ROA)* rate should ideally be higher than its weighted-average cost of capital rate (based on the mix of its debt and equity capital sources).

creative accounting: The use of dubious accounting techniques and deceptions designed to make profit performance or financial condition appear better than things really are. See *profit smoothing* and *cooking the books*.

creditors: One main type of the short-term liabilities of a business, representing the amounts owed to vendors or suppliers for the purchase of various products, supplies, parts and services that were bought on credit; these do not bear interest (unless the business takes too long to pay). In the US, *creditors* or *trade creditors* are usually called accounts payable.

credit crunch: A time when cash is in short supply; businesses find it difficult to raise loans and when they can, interest rates are relatively high.

current assets: Includes cash plus *debtors, stock* and *prepaid expenses* (and marketable securities if the business owns any). These assets are cash or assets that will be converted into cash during one *operating cycle*. Total current assets are divided by total current liabilities to calculate the *current ratio*, which is a test of short-term solvency.

current liabilities: Short-term liabilities, principally *creditors, accrued expenses payable*, corporation tax payable, overdrafts and the portion of long-term debt that falls due within the coming year. This group includes both non-interest bearing and interest-bearing liabilities that must be paid in the short-term, usually defined to be one year. Total current liabilities are divided into total *current assets* to calculate the *current ratio*.

current ratio: A test of a business's short-term solvency (debt-paying capability). Find the current ratio by dividing the total of its *current assets* by its total *current liabilities*.

debits and credits: These two terms are accounting jargon for decreases and increases that are recorded in assets, liabilities, owners' equity, revenue and expenses. When recording a transaction, the total of the debits must equal the total of the credits.

debtors: The short-term assets representing the amounts owed to the business from sales of products and services on credit to its customers. In the US these are known as *accounts receivable*.

deferred income: Income received in advance of being earned and recognised.

depreciation expense: Allocating (or spreading out) a fixed asset's cost over the estimated useful life of the resource. Each year of the asset's life is charged with part of its total cost as the asset gradually wears out and loses its economic value to the business. Either *reducing balance* or *straight-line depreciation* is used; both are acceptable under *generally accepted accounting principles (GAAP)*.

diluted earnings per share (EPS): Diluted earnings per share equals net income divided by the sum of the actual number of shares outstanding plus any additional shares that will be issued under terms of share options awarded to managers and for the conversion of senior securities into common stock (if the company has issued convertible debt or *preference* shares). In short, this measure of profit per share is based on a larger number of shares than basic EPS (earnings per share). The larger number causes a dilution in the amount of net income per share. Although hard to prove for certain, market prices of shares are driven by diluted EPS more than basic EPS.

dividend yield: Measures the cash income component of return on investment in shares of a corporation. The dividend yield equals the most recent 12 months of cash dividends paid on a share, divided by the share's current market price. If a share is selling for £100 and over the last 12 months has paid £3 cash dividends, its dividend yield equals 3 per cent.

double-entry accounting: Symbolised in the *accounting equation,* which covers both the assets of a business as well as the sources of money for the assets (which are also claims on the assets).

due diligence: a process of thoroughly checking every aspect of a business's position, including its financial state of affairs, usually as a prelude to a sale or to raising additional funds.

earnings before interest and taxes (EBIT): Sales revenue less cost of goods sold and all operating expenses – but before deducting interest on debt and tax expenses. This measure of profit also is called *operating earnings, operating profit* or something similar; terminology is not uniform.

earnings management: See *profit smoothing.*

earnings per share: See *basic earnings per share* and *diluted earnings per share.*

earn-out: When a business is sold, buyers often make part of their offer conditional on the future profits being as forecasted. This, in effect, makes the seller earn out that portion.

effective interest rate: The rate actually applied to your loan or savings account balance to determine the amount of interest for that period. See also *annualised rate of interest and rate of return.*

equity capital: See *owners' equity.*

external financial statements: The financial statements included in financial reports that are distributed outside a business to its shareholders and debt-holders.

extraordinary gains and losses: These are unusual, non-recurring gains and losses that happen infrequently and that are aside from the normal, ordinary sales and expenses of a business.

Financial Accounting Standards Board (FASB): The highest authoritative private-sector standard-setting body of the accounting profession in the US.

financial leverage: The term is used generally to mean using debt capital on top of equity capital in any type of investment. For a business it means using debt in addition to equity capital to provide the total capital needed to invest in its *net operating assets.* The strategy is to earn a rate of *return on assets (ROA)* higher than the interest rate on borrowed money. A favourable spread between the two rates generates a financial leverage gain to the benefit of *owners' equity.*

financial reports: The periodic financially oriented communications from a business (and other types of organisations) to those entitled to know about the financial performance and position of the entity. Financial reports of businesses include three primary financial statements (*balance sheet*, *profit and loss account* and *statement of cash flows*), as well as footnotes and other information relevant to the owners of the business.

financial statement: The generic term for *balance sheet, cash flow statement and profit and loss account*, all three of which present summary financial information about a business.

financing activities: One of three types of *cash flows* reported in the *cash flow statement*. These are the dealings between a business and its sources of debt and equity capital – such as borrowings and repayments of debt, issuing new shares and buying some of its own shares, and paying dividends.

first-in, first-out (FIFO): One of two widely-used accounting methods by which costs of products when they are sold are charged to cost of goods sold expense. According to the FIFO method, costs of goods are charged in chronological order, so the most recent acquisition costs remain in stock at the end of the period. However, the reverse order also is acceptable, which is called the *last-in, first-out (LIFO)* method.

fixed assets: The shorthand term for the long-life (generally three years or longer) resources used by a business, which includes land, buildings, machinery, equipment, tools and vehicles. The most common account title for these assets you see in a balance sheet is 'property, plant and equipment'.

fixed expenses (costs): Those expenses or costs that remain unchanged over the short run and do not vary with changes in sales volume or sales revenue – common examples are property rental and rates, salaries of many employees and telephone lease costs.

footnotes: Footnotes are attached to the three primary financial statements to present detailed information that cannot be put directly in the body of the financial statements.

free cash flow: Many people use this term to mean the amount of *cash flow from profit* – although some writers deduct capital expenditures from this number, and others deduct cash dividends as well.

gearing: The relationship between a firm's *debt capital* and its *equity.* The higher the proportion of debt, the more highly geared is the business. In the US, the term leverage is usually used here.

general ledger: The complete collection of all the accounts used by a business (or other entity) to record the financial effects of its activities. More or less synonymous with *chart of accounts*.

generally accepted accounting principles (GAAP): The authoritative standards and approved accounting methods that should be used by businesses and private not-for-profit organisations to measure and report their revenue and expenses, and to present their assets, liabilities and owners' equity, and to report their cash flows in their financial statements.

going-concern assumption: The accounting premise that a business will continue to operate and will not be forced to liquidate its assets.

goodwill: Goodwill has two different meanings, so be careful. The term can refer to the product or brand name recognition and the excellent reputation of a business that provide a strong competitive advantage. Goodwill in this sense means the business has an important but invisible 'asset' that is not reported in its balance sheet. Second, a business may purchase and pay cash for the goodwill that has been built up over the years by another business. Only purchased goodwill is reported as an asset in the balance sheet.

gross margin (profit): Equals sales revenue less cost of goods sold for the period. On a per unit basis, gross margin equals sales price less product cost per unit. Making an adequate gross margin is the starting point for making bottom-line *net income*.

hedge fund: A fund that uses derivatives, short selling and arbitrage techniques, selling assets that one does not own in the expectation of buying them back at a lower price. This gives hedge fund managers a range of ways to generate growth in falling, rising and even in relatively static markets.

hedging: A technique used to manage commercial risk or to minimise a potential loss by using counterbalancing investment strategies.

hostile merger: The term used where a business is acquired against the wishes of the incumbent management.

hurdle rate: The rate of return required before an investment is considered worthwhile.

hyperinflation: A situation where prices increase so quickly that money is virtually useless as a store of value.

imputed cost: A hypothetical cost used as a benchmark for comparison. One example is the imputed cost of equity capital. No expense is recorded for using owners' equity capital during the year. However, in judging net income performance, the company's rate of *return on equity (ROE)* is compared with the rate of earnings that could be accrued on the capital if it were invested elsewhere. This alternative rate of return is an imputed cost. Close in meaning to the economic concept of *opportunity cost.*

income smoothing: See *profit smoothing.*

income statement: American term used for the profit and loss account.

income tax payable: The tax due, but as yet unpaid, on profits earned.

incubator: Usually both a premises and some or all of the services (legal, managerial or technical) needed to launch a business and access seed capital.

initial public offering (IPO): The first offer of a company's shares made to the general public.

insider trading: Buying or selling shares based on information not in the public domain.

internal (accounting) controls: Accounting forms, procedures and precautions that are established primarily to prevent and minimise errors and fraud (beyond what would be required for record keeping).

investing activities: One of three classes of *cash flows* reported in the *cash flow statement.* In large part these are the *capital expenditures* by a business during the year, which are major investments in long-term assets. A business may dispose of some of its fixed assets during the year, and proceeds from these disposals (if any) are reported in this section of the cash flow statement.

junior market: A stock market (such as the AIM) where shares of smaller or younger companies are traded.

last-in, first-out (LIFO): One of two widely used accounting methods by which costs of products when they are sold are charged to cost of goods sold expense. According to the LIFO method, costs of goods are charged in reverse chronological order, one result being that the ending stock cost value consists of the costs of the earliest goods purchased or manufactured. The opposite order is also acceptable, which is called the *first-in, first-out (FIFO)* method. The actual physical flow of products seldom follows a LIFO sequence. The method is justified on the grounds that the cost of goods sold expense should be the cost of replacing the products sold, and the best approximation is the most recent acquisition costs of the products.

leverage: see *financial leverage* and *operating leverage.*

leveraged buyout: A situation where a company is bought by another financed mainly by debt, such as bank borrowings.

LIFO liquidation gain: A unique result of the *last-in, first-out (LIFO)* method, which happens when fewer units are replaced than sold during the period. The decrease in stock requires that the accountant go back into the old cost layers of stock for part of the cost of goods sold expense. Thus, there is a one-time windfall gain in *gross margin*, roughly equal to the difference between the historical cost and the current cost of the stock decrease. A large LIFO liquidation gain should be disclosed in a footnote to the financial statements.

limited liability company (Ltd): Company whose shareholders have limited their liability to the amounts they subscribe to the shares they hold.

listed company: A company whose shares are on the official list of a major stock market, such as the London Stock Exchange.

management accounting: The branch of accounting that prepares internal financial statements and various other reports and analyses to assist managers to do their jobs.

management buy-out: The term used when the management of a business buys out the existing shareholders, usually with the help of a venture capital firm.

margin of safety: Equals the excess of actual sales volume over the company's *break-even point*; often expressed as a percentage. This information is used internally by managers and is not disclosed in external financial reports.

market cap: The total value of a business calculated by multiplying the current market price of its capital stock by the total number of shares issued by the business. This calculated amount is not money that has been invested in the business, and the amount is subject to the whims of the stock market.

net income: American term used to describe profit.

net operating assets: The total amount of assets used in operating a business, less its short-term non-interest-bearing liabilities. A business must raise an equal amount of capital.

net realisable value (NRV): A special accounting test applied to stock that can result in a write-down and charge to expense for the loss in value of products held for sale. The recorded costs of products in stock are compared with their current replacement costs (market price) and with net realisable value if normal sales prices have been reduced. If either value is lower, then recorded cost is written down to this lower value. *Note:* Stock is not written up when replacement costs rise after the stock was acquired.

net worth: Balance sheet value of owner's stake in the business. It consists both of the money put in at the start and any profits made since and left in the business.

notes to financial statements: Notes attached to the *balance sheet* and *income statement* which explain: (a) Significant accounting adjustments; (b) Information required by law, if not disclosed in the financial statements.

operating activities: The profit-making activities of a business – that is, the sales and expense transactions of a business. See also *cash flow from operating activities*.

operating assets: The several different assets, or economic resources, used in the profit-making operations of a business. Includes cash, accounts receivable from making sales on credit, stock of products awaiting sale, prepaid expenses and various fixed, or long-life assets.

operating cycle: The repetitive sequence over a period of time of producing or acquiring stock, holding it, selling it on credit and finally collecting the account receivable from the sale. It is a 'cash-to-cash' circle – investing cash in stock, then selling the products on credit, and then collecting the receivable.

operating earnings (profit): See *earnings before interest and income tax (EBIT)*.

operating leverage: Once a business has reached its *break-even point*, a relatively small percentage increase in sales volume generates a much larger percentage increase in profit; this wider swing in profit is the idea of operating leverage. Making sales in excess of its break-even point does not increase total fixed expenses, so all the additional *contribution margin* from the sales goes to profit.

operating liabilities: Short-term liabilities generated spontaneously in the profit-making operations of a business. The most common ones are *payable creditors*, *accrued expenses payable* and *income tax payable* – none of which are interest-bearing unless a late payment penalty is paid, which is in the nature of interest.

opportunity cost: An economic definition of cost referring to income or gain that could have been earned from the best alternative use of money, time or talent foregone by taking a particular course of action.

ordinary shares: Normal shares in business used to apportion ownership.

overhead costs: Sales and administrative expenses, and manufacturing costs that are indirect, which means they cannot be naturally matched or linked with a particular product, revenue source, or organisational unit – one example is the annual property tax on the building in which all the company's activities are carried out.

owners' equity: The ownership capital base of a business. Owners' equity derives from two sources: investment of capital in the business by the owners (for which shares are issued by a company) and profit that has been earned by the business but has not been distributed to its owners (called *retained earnings or reserves* for a company).

partnership: When two or more people agree to carry on a business together intending to share the profits.

preference share: A second class, or type, of share that can be issued by a company in addition to its *ordinary shares.* Preference shares derive their name from the fact that they have certain preferences over the *ordinary shares* – they are paid cash dividends before any can be distributed to ordinary shareholders, and in the event of liquidating the business, preference shares must be redeemed before any money is returned to the ordinary shareholders. Preference shareholders usually do not have voting rights and may be callable by the company, which means that the business can redeem the shares for a certain price per share.

preferred stock: American term for preference share.

prepaid expenses: Expenses that are paid in advance for future benefits.

price/earnings (P/E) ratio: The current market price of a capital stock divided by its most recent, or 'trailing', twelve months' *diluted earnings per share (EPS)*, or *basic earnings per share* if the business does not report diluted EPS. A low P/E may signal an undervalued share price or a pessimistic forecast by investors.

private equity: Large-scale pooled funds, usually geared up (see *gearing*) with borrowings that buy out quoted companies. This takes those companies off the stock market and makes them private, but the companies are often returned to the market after a few years of financial engineering.

product cost: Equals the purchase cost of goods that are bought and then resold by retailers and wholesalers (distributors).

profit: Equals sales revenue less all expenses for the period.

profit and loss (P&L) statement: The *financial statement* that summarises sales revenue and expenses for a period and reports one or more *profit* lines.

profit ratio: Equals *net income* divided by sales revenue. Measures net income as a percentage of sales revenue.

profit smoothing: Manipulating the timing of when sales revenue and/or expenses are recorded in order to produce a smoother profit trend year to year.

proxy statement: The annual solicitation from a company's top executives and board of directors to its shareholders that requests that they vote a certain way on matters that have to be put to a vote at the annual meeting of shareholders. In larger public companies most shareholders cannot attend the meeting in person, so they delegate a proxy (stand-in person) to vote their shares' yes or no on each proposal on the agenda.

quick ratio: The number calculated by dividing the total of cash, *accounts receivable* and marketable securities (if any) by total *current liabilities.* This ratio measures the capability of a business to pay off its current short-term liabilities with its cash and near-cash assets. Note that stock and prepaid expenses, the other two current assets, are excluded from assets in this ratio. (Also called the acid-test ratio.)

reducing balance: One of two basic methods for allocating the cost of a fixed asset over its useful life and for estimating its useful life. Reducing balance (sometimes called accelerated depreciation) allocates greater amounts of depreciation in early years and lower amounts in later years, and also uses short life estimates. For comparison, see *straight-line depreciation.*

reserves: Another term used for *retained earnings.*

retained earnings: One of two basic sources of owners' equity of a business (the other being capital invested by the owners). Annual profit (*net income*) increases this account, and distributions from profit to owners decrease the account.

return on assets (ROA): Equals *earnings before interest and taxes (EBIT)* divided by the *net operating assets* (or by total assets, for convenience), and is expressed as a percentage.

return on equity (ROE): Equals *net income* divided by the total *book value of owners' equity*, and is expressed as a percentage. ROE is the basic measure of how well a business is doing in providing 'compensation' on the owners' capital investment in the business.

return on investment (ROI): A very broad and general term that refers to the income, profit, gain or earnings on capital investments, expressed as a percentage of the amount invested. The most relevant ROI ratios for a business are *return on assets (ROA)* and *return on equity (ROE).*

road show: Presentations where companies and their advisers pitch to potential investors to 'sell' them on buying into a business.

sales revenue-driven expenses: Expenses that vary in proportion to, or as a fixed percentage of, changes in total sales revenue (total pounds). Examples are sales commissions, credit-card discount expenses, and rent expense and franchise fees based on total sales revenue. (Compare with *sales volume-driven expenses.*)

sales volume-driven expenses: Expenses that vary in proportion to, or as a fixed amount with, changes in sales volume (quantity of products sold). Examples include delivery costs, packaging costs and other costs that depend mainly on the number of products sold or the number of customers served. (Compare with *sales revenue-driven expenses.*)

Securities and Exchange Commission (SEC): The US federal agency established by the federal Securities Exchange Act of 1934, which has broad jurisdiction and powers over the public issuance and trading of securities (stocks and bonds) by business corporations. In the UK, the London Stock Exchange and the Department of Trade and Industry cover some of the same ground.

seed capital: The initial capital required to start a business and prove that the concept is viable.

sole trader: Simplest type of business. No shareholders, just the owner's money and borrowings. Also known as a sole proprietor.

statement of cash flows: See *cash flow statement.*

statement of changes in owners' (shareholders') equity: More in the nature of a supplementary schedule than a fully fledged financial statement – but, anyway, its purpose is to summarise the changes in the owners' equity accounts during the year.

stock: Goods on hand for resale, or held in raw materials, or as work in process. In the US, the term inventory is more commonly used. Stock, in the US, is usually used to describe share capital.

straight-line depreciation: Spreading the cost of a fixed asset in equal amounts of depreciation expense to each year of its useful life. Depreciation is the same amount every year by this method.

true and fair: The auditors' confirmation that the balance sheet and income statement show a 'true and fair' view of the business, in accordance with generally accepted accounting principles.

variable expenses (costs): Any expense or cost that is sensitive to changes in sales volume or sales revenue.

venture capital: Professionally managed funds that buy stakes, usually in private companies, to help them realise their growth potential.

warranties: A guarantee given by the officers of a company to a buyer of that company that all the material facts have been disclosed. Serious financial penalties await if this is found not to be the case.

window dressing: Accounting devices that make the short-term liquidity and solvency of a business look better than it really is.

working capital: The difference between current assets and current liabilities.

zero based budgeting: Where every expense has to be justified in full for an upcoming period as opposed to just accounting for any higher rate of expenditure.

Z-Score: An algorithm that uses various financial ratios to arrive at a figure below which firms have a high chance of failure.

Appendix B

Accounting Software and Other Ways to Get the Books in Good Order

. . . .

*T*his chapter gives you some general pointers for narrowing down your choices when deciding which way to keep your books up to date. The route you choose has to be right for you and right for your business:

✔ Get the person responsible for keeping your books involved in the selection process early on.

✔ Make a list of the features that you need.

✔ Get a recommendation from your business friends and associates who are already using an accounting program, bookkeeper or accountant.

✔ Think about how simple or difficult the program or process is to set up.

Popular Accounting Programs

With the cost of a basic computerised bookkeeping and accounting system starting at barely £50, and a reasonable package costing between £200 and £500, it makes good sense to plan to use such a system from the outset. Key advantages include speedy preparation of VAT returns and having no more arithmetical errors; preparing your accounts at the year-end can be a whole lot simpler.

Sourcing accounting and bookkeeping software

You can find dozens of perfectly satisfactory basic accounting and bookkeeping software packages on the market. Some of the leading providers are:

- **Banana Accounting for European Companies,** www.banana.ch/cms/en: A double-entry accounting program for European small businesses, associations and financial companies, which costs €79. Banana is a Czech firm.

- **Business Management System for Book Publishers,** www.acumenbook.com: Business management software, including royalty accounting and job costing, designed specifically for book publishers.

- **C. A. T.,** www.catsoftware.com: Software packages addressing the specific accounting tasks that are unique to the outdoor amusement and carnival business.

- **CheckMark Software Inc,** www.checkmark.com: Payroll and accounting software.

- **Creative Solutions,** www.creativesolutions.com: Integrated tax, accounting and practice management software designed exclusively for practising accountants.

- **DBA Software,** www.dbasoftware.com: A small business software package focused exclusively on the needs of small manufacturers and jobbing shops.

- **Dosh,** www.mamut.com/uk/dosh: Part of Mamut, a leading European provider of complete, integrated software solutions and Internet services for SMEs. You can download trial versions of the software from the website. Prices start at £49.50.

- **QuickUSE Accounting,** www.quickuse.com: Integrated accounting software with free downloads from the site.

- **Sage,** http://shop.sage.co.uk/accountssoftware.aspx: The market leader in accounting software with packages from £120, plus VAT.

- **Red Wing,** www.redwingsoftware.com: Mid-range software systems designed for small to mid-size businesses, agribusinesses and nonprofits.

- **R. T. I.,** www.internetRTI.com: Accounting and operational software for restaurants.

If you want some help in choosing a system, visit Accounting Software Reviews (www.accounting-software-review.toptenreviews.com), which ranks the top ten accounting packages priced from around $40 up to $2,000. Over 100 criteria are used in their test, which they carry out yearly. At the time of writing, Sage's Peach Tree Complete package, priced at $299.99, is rated as the best of the bunch, which just goes to show that money isn't everything when it comes to counting it!

Using a Bookkeeping Service

Professional associations such as the International Association of Bookkeepers (IAB) (www.iab.org.uk) and the Institute of Certified Bookkeepers (www.book-keepers.org) offer free matching services to help small businesses find a bookkeeper to suit their particular needs. Expect to pay upwards of £20 ($30/€23.50) an hour for services that can be as basic as simply recording the transactions in your books, through to producing accounts, preparing the VAT return or doing the payroll. The big plus here is that these guys and gals have their own software.

Hiring an Accountant

If you plan to trade as a partnership or limited company or look as though you'll grow fast from the outset, you may be ready to hire an accountant to look after your books. Personal recommendation from someone in your business network is the best starting point to finding an accountant. Meet the person, and if you think you could work with him or her, take up references as you would with anyone you employ, and make sure he or she is a qualified member of one of the professional bodies. Take a look at the Association of Chartered Certified Accountants (www.accaglobal.com) and the Institute of Chartered Accountants (www.icaewfirms.co.uk).

Index

• **E** •

• **F** •

• T •

FOR DUMMIES®

Making Everything Easier!™

UK editions

BUSINESS

978-0-470-97626-5

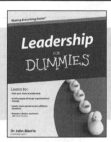

978-0-470-97211-3

978-1-119-97527-4

REFERENCE

978-0-470-68637-9

978-0-470-97450-6

978-0-470-74535-9

HOBBIES

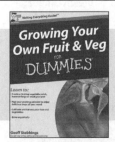

978-0-470-69960-7

978-0-470-68641-6

978-0-470-68178-7

Asperger's Syndrome For Dummies
978-0-470-66087-4

Basic Maths For Dummies
978-1-119-97452-9

Boosting Self-Esteem For Dummies
978-0-470-74193-1

British Sign Language
For Dummies
978-0-470-69477-0

Cricket For Dummies
978-0-470-03454-5

Diabetes For Dummies, 3rd Edition
978-0-470-97711-8

English Grammar For Dummies
978-0-470-05752-0

Flirting For Dummies
978-0-470-74259-4

IBS For Dummies
978-0-470-51737-6

Improving Your Relationship
For Dummies
978-0-470-68472-6

Keeping Chickens For Dummies
978-1-119-99417-6

Lean Six Sigma For Dummies
978-0-470-75626-3

Management For Dummies,
2nd Edition
978-0-470-97769-9

Neuro-linguistic Programming
For Dummies, 2nd Edition
978-0-470-66543-5

Nutrition For Dummies, 2nd Edition
978-0-470-97276-2

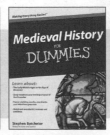

FOR DUMMIES®

The easy way to get more done and have more fun

LANGUAGES

Spanish For Dummies
978-0-470-68815-1
UK Edition

French For Dummies
978-1-118-00464-7

German For Dummies
978-0-470-90101-4

MUSIC

Ukulele For Dummies
978-0-470-97799-6
UK Edition

Guitar Chords For Dummies
978-0-470-66603-6
Lay-flat, UK Edition

DJing For Dummies
978-0-470-66372-1
UK Edition

SCIENCE & MATHS

Biology For Dummies
978-0-470-59875-7

Algebra I For Dummies
978-0-470-55964-2

Genetics For Dummies
978-0-470-55174-5

Art For Dummies
978-0-7645-5104-8

Bass Guitar For Dummies, 2nd Edition
978-0-470-53961-3

Criminology For Dummies
978-0-470-39696-4

Currency Trading For Dummies, 2nd Edition
978-1-118-01851-4

Drawing For Dummies, 2nd Edition
978-0-470-61842-4

Forensics For Dummies
978-0-7645-5580-0

Guitar For Dummies, 2nd Edition
978-0-7645-9904-0

Hinduism For Dummies
978-0-470-87858-3

Index Investing For Dummies
978-0-470-29406-2

Knitting For Dummies, 2nd Edition
978-0-470-28747-7

Music Theory For Dummies, 2nd Edition
978-1-118-09550-8

Piano For Dummies, 2nd Edition
978-0-470-49644-2

Physics For Dummies, 2nd Edition
978-0-470-90324-7

Schizophrenia For Dummies
978-0-470-25927-6

Sex For Dummies, 3rd Edition
978-0-470-04523-7

Sherlock Holmes For Dummies
978-0-470-48444-9

Solar Power Your Home For Dummies, 2nd Edition
978-0-470-59678-4

Available wherever books are sold. For more information or to order direct go to www.wiley.com or call +44 (0) 1243 843291

32812 (p3)

FOR DUMMIES®

Helping you expand your horizons and achieve your potential

COMPUTER BASICS

978-0-470-57829-2

978-0-470-61454-9

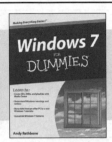

978-0-470-49743-2

DIGITAL PHOTOGRAPHY

978-0-470-25074-7

978-0-470-76878-5

978-1-118-00472-2

MICROSOFT OFFICE 2010

978-0-470-48998-7

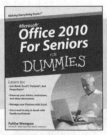

978-0-470-58302-9

978-0-470-48953-6

Access 2010 For Dummies
978-0-470-49747-0

Android Application Development
For Dummies
978-0-470-77018-4

AutoCAD 2011 For Dummies
978-0-470-59539-8

C++ For Dummies, 6th Edition
978-0-470-31726-6

Computers For Seniors For Dummies,
2nd Edition
978-0-470-53483-0

Dreamweaver CS5 For Dummies
978-0-470-61076-3

iPad For Dummies 2nd Edition
978-1-118-02444-7

Macs For Dummies, 11th Edition
978-0-470-87868-2

Mac OS X Snow Leopard For Dummies
978-0-470-43543-4

Photoshop CS5 For Dummies
978-0-470-61078-7

Photoshop Elements 9 For Dummies
978-0-470-87872-9

Search Engine Optimization
For Dummies, 4th Edition
978-0-470-88104-0

The Internet For Dummies,
12th Edition
978-0-470-56095-2

Visual Studio 2010 All-In-One
For Dummies
978-0-470-53943-9

Web Analytics For Dummies
978-0-470-09824-0

Word 2010 For Dummies
978-0-470-48772-3

WordPress For Dummies, 4th Edition
978-1-118-07342-1

32812 (p4)